David Earle Anderson

Merlin House - 2001

D0378985

Experiences in Theology

Experiences in Theology

Ways and Forms of Christian Theology

Jürgen Moltmann

Translated by Margaret Kohl

FORTRESS PRESS
Minneapolis

EXPERIENCES IN THEOLOGY
Ways and Forms of Christian Theology

First Fortress Press edition 2000

ISBN 0-8006-3267-2

Manufactured in Great Britain   AF 1-3267
04   03   02   01   00   1   2   3   4   5   6   7   8   9   10

For Elisabeth

Contents

II. Hermeneutics of Hope

Abbreviations

CD	K. Barth, *Church Dogmatics*, ET Edinburgh and Grand Rapids, 1936–69
EvTh	*Evangelische Theologie*, Munich
HST	Handbuch Systematischer Theologie, ed. C. H. Ratschow, Gütersloh 1979ff.
LThK	*Lexikon für Theologie und Kirche*, Freiburg 1957ff.
PG	J. P. Migne, *Patrologia Graeca*, Paris 1857ff.
PhB	Philosophische Bibliothek, Hamburg
QD	Quaestiones Disputatae, Freiburg
RGG³	*Die Religion in Geschichte und Gegenwart*, third edition, Tübingen 1957–65
STh	Thomas Aquinas, *Summa Theologica*
TDNT	*Theological Dictionary of the New Testament* (trans. by G. W. Bromiley of TWNT), Grand Rapids and London 1964–76
ThLZ	*Theologische Literaturzeitung*, Leipzig
ThQ	*Theologische Quartalschrift*, Tübingen
ThSt	Theologische Studien, Zürich
WA	M. Luther, *Werke*, Weimarer Ausgabe, Weimar 1883ff.
WTJ	*Westminster Theological Journal*, Philadelphia
ZKG	*Zeitschrift für Kirchengeschichte*, Stuttgart, etc.
ZThK	*Zeitschrift für Theologie und Kirche*, Tübingen

Translator's Note

Biblical quotations have been taken from RSV unless a change of wording was required to bring out the author's point. Where English translations of books referred to exist, references to these have been given, but in some cases quotations have been translated directly from the German. The absence in the relevant note of a page number reference to the translation will make this clear.

A few minor changes have been made to the German text, mainly for the benefit of the English-speaking reader. These changes were made in consultation with Professor Moltmann.

This being the final volume of his 'Contributions to Systematic Theology', I should like to express my thanks to the publishers, and especially to Dr John Bowden, for their careful and helpful editing and co-operation. Above all, however, I am grateful to Professor Moltmann for his never-failing patient and generous help in the preparation of the translations. To work on these books has been a privilege and a joy.

Margaret Kohl

Preface

An afterword instead of a foreword

An extensive work on theological dogmatics or systematic theology generally begins with what are called the *prolegomena*. In this introductory discourse, the foundations of Christian theology, the method chosen and the understanding of theology presupposed are all discussed. If the method is clear, it can be applied to every theological doctrine. But ever since the beginning of modern critical thinking, the foundations and methods of theology itself have become questionable; and consequently modern theologians have fallen upon these prolegomena to dogmatics with particular fervour, and have tried to answer the fundamental questions with the help of whatever new philosophy, psychology, or science of religion is to hand. How is Christian theology possible under the conditions of the modern world? And can there be such a thing as a specifically Christian ethics at all?

Up to now these questions about method have not greatly interested me, because I first wanted to get to know the real content of theology. For me, what was more important was the revision of theological issues in the light of their biblical origins, and their renewal or reworking in the challenge of the present. For this there were personal reasons, among other things. My upbringing was not particularly Christian. My Hamburg family – 'Enlightened' ever since my grandfather's freemasonry – was more or less indifferent to Christianity in general and the Christian church in particular, and was pretty much detached from both. So from the beginning of my theological studies – first as a prisoner-of-war in Norton Camp near Nottingham

and then, after my return to Germany in 1948, in Göttingen –
for me everything theological was marvellously new. I had first
to grasp and make my own what others had learnt from their
youth up.

For me, theology was, and still is, an adventure of ideas. It is
an open, inviting path. Right down to the present day, it has
continued to fascinate my mental and spiritual curiosity. My
theological methods therefore grew up as I came to have a perception of the objects of theological thought. *The road emerged
only as I walked it.* And my attempts to walk it are of course
determined by my personal biography, and by the political context and historical *kairos* in which I live. I have searched for the
right word for the right time. I have not written any theological
textbooks. The articles I have contributed to various theological dictionaries and encyclopaedias have seldom been
particularly successful. I was not concerned to collect up correct
theological notions, because I was much too preoccupied with
the perception of new perspectives and unfamiliar aspects. I had
no wish to be a disciple of the great theological masters of
past generations. Nor have I any desire to found a new theological school. My whole concern has been, and still is, to
stimulate other people to discover theology for themselves – to
have their own theological ideas, and to set out along their own
paths.

Because of that I set aside the questions of method which are
dealt with in general prolegomena to dogmatics, and in these
systematic contributions to theology have tried to come directly
to 'the heart of the matter' – the things themselves. In the
forewords to each individual volume I have talked about the
particular path I have taken there; so from these five prefaces
interested readers could certainly detect my implicit method.
But because my method was not fixed in advance of its application, but only as it was applied, at the end of this road I must
now come to talk about it, and instead of the usual prolegomena to dogmatics put down a few final, summary thoughts
about these systematic contributions of mine. Because I am not
used to personal postscripts, it could well be that I shall succeed

only in writing another 'foreword' to new paths. But if that
should be the case, this 'afterword' will by no means have
failed. It will simply have manifested my innermost conviction
that in Christian theology 'the beginning is in the end', and
that Christians in their faith in the resurrection (unlike Jews on
the sabbath) are 'the eternal beginners', as Franz Rosenzweig
once said: they must always start out afresh with their beginnings; for 'all's well that begins well'.[1] The divine promise and
the awakened hope teach every theology that it must remain
fragmentary and unfinished, because it is the thinking about
God of men and women who are on the way and, being
still travellers, have not yet arrived home. That is why the
mediaeval cathedrals and minsters also had to remain unfinished, so that they might point beyond themselves.

Systematic contributions to theology

When I began on this theme-orientated series in 1980, I chose
the title 'systematic contributions to theology' *first* because I
wanted to make the point that theology as a whole is more than
systematic theology or dogmatics. There is biblical theology
too, historical theology, practical theology, and other theologies as well. Systematic theology is only one contribution to a
greater shared theological whole. This means that it cannot be
a closed system, but must indicate the points of contact where
there can be dialogue with the other theological disciplines. The
age-old dispute about 'the crown of theology' is a vain one. The
systematic theologian may be 'an amateur and conductor' of
the whole theological orchestra, as Kornelis Heike Miskotte
once stylized the matter, but of course practical theologians can
be that too, if for them all theological theories come down to
praxis – or historical theologians, if they believe that everything
present and future will one day belong to the past, and hence
become the object of their research. For me, theology comes
into being wherever men and women come to the knowledge of
God and, in the praxis of their lives, their happiness and their
suffering, perceive God's presence with all their senses. It is to

this that systematic theology should, last and first, make its contribution.

Secondly, I chose this title because these systematic contributions to theology are not intended to present 'my system' or 'my dogmatics'. Right down to their very structure, I have tried to seek the truth in dialogue, and to avoid monologistic conversations with myself. Christian theology is the joint task of the shared theologizing of all believers. For that reason I have sought the communicative style of *suggestion.* I was not interested in defending impersonal dogmas or non-subjective truths. Nor did I want simply to express my own private opinion. What I do wish, however, is for my suggestions to be taken seriously in the theological community – that they should not simply be met with agreement or disagreement, but that they should stimulate theology's ongoing dialogue. I myself have also picked up the suggestions of others where these seemed to me fruitful, and where they carried me a step further. This may have been the case more often than I realized. Theology is like a network of rivers, with reciprocal influences and mutual challenges. It is certainly not a desert in which every individual is alone with himself or herself, and with his or her God. For me, theological access to the truth of the triune God is through dialogue. It is communitarian and co-operative. *Theologia viatorum* – the theology of men and women on the way – is an enduring critical conversation with the generations before us and the contemporaries at our side, in expectation of those who will come after us. So what I have written is not safeguarded from every side. It is sometimes 'foolhardy', as some concerned churchmen have thought. In the business of theology it is hard not to be controversial.

Not least, in making *contributions,* the writer recognizes the conditions and limitations of his own place, and the relativity of his own context. It is impossible to say anything that is theologically valid for everyone at all times and in all places. A perennial theology is out of the writer's power. So he must critically resolve the naive, absolute self-centredness of his thinking. That is why in 1980, in the preface to *The Trinity and the Kingdom of God*, I wrote: 'Of course [the writer] is a European, but European theology no longer has to be Euro-*centric*. Of course he is a man, but theology no longer has to be andro*centric*. Of course he is living in the "first world", but the theology which he is developing does not have to reflect the ideas of the dominating nations. On the contrary, it will try to help to make the voice of the oppressed heard. We normally presuppose the absolute nature of our own standpoint in our own context. To abolish this tacit presupposition is the intention behind the phrase "contributions to theology"' (xii). In Part III of the present book, on 'Mirror Images of Liberating Theology', I have tried to keep this promise.

Theology and biography

In this book, I have described the ways my own biography has given me entries into theology – in general, in my own person and in the community of the church and the university; and then in particular, access to the individual theological problems. I have described this process in the introductions to the various chapters, because I have come to see that the biographical dimension is an essential dimension of theological insight. As a student, admittedly, I failed to notice that the determining subject belongs to dogmatics. On the contrary, the pure objectivity of what was said was supposed to guarantee its verifiability at all times by everyone everywhere. It was therefore impossible to tell from the splendid books of my teachers who wrote them, and when, and where. And as the author's subjectivity withdrew, all relatedness to the time receded too. What was allegedly the *Zeitgeist*, 'the spirit of the age', was left to the journalists; and indeed this *Zeitgeist* was certainly no more than a disembodied apparition. But with their contemptuous dismissal of 'the *Zeitgeist*', the contemporaneity of the theologians vanished too. They now felt that here below they were merely 'guests on a beautiful star', as Helmut Thielicke put it. It took me some time, and some effort of will, before – at the urging of my wife – I dared to say 'I' in theology too. In the present state of society, the death of the subject is proclaimed on the one hand – and is also practised in the enormously proliferating number of 'anonymous burials'; yet on the other hand, more and more people are thrusting forward in talk shows to 'come out', casting aside every degree of respectful discretion, and breaking all the bounds of decency. And in this situation to talk about oneself is both necessary and difficult. In the last thirty years I have come to see that it is much harder to communicate to other people *abstractions* drawn from one's own situation and biography than it is to communicate the concrete truth, however subjectively or contextually it may be formulated. It is concrete truth that prompts other people for the first time to find *God's* truth in the history of their own lives. Readers of a book want to know not only what the author has to say, but also how he or she arrived at it, and why they put as it as they do.

At the beginning of the 1970s there was a theological movement in the United States which called for a 'narrative' theology (over against purely argumentative theology) and then, in the context of this narrative theology, went on to demand 'theology as biography' as well. In 1974 Johann Baptist Metz took this up with a wealth of ideas in an article on 'Theology as Biography'.[2] My own experiences with theological thinking have taught me that the two things belong together in Christian theology: the *telling* of God's history with us, and the *argument* for God's presence – biographical subjectivity and self-forgetting objectivity. Because the way – the method – belongs to the perception of the thing itself, I have written biographical introductions to the different themes, not for the sale of the personal subject, but as a way leading to insight into the object of enquiry. Because the subject as person comes from a community and talks within a community, this is not the in-turned reference of a solitary ego, for: 'What have you that you have not received?'.

Theology for the kingdom of God

There are theological systems which do not merely aim to be free of contradictions in themselves, but which aspire to remain uncontroverted from outside too. In these systems, theology becomes a strategy of self-immunization. Systems of this kind are like fortresses which cannot be broken into, but cannot be broken out of either, and which are therefore in the end starved out through public disinterest. I have no wish to live in any such fortress, and I have resisted the temptation to view Barth's *Church Dogmatics* as a fortress of that kind, as the Barthians do. For it is not a fortress, even if some of his followers let Barth think for them, so as to feel safe with him, while other people put him down as neo-orthodox, so as not to have to read him and grapple with what he says. My image of theology is not 'A safe stronghold is our God'. It is the exodus of God's people, on the road to the promised land of liberty where God dwells. For me, theology is not an inner-church or postmodern dogmatics, designed only for one's own community of faith. Nor is it for me the cultural study of the civil religion of bourgeois society. Theology springs out of a passion for God's kingdom and its righteousness and justice, and this passion grows up in the community of Christ. In that passion, theology becomes imagination for the kingdom of God in the world, and for the world in God's kingdom.

As kingdom-of-God theology, it is of necessity *missionary* theology, linking the church with society, and the people of God with the peoples of the earth. It becomes a *public* theology, which participates in 'the sufferings of this present time', and formulates its hopes for God at the places where contemporaries are and exist. Kingdom-of-God theology intervenes critically and prophetically in the public affairs of a given society, and draws public attention, not to the church's own interests but to 'God's kingdom, God's commandment and his righteousness', as Thesis 5 of the Barmen Theological Declaration says. That means that kingdom-of-God theology can neither withdraw to its own community of faith in fundamentalist fashion nor adapt itself in modernist style to society's prevailing trends. It is resistingly and productively concerned about the future of life in the whole earthly creation.

Some people have critically remarked that I think I know more about God and his future than human beings can ever know. They counsel me to more silence before the unfathomable, nameless Mystery, and to more negative theology in 'the missing of God' (J. B. Metz's phrase). I am enough of a mystic to understand what they mean. But just because the disclosed mystery of God's name is unfathomable, one can't get enough of wanting to know about it. The Spirit searches everything, even the depths of God . . .

Other people have ironically criticized my use of the Bible as a 'use *à la carte*', although it is no different in principle from the way Karl Barth or Basil the Great used Scripture – except in the deficiency of my biblical knowledge. In *Theology of Hope* (1964; ET 1967) I was still able to pick up the Old and New Testament exegesis of Gerhard von Rad and Ernst Käsemann with which I was familiar. But then, sometime in the 1970s, the exegetical discussion became hazy and confused for me, and the hermeneutic discussion even more. I found it more of a hindrance in listening to the biblical texts. In Germany, historical and theological exegesis parted company. Historical criticism disappeared almost entirely. Finding myself at a loss, I then doubtless developed my own post-critical and 'naive' relationship to the biblical writings, and tried to find my own way through the texts. As I did so, I discovered how much at home I felt in the Bible, and how gladly I let myself be stimulated to my own thinking by different texts. For the quotations I have more and more kept to the Luther Bible, not because Luther's translation is an especially faithful rendering, but because it was with the Luther Bible that the German people became literate, and because the Luther Bible put a profound impress on the language of German culture from Lessing and Goethe to Thomas Mann and Bert Brecht, from Kant and Hegel to Nietzsche and Heidegger.

But in my dealings with what the biblical writings say I have also noticed how critical and free I have become towards them. Of course I want to know what they intend to say, but I do not feel bound to take only what they say, and repeat it, and interpret it. I can quite well conceive that it is possible to say what they say in a different way. In other words, I take Scripture as a stimulus to my own theological thinking, not as an authoritative blueprint and confining boundary. It is 'the matter of Scripture' that is important, not the scriptural form of the matter, even if it is only through that form that we arrive at the substance. 'God's Word is not bound.' It is not bound to a patriarchal culture and the disparagement of women, or to a slave-owning society, or to the pre-modern transitions from nomadic to agrarian life, and from rural life to life in the towns – even though all this is the context in which the biblical writings were framed. Only what goes beyond the times in which the texts were written and points into our future is relevant – God's history of promise, and the history of his future. This 'matter of Scripture' gives us creative liberty towards the utterances of Scripture which are subject to their time. It is along these lines, I believe, that I developed my use of the Bible. In Part II of the present book I shall put forward for discussion the hermeneutical method that corresponds to it, under the heading 'Hermeneutics of Hope'.

This book can also be read as an *introduction to Christian theology*, so in Part I I have addressed myself in detail to the definition and requirements of historical theology, Christian theology and natural theology, while in Part II I have tried to formulate a 'theological epistemology'. It is only possible to write an introduction to theology if one knows what theology is. That is why this introduction comes at the end of the series. It is not intended to be an introduction to my theology, but it is of course my introduction to theology.

Denominational or ecumenical theology?

In 1948 I came back from the prisoner-of-war camp as a Christian, but I had no relationship to the churches. In the labour camp in Scotland a Catholic professor of philosophy gathered a group of interested people round him. In Norton Camp I studied Protestant theology. In Bremen I worked in a Reformed congregation and was ordained in Leer, East Frisia, as a Reformed pastor. Collaboration with Catholic colleagues in Bonn and Tübingen, the ecumenical conferences of the Faith and Order Commission of the World Council of Churches, to which I belonged from 1963 to 1983, the co-editorship of *Concilium*, the periodical of Catholic reform: all this convinced me that although my origins are Reformed and Protestant, my future is ecumenical. I see the Reformed tradition in which I live and think as part of Christianity's wider, shared whole, which must be ecumenically united; and I have felt no reservations when mixing in Catholic, Orthodox or Pentecostal circles. On the contrary, I have felt accepted and at home everywhere. There is a quotation cartel in theological books whereby popes cite only popes, Catholics only Catholics, Orthodox only Orthodox, and Protestant theologians only Protestants. This has always seemed to me narrow-minded and sectarian. The confessional boundaries which are necessary today no longer run parallel to the traditional denominational demarcation lines – not even in the doctrine of justification, and not in the understanding of the Trinity either. New theological alliances have developed, and new differences. These have to be put to use in the ecumenical theology that is now developing.

Finally, I must apologize to the many doctoral students and reviewers for not being able to enter into their critical assessments. There are so many of them that to do so would have made a book in itself. Those who have sent me their dissertations and reviews may be sure that I have read them. Those who did not send them either had no wish for me to read them, or did not find it necessary to follow the traditional academic style. And yet it would be a pity if academic community were to break down at this point, and if authors were no longer in a position to know what someone had written about them. Here even the Internet is no help.

When, thirty-five years ago, I began my systematic theology

with my *Theology of Hope*, I dedicated the book to my wife; and so this last book in the series is dedicated to her too. My experiences in theological thinking have grown up in the life we share, and spring from my perpetual joy in it.

Tübingen, 23 March 1999   Jürgen Moltmann

1. What is Theology?

Where do we think theologically?
Locations of personal theological
existence

I am beginning with a personal introduction because I have clearly sensed how my theological concerns and the topics I have taken up have been indirectly influenced by a particular situation or *Sitz im Leben* (to borrow an expression from form criticism) and I can also clearly distinguish between these different concerns. Perception of the *locus theologicus* – the 'location' of a given theology – is indispensable for every hermeneutics and for every politically conscious theology.

1. Existential theology

By existential theology I mean one's own theological existence which, out of personal experiences of life and death, seeks the theological answers of faith, and so takes over responsibility for one's own life.

For me, Christian faith began with a despairing search for God and a personal struggle with the dark sides of 'the hidden face' of God. At the end of July 1943, as an air force auxiliary, I experienced the destruction of my home town Hamburg through the RAF's 'Operation Gomorrah', and barely survived the fire storm in which 40,000 people burnt to death. The friend standing beside me was blown to pieces by the bomb which left me unscathed. I come from a secular family, but that night I cried out to God for the first time 'My God, where are

you?' And the question 'Why am I alive and not dead like the
rest?' has haunted me ever since. I had wanted to study mathematics and physics. The heroes of my youth were Einstein,
Planck and Heisenberg. But in 1944, while I was working
through Louis de Broglie's *Matière et Lumière* (published in
German in 1943), I was called up, and after a brief training
found myself on the fringes of the battle for the Arnhem bridge.
Six months later, in February 1945, I was taken prisoner by the
British, and had more than three years to think about the
horrors of war I had gone through, and the German crimes
against humanity in Auschwitz. I searched for some certainty in
life, for I had lost mine. I asked about the knowledge that can
sustain existence, and lost interest in the knowledge that reads
and dominates nature. I needed what the Heidelberg Catechism
calls 'comfort in life and death', and through the chance reading of the Bible and the undeserved kindness of Scottish and
English Christians, I found that comfort in the Christ who in his
passion became my brother in need, and through his resurrection from the dead awakened me too to a living hope.

My experiences of death at the end of the war, the depression
into which the guilt of my people plunged me, and the inner
perils of utter resignation behind barbed wire: these were the
places where my theology was born. They were my first *locus
theologicus*, and at the deepest depths of my soul they have
remained so.

When I returned from captivity in 1948, I had no idea which
church I should go to, or what profession I should take up. I
went on to study theology and philosophy in Göttingen in order
to discover whether truth can be found in Christ, and if so,
what truth.

2. Theology in the congregation

Through my wife Elisabeth and our joint doctoral supervisor
Otto Weber, I then began to train for the ministry, although
really I was completely ignorant about church, congregation
and pastorate. After some search, I arrived in 1953 in the

Reformed congregation of Bremen-Wasserhorst, a little country congregation of about 400 people, 50 farms, and 2,000 to 3,000 cows. We both had our doctorates, and here we came face to face with the life of ordinary, simple people. That was hard but valuable, for after academic theology, I now got to know *the theology of the people*, in their struggle for their families and their efforts to make ends meet, in their memories of their dead, and in their anxieties about their children. In the mornings I found time to go on with my academic studies – I was working on the theology of the post-Reformation and pre-Enlightenment period; but I developed my personal theology as I went from house to house, and as I visited the sick. If things went well, on Monday I learned the text for the following Sunday's sermon, and took it with me on my way through the parish – and then knew what I had to say in my sermon.

Here a new 'hermeneutical circle' grew up – not now between the interpretation of the text and the self-interpretation of the interpreter (as in Bultmann), but between exposition of the text and the shared experience of men and women in their families, among their neighbours, and in their work. In sermons, hymns and prayers, in teaching, and when I talked to people in their homes, I experienced theology as a *shared theology* of believers and doubters, the oppressed and the consoled. Ever since my five years as pastor in that Bremen-Wasserhorst congregation, I have been convinced of the common theology of all believers, and firmly believe that the remote and rarified plain of pure academic theology is a desert.

3. Theology for the church

In 1958, urged by Otto Weber, I accepted an invitation to the Kirchliche Hochschule in Wuppertal. This had been founded by the resisting Confessing Church in 1935, in order to make possible a theology responsible to the church, a theology free of the state and removed from the political grasp of the government; for after 1933 the theological faculties in the German state universities had been made to fall into line. Paul Tillich and Karl Barth had been dismissed, and members of the academic body were organized in the Nazi University Lecturers' Association, unless they had already become members of the party long before that, on their own initiative. Not much was left of the liberal Protestantism which had prevailed up to the end of the Weimar Republic. The theological faculties were dominated by the 'German Christians', Nazis and Nazi sympathizers, the most prominent of them Emmanuel Hirsch in Göttingen. Unfortunately the Kirchliche Hochschule in Wuppertal was closed by the Gestapo the very day after its founding in 1935. Teaching could only be carried on in private houses.

In 1945 the college was opened afresh, so as to give the Protestant church in Germany a double location for theology, one linked with the church, the other under the aegis of the state.* In its spirit and practice, the Kirchliche Hochschule was orientated towards the church. There were still country congregations which sent the students potatoes. We all felt committed to Karl Barth's *Church Dogmatics*, where theology was consciously developed as an ecclesiological study, not as a science of religion. In the years from 1958 to 1963 the unity of the Protestant church in Germany was more important for us than the Federal Republic in the Western part of divided Germany. Solidarity with those we called the 'brothers and sisters' in the German Democratic Republic was greater than loyalty to the provisional government in Bonn, a 'stop-gap' which then, after all, lasted for forty years. So we felt free to protest against political developments which we believed would be a fatal deterrent to reunification, or would at least hinder it. In 1958, during the movement known as the 'Struggle against Atomic Death', the faculty drew up a theological paper protesting against further rearmament in the East–West conflict. In the Kirchliche Hochschule at that time we enjoyed a marvellous freedom from any regard for political expediency,

---

* Universities in Germany come under the ministries of education in the various *Länder*.

and we ran into no difficulty with the leaders and synods of the Evangelical Church in Germany (the EKD).

The isolated character of this rebirth on the 'Holy Mountain' in Wuppertal had a decidely creative effect. We were not obliged to pay reverence to any previous faculty. So here in 1961 my colleague Wolfhart Pannenberg had published a new theological programme, *Revelation as History*, while in 1964 I brought out my *Theology of Hope*. In the established, time-honoured faculties, I might not have permitted myself this audacity. I would have tried to keep myself safe, and in what I said to cover myself circumspectly from every side – as our theological contemporaries generally do nowadays, so as not to go wrong, or lay themselves open to censure, and at all events to remain generally acceptable candidates for further advancement. I was highly conscious of this theological liberty in responsibility towards the church, and missed it keenly when in 1963 I accepted an invitation to a chair in the Protestant theological faculty of Bonn University, and from that time on remained in state universities.

4. Theology in the university

I was first faced with a conflict of conscience when – now a civil servant at a state university – I had to take an oath of loyalty to the state. In 1935 Karl Barth had had to leave Bonn University, because it was only with a personal reservation that he was prepared to take the oath of loyalty to Hitler. In 1963 I myself had the disagreeable feeling of having surrendered part of my liberty as a Christian for the sake of the loyalty required of a civil servant. I was able to live with this, but ran into conflict in 1968 during the protests against the State of Emergency laws. But because the German constitution – the Basic Law – to which I had taken the oath had been passed 'in our responsibility before God' (as the preamble puts it), I knew that in theological criticism of these laws I was at one with the spirit of the constitution.

Did the university location change my theology? I think it

did, because here the demand to be 'scholarly' or 'scientific' made by the other faculties was greater than it had been in a college belonging to the church. I worked on a theological ethic, and began to do theology in a more systematic and scholarly way – for example through a detailed discussion with tradition, and in growing ecumenical fellowship, first with Catholic and then with Orthodox theology. I was always pleased when students from the Catholic theological faculty, and from other faculties too, attended my lectures, not just men and women who were training to become Protestant clergy and teachers. I had no desire to be part of a theological vocational school. I wanted to talk about theology because I was interested in it, and out of a passion for the kingdom of God.

Here I was helped by the great dialogues of those years in which I was able to participate. The Christian-Marxist dialogue was set on foot by the Catholic Paulus Gesellschaft, and took place for the last time in Marienbad in 1967, together with the Czech Academy of Sciences, before in 1968 the troops of the Warsaw Pact put an end to 'socialism with a human face'. We learned theology in dialogue, in confrontation and co-operation. For me in Tübingen, the Christian-Jewish dialogue then followed, and there intellectually I moved more and more away from Ernst Bloch, and more and more towards Franz Rosenzweig. Other discussions were important, too, for the development of my academic theology, among them the discussions between theologians and lawyers and between theologians and scientists in Heidelberg. I participated in a research programme, led by Ernst Wolf and Hans Dombois, on the interpretation of social institutions and later took part in developing a *Theory of Open Systems*, the papers being published in two volumes by Ernst von Weizsäcker. I found particularly lively theological questioning at medical conferences, which I attended with my Catholic friend Franz Böckle, whose field in Bonn was social ethics. These conferences led off with the two jubilee congresses organized by the pharmaceutical concern Hoffmann-La Roche in Basel, and were then continued on local levels and under UNESCO.

Academic theology has to achieve the master stroke of linking *church theology* in the training of clergy and teachers with the offer of a *general theology* for interested people from other faculties, whether they are Christians or not. Because academic theology itself is a combination of different disciplines – historical, philological, philosophical and psychological – various common interests emerge, cutting across the boundaries of the different faculties; and these can be highly fruitful for theology.

But is theology also relevant for the others? Do we need a new general theology which is accessible by nature to everyone, whether they are Christians or atheists, Jews or Buddhists? Is anything of this kind conceivable at all?

2

Who is a theologian?

Like the terms biologist, sociologist, and so forth, the word theologian immediately suggests an educated, academically trained and competent expert. A person 'learned about God' must at all events be learned. There have been theological faculties at European universities since the thirteenth century. Ever since the era of high scholasticism, the expression *theologia* has been the accepted term for the exposition of Christian doctrine, as we can easily see from the *Summa Theologica* of the famous Thomas Aquinas.[1] Academically educated theologians have to pass examinations. They receive degrees or diplomas. The perfect example of the genre is therefore the theology professor, who has a university chair, and is responsible for his own teaching and research. The only thing that is above the professor for theology is the authority of the subject of his theology.

This development of academic theology is historically understandable, but substantially it is of only limited value. It was possible only in the European *Corpus Christianum*, that strange and unique unity of church and state, faith and culture in the *Sacrum Imperium*, the Holy Empire. In the non-Christian and post-Christian worlds, the external conditions for any such union are lacking.

The internal dividing lines in academic theology can be discovered in every theological faculty. Many professors expound their theology in just the way they expect their doctoral candidates and assistants one day to go on expounding it. But most of their students want to be pastors or teachers in the congregations of their church. They are not interested in an academic career. The more they adopt academic theology and make it their own, the greater their difficulty later in bridging the broad gulf between the 'educated' and the 'uneducated' in their congregations. Over against this academic theology, a 'congregational theology' has long since developed everywhere. This is certain that it is closer to the Bible, because the prophets and apostles were not learned theologians either.[2] This is 'popular' theology – the theology of the people. These two theologies, the academic and the popular, must relate to each other, show consideration for each other, and learn from each other. If academic theology does not find its way to ordinary people, it loses its foundation. Without the church, Christian theology cannot exist as a university discipline. It will become diffused and lose itself in the science of religions. On the other hand, popular theology loses its reasonable character if it pays no attention to academic theology, or if it despises that theology's competence.

1. The shared theology of all believers

Theology is the business of all God's people. It is not just the affair of the theological faculties, and not just the concern of the church's colleges and seminaries. The faith of the whole body of Christians on earth seeks to know and understand. If it doesn't, it isn't Christian faith. This means that the foundation for every theological specialization is *the general theology of all believers,* which corresponds to the Reformation's thesis about the universal 'priesthood of all believers'. All Christians *who believe and who think about what they believe* are theologians, whether they are young or old, women or men. That is what Luther meant:

> All are theologians, that means every Christian.
> All are said to be theologians so that all may be Christians.
>
> (*Omnes sumus Theologi,* heisst ein jeglicher Christ.
> *Omnes dicimur Theologi, ut omnes Christiani*)
>
> (WA 41.11).

I should not like to let this universalization of the priesthood and of theology stand in such general terms, and so I would prefer to talk about 'the shared priesthood' and therefore about *the shared theology of all believers* too. On this common ground, not everyone has to do and think the same thing. The fellowship of all believers requires that differentiation of assignments and functions which corresponds to the multicoloured diversity of the Spirit's gifts, or charismata. Even in the shared theology of all believers there are particular commissions and delegations. Academic theology is one of them. But the community of Christians must be able to identify with its delegations. Otherwise alienations arise which have an oppressive rather than a helpful effect.

Oppressive alienations have not merely come about through academic theology, over against the congregation. More serious is the two-thousand-year-old ascendancy in Christianity of *the traditional theology* determined by men. Except for a few famous nuns and women teachers of the church, such as Catherine of Siena and Hildegard of Bingen, the theologians (as well as the bishops) have all been men, and masculine viewpoints, ways of thinking and interests have therefore prevailed in theology. It was only in the twentieth century that an independent *feminist theology* developed, and this is struggling for recognition.[3] It must be taken seriously by men, too, not just by women. Otherwise we can never arrive at a common, *shared theology* of all believers, both men and women. In a first step, feminist theology must free itself of the dominant theology, and develop separately on its own account, before there can one day be a shared theology of free and equal men and women, as Joel 2.28–29 promises.[4]

The same may be said of *theology in ecumenical fellowship*. Here, too, the European logic of theology was initially paramount, because the Hellenistic and Roman *Corpus Christianum* had the whole weight of tradition in theology and church on its side. It is only slowly that, in debate and dispute with this European theology, Asian, African and Latin American theologies are developing, in awareness of their own cultural context and cutting themselves free from Euro-centrism. Here too three steps have to follow on one another: liberation – separation – integration. A shared theology of all believers in the different cultural and economic contexts still seems a long way off, except that – as every ecumenical con-ference shows – the text of the biblical message is the same everywhere. This cuts right across the different cultural con-texts and creates its own ecumenical context, which extends throughout 'the whole of Christendom on earth'.

In the churches, this common theology of all believers also serves the church's *shared teaching ministry* or *magisterium*.[5] On the basis of Scripture and creeds, and in the context of the present at any given time, the teaching of the church formulates orientations and regulating norms for proclamation and teach-ing, as well as guidelines for ethical and political decisions. Trained theologians and the church's leading bodies – the synods and bishops – work together on the formulation of the church's doctrine. This collaboration must not be broken off by the one side or the other: theologians do not merely serve the teaching ministry of the church through their interpretation of dogmas and encyclicals, and through the arguments they pro-vide; nor can they claim this teaching ministry for themselves, and indoctrinate the leading bodies of the church. The teaching ministry in synodal form seems the best way of expressing their 'shared path', and hence the shared teaching office or ministry of all believers.

Academic theology is nothing other than the scholarly pene-tration and illumination by mind and spirit of what Christians in the congregations think when they believe in God and live in the fellowship of Christ. By scholarly I mean that the theology is methodologically verifiable and comprehensible. Good - scholarly theology is therefore basically simple, because it is clear. Only cloudy theology is complicated and difficult. Whether it be Athanasius or Augustine, Aquinas or Calvin, Schleiermacher or Barth – the fundamental ideas of every good theological system can be presented on a single page. It is true that Barth needed more than 8,000 pages for his *Church*

Dogmatics, and even then they were still unfinished, so that kindly disposed critics said, 'surely truth can't be as long as that'. But as we know, theological praise of the eternally bounteous God is never-ending. So the length of a work does not necessarily detract from the simple truth of what it says.

If the people who believe and think about what they believe are – all of them together – theologians, this *theology of all believers* is the foundation for every academic theology. But does that also mean, conversely, that Christian theology can be nothing other than a self-related 'doctrine of faith', to echo the title Schleiermacher gave his modern theology?* Does it mean that only people who are 'believers' or 'born again' can study and understand theology, and that they understand it because they are already in agreement with it from the outset? Now, faith is of the essence for Christian theology, because theology does not purpose to be a theory about the Absolute, devoid of any determining subject, and the rebirth to a living hope is the subjective opening up of God's new future for the world. But that still does not have to mean that theology is only there for believers. God is not just a God of believers. He is the Creator of heaven and earth, and so he is not particularist, in the way that human belief in him is particularist; he is as universal as the sun which rises on the evil and the good, and the rain which falls upon the just and on the unjust, and gives life to everything created (Matt. 5.45). A theology solely for believers would be the ideology of a Christian religious society, or an esoteric mystery doctrine for the initiated. It would be in utter contradiction to the universal God-ness of God, and his public revelation as the God of Israel and the Father of Jesus Christ. It is not theology that has an absolute claim. What does have that claim is the one God, about whom theology talks in human terms. Neither the tolerance required of human beings, nor the situation of the multifaith society in which Christians exist today, can narrow down the universal offer of the gospel, and the

---

* F. D. E. Scheiermacher, *Glaubenslehre* (1821; revised 1830). The title of the English translation, however, is *The Christian Faith*, Edinburgh 1928; Philadelphia 1976.

eschatological invitation to the new creation of all things through God.

Ever since the seventeenth century, Pietist movements have repeatedly set up the ideal of a *theologia regenitorum*, a theology of the regenerate – the reborn – in which personal conversion was made the precondition for theology, and theology was turned into a sectarian in-group mentality. But this withdrawal into the devout self and the self-endorsing conventicle abandoned 'the wicked world' to its godlessness, and was at odds with the gospel's missionary universalism. The withdrawal of Christian presence and theology from society's public institutions may – as it claims to do – preserve the purity of Christian identity, but it surrenders the relevance of the Christian message.[6] This Christian relevance is not self-related. It is related to God's kingdom and his righteousness and justice. What the church is about is something more than the church. The church is about life in proximity to the kingdom of God, and about the experience and praxis of the justice and righteousness of that kingdom. So Christian theology also has to do with more than Christian self-presentation in public life. It has to do with the presentation of public life against the horizon of God's coming kingdom. Christian theology is *theologia publica*. It is public theology for the sake of the kingdom. So it must be aligned and think not just intra-textually, but always correlatively too. It has to be both 'in accordance with Scripture' and contextual.

2. The theology of atheists

In resisting the limitation of theology to believing Christians, we therefore ask: is not every unbeliever who has a reason for his atheism and his decision not to believe a theologian too? Atheists who have something against both God and faith in God usually know very well whom and what they are rejecting, and have their reasons.[7] Nietzsche's book *The Antichrist* has a lot to teach us about true Christianity, and the modern criticism of religion put forward by Feuerbach, Marx and Freud is still theological in its anti-theology. Beyond that, moreover, there is a protest atheism which wrestles with God as Job did, and for the sake of the suffering of created beings which cries out to high heaven denies that there is a just God who rules the world in love. This atheism is profoundly theological, for the theodicy question – 'If there is a good God, why all this evil? – is also the fundamental question of every Christian theology which takes seriously the question that the dying Christ throws at God: 'My God, why have you forsaken me?'

Dostoievsky splendidly presents the two sides of theology, the believing side and the doubting side, in the brothers Karamazov, Alyosha and Ivan.[8] The one submits, the other rebels. The story which Ivan tells to illustrate his rebellion against God is a horrible one. A Russian landowner sets his hounds on a little boy. They hunt him to death, tearing him to pieces before his mother's eyes. 'What kind of harmony is that in which there are hells like this?' accuses Ivan, and replies, 'Is there anyone in the whole world who could forgive, and who is allowed to forgive? I don't like the harmony. I don't like it because of my love for the world. I would rather keep the enduringly unreconciled suffering . . . It isn't that I refuse to acknowledge God, but I am respectfully giving him back my ticket to a world like this. Understand me, I accept God, but I don't accept the world God has made. I cannot resolve to accept it.' Here Ivan does not simply pose the theodicy question with its indictment of God – the question why God permits crimes like this. He asks the question about justice – about guilt and expiation. He asks who could forgive guilt like this, and in doing so he gives Alyosha the word he needs: 'That is rebellion. You say: is there a being in the whole world who could forgive and is allowed to forgive? There is someone, and he can forgive everything, all and everyone, and for everything, because he himself poured out his innocent blood for everyone and everything. You have forgotten him. It is on him alone that the building will be built [he means the 'harmony' of the 'divine world', the kingdom of God]. To him we can cry: "Just art Thou Lord, for all Thy ways have been revealed."'

Protest atheism there – the theology of the cross here. Rebellion over the 'enduringly unexpiated suffering' there – universal reconciliation through the crucified God here. In the dissimilar brothers Karamazov Dostoievski portrays himself. Both can be found in every true Christian theology – rebellion against the God who permits so much meaningless suffering in his world, and faith in the crucified Christ, who suffers with the victims and prays for the perpetrators. The person who has never contended with God like Job does not understand the death cry of the crucified Christ. And conversely, the person who does not believe in God and his justice ends up by no longer rebelling against the 'enduringly unexpiated suffering' in this unjust world either, but gets accustomed to it.[9]

Christian faith in God is not a naive basic trust. It is unfaith that has been overcome: 'Lord, I believe, help thou my unbelief.' In the fellowship of the assailed and crucified Christ faith grows up in the pains of one's own suffering and the doubts of one's own heart. Here the contradictions and rebellions do not have to be suppressed. They can be admitted. Those who recognize God's presence in the face of the God-forsaken Christ have protest atheism within themselves – but as something they have overcome. So they can well understand the atheists who can no more get away from their atheism than they can get away from the God whose existence they have to deny in order to be atheists. Christian theology is theology for Christ's sake, and in Christ it reaches out beyond the alternatives between simple theism and the atheism that corresponds to it.[10]

In the fellowship of Christ the justification of God by way of an 'unflawed world', and the calling God in question through the evil and suffering in this world which is so bitterly flawed, are no longer 'the last word'. So Christian theology does not belong solely in the circle of people who are 'insiders'. It belongs just as much to the people who feel that they are 'outside the gate' (as Wolfgang Botchert puts it). A Christian theologian must not just get to know the devout and the religious. He must know the godless too, for he belongs to them as well.

3. *Theology in interfaith dialogue*

So much for theological existence in the atheism of a secular
society. But what does *the secularity of a multifaith society*
require of Christian theologians?

Dialogue is the concept that has seemed appropriate for the
encounter and co-existence of different religious communities
in modern society.[11] Even though that is not necessarily the last
word, it is true that all multifaith existence begins with the
mutual recognition which leads us to listen to each other and
talk to each other. So we may expect Christian theologians
to be *capable of dialogue*. That means interest in the other
religion, an open-minded awareness of its different life, and the
will to live together – what Theo Sundermeier calls 'convivence'
(Spanish *convivencia*), which is more than mere co-existence.
But the more usual state of affairs in a multifaith society is
indifference towards other religions, the ghettoization of the
others or the self-isolation of one's own religious group, and an
uninterested, silent existence side by side. For of course any
interest in another religion and all open-mindedness towards a
different kind of life makes one's own religion open to change,
and one's own life vulnerable. Studies in comparative religion
are extremely helpful in providing knowledge about other
religions, and every trained Christian theologian should be able
to say what other religion he or she has intensively studied. But
for all that, we have to realize that religious studies do not
make people capable of dialogue, because they present the
different religions with scientific objectivity and are in themselves a-religious. They do not ask the question about God.
Consequently the science of religion does not enable people to
engage in the dispute between the different religions themselves.

To be capable of dialogue also means *to merit dialogue*. Only
people who have arrived at a firm standpoint in their own
religion, and who enter into dialogue with the resulting self-
confidence, merit dialogue. It is only if we are at home in our
own religion that we shall be able to encounter the religion of

someone else. The person who falls victim to the relativism of the multicultural society may be capable of dialogue, but that person does not merit dialogue; for after all, the representatives of other religions do not want to talk to modern religious relativists. They are interested in convinced Christians, Jews, Muslims, and others. Pluralism is not as such a religion. It is not even a particularly helpful theory for interfaith dialogue. People who begin with this motto soon have nothing more to say, and no one will go on listening to them either.

In serious dialogue we perceive our own identity over against the other in the measure to which we perceive that other. Scholars belonging to other religions often perceive the particular character of Christianity more distinctly than Christian theologians. If we wish to know ourselves, it is important for us to see ourselves in the mirror of other eyes too. But in dialogue the partners acquire a new profile in what they themselves *are* – a *dialogue* profile. The better this is worked out in the dialogue, the more clearly the partners will perceive their own selves. This means that dialogue is not an antithesis to mission. In dialogue, the partners involved become mutual witnesses to the truth of their own religion: the Jew witnesses to the Christian, the Christian to the Muslim, the Muslim to the Christian and the Jew.

Serious dialogue is not a cultural forum for talk shows and entertainment. And dialogue only becomes serious when it becomes *necessary*. It becomes necessary in the face of a life-threatening conflict, where a peaceful solution has to be sought jointly, by way of dialogue. 'If we don't talk to each other now, we shall be shooting at each other tomorrow.' All the partners to a dialogue bring themselves into the undertaking with the whole truth of their religion. The exchange of graceful courtesies helps no one. Dialogue has to be about the question of truth, even if no agreement about the truth can be reached. For consensus is not the goal of the dialogue. Once the one side is convinced by the other, the dialogue is at an end. If two people say the same thing, one of them is superfluous. In the interfaith dialogue which has to do with what is of vital and absolute concern to men and women – with the things in which they place the whole trust of their hearts – the way is already part of the goal, provided that it makes living together possible in the midst of the unbridgeable differences. Finally, dialogue cannot be carried on only by experts who speak simply for themselves. Every participant must be able to speak for his or her community too. If the people concerned become too detached from their own communities, they will have difficulty in talking to their own people later.

Many experiences in ideological and religious dialogues suggest that the path of dialogue may be described as follows: from anathema to dialogue – from dialogue to co-existence – from co-existence to convivence – from convivence to co-operation. The goal of interfaith dialogue is not a single, unifed religion, nor is it the transformation and absorption of the different religions into the pluralist service-offer of a religious consumer society. The goal is 'reconciled difference', the difference which is endured and productively shaped.

It is useful to distinguish between *direct* and *indirect* dialogue. Direct dialogue is the religious dialogue between different religions – the religions which we call world religions, because they are not bound to a single people, culture or language, but can be found all over the world. This dialogue has to do with the confrontation and comparison of different religious concepts of transcendence and salvation, the understanding of humanity and nature. Here Christianity must come forward with its trinitarian view of God, its theology of the cross, its doctrine of salvation, and its eschatology, and it must be taken seriously in these convictions. But the idea that through dialogue the great world religions can arrive at peace between themselves, and can make a contribution to the peace of the world, is a Western notion; for 'book' religions are naturally better equipped for spoken dialogue and logical argumentation than meditative and ritual ones. This is already evident from the fact that the animist religions of Africa, Australia and America are virtually unrepresented in the direct dialogue programmes.

Indirect dialogue takes place today at local levels where social questions are at issue, and at global levels in conferences on the environment. Here the purpose is not to exchange religious ideas. The driving concern is a shared perception of the present deadly perils to which the world is exposed, and the search for common ways out of them. How have the world religions helped to justify the modern spoilations of the world? What can they do to save the earth we share? Where do the religions harbour forces hostile to life, prepared for violence, and destructive of the world? And what changes are required to make the religions humane forces which affirm life and preserve the world? This dialogue is indirect because we are not talking about ourselves or each other. We are talking together about a third factor – something outside ourselves. Even if we seek interfaith dialogue in order to find a global ethic for global peace, we are really engaged in indirect dialogue. In this indirect dialogue about social and ecological questions, the sages of the religions which are called 'primitive' or 'animist' begin to find a voice, and are listened to, because they preserve a wealth of social and ecological wisdom from the pre-industrial era, which we have to translate into the post-industrial age if this world is to survive.

This, finally, brings us to a new definition of *what a world religion is*. In the future, only a religion which promotes and secures the survival of humanity in the framework of the earth's organism will be able to count as a world religion. Here it is valuable to remember and respect that hidden 'religion of the earth' about which Israel's sabbath laws tell us. Every seventh year the earth is to remain untilled, so that 'the land may keep its great sabbath to the Lord' (Leviticus 25 and 26). That is the 'divine worship' of the earth.

The frame of reference which the state provides for interfaith dialogue (whether direct or indirect) establishes the following fundamental conditions: 1. Separation between religion and state, through the disengagement of the state from religion, and of religion from the state; 2. State protection for the free practice of religion by the various communities, and for the religious freedom of individuals; 3. A common system of laws equally valid for all religious groups. The secular state – religiously neutral – cannot permit human and civil rights to be infringed in the name of any religion. It must guarantee personal liberty to enter or leave a religious group. Anyone who wishes to participate in the dialogue between the religions, and who wishes to be taken seriously in that dialogue, must respect this framework which the state provides. Freedom of religion is a human right which takes precedence over the different religions themselves.

3

How does someone become a true theologian? Suffering from God and delight in God

Theology is not an objective science which has to do with facts that can be pinned down, and circumstances that can be proved. It does not belong to the field of objective knowledge which is under our control. Its sphere is the knowledge that sustains existence, that gives us courage to live and comfort in dying. Nor does theology fall under the technology which we learn so as to dominate things or control human feelings. Theology has at heart only one problem: God. God is the passion of theologians, their torment and their delight. But God can only be loved 'with all our heart and with all our soul and with all our might'. So a theologian must be wholly concentrated. We cannot do theology half-heartedly, or with a divided mind or soul, or merely by the way. Theologians will bring the whole of their existence into their search for knowledge about God. 'Subjectivity is truth.' That postulate of Kierkegaard's is true at least for theologians.

'To know God means to suffer God', says a wise old theological saying. We suffer God when we experience his absence, when God 'hides his face', and we feel God-forsaken, as Christ did on the cross. The young Luther described this out of his own experience in 1519:

> By living, no – more – by dying and being damned to hell doth a man become a theologian, not by knowing, reading, or speculation.

('*Vivendo, immo moriendo et damnando fit theologus, non intelligendo, legendo aut speculando*', WA 5, 163).

Luther was a professor, and he told his students this in his second lecture on the Psalms.[12] Of course in saying this he was not condemning study, reading or reflection. But reading, reflection and the understanding of Scripture have to be accompanied by this personal wrestling with God, so that theology becomes not just a scholarly study which teaches, but also a *wisdom* which makes wise out of the experience of God. Experience comes first and then the theology; first the passion – then the action.

This kind of theology – theology as wisdom – may be compared with psychoanalysis. One can become a psychoanalyst only if one has undergone an analysis oneself, and if one knows oneself. Much the same is true of theology as wisdom. True theologians must have addressed and worked through their struggles with God, their experiences of God, their fears of God, and their joy in God. They must have laid themselves open personally to the things they maintain, and must neither suppress their negative experiences of their own selves before God, nor hide their positive delight in God (Ps. 37.4). It is good if we can perceive the theologian in his or her theology – good, if in those who have 'the cure of souls' we can sense the soul that has itself been deeply touched.

To know God by suffering God is only one aspect of existential theology. It is one-sided to make it a reason for declaring, as Luther did, that the *theologia crucis*, the theology of the cross, is the only true Christian theology. In the psalms, God is already an object of delight, too, of joy and rejoicing. When God does not 'hide' his face but, in the words of the Aaronic benediction, lets it shine upon those who are his and his whole creation, life comes alive and is filled with inexpressible joy; for this fellowship with the creative, life-giving God is the very 'fullness of life'. We experience an unrestrained and boundless delight in the God 'who surrounds us from every side' (Ps. 139.5) because our limited earthly life can then unfold on every side 'in' God, that 'large room' (Ps. 31.8 AV). Earlier, people called this joy in God (*fruitio Dei*).

In this delight in God, the theology of the people who experience it becomes a kind of intellectual love for God, a 'delight in the Lord' and 'pleasure in wisdom' (Wisdom 6.21). Thoughts no longer just 'flow'. They begin to dance and play before God in what we might call theo-fantasy. They also move along with measured steps, in logical progressions, so that they can think God in ways appropriate to him, avoiding inner contradictions and irrational mental leaps, and can experience truth in these conformities. This then deserves the name of theo-logy. In tense narratives, God's saving history with those he has created is put on stage. A kind of 'theo-drama' then corresponds to God's great drama of salvation.[13] Not least, human theology also participates in the great 'play' of God's Wisdom, which Proverbs 8 says is the true Logos of creation and the real secret of the world:

> I was set up from everlasting, from the beginning,
> before ever the earth was . . .
> Then I was beside him like a master workman,
> and I was daily his delight,
> playing before him always,
> playing upon his earth and delighting
> in the children of men (23.30–31).

The true theology of 'the children of men' is participation in the delighted loveplay of the divine Wisdom, which interpenetrates everything created.[14] It is what Vladimir Solovyev called sophiology. The word 'play' does not mean something superficial or casual. It is the profound, unreasoning pleasure in God's presence, which goes far beyond all the purpose-and-profit rationality of instrumentalized human reason. In the image of play, we express the truth that the creation of the world is in itself meaningful but by no means necessary.[15] With this image we describe the contingency, the uniqueness of existence, its never-to-be-repeated character. The profound sense of human theology is to participate in the play of the divine Wisdom, and thereby to fulfil the destiny of human beings 'to glorify God and enjoy him for ever', as the Westminster Catechism of 1647 put it, in the spirit of Calvin. This also characterizes personal experience in faith: 'He delivered me because he delighted in me' (Ps. 18.19).

Summing up, we may say that the beauty of theology lies in its *doxology*, and delight in God is expressed through joy over existence in nearness to him. According to the New Testament, the gospel of Christ is filled with God's joy, for that gospel is the message about the raising of the crucified Christ from death, God-forsakenness and hell, into the eternally living life of God and of 'the world to come'. That is *God's counter-history* to the world's history of disaster. Easter joy is the doxological utterance of Christian belief in God.[16]

God's grace (*charis*) finds its response in human joy (*chara*), and God's glory (*doxa*) is answered by human thinking and believing (*doko*). The kingdom of God which appeared in the raising of Christ from death is the 'joyful feast of the Lord' (Matt. 25.21), and the biblical greeting 'Rejoice in the Lord always' (Phil. 4.4) is grounded on the presence of the risen Christ. The resurrection of the dead Christ makes the whole of life what Athanasius called 'a feast without end', and a song against death, hell and God-forsakenness. 'Your resurrection, O Lord, illumines the universe. The whole creation praises you, bringing you daily a hymn,' says the Orthodox Easter liturgy.[17]

It is not just human theology which should be understood as an expression of the undreamt-of, exuberant Easter joy in God. The same is already true of the church's 'dogma'. 'Dogma is a component of living adoration itself.'[18] If this is not to remain liturgical esotericism, it must emphatically be stressed that the resurrection faith breaks through the whole pattern of this world, calling in question and entering the lists against the powers of this world, to which human beings have become accustomed. 'Death, where is thy sting? Hell, where is thy victory?' (I Cor. 15.55). Delight in Christ's resurrection makes Christians what Christoph Blumhardt aptly called 'protest people against death'. And that includes the protest against the political and economic forces which have made a covenant with death.

4

Theology of history

In the following sections we shall try to work out the particular character of the biblical – and especially the Christian – belief in God, so as to see whether theology is necessary and, if it is necessary, what characteristics and functions it takes on.

1. *The God of Abraham, Isaac and Jacob: religions of history*

Like Judaism and Islam, Christianity is called a *religion of history*, over against the great Asiatic 'cosmic' religions. If the intention is to emphasize the particular human experience of God which underlies these three religions of history, they are also called *Abrahamic* religions, since Abraham counts as their common 'father' or progenitor, even though they interpret his experience of God in very different ways. We shall first look at these two qualities – historical* and Abrahamic – and shall ask about their positive and negative consequences for the under-standing of reality and the self-interpretation of the people con-cerned.

The God about whom the '*historical*' religions speak is not, like the divine in the 'cosmic' religions, always already so mani-fest and evident in the laws of the cosmos and the rhythms and cycles of life that no special revelation is required for the divinity to be perceived; *this* God reveals himself to the people

---

* German can distinguish between 'the study of history' as a discipline (*Historie*) and 'history' as the historicity of human existence (*Geschichte*). It is in this latter sense that the word 'historical' is used here.

of his choice in contingent events of human history.[19] He is therefore named after the people whom he encounters and whom he has called. That is how talk about 'the God of Abraham, the God of Isaac and the God of Jacob' came about – and it is a way of speaking unique in the history of religion. In the Egypt and Babylon of the same era, kings called themselves after the gods of the peoples in order to have themselves worshipped as sons of God. But with Israel's 'God of the fathers', we find the precise opposite. In the other great religions, any such humanization of the divine counts as blasphemy. So for the 'historical' religions – the religions of history – the naming of God after the people who experienced him must have a particular significance. But this naming does not imply a humanization of God. If we look closely, we see that it is a way of safeguarding the unnameable divine mystery. In the story of Abraham in Gen. 12.1–4, Abraham does not ask about the name of 'the Lord' whose call and promise he has heard. Instead he 'went out as the Lord had told him'. In the story about Moses' call in Ex. 3.13–14, the answer to his question about God's name is: 'I will be the one whom I will be' (v.14), which simply means: follow my call and 'I will be with you' (v.12). God's real presence is not perceived through the contemplation of nature, or through consideration of the ways history runs its course. It is discerned by way of action in history in God's name – action, moreover, that is innovative, without prototype and example. It thus becomes itself the prototype and example for those who come later.

Judaism, Christianity and Islam all appeal, each in its own way, to '*the faith of Abraham*' (Rom. 4.16), and thus to the experience of God particular to Abraham and Sarah.[20] Remarkably, this experience is the experience of estrangement and hope, exile and future: 'Go from your country and your father's house and your kindred to the land that I will show you. And I will make of you a great nation, and I will bless you, and you shall be a blessing. In you shall all the families of the earth be blessed' (Gen. 12.1–3). When Abraham and Sarah 'went out', their experience of God meant for them estrangement from everything which means home for human life: country, people, family, kindred and friendship. In this experience of God they become homeless, lonely, unloved asylum-seekers in an unfriendly, hostile world. Their freedom becomes the freedom of the desert.

This too has no prototype in the history of religion. Everywhere else the religious experience of human beings is, after all, intended to bring them into harmony with the divine laws of the cosmos, and integrate them into the life-furthering rhythms and cycles of nature. Everywhere else safekeeping – security – counts as primal religious experience. But here it is the lack of security and the vulnerability which are the consequence of departure from the shelter of natural and social environments. This price for liberty is indeed high. As the history of civilization shows, it can also lead to the destruction of the nature which has now become alien. This price for the future – the future into which the divine promise given through Abraham and Sarah is to lead 'all the families on the earth' – can entail a breach with the past, which is now no longer deserving of a backward glance.

If, with this in mind, we take a look at the biblical narratives about God, we discover that from beginning to end they are histories of exile and exodus, freedom and estrangement, homecoming and indwelling.

The history of disaster begins when Adam and Eve are driven out of the paradise where they were at home with God.[21] The rest was labour and struggle on an unfriendly earth: 'Cursed is the ground because of you . . . thorns and thistles it shall bring forth to you' (Gen. 3.17f.). The history of violence begins with Cain's fratricide – his murder of his brother Abel. Cain is condemned to be 'a fugitive and a wanderer on the earth' from which his brother's blood cries out to high heaven (Gen. 4.10, 12). Joseph is sold into Egypt by his brothers, and has to live as a prisoner in the foreign country (Genesis 37). After the destruction of the First Temple, Israel is carried off into Babylonian exile, and the Israelites become displaced persons. After the destruction of the Second Temple by the Romans, God's people are scattered among all the nations. That is the *galuth* which endures to the present day, from which, according to some theological interpretations, only the Messiah will redeem Israel.

The histories of salvation show continually new beginnings, so that there may be a homecoming from exile and an arrival at God's rest from unrest, whether this be through a return home to God's country, or through entry into God's time. God's indwelling in the Temple (his Shekinah) represents God's real presence in space, while every interruption of working time on the sabbath represents his real presence in time.[22] Both point beyond themselves to the new, eternal creation which God will indwell. The biblical narratives about God deepen the experience of exile more and more, so that the ardent desire to come home and to arrive at rest grows into the universal and the ultimate. Yet conversely, the more the greatness of God's promises is comprehended, the more restless the hearts and the more homeless the existence of those who have been touched by them.

2. *The experience of time – remembrance – narrative: 'scriptural religion'*

As we can see from every comparison with the cyclical understanding of time found in the Asian religions, the Abrahamic religions of history have developed a unique understanding of *time*. For people who are on the move because they have no homeland, the past is 'behind' them and the future is 'ahead'. The future brings something new and does not repeat what is past. The repetitive element in events is disregarded. What claims attention is the contingently new, because what is expected is the fulfilment of what has been previously promised. Consequently the world exists, not in the great equilibrium of mutually harmonizing forces, as in the world of Tao, but in a disequilibrium of future and past, because it is aligned towards future. This has nothing to do with a modern, linear concept of time, for future and past are not the same in quality. They differ, as possibility and reality. Time is not irreversible, as in the 'ever-circling spheres' of the eternal return. It is irreversible, in the difference between before and after, past and future. The future becomes past, but the past never again becomes future. The time-arrow of the divine promise points from the past into the future. The Abrahamic, 'historical' religions have left sheltering space and have discovered the challenging future.

Religions of exile are always *religions of time*. God's presence is worshipped at certain times. On the Jewish sabbath God 'dwells' in time, and makes of the sabbath 'the Jewish cathedral'.[23] Sanctified spaces give way to sanctification in time. Every moment in time is unique and can never be brought back, and is therefore infinitely precious, for it is one in essence with eternity.

If time is irreversible and nothing ever returns, then the unity of history can only be maintained through *recall and remembrance*. If we only existed from day to day we should lose our identity. It is memory alone which preserves continuity in time. The biblical religions of history live from recall and remembrance. This becomes incomparably clear from the Jewish recollection of history. '*Zachor* – Remember!' These countless appeals are addressed either to Israel or to God, 'for remembrance is incumbent on them both'.[24] The 'historical' religions have developed an 'anamnetic culture'[25] which is largely unknown to religions whose native home is the earthly and cosmic spaces. Who is reminded? On the one hand, *the people* is reminded of God's 'mighty acts', so that every new generation can identify itself with God's promises, uttered to past generations. On the other hand, *God* is reminded of the privations, the persecutions and sufferings of the people in the far-off land, so that he may swiftly set out to their aid. The story of God's unfulfilled promises and the story of the unavenged suffering of the people must be remembered from one generation to another.

The medium of remembrance is first of all *the telling of the story*.[26] Since the story is still unfinished, it is told in such a way that it continues in and with the listeners. The past is remembered because the future it hides is to awaken the hopes of the next generation. So what is told is not really something past, which has had its time. It is something which has gone forth but which still has its time ahead of it. The story of the divine promises is told and passed on in the form of the remembered hopes of the people. This is remembrance in which one can live and which is essential for living.

The medium of the story told becomes afterwards the *writing* which is read and interpreted. Whereas the story-teller remembers what he is telling, and interprets it for his listeners in the same breath, the story which is fixed in writing demands its living interpretation in every new situation and for every new group of listeners, so that these too may be drawn into the story's future. Although it has been written down, the story is not tethered to its past. Nor is it integrated in any given present. Its goal and its criterion is neither its past nor its present but its future. At a time of deportation and exile, the *writing* is important, because the narrating communities have been torn apart. The religions which are called 'historical' have consequently become *scriptural religions*. The point of the long genealogies in these writings is, read backwards, continuity in the origins; read forwards it is their content as promise. In relation to the people's remembrance of God's promises, the reading that points forwards takes precedence – in relation to God's remembrance of the sufferings of his people, the reading that points backwards.

3. *The discernment of God in history*

'The God of Abraham, the God of Isaac and the God of Jacob' was worshipped as the God of the fathers; thus the fact that God is named three times has its particular significance (Ex. 3.6).[27] But 'the Lord' was first manifested to Moses in his liberation of the people from slavery in Egypt. 'I am the Lord. I appeared to Abraham, to Isaac, and to Jacob as God Almighty,

but by my name the Lord I did not make myself known to them'
(Ex. 6.2f.).

The Exodus event is a complex one, but from the account in
the book of Exodus we can clearly see what the *discernment of
God in history* is. The name 'Lord' means a self-lowering on
God's part: 'I have seen the affliction of my people and have
come down' (Ex. 3.8). A cry of suffering out of the depths of
human misery precedes this divine coming. The name of God is
not named, but it is elucidated through the promise of his
faithfulness: 'I will be with you' (3.12). Luther translates the
difficult text 3.14 in the sense of ' "I-will-be" has sent me'. I will
go with you and you will find me there in the place to which I
send you. This present promise must suffice for the trust of the
people as they go out from Egypt. But it demands trust that is
entire, undivided and unsecured. The expression 'the Lord' is
none other than the assurance of freedom for the enslaved
people. It has nothing to do with the lords who are enslaving
them, and nothing to do with male domination either. Moreover, according to the apocryphal Wisdom of Solomon it is not
'the Lord' who led and liberated the people, but 'Wisdom'.
Wisdom 'brought them through the Red Sea and led them
through deep waters' (10.18). According to later rabbinic
writings, it was God's Shekinah which carried Israel out of
slavery into freedom.[28] YHWH; HOKHMAH, RUACH and
SHEKINAH are the terms for the particular historical real
presence of the almighty God seen from its different aspects.
Consequently in the New Testament Jesus can be called 'Lord'
and also the Holy Spirit (II Cor. 3.17). It is not the word 'Lord'
which interprets the Exodus story. The reverse is the case: the
story, with its awakened hopes and the experiences it records,
interprets the word 'Lord'.

Finally, the sequence is important. It is not that God reveals
himself as the Lord, but that 'the Lord is God' because, through
his accompaniment and his liberation, he *becomes* the God of
this people. The uniqueness of the Exodus into the liberty of the
covenant with the Lord then calls into being knowledge, or discernment, of the uniqueness of this God: 'That all the peoples

of the earth may know that the Lord is God; there is no other' (I Kings 8.60). The specific becomes universal, the particular general, the historical eschatological.

Israel is born and called into existence out of this Exodus as the people of the Lord's covenant. Is this happening a *historical event*? It is a historical event; not only, however, because it took place in temporal history and had its time, but because it *opens* the history of 'the Lord' with Israel. This happening threw open the future of freedom for the enslaved people, and is an event powerful in history, as long as the people identify themselves with it, continue to remember it and call it to mind, and 'make it present'. Israel's Exodus only becomes a historical event which is past and gone when the people ceases to assure itself of 'the Lord' and of its own self in that event. 'In every age each must see himself as if he himself has gone out from Egypt,' it is said at the Passover feast (Pessachim 10.5). And with this the covenant on Sinai and the Torah also become present in the presence of 'the Lord' and do not just belong to the human past, from which the human present can cut itself off. In the Passover feast, the event which throws open the future is made present so that every coming generation can find itself in this history, and can continue it.

We can now differentiate, and ask: when and where, and through what, does God's revelation take place? According to the story in the book of Exodus, it takes place through God's own presentation of himself: 'I am the God . . .' (3.6). We meet this 'I am' formula in the first commandment, and frequently later. The people are to know: 'I am the Lord.' That is a self-revelation of God in his self-presentation through his Word.[29] Another possibility would be for God to reveal himself indirectly through his acts in history.[30] Understood as an act of God, the miracle at the Reed Sea, which finally freed Israel from the military power of the Egyptian Pharaohs, casts a revealing light on the One who performs the act: God is the liberator because he has liberated Israel. The question is only: what, then, brought the Israelites to the Reed Sea? It was surely the promise given in the word 'of the Lord' mediated through

Moses. For the hope of liberation which prompted their departure at dead of night, there were no guarantees and no factual
proofs before the Reed Sea miracle. Even afterwards there were
doubts and tribulations enough in the wilderness to make the
people look back and yearn for the fleshpots of Egypt, even as
slaves. The possibility which sums up the two ideas – promise
and act – is discernment of the faithfulness of the God who
performs what he says and fulfils what he promises.[31] In the
harmony between the promise to Moses which is heard,
believed and obeyed, and the 'signs and wonders' accompanying the Exodus which are experienced, the people become
assured of the Lord's faithfulness, and in this perceive his
nature and his truth; for his truth is his faithfulness, and faithfulness is his essential nature.

Just as the Exodus event opens Israel's history with God,
so the event of *Christ's death and resurrection* opens up the
history with God of the fellowship of Christians among the
nations. In the Exodus, God reveals himself as 'the Lord' by
freeing his enslaved people from the religious and political
powers of the Egyptian Pharaohs, making them the people
of his covenant, and leading them into the promised land of
liberty. In cross and resurrection, God reveals himself as 'the
Father' by raising Jesus from the dead and making him 'Lord'
over his kingdom and the redeemer of the nations. There God's
power is liberation from a historical tyrant, here it is liberation
from the tyranny of the power of death in history. There the
Exodus leads into the promised land of liberty, here the resurrection leads into the 'large room' of the eternal life of the
future world, in which death is no more. The parallels and
analogies are manifest. There the event which opens history,
because it throws open the future, is made present in the
Passover feast, so that each new generation in Israel can live in
and with this narrative. Here the event which opens history and
throws open the future – the resurrection of the crucified Christ
– is made present in Christ's feast, so that believers can live 'in'
the Christ who has died 'for them' and has risen ahead of them.

In *the Lord's supper*, the eucharist, what history and life 'between the times' means for Christians is experienced in an exemplary and definitive way. It is the sign of remembrance of Christ's suffering and death 'for many', a remembrance which makes present, and as such it is what Aquinas calls a commemorative sign – a *signum rememorativum*. In its making-present of the new world of the resurrection and eternal life it is also a foreshadowing sign, a *signum prognosticon*. And in the simultaneity of the remembered suffering and death of Christ and the anticipated glory of Christ risen and to come, it is a demonstrative sign – a *signum demonstrativum* – of Christ's present grace.[32] In this feast, in our mindfulness of Christ's history of suffering, his redeeming future is, in anticipation, already given. As the simultaneous presence of the Christ who has come and the Christ who will come, it is the sacrament of remembered hope. 'In it the time is "fulfilled", the past is present *today* and *for us*; in it the One who will come is "there", *today* and *for us*.'[33] The feast is 'open' in a forward direction, because it throws open God's future and sets us in this history, which leads to God's new world. The Lord's supper, the eucharist, is therefore for Christian theology the true 'historical sign'.[34]

Again we can ask about the revelatory moment or element. Is it to be found in the self-identifying 'I am' sayings of the risen Christ, or in the event of his death and resurrection itself? Does the liberating effect lie in the forgiveness of sins through Christ's vicarious suffering and death, or rather in the victory over the power of death through the Christ raised by God and risen? Or do the two liberating acts belong together in the opening up of the future of the new creation and eternal life? In the light of the eschatological future to be disclosed, one-sided theologies of the cross and one-sided Easter theologies are both inadmissible. In distinction from Exodus and Passover, in the Christ event and in the eucharist it is not just a historically remaining future that is thrown open; it is a future *eschatologically new*. And because of that, here history is made *final history*. History is no longer experienced against the horizon of the future in time. Its horizon is now the eschatological future.

'The end of all things is at hand' (I Peter 4.7).

This 'nearness' of eternal life, the kingdom of God and the new heaven and the new earth must not be pinned down chronologically. It is a *category of intimacy*, and means that which touches believers 'nearly' and is closest to their hearts, so that they live from it and act in accordance with it, just as in the 'nearness' of God's kingdom Jesus himself prayed 'Abba', dear Father, and out of the 'nearness' of the kingdom healed the sick, received outcasts and raised the dead.

4. *'Knowing' God – 'forgetting' God*

How do experiences of God in history become a *theology of history?* According to Gerhard von Rad, Israel's earliest acknowledgments of its God were already determined by history.[35] The name of God is indissolubly linked with an experienced and remembered historical act. We always find the name YHWH used in connection with the Exodus event. Originally there were no abstract terms for God – only factual and specific histories with God. But as histories with God these acquire a confessional character which goes beyond the story itself. Von Rad calls them 'salvation history summaries', and has pin-pointed the creed in Deut. 26.5–9 as one of the most important and earliest.

A wandering Aramaean was my father; and he went down into Egypt and sojourned there, few in number; and there he became a nation, great, mighty, and populous. And the Egyptians treated us harshly, and afflicted us, and laid upon us hard bondage. Then we cried to the Lord, the God of our fathers, and the Lord heard our voice, and saw our affliction, our toil, and our oppression; and the Lord brought us out of Egypt with a mighty hand and an outstretched arm, with great terror, with signs and wonders; and he brought us into this place and gave us this land, a land flowing with milk and honey.

Here a special divine revelation is certainly missing, but its place is taken by the prayer that has been heard and the promise thereby fulfilled. The deliverance from Egypt is extolled, and the place where the people who are professing their faith now stand is drawn into the divine history, as outcome of the Exodus God has brought about. That is faith in God mediated through history. A theology of history is the discernment of God which justifies this faith and, as knowledge of history, is necessarily bound up with it. Here faith in God is not celebrated in repeatable ritual; nor, either, is it experienced through a mystical submersion in the ineffable mystery. Because it is based on a unique history, it is dependent on remembrance and remembered knowledge. So what, then, is knowledge of God?

We shall follow the analysis and interpretation which Hans Walter Wolff gave in 1953, in an article entitled ' "Knowledge of God" in Hosea as primal form of theology'.[36]

The prophet repeatedly complains that 'there is no steadfastness, no faithfulness to the covenant and no *dayat elohim* in the land' (4.1). If we were to follow Luther's translation we should read: 'No faithfulness, no love, no discernment of God.' The contrasting term for the discernment or knowledge of God is 'forgetfulness' (2.13; 13.4–6 and frequently) – not blindness, and not ignorance. To say that Israel 'forgets' God means that the people are disregarding God's covenant and precepts; but it also means that they are forgetting God's history with Israel: Exodus, covenant and election. Israel 'has forgotten its Maker' (8.14). In the counter-move to this deadly 'forgetfulness of God', to discern or know God means: 1. faithfulness to the covenant and conduct in accordance with the covenant; 2. knowledge of God's acts in leading the people out of Egypt; 3. knowledge of Yahweh, who 'goes before you' (Deut. 9.3); and 4. knowledge of Yahweh's constant presence. In 'the knowledge of God', those concerned bind together remembrance of God's liberating act, hope for God's guidance into the future, the keeping of his commandments, and love of his presence. 'It is a matter not of historical remembrance as such, but of revering the Yahweh who has been revealed, who is both the present and the coming One.'[37] Without this *knowledge of God*, 'historical' *faith* in God cannot exist at all, and cannot go on existing. The knowledge links present faith in God with past history with God, and intertwines present liberty with the liberating act of God which is its foundation. Conversely, the remembrance of God's saving act does not historicize that act into an occurrence in some far-off past; what it does is to bring the present under its influence.

For Israel, 'the Lord' of Exodus and covenant is 'God' and there is no God other than him, so the people also expect that 'the knowledge of God' will one day lay hold of all the nations *universally*, and guide them: 'Know that the Lord is God' (Ps. 100.3). When Israel's Messiah comes to the nations, he will bring not only justice and righteousness, and hence peace to the world, but also 'knowledge of the Lord'.[38] 'The earth shall be full of the knowledge of the Lord as the waters cover the sea' (Isa. 11.9). But this presupposes that Israel's Lord will assume lordship over all peoples and that 'the whole earth' will be 'full of his glory' (Isa. 6.3). Then the promise of blessing given to Abraham will be fulfilled. Israel's knowledge of God serves the future fulfilment of that promise. This universality of the knowledge of God presupposes God's universal real presence, which is first heralded particularly and *pars pro toto* in God's history with Israel. Another distinction points to this too. According to the story, Moses, the servant of God in the people's Exodus into freedom and the prototype of all Israel's future prophets, saw God 'face to face' (Deut. 34.10–12). In 'historical' faith in God, this leads to the hope that God's presence will not be mediated solely out of remembrance of the history of promise, but will be experienced directly, so that it will be possible to pass from *faith in the Word* to *the eternal contemplation of God*. But this in its turn presupposes a divine presence which is eschatological, no longer historical, a divine presence in which history will be abolished or gathered up, in the double sense of the German word *aufheben*. On the foundation of the discernment of God in history, this is what is expected of the kingdom of glory and the new creation, which God's glory will indwell.

5. *A modern 'end of history'?*

I have described the experience and discernment of God in history in such detail here because our present electronic culture is making every effort to end the *anamnetic culture* of history, and to abolish the culture which lives in remembrance and hope, absorbing it into a *postmodern culture* of 'the eternal present'. 'The future is now!' claims an advertisment for the Internet. If that is true, then this electronic *now* holds all the past within itself, and no longer has any future ahead, other than itself. We are shutting down history, and putting an end to it by transporting its past and its future into present possibilities. This can easily be seen from three trends:

1. Through historical criticism we historicize the processes of historical 'becoming' into hard facts and circumstances of the past. We reify – concretize – the processes which are open to the future, turning them into facts of history which, being finished and done with, have had their time; and these facts are duly filed away. With this, historical remembrances are transferred to processes in museums such as the entertaining *Haus der Geschichte* (House of History) in Bonn. These processes may in fact be unfinished, and their guilt not yet paid off. But – as the name *house* of history shows – this is a way of abolishing time and absorbing it into space, so that the way becomes the final goal.

2. Through unnumbered 'remembrance days' we transform unique events of history – events which open up a new future or call for one – into the eternal return of the same thing.

The solemn hours of which Germans especially are so fond ritualize contingent history. For this, religion was the preparation, transforming unique events of life and death into ritualized rites of passage. Nowadays this is the method of every bureaucracy. There are now no contingent events – only 'instances' which are dealt with 'according to precedent', so that equal treatment can be guaranteed. The present ritual then suppresses the very thing that is made present in that ritual, as when in the Christmas hymn we welcome the 'ever-circling years', or when German children in their Christmas carol sing of the yearly return of the Christ Child.

3. In place of living remembrances and the traditions moulded by memories, today we have data-processing through the computerization of all the facts that we can lay hold of. These are then retrievable at any time. But the computer's 'memory' does not remember, for it does not forget – it merely 'stores'. It can make present the whole of the past we know. It can also extrapolate, and simulate the possible futures which emerge from it. Through the computer we can make the whole of past reality present, and every possible future. That liquidates the awareness of time, brings the different times into the space of eternal simultaneity, and is rightly called 'the spatialization of the world'.[39] Through computers, E-mail, Internet, high-speed trains and supersonic aircraft we vanquish the power of passing time, and try to make all times simultaneous to ourselves. But a present which is no longer aware of any uncompleted past, a past whose business is still unfinished, no longer has any alternative future either. Its endlessness becomes a poor infinity. Omnipresence and simultaneity are apparently the God-complexes of modern men and women when they wish to be 'modern' or 'postmodern'.

And yet, do not the cries of the victims of history, which never really fall dumb, bind us to the past? And do not the promises of the God who judges and saves bring us face to face with the future? And do not both break through the banal and catastrophic illusions of our 'eternal' present?

5

Christian theology

The word theology goes back to pre-Christian antiquity. In the philosophical school of the Stoa, a distinction was made between the mythical theology of the poets (*theologia mythica* – people were thinking of the stories about the gods in Homer), the political theology of statesmen and state priests (*theologia politica*), and natural theology (*theologia naturalis*), in which philosophers enquired about the nature of the gods. The first belonged to the theatre, the second to the government of the state and the public temples, while the place of the third was the schools.[40] Once having entered the Hellenistic world, Christianity very early on adopted the genre of 'theology', and saw *theologia christiana* as the proper and particular task of the Christian faith. The place of Christian theology was pre-eminently worship, and in worship the doxology of the triune God. The Christian doctrine of salvation was called 'the dispensation of God' (*oeconomia Dei*).

What is the specifically Christian element in theology? The first answer may sound somewhat startling. It is the theology itself. Even today, scholars of other religions avoid talking about Jewish, Muslim or Buddhist theology. They prefer to speak of the religious philosophy of their religious community. The terms 'theological faculty' or 'divinity school' are also made over exclusively to Christians. But then what is the specifically Christian factor in Christian doctrine which turns it into theology? Does faith which is specifically Christian lead to theology? Is theology the proper and particular task of the church? Why cannot Christian theologians, like the rest,

confine themselves to the philosophy of the Christian religion,
or to the religious study of Christendom, or to Christian
cultural studies, instead of tormenting themselves with the lofty
and normative claim of a 'theology' – which means the discernment of God, and therefore absolute knowledge?

What is the special thing about the Christian faith? To put it
simply: it is Christ himself. If Jesus of Nazareth is confessed as
the Christ of God, then this acknowledgment presupposes the
world of messianic hope to which the historical faith of Israel
belongs – the faith which we described in the last section.
Christian faith grew up in this world of hope, and that world is
still alive in it.[41] But with the coming of the Messiah in the sending of Jesus, and in his death and resurrection, the world of that
historical faith changes. Out of the open and ambivalent future
of that history, the end of human history and the beginning of
the promised kingdom of God is heralded. With the coming of
the Messiah, historical time is qualified as messianic time. The
times of history become the end-time of history. 'The end of all
things is at hand' (I Peter 4.7); the kingdom of God is 'at hand'
(Mark 1.14). With the eschatological raising of the crucified
Christ, the end-time outpouring of the Spirit on all flesh begins.
Wherever we look in the New Testament – the earliest
Christian writings – we meet this messianic and apocalyptic
solemnity of the ultimate and final. With Christ, God's future
already thrusts into this ambivalent and transient world-time.
'Now is the acceptable time; now is the day of salvation'
(II Cor. 6.2). And with this messianic announcement of 'the
time', the Christian faith stands or falls.

But the end of history has two faces. It can be the *finis* of
history, and it can be its *telos*, either its end or its ultimate goal.
That is not just true in a general sense. It is true quite
specifically. Abraham's and Sarah's history of promise is set
forward on the road to its fulfilment; the history of violence and
suffering among the nations is brought to its end. End and
completion, termination and innovation, are so close to one
another that they are the two sides of the same coin which we
call 'the coming of God'.[42]

If the road leads from open history to the end of history – because in Christian faith we perceive the transition from the God of history to the coming of God, and from the history of salvation to the salvation of history – then we can compare this faith itself with a bridge: it is the *transition* on the one hand from 'historical' to messianic faith, and on the other the *transition* from messianic faith to the eschatological contemplation of God, face to face. Christian faith is 'historical' faith (in the sense in which we have used the word); and at the same time it is more than historical faith. Just as the name of Christ also delineates the way leading from the history of Jesus' life and death to the risen and coming Lord, so Christian faith, too, is a way and a *transition* from believing to knowing, from hoping to seeing, and from loving to understanding. In these transitions we discover the necessity of theology, its pain and its joys.

1. The reasonableness of faith: I believe so that I may understand (Credo ut intelligam)

The first transition is the road from believing to knowing or, to be more precise, from trusting faith to discerning faith. This is the step from 'an assured trust kindled in the heart' to 'certain knowledge', as we have to say, reversing the progression in the answer to Question 21 of the Heidelberg Catechism.*

This discernment belongs essentially to the nature of Christian faith, for one can believe in the sense of confident trust only what is certain. Believing has nothing to do with an uncertain supposing, as modern linguistic usage suggests – in German, especially since Kant.[43] Christian faith is not blind trust. It is faith which sees open-eyed, for it is not without an object but has a nameable 'opposite' in the history, presence and future of Christ.[44] 'We have *believed* and *know* that you are Christ, the Son of the living God,' declares Peter in the name of

---

* Question 21: 'What is faith?' 'It is not only a knowledge whereby I surely assent to all things which God hath revealed unto us in his word, but also an assured trust kindled in my heart by the Holy Ghost through the Gospel . . .'

the men and women disciples, according to the Gospel of John
(6.69). In the Johannine writings, the Christian faith is always
linked with knowledge of Christ, and this knowledge of Christ
is not conveyed merely through the 'remote' senses of eyes and
ears, and through the reason; it is communicated through the
immediate senses of tasting and seeing too: 'The word of life
which we have *seen* with our eyes, which we have *looked upon*
and *touched with our hands* . . . that life has been *made manifest*' (I John 1.1).

The God of Jesus Christ is not a dark and obscure mystery,
which we approach by closing our eyes and by mystical submersion in the inwardness of our own hearts. He is the manifest
God of life, whom we encounter in the history of Christ – open
to the future as it is – because this history draws us into its
process. It is for Christ's sake that Christians believe in 'the
living God'. Without Christ, many of them would be atheists,
as in the nineteenth century Johannes Gottschick said of himself. Those who believe in God for Christ's sake believe in 'the
Father of Jesus Christ' – the name given to him in the New
Testament. They are not people with any special religious
endowment. They hear what everyone can hear, see what everyone can perceive, and believe what everyone can trust in.

Faith and discernment are the two sides of the Christian
faith, the personal side and the objective side. In faith I relate
personally to Christ and link my present with his presence; in
discernment I relate objectively to Christ and perceive him as he
is, and would be even if I did not exist.[45] In discernment I see in
him not just *my* Lord and the Redeemer *for me*, but *the* Lord
and *the* Redeemer *per se*. In discernment I draw back from
myself and seek his truth 'as it really is'. It is only when I discern
the God of Christ as he is in himself that I discern him as he is –
present not just for me but for other people too, and for the
whole world. It is only then that I find his truth, free from my
surmising and the images of my desires, and hence communicable and deserving of worship. The Christian confession of
faith which says 'You *are* the Christ, the Son of the living God'
is therefore more than a subjective value-judgment, with which

believers express the 'value' Christ has for them. This pronouncement is an existential judgment – a judgment about being – with which they intend to express who Christ is in himself. Despite Kant's criticism, believers cannot restrict themselves to saying 'I am certain'. They must express the objective assurance 'It is certain'.[46] It is only in knowing Christ that faith in Christ finds its way to this objectivity, which alone is appropriate for the God-ness of God. Christian theology begins by perceiving what is believed *because it is certain*.

But what does this *certain perception* look like? What perception, and the perception of what, can offer certainty in a world in which, after all, doubt is considered to be the only justifiable beginning of all science? The renowned monastic Father Anselm of Canterbury did not develop his theology in the university world of scholarship, but in the monastery, within the orbit of the church. And it is from him that we have the axiom: Christian faith is faith seeking understanding (*fides quaerens intellectum*). Christian faith seeks to understand what it believes. More even than that: I believe *in order that* I may understand (*credo ut intelligam*). Understanding is the goal of this faith.[47] So the theology towards which faith of this kind presses should not defend faith apologetically against attacks from outside, or against the doubts of our own hearts within; it should say in what way things *are* as the believer believes them to be. It unfolds the inward necessity of the truth of what is believed, and develops itself as a 're-flection' of what faith 'presupposes'.[48] Christian theology presupposes the Christian creed – belief in certain objective truths, the *fides quae creditur* – and unfolds the inward reasonableness of faith, the *intellectus fidei*, within the orbit of the church.

Anselm does not yet have in mind the modern subjectivity of faith, the so-called *fides qua creditur* – faith as intimate personal conviction. But according to his programme for theology the path runs in a single direction, from faith to understanding – *credo ut intelligam*. It does not run in the reverse direction too, from understanding to faith – *intelligo ut credam*, I understand so that I may believe.[49] This one-way street means that only already existent and presupposed faith leads to theology, not that reasoned and reasonable theology also leads to well-founded faith. This restricts theology to an 'ecclesiological study'. It cannot as public theology (*theologia publica*) develop itself in the public sectors of a society, such as a state university, or in the open forum of the truths and values which are of concern to every man and woman. If, on the other hand, the dialectic of faith and understanding/understanding and faith is valid, then in considering mediaeval theologies we have to see Anselm of Canterbury and Thomas Aquinas together, the monastery *and* the theological faculty at the university of Paris, the monastic way *and* its scholastic counterpart. And in modern theology this dialectic must induce us to hold together the modern subjectivity of faith and the modern objectivity of scientific or scholarly knowledge. This is just as important for discerning faith as it is for life in our modern culture, which threatens to founder on its dichotomy between individual and atom, subjectivity and objectivity.[50]

For his programme of Christian theology as 'church dogmatics' and 'ecclesiological science' Karl Barth of course adhered to Anselm, not Aquinas.[51] For him, *fides quaerens intellectum* – faith seeking understanding – meant that theology is a *re-flection* of the truth of God previously revealed and believed by the church. Theology does not take Aquinas's cosmological proofs of God in order to demonstrate that God must be thought as First Cause and Supreme Being if we want to understand the world. It shows only that we have to think God's existence if we think God, because otherwise we have not thought God 'as that than which nothing greater can be conceived'.[52] No one 'must' think God and assume his existence, but if we think God in faith, we cannot think him without thinking his existence.

If we understand intellectually the truth of God which we believe, a great joy springs up over the accord between the heart that trusts and the understanding that discerns, and between the believer who perceives God and the believed and perceived God himself.[53] That is the theological concurrence between the 'object' and the perception of it (the *adaequatio rei et intellectus*). Truth is always accord, correspondence and harmony. Those who are in accord with God and 'correspond' to him in thinking, feeling and action are possessed by an infinite happiness, for they come to themselves and become what as human beings they are intended and destined to be: God's image on this earth. We may define this by adding that correspondence to God means *holiness*, and accord with oneself *happiness*. The two sides of the truth belong together. In the revealed truth of God, the human life which is hidden from itself becomes true and manifest, 'with unveiled face', so to speak.

However, for Anselm the understanding of what is believed is not just a re-flection; as such it is also, at the same time and already, a *thinking ahead*. 'I believe *in order that* I may understand': that indicates the direction. The understanding which believers arrive at theologically along this path constitutes *the bridge* on which they move forward from faith in God's word *here* to the seeing of God 'face to face' *there*. Theology which reflects about faith here, already anticipates through that reflection the seeing there, and is an intermediary between faith and sight, a *medium inter fidem et speciem*.[54] Theological perception of God and his ways with us must be seen as an anticipatory perception, and thus in the literal sense a pro-visional perception, and a perception that runs ahead. Our theological ideas of God and his ways with us are search-images of the One who will come. They are therefore still imperfect and 'in part', as Paul says. 'When the perfect comes that which is in part will pass away' (I Cor. 13.9f.). But as long as 'the perfect' – the 'seeing face to face' – is lacking, we are dependent on the fragments of our knowledge and our prophecy. The coming, perfect perception of God will by no means complete our imperfect, partial perception of God; it will bring that imperfect perception to an end.[55] Here there is a qualitative difference, not merely a quantitative one. *Here* faith hungers and searches for understanding because it longs to see the truth *there*.

What will this seeing of God 'face to face' be like? According to Augustinian tradition, believers who are 'pure in heart' will

come to God and 'see God', as Jesus' beatitude says (Matt. 5.8).
This beatific vision leads believers to find themselves in God
and enjoy one another in God (*fruitio Dei et se invicem in Deo*).
But according to biblical 'preconceptions' and search images,
God will be seen face to face when he comes to us with the kingdom of his glory. Then, at the end, 'God will be all *in* all' (I Cor.
15.28). God's living presence will then so interpenetrate all
things that in all things we shall see, hear, feel, smell and taste
God. The enjoyment of God (*fruitio Dei*) and the enjoyment of
nature in the community of creation will then be intertwined.
The new creation is the glorious perichoresis of God and the
world. 'He will *dwell* with them,' says Rev. 21.3, picking up the
idea of a cosmic divine Shekinah.[56] The whole creation will
become the temple which God's glory will indwell and which
will be lit up by his glory. But this depends, not on a growth in
faith, or progress in the sanctification of the heart, but on a new
real presence of God in the kingdom of his glory, which will
succeed this kingdom of grace here. 'God in all things – all
things in God': the spirituality of ancient and modern cosmic
mysticism gives a foretaste of this eschatological vision, for it
draws everything into reverence for God, and is mindful of the
transcendent inner side of all the living.[57]

This seeing of God in the glory which will fill the new heaven
and the new earth is, then, the goal of the Christian faith which
seeks understanding. But that means that there is *here* no self-
sufficing theological reflection in the 'closed circle' of God's
self-revelation;[58] there is only – or already – the theological
thinking-ahead which belongs to the theology of those who are
on the way, the *theologia viatorum*. The theology of the people
of God, wandering in the faith of Abraham and Sarah, is a theology of the way – a *theologia viae* – not yet a theology of the
home country, a *theologia patriae*. It is a theology of exile and
exodus, and in all its images and concepts it bears the stamp of
the far-off land itself out of which these images and concepts
are to lead us. The lament 'How shall we sing the Lord's song in
a foreign land?'(Ps. 137.4) is the lament of theology, too, in this
world, estranged as it is from God.

The history of Christian theology does not begin with the faith of Jesus' men and women disciples, but with their *seeing* of the Easter appearances – tremendous and *sui generis* – of the risen Christ. After the 'appearances' of the risen Christ had ceased, the women – Mary Magdalene first of all – and the disciples in Galilee who had 'seen' him because he had 'appeared' to them visibly, could certainly say 'Blessed are those who have not seen and yet believe' (John 20.29). And yet the history of the Christian faith which follows begins with their 'seeing' of the 'appearances' of the risen One. According to his own account, the conversion which made a Paul out of a Saul also began with a revelation of God's Son 'in him' (Gal. 1.16). It is understandable that a faith which sprang from a 'seeing' of this kind should be aligned from the beginning towards 'seeing', and therefore aims to run ahead of itself in its provisional nature. What began with Christ's Easter appearances thrusts towards the eschatological appearance of Christ in glory. The parousia expectation of faith in Christ is based on remembrances of his Easter appearances, and therefore belongs indispensably to Christian faith. Faith in Christ's presence – 'We walk by faith not by sight' (II Cor. 5.7) – is neither the first thing nor the last. It follows upon the Easter appearances and is provisional, running ahead towards the seeing of the coming appearance of Christ in glory.

2. *The reasonableness of hope: hope become wise* (docta spes)

Christian hope, even more than faith, has its sights set on the seeing and tasting of the fulfilment of God's promise. Hope asks in its own way about the understanding of why it hopes, and what it hopes for. We call this *intellectus spei* – this understanding of hope – *eschatology*. Eschatology is usually described as the doctrine of 'the Last Things' in this transitory world, and of the first things in the new world of God. But when we sum up the reason for hope, its path and its goal, we understand eschatology as *the doctrine and wisdom of hope*.[59]

Hope is not something which is added to faith, or tags on to it. It is the other side of faith itself, if faith sees itself as Christian faith. For Christian faith itself is the power through which men and women are 'born again' to a *living hope*.[60] 'Unless one is born anew, he cannot see the kingdom of God' (John 3.3). According to I Peter 1.3–9, the *power* for a rebirth or – better – a new birth of this kind is to be found in the mercy of God; the *means* which lays hold of us is 'the resurrection of Jesus Christ from the dead'; and the *goal* is the 'inheritance which is . . . kept in heaven for you . . . a salvation ready to be revealed in the last time'. That is 'the goal of faith', 'the blessedness of souls', 'eternal life', 'glory'. Things 'into which angels long to look' will bring inexpressible, glorious joy. What lays hold of those who hope, out of Christ's resurrection from the dead through the Spirit of life, reaches beyond their death into God's almost inexpressible future: 'What no eye has seen, nor ear heard . . .' (I Cor. 2.9). Whatever the metaphors used to paraphrase this future of God's, it already begins here and now in the birth of the hope which makes us live.

On the strength of their expectation of the imminent end, the first Christians were wholly aligned towards the parousia, so the earliest Christian hope was essentially hope for the coming of God. When this expectation receded – either through disappointment or through untimely anticipation – the cleft between the hope of faith and what was hoped for grew ever wider. In mediaeval theology hope, like faith and love, was viewed as a supernatural virtue conferred by grace,[61] and the hoped-for future was pushed off on to a life after the individual's death, or to the great final Judgment. The living hope here, and what was to be expected there, parted company.

Accordingly, in the church's practice the *ground* of hope in the Easter celebration of Christ's resurrection from the dead, and the *objectives* of hope celebrated at the end of the church's year (All Saints, All Souls and, in the German Protestant church, 'the Sunday of the Dead') drifted far apart. If we compare what is proclaimed and solemnized at the end of the church's year with the great prophetic announcements of

Advent with which the church's year begins, the feeling that takes over is not merely disappointment; it is even bitterness: surely that can't be all!

The unsolved problem is the divergence between the individual hope for eternal life and the universal hope for the kingdom of God. In the *corpus Christianum* the church saw itself as fulfilled promise, as the kingdom of God; and it tolerated no hope for an alternative future of this kingdom apart from itself. Anyone who maintained such a hope was persecuted as a heretic. All that remained in the church was the individual hope for eternal life after individual death. It was no longer the universal coming of God which was declared to be the 'Last Thing' (the *eschaton*); it was death.[62] In the 'Christian world' of modern times, universal eschatology was made over to mythology, because it did not fit into the modern world picture, and people confined themselves to existential interpretation of individual death. 'The world will go on existing, but we individuals will soon depart from it.'[63] It was only the world-wide catastrophes of the twentieth century which first freed the universal eschatology of 'the end of the world' from the suspicion of mythology, and revealed its bitter realism.

The great theologies of the Middle Ages were *systems of love* (*fides caritate formata* – faith formed by love). The theologies of the Reformers, and the Protestant theologies that followed, were a *theology of faith* (*fides creatura verbi* – faith as a creation of the word). But the millenarian spirit of 'modern times' and 'the new world' craves the development of a *theology of hope*. It was not without good reason that Kant demanded of religion an answer to the fundamental question: 'What can I hope for?'[64]

To respond adequately, the theology of hope must solve the internal problems of theological tradition which I have described. It must, first, unfold the unity of hope and what is hoped for, and again make of tired and worn-out eschatology a comprehensive message of hope. Second, it must present the unity of individual and universal eschatologies in a theological eschatology of the coming of God. Third, it must so reconsti-

tute the church's year that at its end the great fulfilments of the
prophetic Advent promises are celebrated, so that the meaning
of Christmas, Good Friday, Easter and Pentecost is made manifest: judgment, universal reconciliation[65] and the new creation
of all things – that is to say, eternal life in the life of the world to
come, and the life of the world to come in the eternal presence
of the living God.

What logos – *what reason – has hope?* What can we know
about the future of God which we hope for? If *logos* means
reality reduced to its definition, then hope has no *logos*, and
what it says and desires must be viewed as unreasonable: an evil
out of Pandora's box. But doesn't reason which wants to grasp
the real as it really is always arrive too late, if this 'real' is
temporal? It is true that Hegel in his later years defined philosophy as 'its own time captured in ideas'; yet he also knew that
this means that philosophy is always too late on the scene.[66] But
cannot philosophy also intervene in the open process of reality,
taking sides and ministering to life? Can it not grasp reality
together with its better possibilities – the unhappy present
together with its redeeming future? Then it would not come too
late; it would hasten ahead of its time. But according to what
criteria, and with what expectations of the future, should
philosophy proceed, if it is to understand not only what things
look like, but the future to which they look? Surely so that every
adequate concept of a reality reaches forward to its future,
ahead of the form of its present life. All our concepts of
historical life in time are temporal concepts, and either come
too late, or are prevenient – anticipations. If they seize reality in
advance, they involve prevenient notions (*praenotiones*) or
anticipations of what is to come. 'Who will draw the proper
concepts from the present without knowing the future?,' asked
Johann Georg Hamann, rightly.[67]

The 'logos' of hope is *promise*. A promise is literally an
advance-sending into the present (a *pro-missio*) of what is to
come.[68] It is not a prophecy drawn from the present about the
future. In his promise, the coming God casts an advance
radiance of his future into the present, and determines the

present by virtue of the hope which his promise awakens. The promise awakens a prevenient understanding of the fulfilment. More than that: a promise of God's is a pledge and a covenant which binds the one who promises, and makes it possible to claim his faithfulness to that promise. One must be able to depend on a promise, for promises must be kept, as every child knows. According to the biblical writings, all God's words and everything God says when he speaks to a man or woman have the character of promise. When the words are positive, they evoke trust, and through the trust lead those addressed to set out into a new, unknown future. For this the exodus of Abraham and Sarah is the prototype. The essential nature of the God who determines human history through promises such as these is not timeless eternity; it is his identity in time – his *faithfulness*. That is the assurance of the hope awakened by his promise: 'God is faithful, he cannot deny himself' (II Tim. 2.13).

The sending-ahead and the fore-taste of God's future bring that future into the present – the past-present and the present-present; and people are roused to hope. But for them the outcome of this hope is a conflict between God's coming world and the world as it exists. The promised future of God awakens their imaginative powers, and calls up counter-images and counter-histories to the present reality. The prophetic visions of peace are turned against this world of violence. The apocalyptic images of catastrophe are turned against this self-complacent, titanically self-deifying world. Counter-histories and counter-images such as these do not constitute immediately real alternatives to the present systems of the world, but they dissever or estrange those who hope from the laws and compulsions of 'this world' so that they no longer permit themselves to conform to it, or to be brought into line (Rom. 12.7). These estrangements bring freedoms where before there were compulsions. Men and women who hope cease to be slaves of the past and become children of God's future, as we see when the New Testament talks about God's children as the heirs of God's new world (Rom. 8.17; Gal. 3.29; Titus 3.7; James 2.5).

Throughout history as the biblical writings tell it, God's history of promise runs like a scarlet thread of hope. It is at once a history in word and a history in act. The promise to Abraham is passed down as a happening in word. Israel's Exodus from Egypt is told as a history in act. Talk about 'the mighty acts of God' is not the language of acts which are finished and done with; it is the language of *history that promises future*. And how much more is the event of Christ's resurrection from the dead, with its conquest of death, *history that throws open the future*. Israel's hope is always a remembered history of promise. The hope of the Christian faith is remembered, eschatological hope: a counter-history to death, and a counter-image to the act of violence of the crucifixion. The remembrance makes the hope present, and makes it certain; and the hope keeps what is past present.

Finally, we can say that the visions of the future of the prophets and apostles display two stylistic elements:

1. The *resolute negation of the negative* in the present. How will it be when God fulfils his history of promise? 'God will wipe away every tear from their eyes, and death shall be no more, neither shall there be mourning nor crying nor pain any more' (Rev. 21.4). Through this resolute negation of the negative the future is thrown open for God and kept open for him. But that alone is not enough, for no positive conclusions can be drawn from negative premises.

2. The *anticipation of the positive*. In every case, the resolute negation of the negative has as its premise the experienced or remembered anticipation of the positive, because without the positive, the negative could not be qualified as negative at all. The passage just quoted from the book of Revelation has this to say about the positive: 'And God will dwell with them, and they shall be his people, and he himself, God with them, will be their God.' That is nothing less than the succinct summing-up of the whole history of promise and covenant in the biblical writings, extended to all peoples. God's indwelling (his Shekinah) in his people Israel, and the 'dwelling' of God's incarnate Word

'among us' are the central statements about God's presence in the Old and New Testaments. It is the redeeming presence of 'Immanuel', God-with-us, but it is not yet his universal omnipresence. In this vision in the book of Revelation, God's historical and particular presence is extended to the whole new creation, or – to put it the other way round – the new creation brings all things into the intimate covenant fellowship of the God of Israel.

3. The resolute negation of the negative cannot exist in isolation. It is dependent on the *anticipation of the positive*. But the anticipation of the positive leads to powerless dreams unless it is bound with every breath to the negation of the negative. It is only through the wise conjunction of the two that hope become wise – *docta spes* – comes into being.

3. *The reasonableness of love* (intellectus amoris)

What we have talked about up to now was the *theoretical* reasonableness of faith and the *historical* reasonableness of hope. Let us now turn to the *practical* reasonableness of them both. For this I am taking over the expression *intellectus amoris* – the reasonableness of love – from Jon Sobrino's liberation theology. Liberation theology purposes to be a theory of the Christian (which means liberating) praxis it presupposes.[69] Sobrino calls this praxis of liberating the oppressed and the poor *love*.[70] But what does love mean in this political and social context, once the intimacy of erotic love and the charitable alms of Christian *caritas* are excluded? If the political struggle for liberation and the economic struggle for justice are called love, then love means a creative and life-giving power whose origin is divine, so it cannot be merged into calculations of success, or experienced defeats, for that sum doesn't come out. 'Love' is then another name for the Holy Spirit, which brings their just rights to people who have no rights, raises up the guilty, comforts those who mourn, and 'renews the face of the earth'.[71] 'Love' is then nothing less than the real presence of the living

God in this world, just as, on the other hand, 'glory' will be his real presence in the world to come.

Love is the praxis of God's coming kingdom and his righteousness and justice in this world. Consequently it is creatively in love with life. Aristotle, indeed, maintains that 'like draws to like', because those who are alike endorse one another. But God's creative love is not directed towards those who are like him; it is focussed on the others, the weary and heavy-laden, the humiliated and insulted, the dying and the grieving. Creative love heals sick life, accepts life that is different and strange, respects life that has been belittled, and makes ugly life beautiful. Creative love reaches its divine perfecting in love of enemies (Matt. 5.43–48). In this way it is like the sun which rises upon the evil and the good, and like the rain which refreshes the just and the unjust. The power of this creative love cannot be kept out of politics and economics, and restricted to private life. It becomes a liberating power in our lives wherever it lays hold of us. And it lays hold of us and other people at the point where we are finished, and give up. The location of its theology – its *locus theologicus* – is the misery of despair, and the blatant injustice which makes us despair; for where else should it display its creative power, the power which raises us up, and puts things to rights? Where else can it manifest itself except in whatever says 'no' to life? The *Sitz im Leben* of creative love is death.

Faith in the God who raised the assailed and crucified Christ from among the victims of violence must, of inner necessity, be active in *creative love*. The hope for resurrection and the life of the world to come must, out of the same inner necessity, be active in *creative expectation*. Creative love and creative expectation are the source of the resolute negations of oppression, and the open visions of liberation.

Is understanding required for this love? In erotic love some people 'lose their heads', as we say. But this creative love stirs up the understanding and all the senses, so that they can perceive the misery, and in order to pierce through our own blindness or the indifference born of familiarity: 'we have got used to it.' In order to understand the misery, we must understand the reasons for it, and analyse the system of violence. Without political, economic and sociological criticism we cannot understand the world of growing inequalities and deadly injustices. One does not have to be a Marxist in order to learn something about capitalism or – to use today's phrase – 'the global marketing of everything' – from Karl Marx's critical analysis of capital. One does not have to be a 'liberal' in order to see through the contempt for human beings in the Socialist state-security and party dictatorships, and to recognize the failure of their controlled economies. Only belief in human dignity and human rights was needed to combat the apartheid system in South Africa. The discussions of the last thirty years have shown that there is not just one all-explanatory root for all the evils from which human beings suffer. Neither capitalism nor racism nor patriarchalism nor anthropocentricism is that single root. These evils interact in the systems of oppression we know, even if they do so in different ways in different places and at different times; and in the same way the movements for liberation must also go forward in several dimensions if they don't want to drive out one devil by another, but aim to minister to justice on every side. Creative love is involvement which opens the eyes of others and is itself open-eyed. Open-eyed love is the intelligent knowledge of how to change things.

Faith which is active in love is always 1. contextual, 2. determined by its *kairos,* and 3. related to its own community. That means that Christian theology which reflects critically about this praxis in the light of the gospel must be consciously contextual, determined by its *kairos*, and have its sights set on particular groups of people.[72] This concrete theology is not comprehensively and judiciously balanced and universal, like abstract theology. But does that then mean that Christian theology, being particularist, transient and determined by party interests, is in contradiction to its own real concern? The answer is both Yes and No.

The forms of theological thinking, theological language and theological metaphors are contextual, always and everywhere.

They are determined by their situation and are guided by particular interests. This is not just true of modern liberation theologies. It applies equally to patristic, mediaeval and modern theology, and to European, African and Asiatic theology. Every form-critical analysis of theological texts proves that on this earth and in this era 'after Babel' (to pick up George Steiner's phrase) there is no perennial theology which is the same everywhere, and at all times, and for everyone. But we undoubtedly come across theologies which, though particularist, nevertheless consider themselves to be absolute and universal, because they fail to consider the personal standpoint of the theologian, and the history of their own beginnings.

But on the other hand, every particularist and contextual theology, every theology which is determined by its situation and its special concerns, is *theo*-logy, talk about the one eternal God of all human beings, all creatures and all times. Even Latin American liberation theology and North American black theology are *theology*, and must therefore be taken seriously by all theologians, all over the world, at all times, and at all social levels. One cannot say to Gustavo Gutiérrez and Jon Sobrino, liberation theology is fine – for you; but it has nothing to do with us. And men cannot say to women: feminist theology may be all right for women, but we aren't women and we aren't interested. If this were possible, and if any such reaction were justifiable, it would be futile to study Athanasius and Augustine, Luther and Calvin, for they have long since had their day. Moreover it would also be impossible to understand American, African or Asian theologians, for they live and think in a context foreign to us. Every theology, however conditioned it may be by its context, *kairos* and culture, says something about God and is important to all who believe in God. Every Christian theology, however conditioned it is by context, *kairos* and culture, follows and interprets the text of the biblical writings. So it is important for everyone who exists within the orbit where the Bible is interpreted, wherever they live, whenever they live, and whoever they may be. For it is the text which determines what for it is the context. Otherwise the word context would have no meaning. So there is a *communio theologorum*, a community of theologians, which spans time, space, cultures and classes, which is engaged in dispute, dialogue, and occasionally also interacts in mutual influence and enrichment. This is not that abstract perennial theology of which we spoke. It is a concrete *theologia viatorum*, a theology of those on the way, who in the differing estrangements of this world and this history are searching for the one coming truth which will one day illumine everyone.

4. Is Christian theology 'revealed' theology?

'Revelation is neither a specifically Christian term nor a theological one.'[73] It plays no central role in the language of the Bible. It was the apologetic theology of the Middle Ages and the opening years of the Enlightenment which for the first time moved 'revelation' into the centre as the foundation of Christian theology, in order to demarcate the knowledge of God particular to the Christian faith from the perception generally accessible to reason, and to emphasize the difference. But in doing so this theology also took revelation out of the general discussion, because 'divine revelations' are not something that can be discussed. One has them or doesn't have them. Christian theology always talked about revelation only in antithesis to human reason. Yet according to the view of the Reformers, the correlative to Christian faith is actually God's promise (*fides et promissio sunt correlativa*). And by God's promise what was meant was the essential content of the biblical traditions; for it is God's history of promise to which these traditions witness.

It was only in modern theology that the terms 'God's self-revelation' or 'self-communication' came to be used as a central concept. Revelation should now no longer be taken to mean the supernatural communication of 'heavenly teachings' (*doctrina coelestis*). It was now the term for the actual living fellowship with God which God grants to those to whom he reveals 'himself'. With this, of course, modern theology also took over the

Idealist reflection philosophy of the absolute subject.[74] If God reveals 'himself', that makes him his own subject and his own object. He differentiates himself from himself, and identifies himself with himself. 'The One God is in Himself not only I but I and Thou, i.e., I only in relation to Himself, who is also Thou, Thou only in relation to Himself who is also I.'[75] But this concept of 'God's self-revelation' is alien to the biblical traditions. According to the Bible, God always reveals 'something' or 'someone'.[76]

It is an error to believe that God's self-revelation is a term in trinitarian theology, and embraces as the three divine Persons 1. the Revealer, 2. the Revelation and 3. the Revealedness, which is the way Barth describes the Trinity at the beginning of his *Church Dogmatics* (I/1, 299), and not at the beginning only. This triad of reflexive subjectivity can also be applied to every human subject who 'presents himself'. For Barth, however, God is supposed to be the 'one acting and speaking divine I', who as such is 'Father, Son and Spirit', 'the one God . . . in three different modes of being' (*CD* IV/1, 205). But according to a biblically based doctrine of the Trinity, God the Father 'reveals' his Son (Gal. 1.16) and the Son the Father (Matt. 11.27), and together, through the Holy Spirit, they reveal the eternal life, the eternal love and glory of the divine nature.

A person's 'self'-revelation is always also a total revelation; the one who reveals himself reveals himself entirely, otherwise he has not revealed himself. Theological tradition talks about a total revelation of God of this kind in eschatology. Only in the revelation and indwelling of his glory will God reveal 'himself', and reveal himself wholly, so that all created being will 'see' him as he is, and human beings will behold him 'face to face'. It is only in the *lumen gloriae*, the light of glory, that God reveals his majesty *'per sese'*, in its very self, as Luther writes at the end of his treatise on *The Bondage of the Will* (*De servo arbitrio*, WA 18,785), whereas in the history which points towards that and leads to it he reveals himself only in the light of the word and faith (*lumen verbi et fidei*), which is the light of grace (*lumen gratiae*). A self-revelation and a total revelation of God in the history of the non-divine world would destroy that world: 'He who looks upon God must die.'

In human history God reveals himself through the consonance of promise and fulfilment, for in that consonance his faithfulness is revealed, and faithfulness is his essential nature.[77] God identifies himself with his promises, and in doing so shows himself as the one who is dependable, steadfast and worthy of trust. 'God is faithful. He cannot deny himself' (II Tim. 2.13). According to the New Testament, the raising of the crucified Christ is the final and eschatological proof of God's essential faithfulness, since this act overcomes the power of death. So with the raising of Christ, the revelation of God's glory begins, the glory which overcomes the force of time, together with the power of death, and which will bring about the eternal creation.

6

Natural theology

The natural category (*genus physikon*) of theology was also called natural theology (*theologia naturalis*) and, as we have said, it was derived from the ancient philosophy of the Stoa. What was meant was knowledge about the nature of things and the natural forces, which were earlier conceived of as gods, as we can see from Cicero's treatise *De natura deorum*. Christian theology took up this natural theology but, because of its belief in creation, it so changed the concept of nature that 'nature' was now taken to mean the finite, contingent and experience-able reality of things which is known, not through contempla-tion of their essence, but empirically. We still have the earlier concept when we talk about 'the nature of things'. We use the second one in our observation of nature, and in the natural sciences.

In the framework of Christian theology, 'natural theology' means a discernment or knowledge of God derived from 'the book of nature', with the help of innate human reason. But how does Christian theology avail itself of this knowledge, and what functions does it have for Christian theology? Having first looked in greater detail at what theological traditions have termed 'natural theology' (see the following section), we shall here discuss three possibilities:

1. Natural theology is the general *presupposition* for specifically Christian theology. There are two ways of under-standing the word 'presupposition': (a) it is something already presupposed to which we relate; (b) we presuppose something which we ourselves determine. In the first case we let ourselves

be influenced by what is presupposed. In the second, we actively exert our influence in advance.

2. Natural theology is the consequence and the eschatological *goal* of historical and Christian theology. The 'Enlightened' transition from the particularist faith of the church to the universal faith of reason makes natural theology the objective of historical and Christian theology, which will of itself be ended and gathered up into natural theology.

3. Christian theology *itself* is the true natural theology. It presupposes nothing other than itself, and prevails of itself, for – as the evidence of itself and of what is false (*index sui et falsi*) – truth in its concrete form is itself universal.

As these three possibilities show, there is no Christian theology without natural theology. If it is to be more than merely a church doctrine confined to its own closed circle, theology must present itself to the public as *public theology* (*theologia publica*). And for this it needs the universal pronouncements and insights of natural theology (or natural religion, as it used to be called), and of the general human rights which, in the eyes of the world, have taken the place of the earlier 'rights of nature', deduced from natural theology.

1. Natural theology as the presupposition for Christian theology

We find the classic expression of this categorization in Aquinas. Christian theology is the theology of supernatural revelation. It presupposes natural theology in the same way that grace presupposes nature, and it therefore sees itself, not as destroying natural theology but as perfecting it. Natural theology belongs in the forecourt of revealed theology, and within it to the preliminaries for the articles of faith (*praeambula ad articulos fidei*).[78] With the help of the five ways of the cosmological proofs of God, natural theology proves to innate human reason that God *is*, and that God *is one*.

The First Vatican Council made a dogma of this natural discernment of God:

The Holy Mother Church holds and teaches that God, the beginning and end of all things, can be known with certitude by the natural light of human reason from created things. [79]

At the same time it condemned any denial of the dogma:

If anyone shall have said that the one true God, our Creator and our Lord, cannot be known with certitude by those things which have been made, by the natural light of human reason: let him be anathema.

Pre-Enlightement, orthodox Protestantism maintained the same view. There is a natural knowledge of God and a supernatural knowledge, the one drawn from 'the book of nature', the other from 'the book of Scripture'. Natural knowledge of God is on the one hand knowledge which is *innate* in the human being; on the other hand it is knowledge which is *acquired* through the observation of God's works and efficacies in nature and history. [80] The first kind of knowledge is directly given in the conscience; the second is mediated through the discernment of nature. Both contribute to an anterior understanding of God's revelation, and both also serve in some degree to regulate the moral conduct of all human beings. 'Human beings possess the awareness, naturally and essentially, that there is a God, and that they have the duty to worship him. Through reason and conscience, this innate knowledge of God, the *notitia Dei insita*, becomes in the human being acquired knowledge, the *notitia acquisita*. That is how there comes to be a natural religion, a *religio naturalis*.'[81] Natural theology and natural religion, like all knowledge, of course create a certain affinity with what is known, but this affinity with God gives only *understanding*, not blessedness. It is only God's supernatural revelation which saves.

The theological interpretation of the presupposed phenomenon of natural religion and theology casts back to creation, as it does in Catholic theology. Natural theology is a remnant of the direct paradisal knowledge of God enjoyed by the first human

beings, which – obscured by the Fall though it is – serves to preserve human beings and their longing for God. If human beings
receive the supernatural revelation of grace, and if they believe
it, they will be all the more able to understand and penetrate
God's revelation in nature.[82] Conversely, this natural awareness
of God shows them what the true revelation of God is, since this
natural awareness of God is 'satisfied' by revelation, so that
there comes to be harmony between conscience and revelation,
or proclamation and existence.[83] In this respect natural theology is *lay theology*, through which pastoral revealed theology
is tested.

The comment taken from Reformed theology shows that the
presupposition of natural theology has also to be understood
actively, not just passively. It is Christian theology itself which
creates this presupposition. That already emerges from the
substitution of the term *creatura* for *natura* when theology as a
natural category (*genus physikon*) was taken over. To say that
the reality of this world as it can be perceived is God's creation
is by no means a self-evident perception which must be presupposed by unprejudiced human reason; it is an assertion of
faith, and after that an insight of reason illuminated by faith.
No one arrives at the notion that this reality is the creation of a
God through mere self-observation of him or herself, or solely
through the observation of nature. Belief in creation had its
genesis in Israel's belief in salvation, and radiated further
through the belief in justification held by the Christian faith. If
this were not so, the Roman Catholic Church would have had
no need to make a dogma of natural theology. Because natural
theology is in actual fact not a *natural* theology at all, but a
creaturely one, it is an active presupposition – a fore-going
postulate – of revealed theology, and would not exist without
the church.

The proposition of the First Vatican Council that God '*can*
be known *with certainty* through the light of natural human
reason' leaves this certain knowledge in the uncertain balance
of the possible. How does this possibility become actuality?
Through the endeavour of natural human reason? Or through

God's grace, which must join company with that natural reason in order to illuminate it? To deduce the Creator God from 'created things' is not difficult; but how are we to discern that the things are created?

The sister of natural theology is political theology, for political theology belongs to natural theology. If we search for the political relevance of the two-tiered character of nature and grace, and natural and revealed theology, we discover in the Middle Ages the Christian church at the centre of the *Corpus Christianum*, and in modern times Christianity in the midst of 'the Christian century' or the civilization of 'the Christian world', to echo the titles of two well-known nineteenth-century periodicals. But that is not the multi-faith and multi-cultural world of the twenty-first century which lies ahead of us.

If we understand natural theology as the forecourt to the temple, which would not exist without the temple itself, this does not mean that we have given up its truth, retreating to revealed theology. For an *active presupposition* of this kind is essential for revealed theology if it is to be theo-logy, and hence aims to present its historical modality as universal. The God of Israel is the creator of heaven and earth, not a tribal God of the Israelites. The God of Jesus Christ is the creator and judge of the world, not a private God of Christians. This universality is, as a kind of advance radiance, projected and perceived in advance from all things and in the conscience of human beings. In this, Christian revealed theology is related to the equivocal nature of reality, and the contentious character of our human relation to transcendence, and intervenes in the interpretations of reality and the illuminations of existential transcending. This 'intervention' does not have to be doctrinaire, as we can see from the articles in Aquinas's *Summa Theologica*. The only question premised, and therefore viewed as common to all, is whether God exists: '*An Deus sit?*' The negating and affirming arguments are then discussed before they are followed by a conclusion.

The knowledge of natural theology is therefore different in kind from the reasonableness of faith. Today more than ever, it takes the form of the open question rather than that of the final answer. The community of enquirers is always greater than the community of the answers found. This community takes no sides and permits both affirmative and negative preconceptions. The community of enquirers even re-assimilates the answers given, and puts them up for discussion. Today, natural theology means this universal community of enquirers, into which the religious and philosophical communities with their answers will have to integrate themselves if they want to be listened to by other people.

The *question about God* is a question for humanity. That, and nothing more than that, is what natural theology is saying, if we see it as one of Christian theology's own, proper tasks. By the question about God we mean the metaphysical and eschatological question of human beings about the unconditioned in the conditioned, the infinite in the finite, and the final in the provisional. But we also mean God's question about human beings: 'Adam, where are you?' and 'Cain, where is your brother Abel?' People experience themselves personally and socially as called in question out of unplumbable depths, and with their whole lives they try to give an answer to the question 'What is the human being?' This *question about humanity* is the reverse side of the question about God. By natural theology as a task for Christian theology we also mean, not least, *the cosmic question* about what gives the universe stability in its contingency, and what holds it together. The history of the universe and the evolution of life are unique, irreversible major processes, with origins, motivations and inherent, already-given objectives. This natural theology is not self-evident, emerging of itself from observations of nature. It springs from a Christian theology of nature. But this must lead to just such a natural theology as a cosmological and biological interpretative suggestion. It cannot remain within the closed Christian circle.

2. *Natural theology as the goal of Christian theology*

In 1946 Hans-Joachim Iwand propounded the thesis that 'Natural revelation is not that from which we come: it is the light towards which we move. The *lumen naturae* is the reflection of the *lumen gloriae* . . . The reversal required of theology today is to assign revelation to our era, but natural theology to the era to come. The theme of true religion is the eschatological goal of theology.'[84] This transposition would make natural theology a goal of Christian revealed theology, no longer its presupposition. The demand for just such a transposition has of course been made ever since the beginning of the German Enlightenment, and it was supported by Lessing and Kant with the emotional and prophetic solemnity proper to the proclamation of a new epoch.[85] The Enlightenment's philosophy of religion radically turned things round: everything in the religions which is supernatural and which precedes reason belongs to what is particular and historical, and serves as 'vehicle' for the development of a natural, generally human religion of reason. It is the theology of this universal moral faith in reason which is now called 'natural theology'. The task of the reasonable study of religion is to read the elements of this future, natural religion out of all the historical, particular religions.

Lessing presented this epochal turn-around of natural theology in his millenarian 'three-act' (or three-stage) construction *The Education of the Human Race*.[86] God's educative providence leads humanity from its 'childhood' by way of its 'boyhood' to 'full manhood'. We can see this today from the sequence Old Testament, New Testament, Enlightenment. Pupils no longer need the primer of the Old Testament once they have learnt its content by heart; and in the same way they will one day be able to dispense with the New Testament, once its revealed truths have been transported into 'truths of reason'. 'When they were revealed, indeed, they were not as yet truths of reason, but they were revealed in order that they might become such.'[87] That is Lessing's interpretation of Anselm's *credo ut intelligam* – I believe *in order that* I may understand. Lessing was convinced that his era was the beginning of the 'Third Age' promised by Joachim of Fiore. This was 'the time of perfecting' because 'now' the transition could be seen from 'historical' faith in the church to a universal faith in reason, and to universal morality. This is, so to speak, 'the time of a new eternal Gospel, which is promised us even in the Primer of the New Testament itself!'[88]

Kant offered a more extensive justification of this viewpoint. His thesis was: 'We have good reason to say that "the kingdom of God is come unto us" once the principle of the gradual transition of ecclesiastical faith to the universal religion of reason . . . has become general.'[89] Belief in pure reason was always already the 'goal' of the church's faith, for the latter is 'the vehicle' for the former. And when we speak of God: it is only the 'pure faith in reason' which fulfils Jeremiah's ancient prophecies, 'I will put my law within them, and I will write it upon their hearts . . . And no longer shall each man teach his neighbour and each his brother, saying "Know the Lord", for they shall all know me, from the least of them to the greatest, says the Lord' (Jer. 31.33f.).[90] The first promise will be fulfilled when everyone obeys the voice of conscience – the 'God within us' – and does the good simply because it is the good. The second promise will be fulfilled when God is discerned through the instrument of reason. This will make every theology so 'natural' and self-evident that 'the mortifying distinction between laity and clerics will cease'. Through the fulfilment of both prophecies 'the general church' will begin to develop into an ethical, divine commonwealth, under the rule of 'the good principle on earth'.

Because this transition is taking place 'now', for Kant his own time is 'the best time' in the entire history of the church as we know it, because it is in the present that 'the seed of the true religious faith is . . . being publicly sown'.[91] The assembly of the nations will bring the commonwealth of humanity with the approach to the kingdom of eternal peace. Universal ethics go hand in hand with the pure religious faith of the religion of reason, which will take the place of all historical religions.

However, the radical transposition which makes natural theology no longer a presupposition of Christian theology but its goal leaves us with a problem: can this goal be fulfilled *chiliastically* – at the end of history, but in time (namely in 'modern' times) – or only *eschatologically*, in the 'new era' in the kingdom of God's glory? From Lessing and Kant onwards, the German Enlightenment was profoundly stamped by Joachim of Fiore's scheme of things, and in its epochal awareness was chiliastically inclined. Progressive, liberal Protestantism also interpreted its 'Christian world' in a millenarian sense, as we can see not only from Richard Rothe but from Johannes Weiss too. Consequently, in the First World War, under the Hitler dictatorship and in Auschwitz, the 'radically evil' of which Kant was still aware fell upon the optimistic faith in progress cherished by Europe's Protestant world and found it unprepared and unprotected.

It is only possible to talk with any meaning at all about a fulfilment of Jeremiah's promises if God appears in a new real presence, and prepares an end for this estranged world in the kingdom of his indwelling glory. Then all will perceive God as he is, and knowledge of God will be so 'natural' that no further theological teaching will be required. Then all human beings will do the good as a matter of course, because God's law is written in their hearts, and no further ethics will be needed. If this *eschatological* theology is the true natural theology, then the 'natural religion' presupposed in nature and in the human conscience can in its turn be understood as the advance radiance and promise of the kingdom of glory. But that means that the 'pre-supposed' natural theology is not a fore*court* of revealed theology itself: it is a fore-*shining* of revealed theology's eschatological horizon, the theology of glory. In this eschatological context, natural theology too is in its own way a *theologiae viae*, a theology of the way. It articulates the 'sighings of creation' (Romans 8) and interprets 'the history of nature' in the vista of creation's future.

The 'traces' of God in nature and human existence are a reflection of the coming new creation of all things. Not every soul is 'Christian by nature', but every soul is by nature made and destined to be the image of God and to participate in his eternal kingdom. This special relationship between the 'pre-supposed' and the hoped-for natural theology can best be seen in the reason Calvin offered: it is the universal efficacy of God's Spirit, which preserves everything created, and fills all the living, preparing it for the coming kingdom of God.[92] The Holy Spirit in its efficacies is the bridge between creation-in-the-beginning and creation's eternal goal. 'Natural theology' is therefore at once a *recollection* of creation and an eschatological *hope* for creation. In the unity of the two it brings us to what must be called a mystical perception of God's presence in all things and in our own innermost being. By virtue of his Spirit, God is present in the heart of the world, and in our own hearts.[93]

In this way natural theology does not merely (as is generally thought) take on significance for a knowledge of God derived from nature and our inmost beings; much more even than that, it has significance for the knowledge of nature and of human existence out of God. If God can be known from the world – in whatever way – then this world becomes *transparent*[94] for God's invisible presence, and potentially a *parable*[95] for his coming kingdom. All created things and all living beings then become in their existence *real promises*[96] of their future in God's world to come. 'Natural theology' understands the world sacramentally as the real presence and advance radiance of the coming kingdom.

3. Christian theology itself is the true natural theology

Inasmuch as natural theology has to do with the universality of God, we might also view it as one dimension of revealed theology, for the universality of the one God is also part of God's revelation.[97] So why the distinction between a 'natural' and a 'revealed' theology? If we assume that God does not reveal parts, but reveals *himself*, there can actually be no presupposed criterion for his revelation in a natural knowledge of God or a natural religion. It is intrinsic to the strict concept of God's self-revelation that God himself is alone the criterion for his revelation. Revelation does not prove itself to be God's revelation because it accords with the conscience, or with a natural religious, already-given understanding, but only because it accords with God himself, as the term 'self-revelation' says. So God's revelation of himself must be seen as God's 'proof of himself', a 'proof' which of itself enforces its own claim. The concept of truth which we can apply here is not the Aristotelian correspondence between the thing and the understanding of it (*adaequatio rei et intellectus*); it is Spinoza's idea of truth as the evidence both of itself and of what is false (*index sui et falsi*).[98] Theology which knows itself to be in correspondence with God's self-revelation then becomes 'the judge and mistress to which all things are subject',[99] for 'it judges everything and is judged by no one', like the 'spiritual human being' according to Paul (I Cor. 2.11) – a formula with which, it must be said, the popes also justified their absolutism at the height of the Middle Ages!

If this is not to be misunderstood as the arrogance of a self-deifying theology, this revealed theology must presuppose the universal revealedness of God: 'Might it not be that Jer. 31.34 is in the process of fulfilment?' asks Barth, when at the beginning of his *Church Dogmatics* (I/1, 5f.) he does not merely assert but also laments the independence of theology over against other studies, and hence theology's separate existence. 'It is indeed unfortunate that the question of the truth of talk about God should be handled as a question apart by a special faculty . . . Philosophy, history, sociology, psychology, or pedagogics, whether individually or in conjunction, all working within the sphere of the church, might well take up the task of measuring the church's talk about God by its being as the Church, thus making a special theology superfluous . . . All sciences might ultimately be theology . . . The separate existence of theology signifies an emergency measure on which the

Church has had to resolve in view of the actual refusal of the other sciences in this respect.'[100]

For Barth, therefore, revealed theology is not a reversion to the particularist inner sphere of the church. In view of the self-revelation of the One God, it is its own kind of public, universal theology. For this, however, Barth brings together in an undifferentiated way God's self-revelation in history and the universal revealedness of God, of which Jeremiah 31 speaks, in the kingdom of his glory. Actually or potentially, all studies and sciences can 'ultimately' be already theology. Actually or potentially, they can make the separate existence of theology superfluous. But once God's self-revelation is universally so manifest that this is possible, then no further 'talk about God' is required either, and no 'sphere of the church'; for all will know God as God is. But if God's self-revelation is not so universally manifest that 'talk about God' and 'the sphere of the church' are still required, then what is meant would surely have to be a 'church' philosophy or a Christian historiography, and so forth. But this is conceivable at most in colleges or seminaries affiliated to the church, in Catholic universities, or at the 'free university' in Amsterdam.[101] And yet, can there be any such thing as a Catholic mathematics or a Protestant biology?

Barth never consistently followed through this beginning of the *Church Dogmatics*, and finally replaced it by his 'doctrine of lights'. But for all that, it turns up again and again. The theological reason for this lies in the universalism of Barth's doctrine of reconciliation, which he understands not just as the hope and intention of the proclamation of the message of reconciliation, but also as an 'ontological declaration about . . . every man as such'. The acknowledgment of Christ has from its very origin 'an inclusive sense': first it embraces those who confess him and belong to him, but in and with itself it also reaches out to other human beings and the whole world. The 'inclusive sense' constitutes the 'ontological connection' between Christ and all human beings, and hence between 'active Christians on the one side' and 'virtual and prospective Christians' on the other. This 'ontological connection' is 'the

legal basis of the *kerygma*'.[102] With the help of this christological ontology, Barth was able to find himself in sympathy
with what Tertullian says about the *anima naturaliter
christiana*, the naturally Christian soul.

But if, according to this view of things, there are only
'actual' and 'potential' Christians, what about Israel, theologically speaking? Is the Christian faith itself really *only*
insight into this universal connection to all human beings in
which God has placed himself through Christ? Is lack of faith
only deficient insight? And is a falling away from faith *only* a
falling back to the status of a 'potential Christian'? For it is then
not easy to gather the universalism of the question about God
in natural theology into this universalism of the divine answer
given in revealed theology. Because, in my view, natural theology is only as yet an advance radiance of the eschatological
theology of glory, Barth's revealed theology, which absorbs
natural theology into itself, takes on the character of a preliminary eschatological anticipation, which conceives itself to be
already existing within the fulfilment of the prophecy in
Jeremiah 31. But if, conversely, and with Barth himself, we distinguish the theology of reconciliation eschatologically from
the theology of redemption (because reconciliation is the anticipation of redemption, and redemption the completion of
reconciliation), then it is no more than consistent also to distinguish again between natural theology and revealed theology,
and to ask whether there can be a new 'natural theology'. It is
just this which, I believe, we find in Barth's so-called 'doctrine
of lights', as expounded in the third part of his doctrine of
reconciliation.

Besides the one word of God there are other words which we
should listen to. Besides the one light of life there are other
lights which we can see. But it is the word of God which makes
these words true, and the light of life which lets those lights
shine.[103] As 'prototype of this order' Barth again takes the New
Testament parables of the kingdom, which are derived from
nature and the world of human beings.[104] Between likeness
and difference, these parables stand as something similar and

corresponding in dissimilarity and difference. Because the subject of these parables is the kingdom of heaven, here it is only the analogy of faith, the *analogia fidei*, which applies, not the analogy of essence, the *analogia entis* of the 'sorry hypothesis of a so-called "natural theology" (i.e., a knowledge of God given in and with the natural force of reason, or to be attained through its exercise)'.[105] Barth thinks that natural theology can have no interest in any such parables of the kingdom; if it had, it would have to deny its own definition. What can be heard and seen in the world, which is in need of parable and is potentially parable, must, he says, be subjected to the criterion of the word of God if it is to correspond to 'the kingdom of heaven'.

In his doctrine of lights, however, Barth goes back a step further, and sees the 'creaturely' world as the framework, the stage, the setting and the backdrop for the drama of salvation: as the *theatrum gloriae Dei*, as Calvin put it, 'the external basis of the covenant', as he himself says. This creaturely world 'has also as such its own lights and truths, and therefore its own speech and words'.[106] But these are 'created lights' which are discovered and characterized and made to shine forth in their truth through the shining of the one true light of life, God's revelation of himself in Jesus Christ. As created lights of this kind, Barth names the general characteristics of creation: existence; existence for one another; the rhythm of nature; 'a certain inner contrariety . . . the encounter and alternation of Yes and No'; the laws of the natural and spiritual world; summons to action, and therefore steps into freedom; as well as the mysterious depth of the cosmos.[107] These are the truths of the stage on which the drama of the great acts of God is played out. In that the truth of God shines out in history, the lights and truths of the created world are lit up also.

Is this 'doctrine of lights' really so different from the Christian 'natural theology' we have described up to now? Emil Brunner rubbed his eyes in amazement when he read this piece written by the enemy of his old 'natural theology' in the pattern of 'nature and grace'.[108] And it is true that, apart from the strict analogy of faith (the *analogia fidei*) and the explicit criterion of the one word of God and the one light of life, the doctrine of lights offers nothing new over against a consciously Christian natural theology. Aquinas certainly began his 'natural' preparation for Christian theology with the open question, 'Is there a God?' (*An Deus sit?*). But he did not answer the question by way of insights provided by reason. He answered with an appeal to God's revelation of himself: because God has said 'I am who I am', he must also *be*. The transformation of the concept of nature into the concept of creaturely being shows very clearly the influence of 'the book of Scripture' on 'the book of nature'. One difference (even according to Barth's own judgment of 'sorry' natural theology) would seem to be the way of arriving at knowledge: the *analogia fidei*, the analogy of faith, moves from above, so to speak, and the *analogia entis*, the analogy of essence, from below. But the angels on Jacob's ladder ascended *and* descended; so could this dispute not be settled as a dialectical play of reciprocal knowing – *analogia entis in analogia fidei*, the analogy of essence *in* the analogy of faith? We shall come back to this in Part II. From the parables, we learn how to understand 'the kingdom of heaven', and in the light of the kingdom of heaven, this world, with its potentiality for parable, becomes transparent and communicable, and acquires its meaning for the future world of God.

The real problem of every natural theology is not its nature, but the use made of it by godless, self-deifying men and women. Luther was right when he pointed to this essential point in his Heidelberg Disputation of 1518.[109] He called natural theology (*theologia naturalis*) the theology of glory (*theologia gloriae*), which is what it really is. If natural theology is not to lead the sinner astray through pious illusions about himself and his God-like capacity for knowledge, then the *theologia crucis*, the theology of the cross, must first put the person who has gone wrong right, and must justify the sinner – make the sinner just. What Luther left out was only that justified sinners are right with God, and in accord with him – and that they have therefore been put in a position to know the creaturely world in its accord and correspondence with God. They can join in the cosmic hymn of praise, and in the world can live out the parables of the kingdom of heaven. *After* the analogy of faith comes the analogy of essence, *after* the theology of the cross comes the theology of glory, *after* the theology of grace the theology of nature, and *after* the theology of nature natural theology.

4. *Natural theology as a task for Christian theology*

If Christian theology sees itself solely as a function of the church (as, in modern times, Schleiermacher and Barth demanded it should), it must withdraw to its own circle of believers, and can present itself to the public forum of its own society or the world-wide community of the nations only through the church's proclamation and mission. It then needs no theological faculties in public or state universities for the training of its theologians. All it needs are theological seminaries, and colleges specifically affiliated to the church. Consequently it does not need the universal horizon of a 'natural theology' either. But if Christian theology sees itself as a function of *the kingdom of God*, for which Christ came and for which the church itself is, after all, there, then it must develop as a public theology (*theologia publica*) in public life. If it is to be present in life's different sectors, and if it is to enter into dialogue with philosophies and religions, it needs the framework of a natural and political theology. For scholastic theology, a framework of this kind was already given in the *Corpus Christianum*. For Enlightened Protestantism, just such a framework was already to hand in 'the Christian world' of a 'Christian era'. Neither *Corpus Christianum* nor 'the Christian era' was really a 'fore-court' for the church. Both were a 'fore-representation' of the kingdom of God – parables of the kingdom in human history. That, at least, was the way the representatives of this Christianization saw the matter: it was 'the taking-form of Christ in the world'.[110]

It was in these contexts that the corresponding natural theologies, together with their political theologies, were at home. That is why the cultural movements of the Enlightenment and Western humanism set out to dissolve the Christian church, absorbing it into the moral commonwealth of humanity and – as we have seen in Lessing and Kant – transforming traditional natural theology from being a presupposition for Christian revealed theology into that theology's future.

This chiliastic naturalization of historical Christian theology met its downfall when it came face to face with the abysses of evil and death in history. The retreat of church and theology from the cultural syntheses and the natural and political theologies of the 'Christian' world was understandable; and this retreat was brought about by dialectical theology, under Barth's leadership. Yet in his 'No!' to Emil Brunner's *Nature and Grace* (1934) it was not so much the 'natural' side of this natural theology which Barth criticized as its political side, evident among the pro-Nazi 'German Christians'.[111] His image of the concentric circles of church and society, with Christ in the centre, shows that his own world of 'parables of the kingdom' in culture and politics is still deeply committed to the stepped structure of nature and super-nature, even if grace is to determine the nature which it presupposes.[112]

Today, out of its own eschatological theology, Christian theology is in the process of drawing up a new creation theology, and out of that a natural theology of its own. This creaturely theology will have to address the new ecological crises and challenges of our time. If we are to have co-operation with other religious communities and philosophies, but above all with the sciences and technologies, we need the framework of natural theology; for it is through a natural theology that others can be brought to the mystery of God's presence in all things and in all the complexes of life, and that Christians can gain an interest in the perceptions and wisdom of others in the ecological crises which threaten us all. If all studies are 'ultimately' theology, as Barth thought at the beginning, then Christian theologians must read scientific books out of their very own concern, so as to learn from them something about the divine mystery of the world. Is not every important scientific discovery a kind of mystical experience? In countries with an unbroken tradition of natural theology, like England, it is a matter of course for theologians to be active as scientists, and scientists as theologians; and on the continent too this practice could help us to overcome the paralysing divide. Of course we cannot expect scientists to turn their science into Christian revealed theology. Even Barth can hardly have meant that. But we ought to be able to expect their science to lead to the out-skirts of the divine mystery of nature, and to approach the inner side of things with respect and reverence. And today natural theology can hardly be more than this.

After a meticulous analysis of natural theology in theological history, and its dissolution in modern critical philosophy, Wolfhart Pannenberg comes to the conclusion that 'relative to every form of religious tradition', it still retains the critical function 'of imposing minimal conditions for talk about God that wants to be taken seriously as such'.[113] 'In this sense it is also perfectly possible to have a philosophical concept which acts as a framework for what deserves to be called God.'[114] Even if a natural 'theology' can no longer be expected of modern philosophy today, 'the phenomenon of the question still serves excellently as a metaphor for the fact that we are referred to a basis for life outside ourselves'.[115] But universal concepts of this kind, which are supposed to serve as a general framework for an understanding of God and life, become theologically more and more abstract, and lose themselves in vague imaginings, the further their proposed outreach. What is really being sought for is a 'general' theology, and this can be defined more closely politically, ecologically and ethically.

1. Today the Universal Declaration of Human Rights of 1948 is authoritative for the United Nations. Every human being is not just a member of a people, the citizen of a country, and, if he or she so wishes, the member of a religious com-munity. Every person is also *a human being*, and possesses inalienable human rights, which today can increasingly be claimed before the international courts. One of these rights is

religious freedom (Article 18). That is the political framework for what is to be called religion.

2. To the degree in which different religious communities live together in multi-faith societies and in a globalized world, they will find some common ground where they can present their differences, because otherwise there is no way of presenting them at all. In Western societies this common ground can be the phenomenon of the questionable character of human existing which is stimulated by the answers of the various religious and secular communities; in societies influenced by Eastern thought it can be the shared reverence for the mystery of life, which is encouraged by Tao. In interfaith dialogues and interfaith co-existence (or convivence), the common ground will always be discovered together with the differences – the shared territory which, after all, is already presupposed in the concept of religion to which all lay claim. But beyond the sphere of the *religious* communities, what is in common will have to embrace all other, secular forms of living as well, if *life* is made the central concept against which talk about God must prove itself, and against which every form of atheism too will have to be judged. Both the religious and the secular must minister to the common life if humanity and the earth are to survive.

3. The universal concept for which theology, philosophy and politics are looking today is undoubtedly *the universe*. The *relative* universe, which we do not only know but also experience, because it determines our lives, is our planetary system, the system of the earth. The earth, as the planet 'in' whose biosphere human life is possible, is for us human beings *relatively total* and *concretely universal*. Now that the scientific and economic age has exploited and destroyed the earth, right down to the foundational conditions of its existence, a new eco-logical age must put the hitherto silent and silenced partner earth at the centre of its economics and politics, and hence at the centre of its form of living and spirituality too. If we want to live and survive, we shall turn to earth economics, to earth politics (Ernst von Weizsäcker's phrase), and to the religion of the earth. For the theological genre of a natural theology, this

context means that a theology of nature must take up and articulate 'the religion of the earth'. This is not a new 'blood and soil theology', on the Nazi model. It is reverence for the sabbath of the earth which, as Israel's Torah describes, the earth celebrates before God, so that it may come alive once more. The general framework for theology today is *the theology of the earth*. There the genre of traditional natural theology will become concrete and manifest, experienced and suffered.

II. Hermeneutics of Hope

In this chapter I should like to clarify some of the terms and concepts which are basic to my book *Theology of Hope*, and which I have used again and again since 1964 – *promise* and *covenant*, for example, *hope* and *future*, and the metaphor of the future which is expected and desired. Going a step further, I should like to sum up the various approaches to a 'hermeneutics of hope' with which I have tried to explore the dimensions of the Christian hope, especially the political dimension on the one hand, and the trinitarian dimension on the other. My purpose with this 'hermeneutics' of hope is not to 'interpret' given reality or temporal and historical reality, and the reality that is open to the future. What I wish to do is to interpret God's promise, out of which the awakened hope makes men and women creatively alive in the possibilities of history. Finally, I should like to engage in the present discussion with a brief theological epistemology.

I shall again begin with a biographical reminiscence, recalling the teachers and teachings to whom, and to which, I owe a debt; for it was they that impelled me to do theology.

The logic of promise

1. *Origins of the book* Theology of Hope

In the autumn of 1948, through the kind mediation of the radical Barthian Helmut Traub, I began my studies in Göttingen. Traub was a pastor in my home town after the war, and gathered aspiring students of theology round himself.

In the winter semester of 1948/49 Hans Joachim Iwand was lecturing in Göttingen on 'the theology of the young Luther', talking by candlelight during the electricity cuts that were still usual at that time. Iwand fascinated us all by his enthusiasm and his prophetic language. He himself was like a young *Luther redivivus*, Luther revived. Under his spell, we discussed among ourselves Luther's Heidelberg Disputation of 1518, and for ourselves took over his early theology of the cross. For us that was true Christian realism: *theologia crucis dicit quod res est* – the theology of the cross says what is truly the case. And here too was the true doctrine of justification: 'Sinners are not loved because they are lovely; they are lovely because they are loved.'[1]

I was soon one of the the band of Iwand's disciples. I was often at his house, and with others of the 'prophet's disciples' tramped the Göttingen forest in his wake. Up to 1951 I attended all his lectures and seminars, and also tried to write a thesis under his supervision. I did not succeed, because he was continually exposed to new ideas. Iwand's theology had two centres of gravity: the early period of Luther's Reformation (to which he also assigned Melanchthon and Calvin), and Protestantism in the era of the German Idealism of Kant,

Schleiermacher, Fichte and Hegel.[2] He himself came from the Luther renaissance of the 1920s and was influenced by Rudolf Hermann. But in the struggle between church and state in East Prussia he then drew close to Karl Barth, Barth's dialectical theology and the *Church Dogmatics*, Iwand's aim being to bring the new political experiences and theological insights gained in the struggle between church and state into post-war theology.

Iwand was at his liveliest when he was challenging existing reality, and in his hope for the promised future: 'Because this world is ready for demolition, our life in the world must be ready to start out afresh.'[3] He formulated the contradiction to 'this perverse world' by way of Luther's theology of the cross. God is known in this godless world through his suffering and cross – that is to say *sub contrario* – in contradiction – and through his cross he destroys our godless ties with this world, freeing us for himself and turning us from proud, unhappy gods into true human beings, who accept their humbleness and weakness. Iwand took his hope from the Reformation concept of promise (*promissio*), which he justified christologically. It is the promise of the world of the resurrection, which shines out beyond Christ's death. The coming Christ is himself present in his promise, and through the awakened hope wins power over our lives. 'The reality of Christianity is determined in the light of what will come, not in the light of what has been.'[4]

Iwand wrote no closely knit work on dogmatics. He developed his theology at that time in his Göttingen Sermon Meditations. These are a treasure-trove of theological perception, which has been won, and can only be won, 'between' the biblical text and proclamation for the time. It is to Iwand that I am indebted – certainly more unconsciously than consciously – for the theological thrust towards the 'coming' kingdom and the 'coming' Christ.[5] In his sermon meditations (1945 onwards) and his short piece on 'The Presence of the Coming One' (*Die Gegenwart des Kommenden*, 1955), these are the passages I marked. In the orientation of his own theology towards the future he was influenced by the book *Jesus the Coming One*,

written by the Russian Dimitri Merezhkovski. It was from
Iwand that I first heard Merezhkovski's name.[6]

Reformed theology in Göttingen was taught by Otto Weber.
He was a wonderful preacher and a gifted teacher. He gave
theologians the courage to preach, and students an appetite for
theology. He had a sovereign grasp of all the different theological fields, and could bring out the unity of exegesis and
dogmatics, and the coherence of history and the present.[7] His
lectures were full to overflowing. I came to him out of love for
my future wife Elisabeth, and he gave me the subject for a
thesis: 'Moyse Amyraut and the theological school of Saumur',
of which I had never heard. However, I soon struck gold, and
became increasingly interested in that unknown period between
the late Reformation and the early Enlightenment.[8] In 1957 I
pursued this line further in a professorial thesis on Christoph
Pezel and Bremen's transition to Calvinism.[9] I discovered the
Reformed 'prophetic exegesis' (which Oscar Cullmann later
called 'the exegesis of salvation history'), and found my way to
Reformed federal theology through the work of Johann
Coccejus, and to federal politics through Johann Althusius.
Jacob Brocardus showed me the link between the mediaeval
eschatology of Joachim of Fiore and the modern theology of the
kingdom, which is indebted to Coccejus.[10] Otto Weber guided
me as a faithful supervisor.

Weber concealed his own theological views behind his teaching, which he put entirely at the service of Karl Barth's *Church
Dogmatics*.[11] His main work therefore bears the modest title
Foundations of Dogmatics. It became a much-used textbook of
systematic theology. In the first volume he withdrew entirely
behind Barth, thereby winning Barth's approval. In the second
volume he came forward with his own ideas, not greatly to the
delight of the master in Basel. Weber's doctrine of the Lord's
Supper influenced me deeply.[12] Whereas in tradition the spatial
view of Christ's real presence was dominant, Weber developed
the complementary eschatological doctrine of time: 'The spatial
interpretation of the happening of the Lord's Supper is one-
sided; for the primary problem is the problem of time.' The

presence of Christ in the feast is 'the presence of the Coming One'. The feast is 'the first gleaming of the Eschaton'.[13]

Weber translated the 'Foundations and Perspectives of Confessing the Faith' issued by the Dutch Hervormde Kerk in 1949, and discussed it with us.[14] Over against the christological concentration of the Barmen Theological Declaration of 1934, the Dutch Confession brought out the universal horizons of creation and the kingdom of God, and was the very first Christian confessional document to include a positive article on Israel. The corresponding church order of 1949 distinguishes between mission to the nations, dialogue with Israel, and the Christianization of one's own society;[15] and from this I have always taken my bearings.

In 1956, through Otto Weber, I came into contact with the Dutch theologian Arnold van Ruler in Utrecht. He freed me from the impression that after Karl Barth there could no more be a new theology than there could be another philosophy after Hegel, because Barth had said everything, and said it so well. From van Ruler I learnt that in his theology of reconciliation Barth had neglected eschatology, just as Hegel, the philosopher of reconciliation, had also done in his time. I was fascinated by van Ruler's 'theology of the apostolate', and by the 'taking form of Christ in the world'.[16] He once began a lecture with the words: 'I smell a rose, and smell the kingdom of God.' I had never heard anything like it before. When my *Theology of Hope* appeared in 1964 (ET 1967) I had the happy feeling that – as the Dutch say of good friends – we were 'like two hands on one belly'. Later we drifted apart, because according to van Ruler's radical Anselmian view, sin is 'the emergency' and Christ 'God's emergency measure' for its elimination, so that at the end everything is once more just as good as it was at the beginning.[17] Consequently for him the state was an element in creation and belonged to the kingdom of God, whereas the church was only a provisional 'emergency measure' on God's part. For van Ruler, paying taxes was like a sacrament. That was more loyalty to the state than I could do with, in the light of my negative experiences of the perversions of state power in

Germany. For me the universal church was more important than the particularist state. But from early on I was convinced by what van Ruler wrote about the Christian church and the Old Testament, and what he presented as the Old Testament's surplus of promise towards the New.[18]

In 1959 I took my first tentative steps into the systematic theological discussion. Through Ernst Wolf I was able to take part in discussions held in Heidelberg between lawyers and theologians, and in 1958 gave a lecture there on Dietrich Bonhoeffer's doctrine of mandates, as a contribution to a theological doctrine of institutions. This lecture was published in 1959. In mild criticism, I tried to get over the deplored rigidity of Bonhoeffer's mandate inventory by integrating these mandates into 'the living stream of the divine history'.[19] 'The goal of all mandates is found in the history of the happening of God's will in the expectation and hope for the one, coming kingdom of God, the new heaven and the new earth.'[20]

I summed up what was exercising me theologically at that time in a short book on 'The Community of Christ in the Context of Christ's Rule. New Perspectives in Protestant Theology' (*Die Gemeinde im Horizont der Herrschaft Christi. Neue Perspektiven in der protestantischen Theologie,* 1959). When I read this again today, I can see that here all the themes of my later theology are really already sounded: the eschatological horizon of history in the kingdom of God; faithfulness to the earth; new partnerships for the church in the world; and 'the narrow wideness of the cross of Christ'. 'That means among other things that we win back hope for the Last Things, and break out of the demythologized, late-bourgeois individual culture. It means that we dare once more to explore the space of freedom into which we are permitted to step out on this earth, and to move towards this future of ours – the space encompassed by the creation of the world, the reconciliation of the world, and the judgment of the world' (34).

My first lecture at the theological college in Wuppertal in 1958/59 was really supposed to treat Zwingli's theology historically; but I settled for a systematic subject: 'The Theology of the Kingdom of God'. I finally took my departure from the quiet waters of historical studies in a book on 'Predestination and Perseverance. The History and Importance of the Reformed Doctrine of the Perseverance of the Saints' (*Prädestination und Perseveranz. Geschichte und Bedeutung der reformierten Lehre* 'de perseverantia sanctorum', 1961). After that I found the theological discussions that ranged round Bultmann and Barth, Gogarten and my Wuppertal colleague Wolfhart Pannenberg, so fascinating and exciting that I was never able to turn back to the peaceful realm of historical studies.

I have written about Ernst Bloch so often that here I shall only touch briefly on what I owe to his messianic philosophy.[21] I met him at the end of a lecture in Wuppertal, he having come from Leipzig. I got hold of the first two volumes of his *Principle of Hope* in the East German edition (the third volume was not allowed to appear because of the chapter on religion), and during a Swiss holiday in 1960 immersed myself so deeply in it that the beauties of the mountains passed me by unnoticed. What fascinated me was not Bloch's neo-Marxism; it was his Jewish and Christian messianism. 'The eschatological conscience came into the world through the Bible.' 'All Christians too know it in their own way . . . from the Exodus and the messianic parts of the Bible.'[22] For Bloch, thinking meant crossing frontiers – 'going beyond' – and with this transcending thinking he was able to make hope 'comprehended hope, *docta spes*'.

My *Theology of Hope* was written in 1962–63, and was published in 1964. From Bloch's philosophy of hope I learned basic categories for this theology, but without engaging in his atheism. I did not 'baptize' his *Principle of Hope*, as Karl Barth suspected at the time.[23] What I did do – taking as my basis the biblical hope, the Jewish faith in the promise and the Christian resurrection hope – was to initiate a deliberately parallel theological act: following the mediaeval theology of *caritas* and the Reformation theology of *faith*, my aim was to help the *hope* of modern times to come into its own, theologically speaking. I had no wish simply to write a theology *about* hope. My purpose was a theology *out of* hope – theology as eschatology, theology of the liberating kingdom of God in the world.

2. *Promise not prophecy*

Promise and prophecy are so close to one another that they are often confused. In the Sistine chapel, Michelangelo has painted prophets and sibyls alternately, side by side, because the patristic church believed that Christ was the fulfilment of both Israel's prophecies and the prophecies of the Hellenistic and Roman world. The post-Reformation 'prophetic interpretation' of the Bible began in England and Holland with the postulate that prophecy was 'anticipated history' (*anticipata historia*):[24] all the Bible's prophecies have either already been fulfilled, or will be fulfilled shortly, in the apocalyptic era soon to come. The Bible is 'the divine commentary on the divine acts in history'.[25] The Bible is 'inerrant' not because it is the repository of divine truth but because all its prophecies come true. In present-day theology, Oscar Cullmann has made out of this his 'hermeneutic of salvation history'.[26]

But a prophecy is not a promise, for prophecies have a different determining subject from the event which they prophesy. Nostradamus prophesied diverse future events, but he did not make them. It was history that made them, or 'Dame Fortune', as people once said, or divine providence. Seers and soothsayers are fortune-tellers, and must at all events claim particular insights into 'God's plan of salvation' or 'the operation of providence', or 'the laws of history'. The prophecy has no influence on the future event. It influences only the subjective attitudes of the people who believe in it. It is in this sense that there is self-fulfilling and self-destroying prophecy. In German one does not actually talk about a prophecy being 'fulfilled'. One says that it 'comes to pass' or 'has not come to pass'. Soothsayers are not made responsible for the happening or failure to happen of what they have prophesied, for they only prophesy the event; they do not make it. So they can be wrong, but bear no guilt for their error. Consequently prophecies are usually so equivocal (as they are in Nostradamus or in fairy tales) that they can be related to either the one event or the other. It is only after the event that they are described as true or false; but by then it is already too late, for they are then no longer prophecies. We generally remember dreams about the future, too, only if what we dreamed of has come true.

And yet in the biblical traditions, for human beings to prophesy the future is evidently viewed as a special gift of the Holy Spirit (see Joel 2). On this level, we find in the New Testament the so-called prophetic proof. When what was prophesied has come about, the prophecy has proved to be true; and because it has been prophesied, the event is supposed to *come* true. But as the prophetic proofs in the New Testament also show, prophecies of this kind are usually prophecies after the event. If something important happens, people afterwards search for the prophecies which the event has proved true. The process can also be reversed, because prophecies naturally trigger off certain search-mechanisms. But these remain in the dark, and can easily be forgotten.

The great *promises of God* witnessed to by the prophets in Israel who succeeded Moses, the prophet of the covenant, belong to a different dimension and must not be confused with human prophecies.

A promise is a speech-act, which is authenticated by the person who promises.[27] It is performative, not interpretative (a '*Tat-Wort*' not a '*Deute-Wort*', in Luther's terminology). The person who promises keeps his word and performs what he has promised. If he fails to keep a promise, he breaks his word. We can only promise what we ourselves can perform, if we wish to avoid causing disappointment, and want to win trust. In their promises people commit themselves and make themselves dependable. They emerge from their equivocal hiddenness and become unequivocal – for other people, but for themselves too. In promising, a person becomes someone who can be appealed to. He or she acquires a firm form, or configuration. Through faithfulness to their promises, people acquire continuity in the flux of the times, because whenever they remember their promise, or are reminded of it, they remember themselves.[28] The person who gives his word, and knows that he is bound to it, gains identity by so doing. The person who breaks his promise loses his identity. The person who forgets his promise forgets himself. But the person who remains faithful to what he has promised, remains true to himself. If we keep our promises we are trusted; if we break our promises people mistrust us, we lose part of our identity, and in the end no longer know who we are. Our name stands for the identity of our life history. Through my name, I identify myself with what I was in my past, and anticipate the person I want to be in my future. With my name I can be addressed and appealed to. With my name I sign my contracts and vouch for what I have agreed to. Life together in society is possible only on the basis of promise and faithfulness, dependability and trust. Control is good, trust is better; for without a minimum of trust, no controls work either.

What is promised can be immediate to our own selves, or more remote from us, but it always involves our self-commitment to keep the promise. 'I promise you a bunch of flowers.' Directly speaking, what is promised is only the bunch of flowers, but indirectly, and as presupposition, the self-commitment of the person promising is part of the promise. The promise made in marriage, 'I take thee to be my wedded wife/husband . . . for better for worse . . . until death us do part', directly involves the self of one's own person, and the identity of one's own faithfulness. The self-commitment coincides with the promise of one's own person. 'I promise myself to you' or, as used to be said of people who were engaged to be married, 'they are promised to one another'. A promise which has one's own person as object is also called a *vow*, because it calls forth unconditional trust and faith. It is often linked with an *oath*. Whatever the endorsements may look like, they are always *covenant formulas,* orientations which look for, and are dependent on, 'good faith', whether it be in the marriage bond or in the ties of social and political life. Every promise of this kind binds the person who promises, and offers him or her the trust and faithfulness of the partner, or partners, to the bond.[29]

3. *The covenant oath*

God promises but he does not prophesy. As the Old Testament
story about Abraham shows, it is the divine promise (Gen.
12.1–3) which leads to God's covenant with Abraham (Gen.
15.18; 17.2, and frequently elsewhere). God's promise already
involves a self-commitment on God's part, and a command to
Abraham. The transference of the promise into the covenant
makes the promise unwaveringly and unbreakably *God's oath*
(Gen. 22.16: 'By myself I have sworn. . .'; Deut. 7.8: 'sworn to
your fathers. . .') and makes it permanent. For human beings
what emerges from this is a certain space for living, under God's
blessing, and in an atmosphere of trust and security within the
divine protective sphere. In the covenant with Noah (Gen.
9.9–14), this space embraces the people alive at the time, their
descendants, and everything living on earth. So it is not limited
to God's relationship to human beings. The initiative for the
divine covenant proceeds from God's side: God establishes the
covenant and commits himself to keeping it. But the covenant
itself is aligned towards reciprocity, and requires of men and
women the conduct which accords with it.[30] When God establishes the covenant, that puts the reciprocity of the covenant
relationship *into force*; it does not do away with the reciprocity.
And yet a breach of the covenant on the human side does not
automatically revoke the covenant which God has established.
This distinguishes the covenant from a contract between
human beings. Only God himself could revoke his covenant
oath, if he were then to 'repent' of having entered into his self-
commitment towards human beings.

The primal form of the real covenant is the covenant on
Sinai, which runs: 'I will be your God and you shall be my
people.' Inherent in the covenant formula is, on the one hand,
the self-binding promise of God's presence in that covenant
and, on the other, the election of his people to be his own
possession. Inherent in it also is God's *indwelling* in the people
of his covenant: 'I will dwell in the midst of the Israelites.' We
may leave on one side here the question whether an indwelling

of the people in God is thought of too. Because the covenant on Sinai is the goal of Israel's Exodus from slavery in the land of the theocratic Pharaohs into the promised land of human freedom, this covenant represents the historical root of Israel's history with God. Promise, Exodus and covenant are the historical paradigm for Israel's prophets and history-tellers. They are the historical framework for Israel's Torah, and in the Torah for the Ten Commandments. The God who makes himself dependable through his covenant promises is fundamentally differentiated from the moods and caprice of other gods or forces of destiny. His essential nature is his faithfulness. His name is his identity, which is manifested in historical continuity. The person who 'hallows' – sanctifies – God's name relies on God's promise, which he has sworn in his own name to keep. A relationship to God which is based on a covenant with him like this is a kind of 'elective' religion, a religion of choice, as distinct from a 'natural' religion.[31] It appeals to the will to keep the covenant precepts in freedom, not to the natural affiliations of people, race, region or nation.

The 'sovereignty' of God which proves itself a liberating power when the people are freed from slavery is given permanence through the covenant on Sinai. God rules through his covenant, which respects and preserves the liberty of his people which has been won. This is a totally different divine rule from that of the Egyptian or Babylonian theocracies, where the deity 'rules' through the despots who resemble him, and demands submission. The God of the Exodus who is named in the First Commandment chooses his liberated people. The reason given is this: 'For all the earth is mine' (Ex. 19.5). This statement can be understood in a causal sense and in a final or purposive one: *because* the whole earth is God's possession, he can choose Israel to be his 'possession before all peoples'; and *in order that* the whole earth may become this God's possession, Israel is chosen to be 'a kingdom of priests and a holy people' for all the nations and for this earth. Then the election of Israel is not an end in itself. It serves the liberation of all peoples, and the blessing of the earth. From this we may conclude that all God's particular, historical covenant promises serve his universal, coming and enduring kingdom, so that in each case they point beyond themselves.

This universal and eschatological alignment of all God's covenant promises is already implicit in God's self-commitment: '*I* will be *your* God.' For the eternal God described in the saying 'I am who I am' is more than just 'your' God. The one who chose Israel to be his 'possession' is the creator and possessor of the whole earth. The particularist covenant promises come from the one, eternal God, and their sights are therefore set eschatologically on the universal real presence 'in all things' of the one and eternal God.[32] Consequently God's covenant promise is never 'fulfilled' in history in the sense that it is factually finished and done with, and can be set aside in time, in the way that a prophecy can. The promise 'I will be your God' is always merely endorsed, for it bears within itself its own 'fulfilment' in the fullness of God's real presence. What it promises happens through its promising, Immanuel, God-with-us: we his partners to the covenant and companions on the way.

4. Promise makes God's future present

If we look first at the history of promise in the Old Testament traditions, we can say that in history the divine promises are communicated to particular people such as Abraham, and are therefore made present through remembrance and narrative.[33] In the new situations in which they are remembered and told, they are also newly interpreted. The fulfilments experienced and the disappointments suffered interpret them. Together with the promise, the reality which corresponds to it – or which contradicts it – is made present. As the Abraham story itself already shows, God's promise that he will make of Abraham and Sarah 'a great nation' is, if one looks at experience, confuted by their *de facto* childlessness. On the other hand this facticity is confuted if one listens to the promise, and looks to the God who promises, for whom all things are 'possible'.

Abraham's history of promise is then interpreted as a history that runs counter to experienced reality.

But God's promises must be understood historically not merely because they were uttered in history, and must ever and again be interpreted afresh in history, but also because they *throw open* a particular history. For the people who are concerned and who trust them, they throw open history in the possibilities of the promising God. These are not the 'unlimited possibilities' of a human utopia. They are possibilities with limited substance, determined by promise and by God's commitment in a covenant. Abraham believed the promise of his God contrary to all appearances, and 'God reckoned it to him as righteousness' (Gen. 15.6). Paul calls this 'the faith of Abraham': 'He believed the God who gives life to the dead and calls into existence the things that do not exist' (Rom. 4.17). The opening up of history in the possibilities of the promising God means the opening up of a history of the creative God for whom creation out of nothing and new creation from the dead is possible. Faith in the promise does not just count on the objective or subjective possibilities of history; it reckons with the presence of the one who makes the impossible possible. Hence the question to the prophet Ezekiel (37.3) when he is faced with the fields of the dead of Israel's history: 'Son of man, can these bones live?' And hence the directive: 'Say to these bones . . . hear the word of the Lord . . . Behold I will cause breath to enter you, and you shall live' (37.4, 5). According to the Epistle to the Hebrews (11.1), faith in the promise means having no doubt about what one does not see. Paul calls this hope (Rom. 8.24, 25), and confronts hope with seeing. 'But hope that is seen is not hope . . . But if we hope for what we do not see, we wait for it in patience.'

We can only talk about the *fulfilment* of these divine promises when in the new creation of all things death is no more, and time (*chronos*) has found its end; for the power of time and the inescapability of death are forces of history; and death and time pass away only in confrontation with that new divine Presence which is described as God's eternal dwelling in all things: 'God all *in* all' (I Cor. 15.28). Then faith and sight will coincide; then the promising word and experienced reality will concur, then God's truth will fill heaven and earth. But until then these things will not coincide. The contradiction between God's promise and the ravaged fields of the dead in human history remains. In history the theology of promise will not be transported into a theology of accomplished facts. The contradictions of the history that runs counter to the promise hold its true future open for experienced history, and keep human hoping in suspense.

But what do exist in history are the accompanying 'signs and wonders'. They strengthened the people in the dangerous Exodus, sustaining them against the resignation that threatened them. They convinced John the Baptist that Jesus was the promised one who was to come (Matt. 11.5). They also accompanied the path of the apostles. On the other hand, the history of promise moves purposefully towards the messianic consummation of the divine covenant. Just as God's covenant on Sinai was concluded through Moses, so God's covenant is finally and universally put into force through Christ: 'For all the promises of God find their Yes in him' (II Cor. 1.20). They are not 'fulfilled' in the sense that they have lost their promissory character, but through the fullness of the Godhead which indwells Christ they are put into force in such a way that 'by grace alone' they are unconditionally valid, and 'by faith alone' are universally open to everyone. 'To believe in Jesus Christ means *living* from the promises of God.'[34] This life is the presence of God's life-giving Spirit, which for its part is experienced as the pledge or 'down-payment' of glory, and as the springtime of the new creation of all things. The promised life becomes lived promise and living hope, and the life lived in hope becomes *the real promise* of its own fulfilment in 'the life of the world to come'.

My stress on the *contradiction* between promise and reality, and between hope and experience, has often been misunderstood and criticized as 'abstract'. However, for me it is concrete, determined by the crucifixion on Golgotha of the bearer of the promise by the imperial powers, and by his raising from the dead through the God of hope. Yet in the discipleship of the crucified Christ, by virtue of the life-giving Spirit, there are varying historical situations. There are situations which must be called *messianic* – situations where the world is actively changed so that it may be brought to manifest its character as God's world, in correspondences to God's kingdom and his righteousness and justice. But there are also what we have to call *apocalyptic* situations of passive resistance to powers and situations opposed to God, in which all that remains is suffering and martyrdom. In the first case the world offers possibilities for action which accords with God; in the second case, the door to these possibilities is closed. But in no case is there compulsion to a total rejection of the world and to suicide. On the contrary, changing the world and resistance to the powers that destroy the world and themselves belong together in an ethics of hope for the future of this world in the kingdom of God. Today it is precisely active effort for the liberation of the oppressed that often leads to persecution and martyrdom – effort to free them for life that will be in accord with God, in justice and freedom.

In the language sector, awareness of the contradiction and the thrust towards correspondences leads to the linking of 'hope sentences' with critical statements about reality, but not to a link with what are allegedly purely 'descriptive sentences'.[35] In a historical reality, purely 'descriptive sentences' take on the character of a legitimation of what exists, if we view them in their social context, and ask who uttered them, and when, and for whom. They then do not just describe what exists. They also justify the way the existent comes to be what it is; for social reality is always determined beforehand by particular interests, as every government spokesman and every marketing manager knows.

5. *Promise opens up history in the possibilities of God*

Every promise thrusts towards the fulfilment of what is
promised. Every covenant with God thrusts towards God's all
fulfilling presence. From the standpoint of the fulfilment, every
promise is therefore literally a *pro-missio*, a sending-ahead of
what is to come, in the way that the daybreak takes its colours
from the rising sun of the new day. In this respect God's
promise is 'gospel' in the heralding of his coming (Isa 52.7:
'How beautiful upon the mountains are the feet of him who
brings good tidings . . .'). The gospel of the kingdom heralds the
coming kingdom itself. Inasmuch as the gospel heralds Christ's
coming parousia, we can see it as Christ's parousia in the word
that heralds it.[36] If we are to be able to rely on the promise of the
gospel, then what is promised – in this case 'the future of Christ'
– must itself already be made present in that promise. For all the
differences, there must already be an identification between
what is to come and the promise in which what is to come is
announced. As the one who will come, Christ is present now in
his word and Spirit. In the present promise, the future is made
present. That does not put an end to the difference between
present and future, which is identical with the difference
between the faith that looks towards the word of the promise,
and the seeing face to face; but it bridges the difference.

The historical present and the eschatological future can only
be bridged in *the language of promise*, not in *the language of
concepts*. The concept presupposes a finished, completed
reality. Only such a fixed reality of facts and circumstances
can be reduced to a definition. 'As the thought of the world it
[i.e., philosophy] appears only when actuality is already there
cut and dried after the process of formation has been completed
. . . When philosophy paints its grey in grey, then has a shape
of life grown old. By philosophy's grey in grey it cannot be
rejuvenated but only understood. The owl of Minerva spreads
its wings only with the falling of dusk.' So wrote Hegel, rightly,
in the introduction to his *Philosophy of Right* (1820).[37]

Over against a definition of 'concept' like this, a promise

reaches out beyond what is existently real into the sphere of what is not yet real, the sphere of the possible, and in the word anticipates what is promised. In so doing it opens up what is existently real for the futurely possible, and frees it from what fetters it to the past: if things are fixed and finished (*rebus sic stantibus*) reality can be reduced to a concept, and defined; if they are in process (*rebus sich fluentibus*) they can be influenced only through anticipations of a possible future. If it is the owl of Minerva which through concepts perceives 'the shape of life' that is already 'completed, cut and dried and grown old', then it must be the lark at daybreak which 'rejuvenates' the shape of life in such a way that in promises it heralds the possibilities of the new day. If 'what is reasonable is real, and what is real is reasonable', Hegel is right.[38] But this reasonably real and really reasonable can only exist in the past, and in that present which no longer has any future ahead of it. Yet from the aspect of 'the shape of life' in time, this is death, and, from the angle of historical reality, petrification. As long as there is future, and as long as we experience reality as history only together with its possibilities, all the concepts of reason are at the same time preconceptions, which reach out to grasp the future of a thing, a person, or complex circumstances. The person who says 'this is the way things are' is always already saying in the open world of process: 'this is the way they must be' – and is appropriating the future.

In modern hermeneutics the question generally asked is only *how* texts belonging to the tradition should be interpreted, not *why* we should interpret them at all, or what *compels* us to explain and apply them. I considered this question in some detail in 1963 in an essay entitled 'Verkündigung als Problem der Exegese' ('Preaching as a Problem of Exegesis').[39] Unfortunately it was never published in English.[40] Only a view of reality in the context of promissory history discloses the need to interpret and apply the subject of the texts at the present day. The historical view of history has no knowledge of this, and existential hermeneutics assumes only that it is possible, not that it is necessary.

'History as remembrance' underlies all 'history as a scholarly discipline'. Once the living remembrance is lost, the result, as Alfred Heuss said, is a 'loss of history'. But what keeps the remembrance of history alive? Not the archives and museums, but the past itself in so far as it is not a question of facts which are finished and done with and have had their day, so that their testimonies can be filed away and the processes surrounding them can be wound up. We *can* survey a distanced past of this kind, but there is no *need* for us to do so, because no remembrances of it crowd in upon us. What is really remembered, in contrast, is only what has still not been paid off, and is incomplete, for itself and for the people concerned. What is still unfinished – what is still in the process of becoming – what is still in dispute: these things are still open. Their end has not yet come. The final judgment has not yet been pronounced. It is in this way that guilt is remembered, because the burden of it is felt. The execrable German expression for this is 'the unmastered past' – *unbewältigte Vergangenheit*. What gives us pain and hurts us is remembered. What is remembered in this way is the past which points beyond itself into a future not yet reached by the present either – undertakings, promises, and the hopes of past generations. This may be called 'future in the past' or 'past future'.[41] Remembrances of this kind 'force themselves upon us', as we say. They compel us to engage with them, because in them something is inherent which is not yet finished, the meaning of which has not yet been disclosed. In history no final line is drawn under them, to say that their debt has been paid off.

History as a scholarly discipline is based on history as remembrance, and history as remembrance is based on openness to the future of historical processes, that is to say of 'past future'. Hermeneutics based on promissory history interprets this 'future in the past' for the present of that future today, thereby obeying the inward compulsion of the promises that have been uttered. This hermeneutics perceives the *uniqueness* of their utterance, together with the future towards which they point. The divine promises uttered in the past are not past but make their future present. To discover this and to apply it interpretatively is the task of the hermeneutics of promissory history. This also makes it evident that the texts of once uttered promises must of necessity be proclaimed today. 'What makes text and preaching necessary is the *promissio*.'[42]

God's great promises do not correspond to reality as it can be experienced, but always reach out beyond that into the future. They contain a surplus of what is promised over and above experienced reality, for they emanate from the economy of God's superabundance – the fullness from which men and women in the course of their own time receive 'grace upon grace' without its ever being exhausted. Consequently the texts of the history of promise also contain so much 'added value' that no new interpretation exhausts them but merely makes them greater. The incompletion of the promise and what it promises (the *inadaequatio promissionis et rei*) is grounded on the fact that the divine promises are eschatologically aligned towards the coming of God, whereas historical reality is temporal and transitory, and so cannot exhaust the future potential of the promises. Paul Ricoeur has seen this future potential of the promissory texts not only in the processually open event of interpretation (as did Gerhard von Rad) but also, with *Theology of Hope*, in the surplus of the eschatological raising of Christ from the dead over against his historical death on the cross: 'How much more,' as Paul stresses.[43]

The interpretation of historical texts in the light of this hope therefore neither opens the door to the absolute knowledge which gathers up and ends history; nor does it conduce to the anticipation of any such absolute knowledge. What it does lead to is the awareness of history's new possibilities in the unexhausted potential of God's promised future, which is already present in the Spirit of life. The human hope to which the historical texts of the promise witness is transmitted through transferral into new historical possibilities, and experienced in new forms of suffering and action. The 'meaning' of a text is not exhausted either in its own time or in its interpretation in a new *kairos*. If it is a text belonging to the history of promise and hope, an enticing surplus of 'more' always remains in the text and in its interpretations. If this is true especially of the unique character of the biblical history of promise, it also applies in general to the appropriate understanding of human history.[44] What today we call past is only the past of our present. But the generations which are present in our past had their own past, and their own future too. When we explore their past-present, we shall also have to explore their own past, and the future which they hoped for and for which they worked. What past did the Reformers see as their past? And what future for the church and Christian society did they have as goal when they entered upon reformation? What is the relation between present reality and that future-in-the-past? How have present hopes changed the hopes of past generations? Future-in-the-past must be compared with future-in-the-present and be critically received into it. In this perspective we perceive history as history of the future, not as the quintessence of the transitoriness of all things.

6. *A critique of the Reformation concept of* promissio

The Reformation viewed the justifying word and justifying faith in correlation ('*Promissio et fides* are correlatives', said Melanchthon). This understanding developed out of criticism of the mediaeval sacrament of penance. There, three acts on the part of the penitent man or woman went together: the contrition of the heart (*contritio cordis*), oral confession (*confessio oris*) and satisfaction through the performance of good works (*satisfactio operum*). The question was: when should the word of absolution (the *remissio peccatorum*) be spoken? Following inner contrition? Following the confession of sins? Or only after the atonement through good works? The young Luther made of the priestly word of absolution the gospel of the forgiveness of sins, which justifies 'through faith alone'.[45] The gospel of the forgiveness of sins is a performative word which effects what it says, and a pronouncement of sacred law: 'If you forgive the sins of any, they are forgiven.' For Luther, the stages in the sacrament of penance were then replaced by 'the merry exchange', in which Christ takes the sins of men and women on himself and confers his own righteousness on believers.[46]

And yet, for all that, the Reformation interpretation of the justifying promise *(promissio)* remains anchored to its place of origin: the word of absolution in the sacrament of penance. Although in his dispute over the sacrament of penance Luther prefers to use the term promise, substantially it is still only a matter of the remission of sins *(remissio peccatorum)* and the formula 'I absolve you' *(Ego te absolvo)*. This becomes unmistakably clear in the christological reason which Article IV of the Augsburg Confession gives for the forgiveness of sins – Christ's vicarious suffering and death:

> . . . that men cannot be justified before God by their own strength, merits, or works but are freely justified for Christ's sake through faith when they believe that they are received into favour and that their sins are forgiven on account of Christ, who by his death made satisfaction for our sins.[47]

To explain the justification of the sinner in this one-sided way through the Anselmian doctrine of satisfaction and the theology of the cross reduces the event of justification to the forgiveness of sins, just as it is reduced in the sacrament of penance. But that is only half the truth. According to Paul, whose Epistle to the Romans became the foundational writing of the Reformation, Christ 'was put to death for our trespasses and raised for our justification' (Rom. 4.25). The salvific significance of Christ's death on the cross is most certainly manifested in the present forgiveness of sins, but the significance of Christ's resurrection cannot, for all that, be reduced to the divine endorsement of this salvific significance of his death. The resurrection of Christ has a saving significance of its own, which goes beyond the forgiveness of sins and is termed 'righteousness', 'rebirth', 'new creation', and 'the outpouring of the Spirit'.

As early as the seventeenth century, the Lutheran reduction

of justification to the forgiveness of sins was already supplemented by early Pietism in the doctrine of regeneration.[48] But the two sides, forgiveness of sins and new life in the Spirit of the resurrection, belong together in the same way as death and resurrection in the person of Christ. Christ's historical death and his eschatological resurrection certainly do not belong qualitatively on the same, single line, so that we could add them together; but for that very reason Paul saw a 'how much more' in Christ's resurrection. That is the surplus of grace over and above the forgiveness of sins, and an 'added value' of the resurrection over and above death.

The close tie between Christ's resurrection and our justification goes back to Augustine: 'In the same sense in which his resurrection is real, so also in us is there authentic justification.'[49] In the Easter liturgy of the the Orthodox Church, the forgiveness of guilt is included in the jubilation over the resurrection. If we wish to hold the two together, we can say: the event of justification consists of a unified, indivisible movement springing from the remission of sins (*remissio peccatorum*) and from the promise of justification (*promissio justificationis*). The shadows of the night withdraw and the new day begins. The forgiveness of sins is the presupposition for the justification of the whole person and that person's rebirth to a living hope. The negation of the negative paves the way for the position of the positive. It is true that in his Small Catechism Luther says: 'Where there is forgiveness of sins, there are also life and salvation';[50] but logically speaking it is impossible to draw any such positive conclusions from the negation of the negative. The word which forgives sins and 'sends them away' (*re-mittere*) is the word of the cross. That is true. But the word that 'sends ahead' (*pro-mittere*) righteousness and new life is the word of the risen One: 'I live and you shall live also.' In the *pro-missio* of justification, the risen Christ enters our lives and takes us with him into the future of his kingdom.

This event of justification, understood as new creation and new birth, is the actual hermeneutical category of Christ's resurrection. We cannot understand the truth of Christ's resurrection appropriately either historically or metaphorically, but only through our empowerment for new life. The event of a person's justification is *pro-missio* – the promise and sending-ahead of the kingdom of God and his righteousness and justice. The eschatological horizon of the present event of justification is not the 'Last Judgment' in itself, as Melanchthon thought. It is the new creation of all things which that judgment inaugurates.

7. The real promise of creation

Having looked at the special theology of promise, we now come, finally, to a 'general theology' of promise. With this we leave the special history of promise in Israel's history and in the Christian faith, and pass to the universal history of creation, asking about the promise of existence and life. One may dispute whether Israel first recognized the God of its hope and of the people's exodus, and only afterwards perceived God as the Creator of heaven and earth. What is at all events certain is that the two acknowledgments belong together – the acknowledgment of the God of history and the acknowledgment of God the Creator – and that the one cannot exist without the other. But is there anything in creation which corresponds to the openness to the future of the history determined by God's covenant? Or do other laws prevail there?

'In the beginning God created the heavens and the earth' (Gen. 1.1). So begins the story of creation. What beginning is meant, and the beginning of what? And what end (*acharith*) does this beginning point to? This is an age-old question. Some scholars believe that creation-in-the-beginning already necessarily means thinking about 'the creation at the end', since there is an end to every beginning. The Priestly Writing may well have thought of 'God's rest' on the sabbath as the goal of that beginning, and the Yahwist may have been thinking of the blessing conferred on Abraham on behalf of all generations on earth. But at all events, the goal set for that beginning has to be called eschatological, for the end is as final as the beginning is unique. In the later history of tradition, the new creation of heaven and earth to be the kingdom of glory was viewed as the future of creation, whose beginning had been told. We can already see this in Isaiah. 'To the beginning there corresponds an end, to creation completion, to the "very good" here the "wholly glorious" there.'[51] Systematically, this also emerges from the creation of time, which is established with that 'beginning'.

Augustine rightly rejected creation *in* time (*creatio in tempore*) and talked about creation *with* time (*creatio cum tempore*).[52] But that presupposes a mutable creation, for time can only be perceived from change. In what way is creation-in-the-beginning open to change? By being open for its own history which can bring salvation and disaster, consummation and destruction. Which concept of time we should associate with creation is not clear. If we imagine creation-in-the-beginning as a paradisal condition, then the concept of 'reversible time' would be appropriate, time as a circle; for the circle is the geometrical image of completion, perfection. From time immemorial theological tradition has here used the term 'aeon' or 'aevum'. It turns up again when the time of the new eternal creation has to be described. This does not have the same eternity as God himself. Its eternity is relative and participatory, through the indwelling of God in it. Here too the scientific concept of 'reversible time' could be applied.

However, if we view creation-in-the-beginning from the perspective of its goal and end as the beginning of a history, then the concept that suggests itself is the concept of *irreversible* time, the time-pointer, with which we can distinguish between before and after, and between past and future. If it is true that 'in the theology of the Old Testament creation is an eschatological concept',[53] then God's history with the world does not begin only with the Fall. It already begins with creation itself, and the time of creation is irreversible time; and we must then talk about a 'future of creation'. This means too that we have to talk about a 'past of creation', as do the eschatological creation promises: 'The old has passed away, behold, the new has come'

(II Cor. 5.17; Isa. 43.18f.). 'I saw a new heaven and a new earth; for the first heaven and the first earth had passed away' (Rev. 21.1).

If we turn back from the new creation of all things at the end to their creation 'in the beginning', then heaven and earth, and all created being in heaven and earth, appear as *real promises* of their future in the kingdom of consummated glory. In all earthly systems of matter and life we can detect an openness for each other and for their own possibilities. The earthly community of creation is like a great participatory and anticipatory community system. We can also describe these relationships poetically, as in the so-called physico-theological proof of the existence of God, the aesthetic form of which we find in Augustine:

> I asked the earth and it answered, 'I am not He', and all things on earth declared the same. I asked the sea and the deeps and the living things that creep in them, but they answered, 'We are not your God. Look above us'. . .I asked the sky and the sun, the moon and the stars, but they told me, 'Nor are we the God whom you seek'. . . With a loud voice they cried out, 'It is he who made us.' My question was my thought about them, and their beauty was the answer they gave me (*Interrogatio mea intentio mea et responsio eorum*).[54]

All created beings, simply as created beings, point to their Creator. But all created beings, as creatures of the beginning, also point to their completion at the end. In these intertwined references, theological and eschatological, to the Creator and to the end, they speak as real symbols.

In 'the bondage' of creation (Rom. 8.19–23) Paul recognizes correspondences to what hoping men and women filled by the Spirit of Christ's resurrection perceive in their own bodies, which are subject to the destiny of death: the longing for redemption, for freedom, and the glory of God. The enslavement under which created being suffers is transience. The enslavement under which believers suffer is their mortality, for 'the redemption of the body' can only mean 'giving life to mortal bodies' (Rom. 8.11). Transience is the time of death. Futurity is the time of life. Among human beings there is a conflict between the two because of the 'first fruit' of the Spirit of the resurrection – manifest in non-human creation through a presence of the life-giving Spirit of creation. Here there is not just a 'oneness with unredeemed creation'.[55] There is a fellowship of unredeemed creation with believers too, in the drive of God's Spirit. Hoping, longing, groaning, waiting are words used of both, and the sighings of the Spirit (8.26) find their resonance both in the hope of believers and in the longing of suffering creation. Here too there is an underlying irreversible time-structure.

This has consequences for the discussion with the sciences. It means that theologians are particularly interested in the 'history' of nature. Natural processes with an irreversible time structure engage their attention especially. These processes correspond to the historical happening of tradition and innovation, in which theologians develop their biblical hermeneutics. This happening is the universe itself, which is the subject of cosmology. If we take the 'Big Bang' and 'expansion' as premise, the universe is unique and has an irreversible history. 'The development of the cosmos is a unique phenomenon. With this development we can have no repeatable experiences.'[56] Something similar may be said of the origin and evolution of life. Biological evolution too is a unique process, comparable only with the uniqueness of historical events. But within these 'great scientific narratives' too there are systems of matter and life which work with irreversible time structures and can therefore on their own levels distinguish past and future. The 'theory of open systems'[57] is an attempt to apply the concept of irreversible time to the diverse systems of matter and life, and thus to demonstrate the historicity of the world known to us in nature.

The attention of theologians is therefore directed in natural events to the phenomena of 1. fortuitousness, 2. uniqueness, 3.

future, and 4. the new. They are less interested in phenomena of 'the eternal return of the same thing', with a reversible time-structure. But since scientific proofs presuppose the repeatability of the experiment, scientists are primarily interested in processes where repeatability can be presupposed: although as everyone knows, and as Heraclitus said, 'no one enters the same river twice'.

2

Historical hermeneutics

1. The genesis of the new political theology and of political hermeneutics

In 1967 Johann Baptist Metz introduced the term 'political theology' into the theological and public debate.[58] With it, he wished to break out of the narrows of bourgeois 'religion as a private affair' and the confines of the transcendental, existential and personalistic theologies of post-war Germany.[59] On the other hand, he wanted to formulate critically and prophetically the message of Christianity, newly understood as eschatological, in the conditions of modern society: 'Every eschatological theology has to become a political theology, as a theology critical of society.'[60] Metz came from the 'new anthropological direction' of Karl Rahner's theology. With theology's eschatological horizon and its political relevance, he won for himself an independent group of contemporaries to add to the clashing social and ideological forces of those years – and not those years alone. It was not a matter of politicizing the church, as some people feared – people for whom, otherwise, political Catholicism and Vatican politics were a matter of course.[61] The purpose was 'a theology with its face turned to the world', and 'talk about God in our own time'.

I first met Metz in 1965 in Tübingen, on the occasion of Ernst Bloch's eightieth birthday. It was to the old 'atheist for God's sake' that we owed our ecumenical friendship. In 1967 we then both took part in the last Christian-Marxist dialogue in Marienbad. Eschatologically orientated talk about God in critical social responsibility was the bond between us. At the centre was insight into the political dimension of Christ's cross and the political relevance of God's kingdom. 'It was not between two candles on an altar that he was crucified . . .' and 'the prices of world trade are not a matter of indifference for the kingdom of God'. These sayings of Metz went the rounds at the time, and opened the eyes of a good many.[62]

On the Protestant side, the different paths of Leonhard Ragaz and Karl Barth, Ernst Käsemann and Helmut Gollwitzer led in the same direction.[63] The time was ripe for a new active political involvement by Christians in the affairs of the time. In the Latin American 'continent of a new beginning' liberation theology came into being, and in 1968 convinced the Bishops' Conference in Medellin that the 'preferential option for the poor' was a necessity. In Europe, the East–West conflict took on new severity, now becoming the Cold War; and this required an unequivocal witness for peace. In America the great civil rights movement was augmented by the widely supported movement against the war in Vietnam. New democratic and socialist ideas at grass-roots level kindled student criticism of the condition of the universities, and the conservative political restorations in West German society. At that time, together with the new political theology we of course also took up the messianic hopes of Ernst Bloch and the apocalyptic dialectic of T. W. Adorno, and grappled with them theologically.

But what motivated the development of the new political theology most profoundly was horror over the failure of churches and theologians in the face of the German crime against humanity which is indelibly associated with the name of Auschwitz. Why the appalling silence of Christians? Why did Christians turn a blind eye with such deadly consequences? Had the bourgeois privatization of religion secularized politics to the depths of such abysses? Was it conscious or unconscious antisemitism which kept Christians mute when the Jews were 'taken away'? Was it the misused doctrine of 'the two king-doms' which helped the churches 'to keep out of things'? As can be seen from the publications of Metz, Dorothee Sölle and myself during those years, the programme of 'talk about God with a face turned to the world' and 'talk about God in our own time' became for us the painful task of talking about God with a face turned to the Jews and to Auschwitz. For Metz this developed into the steadfast insistence on an 'anamnetic culture' of 'dangerous remembrance', and a theology in the open theodicy-process of the political history of modern times.[64] What became important for me was a theology of the cross in which God is apprehended as the God who suffers with us. Important too was Christian criticism of the idols of political religion and the constraints of civil religion.[65] The name Auschwitz became for us the term for the hermeneutical conditions in which we had to think about Christian talk of God in post-war Germany.

The term 'political theology' was not new. It was unfortunately already disagreeably encumbered by its previous history. In 1922 and 1934 Carl Schmitt, the later National Socialist and extremely antisemitic constitutional lawyer, made it the catchword for his anti-revolutionary, anti-liberal and anti-democratic predilection for political dictatorships.[66]

Schmitt's political theology was nothing other than a theologically legitimated doctrine of political sovereignty: 'That one is sovereign who can declare the state of emergency', he pronounced, meaning by this in 1922 'the dictatorship of the President of the Reich, according to Article 48 of the Weimar Constitution'; while after 1933 his reference was to Hitler's Enabling Act. Theologically he justified the need for a political dictatorship by way of a secularized doctrine of original sin: 'In the face of the radically evil, there can only be a dictatorship'[67] – as if dictatorship were not itself 'the radically evil', with its 'non-self-justifying, absolute decisions created out of nothing'! Because human beings are 'evil' by nature, they need a strong hand to control them. This negative anthropology has always served to justify the dictator's tyranny. For Carl Schmitt, according to Nicolaus Sombart's acute analysis, this was the anti-revolutionary, conservative trinity of 'monotheism, monarchy and monogamy'.[68] Michael Bakunin, the anarchist, had cried, 'Neither God nor state!'[69] and Schmitt, setting up to be his adversary, fabricated a political theology 'for God and state', so as to be equipped for 'the decisive bloody battle' in the clash which 'has flared up today between Catholicism and atheistic socialism', as he believed, in the fashion of the nineteenth-century Spanish and French counter-revolutionaries.[70]

The determining subject of Schmitt's political theology is the authority of the state, not the church. However, for Metz and myself the church and Christianity in the world are the determining subjects of the political theology we were seeking. In view of the permanent distinction between us and Carl Schmitt, with his new adherents, it was well that from the very beginning we talked about the 'new' political theology. But unfortunately this differentiation, obvious though it is, has not prevented confusions in recent years.

In the new political theology, new theological ideas were certainly put forward, but not enough effort was made to arrive at a definition of what the word 'political' really means. Perhaps at the end of the 1960s political influence was overestimated, both by the politicians and by the theologians. The revolutions in Latin America, the Vietnam war, and the build-up of nuclear arms in Europe also made politics the largely dominant theme. In 1934 Carl Schmitt had even believed that 'the political' was the whole (*'das Totale'*)[71] – which was an accurate enough description of Hitler's totalitarian rule. But after the all-dominating East–West conflict came to an end in 1989, politics deregulated the economy. The result was a globalization of the economy through the world-wide marketing of everything and, along with that, a 'totalization' of the economy. This means that political decisions become the locally restricted sub-system of globalizing economic forces. Politics control neither the economy, nor the commercial and business associations, nor the financial markets. On the contrary, political decision is in danger of being controlled by these other forces. Politics are still important but they are no longer the only 'world' to which theology must 'turn its face'. That restricts the scope of 'the new political theology', and of the 'historical hermeneutics' to which we shall now turn.

2. *Historical hermeneutics of the future*

By the word 'historical' we mean here the unity of past and present in the vista of the future. It includes political life. The historian's concern with the past as scholar is only one part of the 'historical' interpretation of history. By hermeneutics we do not just mean, like Wilhelm Dilthey, 'the theory of understanding utterances of life which have been fixed in writing'.[72] We mean the comprehending experience and praxis of present history. The theoretical understanding of written testimonies to the experience and praxis of past history is one part of this. We 'understand' not just through observation but through participation too, and not just through participation, but also through our own responsible action in history.[73]

Every historical hermeneutic presupposes a concept of history. All noetic dealings with history imply an ontology of history. Hegel was able to 'grasp time in ideas' because for him history was 'the self-unfolding of Absolute Spirit'. In the knowledge of its history the World Spirit comes to consciousness of itself. Because reason has become reality, the real can be understood through reason. But of course that is only possible when reality 'has finished its process of development and has completed itself'. It is only from the perspective of its end that the whole of the form or configuration of a life can be discerned.

In a very similar way Dilthey embedded his 'utterances of life fixed in writing' 'in the great stream of unfathomable life'. 'It is only through the idea of the objectification of life that for the first time we acquire insight into the nature of the historical . . . Whatever aspect of its own character Spirit transposes into its expressions of life today, is tomorrow, when it stands there, history.'[74] We can 'understand' the 'utterances of life' of the past to the degree in which we ourselves 'live' and search for the utterances of life which are appropriate for ourselves. As far as history is concerned, 'we are historical beings first of all, before we become observers of history'. We can only understand past history because we participate in present history, and to the extent to which we do so. The relationship of the comprehender to that which he seeks to comprehend is pre-eminently determined by his own interest in life and his own participation in history. The 'prior understanding' with which the hermeneutical circle begins, according to Heidegger and Bultmann, is only one aspect of this interest in life and this participation in the history of life.

I am taking up this early hermeneutic of the philosophy of life so as to relate text and life to each other, and in order to avoid narrowing things down to what is existential and personal. Political hermeneutics is aligned towards the liberation from oppression, for life. God's Spirit is 'the source of life'.

But if, as Dilthey maintains, the objectifications of past life are objectifications of the stream of life which flows on further, then they can only be understood adequately in their connection with other expressions of life. Historical testimonies of the past become comprehensible only in association with other historical phenomena. Is there any independently existing 'form or configuration of life' which can complete its process of development independently? If everything in history is bound up with everything else, then the meaning of every individual in history can be understood only from the perspective of the end of the whole. This eschatological horizon for the understanding of history is already implicit with Hegel's philosophy of history. For Dilthey it was clear: 'We should have to wait for the end of our lifespan, and could only in the hour of death survey the whole from whose standpoint the relations of its parts could be ascertained. We should first have to await the end of history before we could possess the complete material which would allow the meaning of history to be determined.'[75]

But since we ourselves are historical beings and do not sit on the throne of judgment, for us a moment in the past becomes 'significant if it establishes a bond with the future through the act of that moment or through an external event. Or if the plan for future conduct was realized. What we set before our future as goal, conditions our decision about the meaning of the past.'[76] Here Dilthey described better than his existentialist successors the connection between an understanding of the past and expectation of the future, between remembrance and hope, putting present understanding into the context of present historical life, which requires concern and participation, not just observation. But for all that, no more than Hegel and, later, Wolfhart Pannenberg, did he perceive that in our time death by no means 'completes' the form or configuration of a life, rounding it off into a whole; generally speaking, death cuts life short by brute force. Even the end of history can only determine the meaning for the whole of the individual in history if that end is a felicitous 'consummation' of history, not a catastrophic rupture. Only a millenarian 'consummation of history' lends history meaning; an apocalyptic end robs it of meaning altogether.

The existential interpretation of historical texts in Heidegger and Bultmann is positioned in the ontology of 'the historicity of *Dasein*', *Dasein* and existence here initially meaning only human *Dasein* and existence.* Because human *Dasein* is in its origin historical, it is interested in '*Dasein* that once was'. Historical testimonies of life are therefore viewed in the perspective of the possible self-interpretations of past existence, not in the perspective of detectable developments or tendencies in political, social or world history. With this perspective, the meaning of history becomes detached from the total history in which human existences participate, and in which human existence has its *Sitz im Leben*; it is now sought exclusively in 'one's own history' and 'one's own present' in each given case. The decision in one's own particular existence is the end and beginning of history in the moment, and this moment is 'an atom of eternity', as Kierkegaard said (in opposition to Hegel), and is therefore eschatologically qualified. There is then no eschatology of world history. The theodicy question which seeks the divine final Judgment is replaced by the question about the identity of the human *Dasein* which is one with itself. The goal

---

* For the word '*Dasein*' used to express the being of persons, see M. Heidegger, *Being and Time*, trans. J. Macquarrie and E. Robinson, London 1962, 27 n.1.

of the eschatological process is not an 'end of the world'; it is a detachment of human existence from its 'worldness' (an *Entweltlichung*, in Heidegger's terminology). But this substitution provides no answer to the historical questions of the victims about justice; it merely suppresses the questions. The existential interpretation of historical texts must therefore again be thrown open for Dilthey's questions about world history, which advance a step further, and which we shall now pick up.

Historical *Dasein* is *Dasein* in history, not just the historicity of *Dasein*. We live in history, inasmuch as we participate in history, in our suffering or our action, not just by relating history to ourselves but also by relating ourselves to history. But the person who participates in history takes over responsibility for its future, expects a particular future, and exerts him or herself on its behalf. 'What we set before our future as purpose, conditions the way the meaning of the past is defined,' said Dilthey. That is not of course a one-sided affair; it is a reciprocal process between hope and remembrance. Participation in history cannot exhaust itself in the observation of history. The pure historian is not usually a politician, and the politician is seldom a good historian. Participation fuses theory and practice in the experience of history – which means in *the shared experience of history*.

Historical suffering moves from practice to theory, historical action from theory to practice. Theory and practice are dialectically linked, and that link cannot be unilaterally broken, either idealistically or materialistically.[77] There is neither 'the theory of a particular practice' nor 'the practice of a particular theory'. For theory cannot presuppose a blind practice, since there is no such thing among human beings; nor can practice presuppose a pure theory, because there is no intuitive notion without a determining subject.

The experience of history and participation in history are *shared between people*, as are the testimonies to the life of the past. Every form-critical analysis of historical texts discloses their *Sitz im Leben*, the community in which they are embedded. The analysis of texts from the standpoint of social history has taken form criticism a stage further. If that is true of 'Dasein that has once been', then it is also true of present *Dasein*, which tries to understand history by participating in it.[78] Every present *Dasein* has its own *Sitz im Leben*, and its interests in understanding past history are determined by its social context.

Not least, as well as the passive and active participation in history in a particular *situation* (*kairos*) and in addition to *social conditioning* (context), a human being's *natural constitution* as woman or man must be taken into account when we try to understand the past and its historical testimonies. It is true that masculine and feminine ways of looking at things, masculine and feminine modes of experience, and the differing interests and concerns of men and women are culturally determined; and in the history of our own culture, the determination is largely one-sided and takes the form of patriarchalism, as we can see from the nineteenth-century slogan 'men make history'. There is no purely masculine or feminine nature untouched by cultural history. To this extent femininity or masculinity is not an inborn fate. But for all that, it is still the genetic nature of the man or woman which receives this cultural impress. Consequently there has to be feminist criticism of a one-sided androcentric or patriarchal hermeneutics, if this purports to be universally human. In the rich diversity between the human sexes, proper attention must be paid to the insights and concerns of a feminine hermeneutics.[79] Since hermeneutics generally interprets traditions in the light of their masculine reception (*secundum hominem recipientem*), regard must be paid to the differences between the sexes, without nailing men and women down to particular roles through hard and fast expectations.

Up to now the ontological presupposition of historical hermeneutics was the assumption that history has a *transcendent subject*, and that it therefore constitutes a unity and can be talked about in the singular. It is the divine history, the history of Absolute Spirit, the history of life or of the *Dasein* of being, the history of humanity – or of the earth – or of matter;

and so forth. With this presupposition, hermeneutical authority could be claimed for the correct interpretation in the name of that higher authority. Totalitarian views of history were the result. These replaced the imperialist presentations of history put forward in nineteenth-century Europe.

Empirically, however, up to now there have been only human histories *in the plural* on this one single earth – histories which were relatively loosely connected, or not connected at all. We need only think of Japanese history and European history, or the history of the indigenous inhabitants of America before they were brought into contact with European history in 1492. In this respect history has always had a multiplicity of determining subjects. It was only through the industrialization and European imperialism of the nineteenth century that the diverse histories of the diverse peoples and empires became fused with European history. It was in the twentieth century that for the first time *one, single humanity* became the object of 'mutually assured destruction' through the great nuclear powers, by way of the weapons of mass annihilation. This led to the compulsion to build up responsible common structures for survival in what had been a passive object of collective suicide. Since the end of the deadly East–West conflict in 1989, the globalization of the economy has gone ahead, and – whether we like it or not – will lead to a unification of the worlds in which people live.[80]

These concentrations between the nations, for good or ill, could make of their histories in different ways a *single* world history, either 1. through a *super-state,* which would represent human mega-history and would rewrite and reinterpret the history of humanity according to its own established future goals; or 2. through a *pluralist interlacing* of the different histories, which would dispense with a centre and in its place make covenants which would leave 'to each his (or her) own' so as to develop the wealth of human cultures and potentialities for the future. This second possibility is more conducive to life. And here it would make sense to dispense with a dominating subject of history, and a simple unity in history, and history in the singular, in order to relate and interweave the differing subjects of differing histories through hermeneutics with multi-perspectives. Then in place of the simple unity of history we should have a co-ordinated, 'covenanted' community of the different histories and the different perspectives from which they are interpreted; and out of these 'the conflict of interpretations' (to take Paul Ricoeur's phrase) could fruitfully be shaped.[81] For this it would be wise for us to confine ourselves to limited goals for our future, so that we could determine the 'meaning' of a surveyable past – wise too to dispense with wholesale interpretations, so as to keep unoccupied the place of the *one* subject of the *one* history.

If interpretation is translation, in the literal sense – the transfer of a text from a context belonging to the past into a context in the present – then of course the text and the thing it talks about will not be able to remain unchanged either. *Hermeneutics does not merely interpret. It also transforms.* This transformation can take the form of a simple adaptation to one's own needs. That is then bad hermeneutics, because the interpretation does violence to its subject and ultimately makes itself superfluous, since if something simply corresponds to our own needs we can think it for ourselves. If, conversely, hermeneutics respects the particular character of the text and the different subjectivities of the people in the past who in the text speak to the present, then it is the interpreter who changes, and those for whom he or she is interpreting, rather than what is interpreted.[82] The people concerned do not apply the text to themselves and their situation as if it were a means to their own ends; they rediscover themselves in the text, and identify themselves with the history it relates. The text can be localized in one's own situation, but one's own situation can also be localized in the text. Only when this latter transposition takes place first does it lead, in a second act, to a change in one's own situation.

But going beyond these two aspects of the so-called hermeneutical circle is the dialogue with the text for the sake of the thing it is talking about, provided that this concern is something we share. Then the hermeneutical process begins with our listening to the text and our understanding of what it says. The next step is to think about the way the text talks about the matter we have in common. Out of this there may perhaps develop an objective criticism of the text which changes it if we adopt it for ourselves. We must not 'always write the Bible afresh' in the way that 'we must always write history afresh' if the perspectives of the present day have undergone some lasting change. But if the objective criticism is justified, we have to express our common concern differently. The 'anti-Jewish' pronouncements of the early Christian communities which were being persecuted by the Jewish synagogue are an example. To take these pronouncements over and repeat them unchanged in the twentieth century would not be in conformity with 'the cause of Christ' which we have in common. There is no need to sanitize the Bible, but in a contemporary situation in which Jews are being persecuted we must consider the opposite to be right, and must express 'the cause of Christ' in a way that is expedient and helpful for a positive relationship of Christians to Jews.[83] The androcentric and patriarchalist texts in the Bible, which are humiliating to women, are a further example.[84] They have to be modified in line with the creation of human beings to be God's image as 'male and female', and in accord with the community of equal rights shared by women and men 'in Christ' (Gal. 3.28) – that is to say, in their liberation. In cases such as these the appropriate translation process does not just interpret a historical form; it also transforms it.

3. The hermeneutics of the Bible's promissory history

Looked at in the context of the history of religions, the foundational document of the Christian faith has two unique characteristics. The first is *the duality of the Old and New Testaments*. This links Christianity indivisibly with Judaism, since for Judaism this Old Testament is its own Tenach. The second notable feature of the biblical traditions is their unique character as promissory history, which points beyond itself to the eschatological *coming of the kingdom of God*.[85] The first

characteristic means that Christian hermeneutics of the Old
Testament is always dependent on Jewish hermeneutics of the
Tenach, and can be properly developed only in dialogue with
that hermeneutics. How does its messianic reading of these
writings relate to the Mosaic reading? How can the Torah
be understood in the light of the gospel, and the gospel in
the light of the Torah? With regard to the second question, it is
not unimportant to note that in the history of Christian
hermeneutics this duality of Old and New (Testaments) has
always awakened eschatological expectations of the future of
God in history. The prophetic promises point beyond the
coming of Christ and the advent of the church to a future fulfilment.

Christian theology has always worked on this surplus of
promise in the Old Testament, because it calls in question the
solemn and passionate Christian claim that Christianity is itself
the fulfilment. Either these promises have been 'fulfilled' in
Christ's coming – ended and now dismissed (in which case they
must be combatted as 'Jewish dreams'), or they are still in force,
like God's covenant, to which they belong – and are in force not
only for the Jews but for Christians too. And in this case they
cannot have been 'fulfilled' in Christ in the sense used above;
they can only have been given final and universal force: 'All the
promises of God find their Yes in him' (II Cor. 1.20). Jesus'
messianic history, the coming of the gospel and faith, and the
beginning of the outpouring of the Holy Spirit 'on all flesh' then
enter into Israel's promissory history, bringing it to its final
eschatological history for the peoples of the world. 'The gospel
of Christ' (Rom. 15.19) is always already 'the gospel of the
kingdom of God' (Mark 1.15), for Christ is the kingdom of
God in person and, being so, gathers into himself the promises
of the Torah and the prophets, and must be comprehended as
'the future of the kingdom clothed in the Word and present in
the Word'.[86] If the kingdom of God is 'at hand', then Christ also
makes the past-future of that kingdom present – that is to say,
Abraham, Moses, Elijah and the prophets.

The Old Testament surplus of promise directs the apprehension of Christ and the experience of the Spirit to the future of the kingdom. It is in the eschatological symbol of the kingdom of God that the future of Scripture is formulated, and that also means the unity of Old and New Testaments. The search for a 'centre of scripture' began when, with the Reformation, scripture became 'the preceptress' of church and theology. The Reformers, with Luther, found that centre in 'what furthers – what ferments – Christ' (*'was Christum treibet'*),[87] and found it not only in the New Testament but in the Old, too; for in the promissory history of the Old Testament Luther already saw 'the gospel'. 'What ferments Christ' was for him the divine righteousness which justifies the sinner, and the justifying faith which is its counterpart. This faith did not come into the world for the first time through Paul; it is the original faith of Abraham (Gen. 15.6).

The image of the centre is in fact not very helpful because every centre presupposes a closed circle of which it is the middle point. But the biblical traditions are not a closed doctrinal system, and the duality of Old and New Testaments even less so. The very reason that 'the biblical histories of promise and gospel can be called historical is that they point *excentrically* beyond themselves into God's future. They are remembrances of this future, which was heralded in the history of the past. They all point to that future in which 'the scriptures will be fulfilled', when it will no longer be a matter of 'it is written', because now 'it has happened' and 'behold, all things have become new'.[88] We shall therefore replace talk about a 'centre' for Scripture through the perception of 'the future of scripture', and shall draw into the expectation of God's coming kingdom and its righteousness what Luther termed the driving force of Christ (*'die treibende Kraft Christi'*), by which he meant the righteousness of God which justifies and creates justice in the history of sin and suffering, the violent and their victims. In the justification of the God-forsaken, God establishes his right to his world, and asserts the righteousness and justice of this new world of his.

If the future of Scripture is apprehended in the symbol of the kingdom of God, then this becomes the scarlet thread of a biblical theology which does not just read the Old Testament in the light of the New, and the New Testament in the light of the Old, but reads both in the light of God's coming to his whole creation. With this, Israel is recognized as the other, the original, community of hope. Then, together with the Jews, Christians testify 'to all nations' and to the whole of creation on earth the righteousness, justice and peace of God's coming world.

The Reformation's hermeneutical principle was that 'Holy Scripture is its own interpreter' (*Scriptura sacra sui ipsius interpres*).[89] Scripture is supposed to be not only the *object* of interpretation but the interpreting *subject* too. This meant disputing the church's authority to interpret scripture. It is not the church which interprets scripture but scripture which interprets the church. But the same tenet also meant that the interpretative authority of enlightened or inspired reason was denied too – not only rationalist interpretation, but 'pneumatological exegesis' as well.

To say that Holy Scripture is its own interpreter can initially mean in practical terms that it discloses itself to the reader of its own accord, provided that the reader lets Scripture speak to him or her, and thereby recognizes its authority or, better, its character as subject. Throughout the whole of church history, the Bible has continually made its own way, in opposition to the interpretative authority of the church, among the Waldensians as well as at the Reformation, in the Catholic Bible movement today as well as in the Pentecostal movement in Latin America. That is why the church repeatedly forbade the laity to read the Bible for themselves. They were permitted to read and listen to it only under the guidance of the church's magisterium. The texts chosen for preaching had to be restricted to passages selected by the church. Christian rulers too forbade the independent reading of the Bible because it was 'a subversive book', to which the rebellions of the oppressed often enough appealed. It was not for nothing that the Reformation acquired its wide influence, not through Luther's theology, but through his translation of the Bible, made during his months as a fugitive in the Wartburg, under the ban of church and empire. Translations of the Bible into the vernacular and their dissemination brought the Reformation to France, Spain, Italy and the countries of south-east Europe. The Reformation was a Bible movement, and is the proof that scripture does in practice interpret itself. It comes close to all who read it and who can form their own judgment. But does that make it a kind of Protestant pocket-pope, infallible and inerrant?

The self-interpretation of scripture does not mean that interpreter and the text to be interpreted are one and the same, and that there is no 'matter of scripture' against which scripture has to be tested. If a text 'interprets itself', there is evidently something in it which thrusts and ferments, something which has to come out and must be e-lucidated, because it cannot remain within itself. It is not finished and done with, and fulfilled of itself. There must be some kind of unrest in 'the matter of scripture' itself which 'wills' to issue from scripture and to go beyond it. Why otherwise should scripture come to interpret itself? If 'the matter of scripture' is God's promissory history, then its self-interpretation is self-explanatory, for 'the promise is an event which is already in the process of its coming',[90] and scripture is an essential factor in this event. What is in the process of becoming event, and is only comprehensible if the comprehension sees itself as a function of that event, is told from generation to generation, so that in the telling the reader is drawn into the event that is still incomplete. It is written down, and its writing must afterwards again be related in such a way that its hearers are drawn into the event which 'is already in the process of its coming'. This happens if in the telling of what is past the future is heralded, so that what is proclaimed is future in the past. It is then also understandable why 'the event which is already in the process of its coming' and to which the writing testifies, has to be believed and understood, and also understood and acted upon.

If 'the matter of scripture' is God's history of promise, then scripture is part of it, and points beyond itself to the time of fulfilment. If it is not the church which interprets scripture but Scripture which interprets the church, then the church becomes the people of God's coming kingdom and acts upon the event of God's promise 'which is already in the process of its coming'. If 'the matter of scripture' is the promissory history of God's kingdom, which renews the world, then Christ is the door to the understanding of scripture, since he is 'the kingdom of God in person': '. . . and he opened their eyes'. If 'the matter of scripture' is the new creation of all things and the rebirth of the cosmos (as the goal of the promise is also called in the New Testament), then our own experience of liberation, of raising up, and the birth to new life becomes the key to an understanding of the words and texts which witness to God's promise; for with experiences such as these the new creation begins, and with it the time when what was written in former times will be fulfilled, as Joel 2 and Acts 2 say.

This self-interpretation of Holy Scripture in the context of promissory history was traditionally termed the 'anagogical sense' (*sensus anagogicus*), which points to eternal glory. The typological interpretation of the Old Testament as the fore-shadowing of what is to come also contains similar elements. But over against this, the self-interpretation of scripture in the light of promissory history takes scripture literally in the sense that in 'the matter of scripture' it takes God at his word:

His Word is true without deceit
and holds its promise sure.

In the words of the English hymn: 'Lord, thy Word abideth.'

This brings us to the present *kairos, context and involvement in history*. Interpreters must identify themselves with 'the matter of scripture' in complete self-forgetfulness; but on the other hand they must be equally aware of their personal, social, political and historical situation. In the school of existential interpretation, interpretation of scripture and interpretation of the self reinforce and deepen each other mutually; and in the hermeneutics of political and liberation theology the same may be said about textual exposition and contextual analysis. The interpretation of scripture in the light of social history requires a form-critical exposition of the present situation of the interpreter and the community to which he or she belongs, an exposition which will translate the biblical traditions into the life of both interpreter and community. The word 'interpretation' is inadequate. It is too feeble, because its sights are set only on the noetic aspect of the 'understanding' of scripture, without regard to practical participation in history. But the biblical testimonies are by no means theoretical testimonies. They do not aim simply at comprehension. They are witnesses to a suffered, experienced, acted-out promissory history, which prompts our own suffering, experiencing and acting within that history. The road of hermeneutics does not merely lead from text to preaching (important though this is for preachers); it leads from a text springing from a past praxis to the praxis of our own lives today. It is only through our own participation in history that we learn to understand the history of the past; and, conversely, the attempt to understand past history leads us to participate in our own. If this is true in general, it is true in particular for 'the event which is in the process of its coming', which we call God's promissory history.

Liberation theology, political theology and feminist theology have pointed out that the divine promissory history which we find in the Bible is a kind of *counter*-history to the victory parade of the rulers of this world, because it is meant 'preferentially' for the poor, the weak, the lost and the victims of the history of human violence. As is evident from the history of Israel since the Exodus from Egypt, and the history of Christ from the manger to the cross, there is a continuing, ongoing 'preferential option' for the poor on God's part. God's promises are understood best by those without hope. The poor understand Jesus' beatitudes, the sick experience Jesus' healings through the life-giving Spirit, the sad feel God's consolations, and sinners God's saving righteousness. The apocalyptic writings speak to the persecuted, the victims and the martyrs.

To read scripture's promissory history with the eyes of the poor – if we may use that term in its most comprehensive sense for a moment – does not mean charitably stooping down to them. It means recognizing 'the messianism of the poor' or 'the apostolate of the poor', and listening to them as their own determining subjects of an authentic interpretation of scripture, not as objects of our own endeavours.[91] According to the scene set in the Bible for the Sermon on the Mount, and according to the Beatitudes themselves, the people of Jesus' Beatitudes were the men and women disciples who followed Jesus, and the poor, abandoned, sacrificed people (*ochlos*) – that is to say, mourners and the merciful, the poor and those who hunger for righteousness, the peacemakers and those who are persecuted for righteousness' sake. This, at least, is what we find if we put together the passive and the active Beatitudes listed in Matthew's Gospel.[92] In the discourse about 'the Last Judgment' in Matthew 25, where Jesus identifies himself with the Son of man-Judge of the world, we again find these two groups among Jesus' people. On the one hand there are the hungry, thirsty, homeless, naked and imprisoned; on the other there are 'the righteous' who act justly towards them. The Son of man-Judge of the world calls the first 'the least of his brothers' (and sisters), the others 'the blessed of my Father', who 'inherit' the kingdom and eternal life. Jesus identifies himself with both.

We can extend these two observations and apply them to the church. The church is *the people who are believers,* to whom the risen Christ says, as he once said to the disciples: 'He who hears you hears me.' But on the other side of the church are *the people who are poor and suffering.* About them he says: 'He who visits them visits me', and with these people he identifies himself through his humiliation to the point of death on the Roman cross.[93] In the crucified people, the crucified Christ is present and calls the righteous to himself.

If this viewpoint is correct, there is no ecclesial hermeneutics commensurate with 'the matter of scripture' without the hermeneutics of the poor, and no appropriate hermeneutical praxis without the fellowship of the poor and their liberation.

This makes it clear that there is no all-encompassing herme-neutics of the Bible's promissory history of the kingdom of God without ethics and politics – the ethics of life and the politics of the righteousness which puts things to rights and creates right-ful justice.

3

Trinitarian hermeneutics of 'holy scripture'

I. What makes writings 'holy scriptures'?

Theological and – in the wider sense of the word – religious hermeneutics is concerned with the understanding and interpretation of the sacred writings of religious communities. Jews, Christians, Muslims, Hindus, Jains, Buddhists and others all have these 'holy scriptures', in which the relationship to God is formulated and also, in the wider sense of the word, the religious community's primal history. These writings can be the documents of a revelation, they can relate myths of origin, or they can record sayings of a fundamental wisdom. In what are called the founder religions, the writings preserve the initial religious experiences of the founder, as in the case of Moses or Buddha.[94] The writings are kept sacred through their reverent use, and because they determine the worship and religious rituals through which the life of the community is brought into harmony with its foundation and origin. They acquire practical authority through the concurrence between text and life: the text determines life, and life interprets the text.

If we consider these writings from the angle of their acceptance into the life of the community, they are not *holy*; they are *hallowed* – sanctified. The community can change them, or can express itself in other hallowed writings too. But viewed from the angle of 'The Holy' which they represent, they are holy through concurrence with their content.[95] There is really no contradiction between an *objective or generative hermeneutics* (which investigates the genesis and growth of a text) and a *reception hermeneutics* (which has in view the reception history). However, the person who wishes to change sacred writings or replace them by others prefers the generative view; while for the person for whom the writings are holy because they witness to an enduringly efficacious 'fact', these writings are permanently valid, because they generate faith, call the religious community to life, and sustain it.

In the case of the holy scripture of Christians, we have to consider the question of precedence: does scripture take precedence over the church, or the church over scripture?[96] If we start from the historical genesis of the writings of the apostles and evangelists, then the church comes first: it produced the writings, sanctified them in worship, and gathered them together in a canon of holy scriptures according to recognizable criteria. The Christian community is therefore really also entitled to go on writing them, provided that it experiences a further revelatory history. Like Roman Catholic dogmatic hermeneutics, it can develop or augment the divine truth which it 'sanctifies' according to 'scripture – tradition – and the present understanding of faith of believers'.

If we start from 'the matter of scripture', however, then it is this which has called to life the oral traditions and their fixed written forms; and in origin this precedes the church. The *im*pression of divine revelation factually precedes the *ex*pression by the people it touches. It was 'for Christ's sake' that Paul wrote his letters, and the evangelists their Gospels.

In comparing the different traditions, we have to examine the scriptures with a view to seeing how they bring out 'the matter' they share. Objective hermeneutics presupposes the difference between 'the matter of scripture' and the scriptural text, and the interior circle of the two; and it is open to objective criticism of what is written. 'The matter of scripture' in the Tenach/Old Testament is God's covenant with Israel and the divine promises given in that covenant, promises which point beyond Israel to the salvation of all peoples and the peace of the whole creation. With the covenant, the history of God's great promises is opened. It was in this experienced, narrated and hoped-for history that the promises had their genesis, and it is in that history that they acquire their 'sacred' function for God's future.

In the New Testament 'the matter of scripture' is the unconditional endorsement and universal enactment of God's promises through and in Christ, and the beginning of their fulfilment in the experiences of God's Spirit. The Christian scriptures are 'holy' inasmuch as they correspond to God's promise in Christ and in the Spirit; they are 'hallowed' or sanctified by their function for the proclamation of the gospel to the nations, and for the new life in the Spirit. They are writings on which the church is founded, and life-renewing texts of the promise.

If, comparing the two views of scripture, we look at the genesis of the written form given to the Word of God, *the early church* has to be viewed as the determining subject of scripture; but if we look at the 'matter' which called the church to life, *scripture* is the determining subject of the church. Scripture and church have to be seen in a dialectical process, where the salient point is the understanding of 'the matter of scripture'. For either scripture or the church to stand alone has far-reaching consequences.

We find independent status being given to scripture in the various doctrines about the *verbal inspiration* of scripture.[97] These writings are then holy in the literal sense, because the Holy Spirit itself guided the pens of the writers. But according to biblical understanding, the Holy Spirit is the beginning of the eschatological 'fulfilment of scripture' and of the coming glory of God, which will 'sanctify' the whole creation. To see the Spirit at work only in the verbal inspiration of scripture is a reduction of the mighty efficacy of God the Spirit which does not accord with 'the matter of scripture'. 'The matter of scripture' does not receive its due through fundamentalism.

For the church to be given independent status over against 'the matter of scripture' is a position found throughout church history. For a long time the laity was forbidden to read the scriptures without the guidance of a priest of the church, because the Bible is a book with 'dangerous reminders' for the rulers. When the church put together the canon, it selected from a wealth of Christian writings and traditions according to certain viewpoints. According to their avowed intention (*intentio recta*) these viewpoints were related to the matter of scripture, but in their veiled intention (*intentio obliqua*) they at the same time asserted ecclesiastical domination and male supremacy. The lectionary laying down the passages of scripture to be used in worship during the church's year also selects and eliminates undesirable texts from the church's proclamation. The Reformation therefore translated the Bible into the vernaculars, so that all Christians could read it as a whole, and believe 'the matter of scripture' independently. For it is 'the matter of scripture' which alone prompts the desire to read the scriptures, understand them, live in accordance with them, and proclaim them. The great promises of God set even our own little restricted lives in the light of God's all-embracing future.

Another critically and objectively justified re-vision of holy scripture has been occasioned by changes in the religious community and is emerging today in *the feminist movement*. The point at issue now is no longer the relationship between scripture and the church; here we are dealing with altered and additional 'holy scriptures'.[98] The first Christian feminist theology is now being replaced by a new interfaith, feminist theory of religion. Hitherto only the androcentric and misogynous 'texts of terror' in the Bible were criticized, and that rightly so; for the myth in Genesis 3 about the Fall brought about by the serpent and the woman (to take one example) was already falsely interpreted in I Tim. 2.11–15 as a justification for the repression of the woman: the woman was created second and was the first to fall into sin, so she ought to keep silent, and 'will be saved' by bearing children. But any such interpretation is false, being in contradiction to 'the matter of scripture' and to Christian experience of the Spirit.

Now, however, an interfaith feminist community is developing which makes other, new, texts their 'holy scriptures', in
addition to and outside the Christian Bible. This reverses the
relationship between text and context: 'We are the text,' says
Chung Hyun-Kyung, and the 'holy scriptures' are our changing
'context'. This goes far beyond the original Roman Catholic
generative view of the Bible, and the precedence of the church
over scripture. The newly developing interfaith community of
women becomes the determining subject of the writings which
it considers sacred, without there being any 'matter of scripture'
as the determining subject of this community. But why should a
liberation movement or an interfaith community see itself as
religious at all, and express itself in 'holy scriptures'? If the
determining subject is the community of people which produces
these scriptures and then sanctifies them, then this community
could just as well express itself in other ways – poetically,
dramatically, ideologically or scientifically. It would thereby
avoid handicapping itself in its productivity through the
'sanctification' of particular writings. But, as Ludwig Feuerbach's criticism of religion already made plain, the anthropological element then becomes the constant, and the religious
element the variable. It is difficult to discover a theological
dimension here, except – as some people say nowadays – the
divine authority of the oppressed and suffering people who
hunger to be free for life and for their full humanity.

The modern fundamentalist phenomenon on the one hand,
and this extension of the scriptures on the other, raise the
question whether the canon of Christian writings is closed or
open.[99] If, with these two movements, we look only at the
scriptural texts themselves, we have to consider the canon to be
closed, or at most open for the addition of other writings. But if
we look at the scriptural texts from the angle of 'the matter of
scripture', then the canon remains open: we can, for objective
reasons, judge the Epistle of James to be 'an epistle of straw', as
Luther did, and might prefer to exclude the book of Revelation;
but we can also preach from non-biblical texts if they accord
with 'the matter of scripture'. A quotation from the Bible is not

enough to guarantee the truth of what is said. And what would happen if someone found what proved to be a Third Epistle of Paul to the Corinthians?

2. Is the Bible the Word of God or a human testimony of faith?

We shall now turn to the special Christian hermeneutics of the Bible. Here, at latest since the beginning of historical-critical research, there has been a conflict between a 'hermeneutics from above' and a 'hermeneutics from below'.

For post-Reformation theology, in its conflict with the Roman Catholic 'tradition' principle, the article or statement of faith about holy scripture (*articulus de scriptura sacra*) became the article by which the church stands and falls (*articulus stantis et cadentis ecclesiae*) – a status which, as we know, Luther assigned to the article about justification. This indicates a shift away from 'the matter of scripture' to the scriptural text. With the help of the theopneustic doctrine (the doctrine of divine inspiration), orthodox Protestantism, and in Protestantism the Reformed tradition particularly, developed a doctrine of the authority of scripture which placed that authority within the sovereignty of God himself: scripture is divine because it is God's written Word. The incarnation of God's eternal Word is followed by the 'inscripturization' of that Word. So the Bible is no less than 'Jesus Christ existing as scripture'.[100]

In our own time, it was Karl Barth above all who maintained this synoptic view of 'the sovereign God and holy scripture'. Opposing the relativizing historical criticism of scripture, which creates distances of time between text and reader, and as early as the Preface to the second edition of his *Epistle to the Romans* (1921), he declared his intention to wrestle, like Calvin, with the text 'till the walls which separate the sixteenth century from the first become transparent, until Paul speaks and the man of the sixteenth century hears, until the conversation between the original record and the reader is wholly concentrated on the subject matter . . . In understanding, I must thrust forward until I stand with almost nothing before me but the engima of the *matter*, hardly any more before the enigma of *the document* as such.'[101] In the development of his *Christian Dogmatics* (1927) and then of his *Church Dogmatics* (from 1932 onwards), this 'matter of scripture' was for Barth always the sovereign God. He also called him 'the God who stands before us in the Bible' and saw the authority of scripture grounded on the '*Deus dixit*' – God spoke.[102] 'God reveals himself as the Lord' became for him the divine origin, first, of God's trinitarian 'revelation of himself' and, second, of the biblical-hermeneutical circle of revelation-scripture-proclamation.

Barth maintained the distinction between 'the matter of scripture' and the scriptural text, and did not identify the two directly and without mediation, as did orthodox Reformed tradition. He followed, rather, the monarchical trinitarian order, which Basil the Great had already employed as a way of presenting the unity of the triune God in the unified movement of his divine sovereignty: the Father *through* the Son *in* the Holy Spirit.[103] With Barth, we can draw out this sovereign movement of the trinitarian sovereignty of God further: from the Holy Spirit *through* scripture *in* the proclamation. These are trinitarian and hermeneutical sequences of identifications which by no means put an end to the differences. On the basis of the identifications in the sovereign movement of God's self-revelation and self-communication, we can then say: scripture *is* God's Word, God's Word *is* God himself. Barth always stressed the unity of the subject of the self-revealing and speaking Person of God: one divine subject in three divine modes of being: Father – Son – Holy Spirit. With this, scripture belongs wholly within the implementation of the sovereign address 'from above' to every human being in time through the eternal God.

Out of the unity of the triune God and the unity of his self-revelation there emerges a *unified view* of scripture which is no longer able to perceive any essential distinction between the Old and the New Testaments. In the light of the divine address and divine history to which the biblical writings witness, this is not wrong; but it means that the differences between the human vehicles of the writings are no longer taken seriously. The Old Testament of Christians was and is and remains Israel's Tenach. Until the coming of the Messiah in glory, the church and Israel remain distinct, each of them witnessing in its own way to the divine Name. If we were to follow through the unity of God's self-revelation consistently, we should have to assume a unified people of God, brought into being either through the testimony to Christ in the Old Testament or through the testimony to the Torah in the New. Did the eternal God reveal himself through Christ or through the Torah of Moses? Is it the covenant with Israel which is the one, eternal covenant of God, or is it the 'new covenant'?

These questions about the relationship between the church and Israel, Christians and Jews, was an internal theological problem from the outset for the Reformed doctrine of the scriptures and its biblical hermeneutics. On the basis of the unity of scripture in the unity of the authority of God, the Reformed church always knew itself to be closely linked with the synagogue, and never vilified it as the 'synagogue of Satan'. When, after 1650, under the influence of Manasseh ben Israel's tract *Spes Israelis,* the Jews were readmitted to England under Cromwell, a new messianic doctrine of Israel took form in Puritanism: the Jews are no longer representatives of the Antichrist; they are agents of the redemption of humanity in the parousia of the Messiah Jesus at the end of days.[104]

A 'hermeneutics from below' develops once the biblical writings are viewed as *human testimonies of faith*, which have been historically, socially and culturally conditioned. Then their determining subject is not the sovereignly self-revealing God; it is the historically existing and responding human being. Over the historical and cultural divides, we can understand the men and women of the past because our existence, like theirs, is historically conditioned.[105] The fundamental metaphysical questions of human existence are the same, so we can understand and adopt their answers.

For Christian hermeneutics, this general hermeneutics of the historicity of existence is supplemented by the history of the kerygma, which from the very beginning has faced human beings with the decision of faith.[106] Inasmuch as we know ourselves to be faced with this decision, we can understand the testimonies of faith of the early Christian communities and, understanding them, can make them our own. Existential-historical, socio-historical and psycho-sociological exegeses of the texts passed down to us enable us to discover how people and human communities expressed themselves, and how they shaped their lives.

Because this 'hermeneutics from below' is the hermeneutical method most employed, having given rise to a motley variety of further methods,[107] we need not expound it any further. But we have to establish that here it is not the eternity of God which is made the constant; it is the constitutional historicity of human existence, while the religious self-interpretations of human existence in history are variable. Whereas in hermeneutics 'from above' it was the one divine determining subject which utters and 'reveals' itself, in hermeneutics 'from below' it is the one human subjectivity. With this, the way of looking at many texts alters. Whereas a text talks about the resurrection of Christ, for example, it is the author's faith in the resurrection expressed in this discourse which is investigated. The text's avowed intention (its *intentio recta*) is examined with the aim of detecting its veiled intention (its *intentio obliqua*). What the text is talking about is neglected in favour of the person or community which speaks in the text. While a congregation gathers together for worship, the hermeneut investigates its social status. While a person praises God, the androcentricism or mysogenist sexism of which he is unconscious is probed. This kind of hermeneutics, which derives from criminology and psychoanalyis, is known as the 'hermeneutics of suspicion'.[108]

On the other hand the biblical writings by no means comprise solely preaching texts for a hermeneutics 'from above'. There are also many stories to be told, and prayers, psalms, hymns and doxologies to be prayed, sung and danced, and where God is extolled. The texts must therefore also be interpreted 'from below', for in these writings people do not only listen to God's Word; they also want to open their hearts before God. God does not just speak; he also hears. This hermeneutics 'from below' does not have to be justified by way of an existential ontology or through the assumption of anthropological constants. We can also understand it in trinitarian terms. Then these are testimonies of faith and expressions of the life of persons and human communities, which have been gathered together and passed down to us in the biblical traditions, expressions of life and testimonies of the Spirit, who is 'the giver of life'. The rich variety of the charismata, callings and energies of God's Spirit find expression here, but also its sufferings and sadnesses; and their *ex*pression follows the traces of the *im*pression of God which called the expression forth. 'The way to the knowledge of God therefore proceeds from the one Spirit through the one Son to the one Father,' said Basil, explaining the 'eucharistic Trinity'.[109] It is a movement of thanksgiving and praise, but a movement too of lament and doubt, which proceeds from the indwelling Spirit, through the Son/the eternal Word/the eternal Wisdom, to the Father.

In this eucharistic movement, which runs counter to the monarchical Trinity, it is not the identifications 'from above' which are perceived, but the differences 'from below', the inadequacy of the ways we express life before God, the dissimilarities in the metaphors in which we express ourselves, and the disharmonies in the harmonies with God which we seek. Here the experience of the identification of God with his Word in the monarchical trinitarian movement finds its correspondence in the experience of differentiation in the eucharistic movement of the Trinity. What there leads to speech in the name of God, here leads to the apophatic silence before the divine mystery. It is of course true that the trinitarian version of a hermeneutics of the Bible 'from below' such as I have suggested here presupposes a new, extended version of the Calvinist doctrine about the inner testimony of the Holy Spirit (*testimonium Spiritus Sancti internum*).[110]

In actual fact both heremeneutics, the hermeneutics 'from above' and the hermeneutics 'from below', live from the same monistic premise: history is the work of a single determining subject which determines the whole, whether this be God's self-revelation or the self-expression of human beings. But does this premise accord with the biblical history and the history in which the Bible acquires its intended efficacy? I have therefore proposed a 'trinitarian hermeneutics' for the New Testament: 'According to the witness of the New Testament Jesus is manifested as "the Son". His history springs from the co-efficacy of the Father, the Son and the Spirit . . . The history in which Jesus is manifested as "the Son" is not consummated and fulfilled by a single subject. The history of Christ is already related in trinitarian terms in the New Testament itself. So we start from the following presupposition. *The New Testament talks about God by proclaiming in narrative the relationships of the Father, the Son and the Spirit, which are relationships of fellowship and are open to the world.*'[111] This can easily be recognized from the co-efficacy of the Spirit in Jesus' life and sending, and the co-efficacy of Jesus with the Spirit in his raising and exaltation. We recognize it from Jesus' Abba prayer in the Spirit, and from the sending of the Spirit from the Father.

But to discover the co-efficacy of the divine Persons according to the testimony of the history of God in scripture is only the one side; the other side is the perception of the function of scripture *in the trinitarian history of God*, into which human beings are integrated through baptism and the rebirth to a living hope. In the perspective of the eschatological finality of the death and resurrection of Christ, scripture is *closed* and complete. Christ 'died to sin once for all, but the life he lives he lives to God' (Rom. 6.10). The christological *ephapax* – the once for all – applies to the christological witness of scripture too, as Heb. 1.2 intimates. But in the perspective of the Pentecostal beginning of the eschatological experiences of the Spirit, scripture is *open*. The eschatological experience of the Spirit is itself *the future* of scripture. It is for this, and looking towards this, that what has been passed down has been told, written down, read and continually interpreted afresh. With this future 'the fulfilment of scripture' in the kingdom of God begins. In this respect we have to understand 'what is written' in the great framework of God's economy of the Spirit. Nothing less than that should be meant by the demand for a 'spiritual inter-pretation of Scripture'.[112] So seen theologically, *God the Spirit* is the real interpreter.

3. The Spirit of life as the real interpreter

It is not only the Gospel of John which provides good argu-ments for this view. According to Jesus' farewell discourses in John 14–16, the Son dies so that the Paraclete may come. The Son prays the Father to send the Comforter. That is *the Spirit of truth*, who reveals what is hidden. In him men and women will know Christ and the God who sent him. 'Whatever he hears he will speak, and he will declare to you the things that are to come' (John 16.13), thus mediating past and future. He will 'glorify' Christ by 'declaring' Christ (16.14).

What the Spirit of truth communicates is knowledge of Christ the Lord and of the God who has raised him. But the fact *that* the Spirit communicates this is something new and specific to the Spirit, over against what Christ and God the Father have done and do. Why did Christ come, die and rise again? The answer is: in order *to send the Spirit* who sanctifies life and opens up the future of the eternal kingdom. The faith which the Spirit awakens is in content wholly related to Christ and God, but in the coming of faith the new day of God already begins. From time immemorial, the Holy Spirit has been understood as the *eternal light* which enlightens and illuminates. Because, as we are told, God is known only through God, it is in his light alone that we see light (Ps. 36.9). It is not only the *knowledge* of God which proceeds from God; it is the knowing too. Just as no one knows the Father except the Son (Matt. 11.27), so no one confesses Jesus as Lord except *in* the Holy Spirit (I Cor. 12.4). This is formulated as if it were a limiting condition, but what it means is the very reverse – a marvellous de-limitation of the trinitarian circle: the person who knows Christ and believes the God who raised him from the dead is illuminated by God the Spirit, and enters into the eternal light. And with this, the light of God's new day of creation shines in that person. Knowledge of Christ is the first flush of dawn, the daybreak colours of the future world. This 'knowing' with the enlightened eyes of reason is not the cold light with which we rationally know things in order to master them. It is the warm light of the knowing which is loving, participatory and uniting.

For the consequence of this view, we can look at the other saying from the Gospel of John which describes the goal of Christ's coming. What God brings into this world through Christ is *life*. 'I live and you shall live also' (14.19). God the Spirit is the source, the wellspring of life *(fons vitae)* – life that is healed, freed, full, indestructible and eternal. Christ himself is 'the resurrection and the life' *in person*. Those who believe in him will live even though they die, because to them 'life has been made manifest' (I John 1.2). They experience it with all their senses. So the sending of the Spirit is at the same time *the sending of life*.[113] From this we can conclude that a 'spiritual interpretation of scripture' has to be a *biographical* interpretation. Through the ways in which we express our lives we interpret the scriptural texts we live with. These utterances of life (as Dilthey called them) find expression through language and logic – through the praxis that furthers life – through our bodily configuration and the body language of mimic and gesture – through the experiences and remembrances which have shaped our lives – through our relationships in the communities we live in; and so forth. The book of the Bible is interpreted by our lived lives, for it is 'the book of life', as it has been called from time immemorial. The sending of the Spirit *(missio Dei)* awakens life and multifarious movements of revival and healing. So *life* is the true interpreter.

But what is life? Greek distinguishes between *bios* and *zoe*. *Bios* means the vegetative life which human beings have in common with animals and plants; *zoe* means conscious and specifically human life. God's Spirit, 'the giver of life', reaches everything living, as in creation, and fills it with the divine life-force (*ruach*) and with earthly joy in existence (Psalm 104). So when the energies of the divine Spirit 'are poured out on all flesh', it is *all* the living that are meant. But as 'the Spirit of Christ', 'the Spirit of God' has the impress of the form and ministry of Jesus Christ, and is efficacious as 'the power of the resurrection'. The Spirit who in accordance with Christ gives life, brings *zoe* into being, as immortal life and the eternal livingness of love. In the field of force of God's love, earthly, created, human life becomes eternal life, which participates in the living God. So we can talk about an 'increase of life' (if we like to use this category from Nietzsche's philosophy of life), from all the living to human life, and from human life to participation in the divine life. How does the Spirit who is 'the giver of life' act on life?

As the Spirit of Christ, the life-giving Spirit carries on the ministry of Jesus Christ: 1. He heals sick life and gives renewed health by expelling the demons of chaos from body and soul. Just as in the ministry of Jesus the Spirit healed the sick, so Jesus goes on acting in the Spirit, and through the Spirit heals those who are sick. In this sense 'life' means health, with organs that function, a clear mind, and well-being of body and soul. 2. The Spirit forgives sins and lifts the oppressive burden of guilt from life. Guilt fetters us to the past and takes away the breath we need for living. To be imprisoned in guilt robs life of its future. Just as in the ministry of Jesus the Spirit forgave sins and absolved the guilty, so Jesus continues to minister in the Spirit, and 'bears the sins of the world', so as to give future in which they can live to the guilt-ridden. 3. The Spirit frees the oppressed and exploited people from unjust structures and the brutality of human beings. Just as in the ministry of Jesus the Spirit gathered the impoverished and helpless people (*ochlos*), making them the people of the Beatitudes, so Jesus continues to act in the Spirit and in the community of his people gathers the 'foolish', 'weak', 'low and despised' and those who are of no account in the eyes of the world, in order to put to shame the violent, the people of noble birth, and the wise of the world

(I Cor. 1.26–29). 4. As the power of Christ's resurrection the Spirit gives life to our mortal bodies (Rom. 8.11), and will drive out godless death from creation. The raisings of the dead during Jesus' ministry were restorations into this mortal life. Lazarus too died later. But as such, they are signs of the raising of the dead into the eternal life of God's coming world. The Spirit of Christ is the power and energy of the resurrection. It is already experienced here and now in the love which is as strong as death, and it makes believers experience in love the livingness of eternal life. In it, life becomes indestructible, unfading and immortal. What makes life living is not Nietzsche's deadly 'will to power'; it is the creative love for life.

Compared with other forms of the living, human life is life that is aware of death. It is therefore dependent on the acceptance and affirmation of death. Because human life can be negated, denied and rejected, it must be affirmed, accepted and chosen. Because human life can suffocate in self-hate, it must develop self-love, which grows out of the experience of being loved. Life is kept living through interest in life. If interest in life flickers and dies out, then life loses its human quality, and dies biologically too. Human life comes from love, comes alive through love, and through love is able to make other life living. If this experience of love disappears from a human life, that life becomes petrified and dies even while the body lives.

4. *The biblical texts as furthering life*

'Life is robbery,' said Nietzsche, Whitehead and, in another form, Albert Schweitzer too, Darwin having made them familiar with the animal world as a 'struggle for existence'.[114] Life always lives at the expense of other life, and the struggle to live heightens life, though only the life of the stronger. That was not just an observation; it was a biological justification for the modern imperialism of 'the white man'. But every mother and every child knows that life is born and is a gift. It is only for the masculine arrogance of the will to power that life and death are one. What distinguishes life from death, however, is love. It is 'nativity' which gives life hope, not cynical morbidity. Whenever a life is robbed, life is the premise. So life is above death. We can only kill what was once born.

Nietzsche's 'will to power' and to the growth-orientated 'increase of life' manifests a climber mentality which is contrary to nature, destructive of nature, and suicidal; it aims to tread underfoot anyone who is weaker, or different, or alien, and it digs its own mass grave. The German 'will to power' ended up in two world wars, in Verdun, Stalingrad and Auschwitz. Can life be 'increased'? What is 'increased' life? Does it mean living longer, living faster, living more intensively, or living with more power? An increase means something quantitatively more. But do we not need something different – a new *quality* of living in a life filled with meaning? The Gospel of John talks about 'the fullness of God' from which we receive 'grace upon grace', and speaks about 'the fullness of life'. That is another phrase for 'eternal life', and a completely different category from Nietzsche's 'increased' life.

What does this mean for a hermeneutics of the biblical writings in the coming of the Spirit who is 'the giver of life', and in the context of our own life-stories? We shall take our bearings from the following guideline. We shall work out what in the texts *furthers life*, and we shall subject to criticism whatever is *hostile to life*.

1. What furthers life is whatever ministers to the *integrity of human life* in people and communities.

2. What furthers life is whatever ministers to the *integration* of individual life into the life of the community, and the life of the human community into the warp and weft of all living things on earth.

3. What furthers life is whatever spreads *reverence for life* and the *affirmation of life* through *love for life*.

4. What furthers life is whatever heals *broken relationships* and *liberates life* that has been oppressed.

5. What furthers life is whatever leads to the *new beginning of life* in hope.

6. What furthers life is whatever ministers to *God's covenant*

with life, and whatever breaks the covenant of human beings with death.

7. What furthers life is, first and last, whatever makes *Christ* present, Christ who is *the resurrection and the life in person*; for in and with Christ *the kingdom of eternal life* is present, and this kingdom overcomes the destructive powers of death.

8. But life from the divine source of life does not just mean full human life; it means 'deified' life too, the life Paul and Athanasius saw in the children of God – in the sonship and daughterhood of those 'driven' by God's Spirit (Rom. 8.14). This driving power, this leaven of the Spirit, is to be found not in the Spirit's eternal essential nature but in his energies. As I see it, these are not the 'uncreated energies' about which Orthodox tradition speaks, nor are they the 'created energies' with which Western mediaeval tradition was concerned. They are the *creative energies* of the Spirit in which the uncreated and the created are bonded, and which renew human life from its foundations, making it immortal in the eternal fellowship of God.

4

Theological epistemology

In this section we shall be looking at the different ways of knowing and talking theologically before God. We shall begin with the Aristotelian axiom that 'like can only be known by like', and examine the ways in which human beings, who are not like God, try to know God and talk about him, on the one hand with the help of analogy and metaphor, and on the other through negation and apophaticism. We shall then develop the counter-axiom, that in reality 'only the unlike can know each other', and shall consider the dialectical knowing of God *e contrario*, and dialectical talk about God. Finally, we shall look at the counter-images of subversive talk about God and the assertoric proclamation of God.

1. *The axiom of likeness*

Ever since Aristotle, the cognitive principle has been 'Like is only known by like.'[115] Correspondingly, the principle of community is 'Like draws to like,'[116] and the principle on which justice rests is 'Like must be repaid by like: good by good, evil by evil.'

Strictly understood, the axiom of likeness in epistemology means that what is other and alien cannot be known at all.[117] All cognition can then only be a re-cognition of what is already known or familiar. The early Greek philosophers therefore expanded this principle to cover what is similar and corresponding, and turned the axiom *par a pari cognoscitur* into a *similis a simile cognoscitur*: now it is not just like that is known by like, but similar which is known by the similar. If likeness is understood in its strict sense, cognition takes place in a closed circle. If the principle is expanded to cover what is similar and corresponding, cognition can become an open circle for learning, into which something new can be absorbed, and in which progress in knowing can be made. But at the same time, according to the criterion of analogy, we know only if in the 'other' we ask about what accords with ourselves, and if in what is alien we enquire about what corresponds to us. Then in the sphere of what is other and alien the knower perceives only that which resembles him and corresponds to him. He sees only that which binds in what divides, not that which divides in whatever binds. We adopt for ourselves what fits in with ourselves, but we do not change in order to understand what is different. Why does this way of understanding cognitive perception seem so convincing?

If the knower wishes to hold his ground and preserve his identity, whatever finds some correspondence within himself is perceived, while everything else is filtered out and excluded. All knowledge of phenomena in the external world perceived through the senses evokes a resonance in the inner world, if the phenomena are received. If they evoke resistance and contradiction, they will not be received at all, not even perceived. The macrocosm outside finds its correspondence in the microcosm within. That is why Empedocles (from whom the epistemological 'likeness' principle derives), said, 'Thus sweet reached out for sweet, bitter rushed to bitter, sour to sour, the warm poured itself into the warm. Thus fire pressed upwards, striving towards what was like it.' For: 'With the earth we see the earth; with the water, water; with the air the divine air; but with fire the destroying fire; with love, love; strife with sorry strife.'[118]

Here the concern that prompts knowing (Habermas's 'knowledge-constitutive interest') is the power of *eros*, which makes like strive to be united with like. What draws love is worthy of love. What charms, awakens desire. What is valuable evokes appreciation. The power of eros is the cosmic force of knowing and of union.

If we apply this principle to the knowing of other people and union with others, then I will recognize in the other only what corresponds to me myself, not what is different in kind and alien. 'True friendship rests on the foundation of likeness,' said Aristotle. It is true that some heroes who died young in battle were called 'friends of the gods', but no one could seriously speak about friendship between a human being and Zeus, the father of the gods. On the foundation of likeness, 'friendship' is effectively *exclusive*. There can be no friendship between freemen and slaves, or between men and women. Likeness issues in closed societies, where people who are alike confirm their identity through mutual self-endorsement and by excluding others. But because they are alike they also make each other superfluous, and become bored through the eternal repetition of the same thing. Even if societies of this kind are thrown open to those who fit in, or correspond to them, this does not lead to increased vitality, for interest is directed, not to what is dissimilar in the similar, or to the discrepant in the corresponding. It is concentrated on what is similar in the dissimilar, and what is corresponding in what is discrepant. In principle the mutual self-endorsement and exclusion of anything different and alien remains as it was.

If we apply the likeness principle to knowledge of God, the result is either a divinization of the perceiving human being, or a humanization of God. We can know the divine *above* us only with the divine *within* us, for according to the likeness axiom, God is only known by God. Knowledge of God and knowledge of the self therefore belong together in such a way that human beings perceive themselves in God and God in themselves. In this sense, and following Empedocles, Goethe wrote:

Were the eye not like the sun,
how could we the sun descry?
Were not God's own power within us,
how could the divine delight us?[119]

Goethe added a distinctive touch of his own to the principle of theological likeness that 'God is only known through God' by reversing the axiom. It now read '*Nemo contra Deum nisi Deus ipse* – no one is against God unless it be God himself.'[120] He took this as the motto for the fourth book of his auto-biography *Dichtung und Wahrheit* ('Poetry and Truth'), and was probably thinking of his revered Giordano Bruno, who fought 'with the universe'. 'A glorious dictum of endless appli-cation,' was Goethe's interpretation: 'God encounters always himself. God in man encounters himself again in man . . .' Like Spinoza, he saw God pantheistically, as already present everywhere in the universe. God is already all in all, so if there is anything counter-divine in the universe, the contradiction lies in God himself. For outside God there is no one who could fight against God. Even in the harshest *contra Deum* he can be perceived: *Deus ipse* – God himself. Taken by itself, however, this assertion makes God the only conceivable atheist in the world. If no one in the world can be against God other than God himself, then human atheism is impossible – either that or through his *contra Deum* the human atheist will himself become God.

On the other hand, in the knowing of God the principle of likeness leads to the humanization of all images and concepts of God. Human ideas and concepts of the divine are no more than human products and tell us nothing about the divine itself. Even in what they suppose to be their knowledge of God, men and women remain in the hall of mirrors of their own selves. 'You are like the spirit you understand, not me,' cries the Earth Spirit to Dr Faust in Goethe's drama, after Faust has conjured it up. 'What you call the spirit of the times is simply your own spirit,' says Faust ironically to Wagner. So the vista 'beyond' is closed to us. Human beings create their gods, fetishes and idols in their own image: men fashion male gods, women female gods, white people white gods, and so on. The 'Other' or, as the young Karl Barth said, following Rudolf Otto,[121] 'the Wholly Other' of the divine is for us so unknowable that it cannot even be thought, so that even unknowability cannot be a divine attribute. But when modern men or woman, everywhere in society, perceive on earth and in heaven only the traces and projections of themselves, their narcisstic self-love can swing over into self-hate, and their hybrid sense of omnipotence can issue in a feeling of utter loneliness. And then, if only occasionally, a 'longing for the Wholly Other' may spring up in them.

2. *The principle of analogy*

The classic philosophical formulation of the principle of analogy can be found in the text of the Fourth Lateran Council of 1215:

> Between the Creator and the creature so great a likeness cannot be noted without the necessity of noting a greater dissimilarity between them.[122]

The similarity between the creature and its Creator in spite of still greater dissimilarity is based on a continuum of being. The created being is a being mingled with non-being; God is pure and supreme Being. The still greater dissimilarity between the Creator and his creature is based on the Creator's unfathomable freedom. The analogy between creature and Creator is therefore called an analogy of being or essence (*analogia entis*). Creation corresponds to God but is not the same as him. None the less, it is a parable of its Creator in spite of the Creator's incomparability with what he has created. Although different from its Creator, creation is capable of being a parable and, in being so, is also in need of being a parable for him. On the basis of this unique character of creation, created human beings can talk about the incomparable Creator in analogies, metaphors, parables, images and narratives. All creaturely talk about God is therefore at best – which means when it is appropriate to God – speech that is indirect, analogical and metaphorical. This is only true, however, if and inasmuch as human beings are only God's *creatures*, and nothing other than that, created to be his image. In a supralapsarian sense it can be said only about human beings without sin. It is only true of God if he is nothing other than the transcendent Creator of human beings, but not also their crucified Redeemer.

For a more precise explanation of the principle of analogy, let us turn to ideas put forward by the Jesuit writer Erich Przywara.[123] For him, and hence also for his Protestant adversary Karl Barth, 'the basic principle of the *analogia entis*' was the foundational principle of Catholic thinking in general. With its help, the relationship between God and created being is grasped as a relationship which is 'open upwards'. That means on the one hand that God is not the absolutization of anything individually created. God is neither the Universe nor Absolute Spirit – neither the supreme Idea nor Unity; for God is simply and *per se* 'beyond' all conceivable concepts. But this means, on the other hand, that the totality of created being is God's 'revelation' 'from above' – not a 'parable' from which God's presence and efficacy could be inferred, but a 'parable which points beyond itself into a God who is above parable', who in his free, unfathomable resolve has chosen precisely this 'parable' from unnumbered other possibilities.[124] Thus God is at once the mysterious meaning towards which the totality of what is created points as in a parable, and yet not an inner meaning of this being which he has created.

'God is therefore differentiated and divided from everything outside himself, and yet there is nothing outside him which is not in his total essence (i.e., *essentia*) and his existence (i.e., *esse*).'[125] We cannot therefore deduce the Creator and his attributes from creation and its attributes. Creation is not 'the metaphorical language of the divine Being'. Its livingness in the process of its becoming is not a reflection of the divine *actus purus*. Only creation as a whole can be understood as a parable of the Creator. 'The question about the parable relationship between God and creature can only be asked on the basis of the whole.' As long as this unity in created being does not exist, no *analogia entis* can be discovered either. The created being only becomes 'similar to God through the common factor of a unity of essence and existence, but it is precisely in this similarity that it is essentially dissimilar from God, because in God the form of unity of his essence and his existence is "an essential identity" whereas in the creature the form of unity is "a unity in tension".' [126]

Analogia entis is intended to be the philosophical term for the theology of creation out of nothing (*creatio ex nihilo*) and continuous creation (*creatio continua*). The fact that creation 'is' and 'is becoming' is inconceivable without its source in pure, absolute Being; otherwise creation would be 'left in the air' and its becoming would be undecided – in the balance. When we consider this problem of the existence of created being, the statement 'God in us *and* above us' is the succinct answer offered by the doctrine of *analogia entis*. This leads to a final idea implicit in the doctrine: the *analogia entis* gathers together everything created into a 'total parable' of God, but in such a way that everything created is open towards God in its enduring capacity for obedience to him (*potentia oboedientialis*). So God is the One who, above and beyond his parable-like reflection, is 'always greater' – *Deus semper major*, as Ignatius Loyola said.

The usual Protestant criticism maintains that the *analogia entis* means thinking 'from below'- from the creature to the Creator. But in my view that is not correct. The unity of the creature with the Creator God who is above what he has created is 'never deducible "from below", i.e., through human calculation, but only "from above", i.e., in the light of his free revelation.' [127] But it is always 'open and receptive' as a permanently received potentiality.

This is where serious criticism has to begin. The doctrine of the *analogia entis* talks about a potential condition of created beings, their *potentia oboedientialis* – their capacity for obedience – but not about their actual condition, which Paul in Rom. 8.17ff. discerns as being 'the groanings of enslaved creation'. The doctrine talks about a *possible* knowledge of God which accords with him and is analogical, and which can be attained by created men and women. But it says nothing about the knowledge of God of the truly Godless and God-forsaken – in theological language 'sinners'. [128]

But now it is not as if the 'sinner' were no longer a human being and a creation of God's. The sinful human being is a human being too, and is still God's image. His character as God's image is not lost as long as God remains faithful to him and thus accords with himself. In considering the human being as God's image, we must go on to distinguish between God's relationship to the human being, and the human being's relationship to God. Sin turns the human being's relationship to God upside down: correspondence becomes contradiction. With the human being's contradiction, his capacity for obedience (the *potentia oboedientialis)* ceases in his particular case, for his free will then becomes an 'unfree will', as Luther rightly said. But God's relationship to the human being, and the character of the human being as image of God which is implicit in that relationship, do not cease. Only God himself can end his relationship to the human being who bears the name of human being, neither sin nor death can do so, for God is God. Out of his relationship to the human being, and through an act of grace, God can restore the human beings's *potentia oboedientialis*, and make what was for him impossible, once more possible: it becomes possible for him to correspond to his Creator and the source of his life. The *potentia oboedientialis* is a divine reality before it becomes a human possibility.

If the 'relationship of parable between God and created being' can only be established 'on the basis of the whole', then the 'eschatological proviso' on which Erik Peterson insisted must not be disregarded either, for according to that, the whole is not yet there – neither the whole of continuous creation nor the Real Presence of God 'all in all'. Paul talks about both eschatologically in the promises of hope, not ontologically in terms of the *analogia entis*. Only a world pregnant with future can be a world capable of parable for the kingdom of God.

Yet 'God in us *and* above us' is already, here and now, the experience of God and one's own self *in the energies of the Holy Spirit,* which is the beginning of the rebirth of the whole creation in the kingdom of glory. So seen theologically, ought the parables of the doctrine of the *analogia entis* not to belong to a doctrine about pneumatological energies, instead of to a doctrine about Creator and creature? In the sufferings and the sighings of enslaved creation, the newly-creating divine Spirit already evokes the first correspondences and parables of their redemption in the kingdom of God. In the energies of new life we recognize ourselves in God and God in us, what is beyond in what is here and now, and what is now in what is beyond, and we perceive God in all things and all things in God – that is to say, we perceive the God who is beyond parable in the parables of his eschatologically awakening creation.

Erich Przywara declared the doctrine of the *analogia entis* to be the 'Catholic form of thinking', equivocally relating the term 'Catholic' both philosophically to the whole of being and theologically to the Roman Catholic Church.[129] This led to Barth's misunderstanding, expressed in his much-quoted dictum: 'I regard the *analogia entis* as the invention of Antichrist, and I believe that *because of it* it is impossible ever to become a Roman Catholic.'[130] He felt that the perception of his early dialectical phase about God as 'the Wholly Other' and the 'infinite qualitative difference between time and eternity' was threatened by his opponent's doctrine of analogy; but he overlooked the fact that as long before as 1921, in *The Christian in Society*, and explicitly later, in 1926, in *Church and Culture*, he himself had developed his own doctrine of analogy in talking about God; in the *Church Dogmatics* this then led to a comprehensive system of God's self-correspondences, and the correspondences to these in created being.[131]

It is true that Barth preferred the *analogia relationis* and the *analogia proportionalitatis*, and began with the *analogia fidei*, with which Przywara concluded his train of thought, maintaining that the unity of the creature with his transcendent Creator comes about 'solely from above' out of God's 'free revelation', so that all analogies to God are perceived only from this undeducible and unhoped-for divine event, since they are literally 'pre-ceded' by this event of divine revelation and in that really 'are'; it is not that they just 'can be'. All analogies of the creaturely essence, however, are based on the analogy of its existence to the divine Being. Because and inasmuch as creaturely existence partakes of the Being of the divine Creator (since it is sustained by that), there are correspondences in the nature and in the relationships of created being to its Creator.[132] The possibility of human, analogical knowledge of God is given when human beings are created to be the image of God.

The principle of analogy is not an instruction for building up a theological system. It describes a theological movement or train of thought. Knowledge of God comes about in the rhythm of perceived similarity and perceived dissimilarity to God. The more we know of God, the more we perceive that we know nothing of God. Analogical knowing of God takes place in approaches to the divine mystery. But the closer we come to God, or – better – the closer God comes to us, the more unknowable for us he is. Strangeness is a category not of distance but of *closeness*, for it is the closeness which first makes the strangeness apparent. All knowledge needs a certain distance from what is known. Every picture and every image creates a distance of this kind. If, in his all-interpenetrating Spirit, God comes closer to us than we ourselves can come – '*interior intimo meo*', as Augustine acknowledged (*Confessions* III, 6, 11) – then for us he becomes *per se* unknowable, inexpressible, and incapable of apprehension through image. God is then so present to us that we are in God.

The approach to the divine mystery can have two different emphases. On the one hand it is a perception of the similarities in the still greater dissimilarity of God, as Erich Przywara stresses. Analogical knowledge of God is thus constituted from Yes and No, and out of infinite progression. The ever-greater dissimilarity of God relativizes all perceived similarities. On the other hand it is a perception of 'the ever-greater similarity between God and human beings in the midst of however much greater a dissimilarity', as Eberhard Jüngel puts it, with good Protestant reasoning.[133] The still greater similarity then identifies the dissimilarity of God, however great it may be. Both emphases are important for the rhythm of analogical knowledge of God: the identification of God in his Word, and the relativization of all our own words.

3. The play of metaphors

Metaphorical language is the language of images and comparisons.[134] A metaphor is an abbreviated parable, which takes the form of 'just as – so'. Let us look at two biblical examples:

> As a father pities his children,
> so the Lord pities those who fear him (Ps. 103.13).

And:

> As one whom his mother comforts,
> so I will comfort you (Isa. 66.13).

It is a fundamental characteristic of *religious* speech to try to make the unexperienceable divine reality comprehensible with the help of metaphors taken from the world which human beings experience. With metaphors, this kind of language reaches out beyond existing reality into the sphere of the possible. On the other hand metaphor is *ordinary* language. Our everyday colloquial way of speaking is so full of metaphors that it can itself be called metaphorical language. It is like a 'dictionary of faded metaphors'.[135] Because we have been familiar with them since childhood, and continually use them, we no longer notice this special character. Nor do they achieve a surprise effect any more, as new metaphors do, particularly if they are drastically graphic ones. *Poetic* language is metaphorical language as an art form. The abstract or ideational *language of concepts* presupposes a multiplicity of metaphors which present the similar in the dissimilar, and yet it generalizes only the similar, reducing it to the concept of 'the same'. 'A concept is an abstraction of the similar from a sea of dissimilars.'[136] The modern scientific language of symbols is to a high degree metaphorical, even if it is not poetical.

Metaphors can be equivocal. They have to be if they want to achieve a surprise effect – in a joke perhaps, or in some grotesque expression. *Concepts*, in contrast, have to be unequivocal, and must always mean the same thing. Metaphors can be equivocal, concepts must be unequivocal. But if concepts are not 'above' history but belong to it, their meaning also changes as time goes on, and they become not very far removed from the metaphors whose abstraction they are. Great philosophers have therefore readily clothed their profoundest insights in felicitous and memorable metaphors. In this Hegel was a master. In theology too it is useful to turn back again from the level of abstract conceptualization to the level of metaphor, so as to express with poetic imagination something which escapes both the unequivocal character of the concept and its abstraction from time.[137]

Conceptual definitions limit and demarcate – they are, in fact, distinctions. But metaphors can also *de*-restrict and can throw open the realm of possibilities. As Gregory of Nyssa already perceived, concepts can become idols. Metaphorical language dissolves them again, makes them fluid, so to speak, for it is open to the future – emendable, experimental, indirect, iconoclastic and transformable.[138] Metaphorical language knows no 'infallible and unreformable' dogmas, which are the same and equally valid everywhere and at all times, as the First Vatican Council attested,[139] for metaphor always links the comparison of what is similar ('just as – so') with the comparison of what is not similar ('not as . . .'). Consequently the metaphors from the Bible I cited above do not contradict each other: God acts 'like a father', but he also acts 'like one's own mother', for he is at the same time 'not like' my father, or my mother. Because it is a matter of similarity in one respect only, within the sphere of greater dissimilarity, these two metaphors are not legitimations for patriarchal or matriarchal language; if they were, they would no longer be metaphors.

With this, of course, the metaphors also assume forms of *play*. We experiment and 'play' with the comparisons just because we are aware that they are inappropriate. 'Metaphors are events of direct learning. They teach us to learn through play.'[140] The 'element of play' should then also be 'the anthropologically most convincing primary motivation' of the metaphor.[141] If for this we only construct the ontological background of the similar in greater dissimilarity, all metaphors are equally appropriate and inappropriate. Yet there are 'unfortunate' metaphors, which make us laugh and which we quickly forget, and there are 'felicitous' metaphors, which we remember because they make us see something new. They become 'familiar quotations' because they expand the language, and in so doing also extend our possibilities of understanding.

The conceptual background of the tradition about similarity in still greater dissimilarity which is used for analogy and metaphor is not the only one possible. It presupposes a graduated order of being, in which we can advance by a process of inference from the lower to the higher by way of analogy or in the play of metaphors. A different conceptual background is offered by the *historical time* of *present and future*. Metaphors go beyond what is at hand, and reach out in anticipation to the possible future by imagining what might be. In the historical interlacing of present and future we form metaphors of what is to come. The future is 'like . . .'. These analogies of the future are formed out of remembrances of the past and must have the same playful, experimental, transformable and emendable character as metaphors if they are not to lead to prejudice and to prejudgments towards what is surprising and new in the future. They are imaginations which are supposed to prepare the way and open the door to expectation. They must themselves be revised as they go, just as the expectations are changed through the experiences and disappointments which then actually come to meet us. Metaphors of the historical future are *movable symbols*, as Ernst Bloch made clear.

If a metaphor can be called 'a kind of abbreviated parable', then a parable can be understood as a kind of 'expanded metaphor'.[142] In the metaphor, only a single image is used in the comparison, generally speaking, whereas the parable uses a series of images or a 'short story' with dramatic intent. What the parable is meant to bring out are not facts but a story. In Jesus' parables in the New Testament about the kingdom of heaven, God's actions wait for some corresponding action on the side of the human being.[143] In the parable of the Ungrateful Servant in Matt. 18.23–35, the kingdom of heaven is 'like' a human king who has mercy on his defaulting servant and remits the huge debt he owes. But when this servant refuses to remit the paltry debt of his own debtor, the king has him thrown into prison: 'So also my heavenly Father will do to every one of you, if you do not forgive your brother from your heart.' The debt remitted by the king (a Jewish metaphor for God) passes all bounds: 100 million dinars. The debt which the servant does not remit is minute: 100 dinars. The point of comparison is that our guilt before God is infinitely greater than anything other people owe us; God's mercy with us is infinitely greater than the mercy which God can expect of us. The parable therefore has to do with correspondences between the way God acts and the way human beings act. The sequence of scenes in the short stories in the parables is so arranged that the disproportion in the contrast, or the unusual in the customary, strikes the listener immediately. That is the point of the parable.

'The synoptic parables generally take the form of a game.'[144] They have leading roles and minor ones, dialogues and questions to the listener. These parables can therefore be acted out, as they are in the 'bibliodrama'. They are conceived for the sake of their own interpretation, as it were. That is why the *listeners* to the parable belong to the parable itself. The metaphorical language is the everyday language of Palestine. The stories about the man who went out to sow, or the seed that springs up of itself, were familiar territory to everyone at the time of Jesus. The parables often take the form of a question to the listeners: 'Which of you . . .?' These are the so-called 'question parables'. Some characters in the parables are closely modelled on the listeners, so that they could see themselves as if in a mirror – in the character of the Rich Fool, for example (Luke 12.16ff.). In the short story which the prophet Nathan tells (II Sam. 12.7), King David is led to condemn himself, for:

'You are the man!' So the listeners are part of the structure of the parables themselves.[145] These are not parables addressed 'to whom it may concern'. They relate to their *kairos*, their context, and the group to which speaker and listeners belong, in the community where the parables are told. To turn them into a general 'metaphorical' or 'analogical' theology is an abstraction similar to the one that wants to make a 'kerygmatic theology' out of sermons preached to a congregation.

It is therefore not unproblematical to base the parables of Jesus on *the person of Jesus as 'parable of God'*, as both Eberhard Jüngel and Sallie McFague do, the latter following Leander Keck.[146] 'Jesus concentrated on parabolic speech because he himself was a parabolic event of the kingdom of God.'[147] 'The *son* is the *personal parable of the father*; he represents the father.'[148] But whereas Sallie McFague seems to mean by this the historical Jesus, for Jüngel it is the Son of God, recognized as such and believed in after his death and resurrection, who is the parable of God the Father.

Was the Jesus who speaks in the parables of the kingdom really nothing more than 'a' parable of God himself, or 'a' parable-like event of God's coming kingdom? We can only arrive at this conclusion if we disregard the other kingdom-of-God actions of the synoptic Jesus – the healings of the sick, the expulsion of demons, the receiving of the outcasts and – the forgiveness of sins. Without these anticipatory acts the parables would remain in the air and unresolved. But they are often told in order to interpret Jesus' actions. Nor can we isolate the Jesus who told these parables from his fate: his crucifixion by the Romans and his raising by the God whom he addressed as Abba, dear Father, and in the closeness of whose kingdom he lived and preached. It is of course true that the acts of Jesus in the Gospels are told as parables: as Jesus acts, so God acts. But Jesus' relationship to God is more than a parable, as the exclusive Abba relationship shows. In the relationship conferred at creation, every human being is the image and parable of the Creator. But Jesus' relationship to God is more than a human relationship given with creation. It is designated through the

divine Sonship of this unique 'messianic Child'.[149] But is 'the
Son of God' the same thing as 'the parable of God'? In trinitarian thinking, is 'the Son' the 'personal parable of the Father'?
If that were meant, it would mean bursting apart the concept of
parable as 'similarity in spite of still greater dissimilarity'. For in
trinitarian thinking the Son does not 'resemble' the Father; he is
the same in essence, *homousios*, 'God of God, light of light . . .',
as the Nicene Creed solemnly extols. 'No one knows the Son
except the Father, and no one knows the Father except the Son
and any one to whom the Son chooses to reveal him' (Matt.
11.27).

I should therefore like to distinguish the parable-like features
in Jesus' life, acts and sufferings, his prophetic sign actions, and
his indirect pointers to God, from his own personal relationship
to God, and God's special relationship to him. And where the
parables of the kingdom are concerned, I think it is more
correct to call Jesus 'the kingdom of God in person', rather than
to make him one parabolic kingdom-of-God event among
others. We might say that a metaphor begins to illuminate only
if not everything is metaphorical; and so the parables of Jesus
too begin to speak only if he himself is not a parable.

4. *Negative or apophatic theology*

We cannot say what God is – only what he is not. Negative
theology is the necessary corollary of analogical theology if it is
true that the 'similarities' of which we have spoken are formulated 'in still greater dissimilarity' to God. The statements 'God
is like a father' and 'like a mother' must necessarily be accompanied by the negations 'God is not like a father' and 'not like a
mother'; otherwise the 'like' is open to misunderstanding. To
leave the negations out is to make an analogy-in-non-analogy
into a concept which parts company from the unlike and dissimilar in God, and in so doing puts itself in God's place.
It is then an idol. *Negative* or, as the Eastern Church says,
apophatic theology has two roots; philosophical criticism of
anthropomorphic talk about God, which already begins with

the Greek pre-Socratic philosophers, and the prohibition of images in the Old Testament.

The pre-Socratic theology of essence – *genus physikon* – asked about the essential of the Deity behind the manifold appearances of the gods, and found this divine essence – hidden, unknowable and ineffable – as the One in the Many, which can only be periphrastically described through negations. Xenophon criticized Homer's mystical theology and Hesiod's anthropomorphic polytheism: 'There was never a man, and there never will be one, who knows the truth of the gods and everything on earth. For even if he should some time or other hit the mark perfectly, he would not know that he had done so. For all that is granted to us is imagination.'[150] For Xenophon, the divine Being was one, homogeneous, immovable, impassible, imperishable, immutable. The One is inexpressible because it is indivisible. All that can be said of it is what it is not. It has no name and is unattainable by human knowledge and thought. It is nevertheless omnipresent and therefore the absolute mystery of the world: so said later Platonic and neo-Platonic philosophy. This negative theology of the Greek religious Enlightenment has left profound traces in Christian theology, which adopted it and combined it with its own biblical traditions.

Israelite and Christian criticism of religion in the name of the one God was under the spell of the Second Commandment: 'You shall not make for yourself any graven image, or any likeness . . . you shall not bow down to them or serve them . . .' This prohibition of images belongs to the service of the God of Abraham, Isaac and Jacob, and protects the promise of that God. As the 'Second' Commandment, it presupposes the proof of himself given by God 'the Lord' in the liberation of the people from slavery in Egypt, the proof given in the 'First' Commandment, 'You shall have no other gods beside me.' Whereas Greek philosophy strove to protect the immovability and immutability of the One over against the diversity, mutability and transience of the world of phenomena, Israel's prohibition of images preserves the historicity of God's faithfulness to his promise from human attempts to assure themselves of the divine power in images and likenesses.[151]

For the Greeks, 'truth' is *the One* which always remains the same in itself, but biblically it is *God's faithfulness* to his promise and thus to himself. God is not immutable; he is faithful. God is not immovable; he is in his own movement to his kingdom. God is not impassible; he is full of the passion of love for those he has created. We can bring out the differences still further by comparing the attributes. But the profoundest difference is in the namelessness and unnameability of the divine One in the negative theology of Greek philosophy, and the sanctification of the Name of God in the biblical traditions, which the prohibition of images serves. Even the 'hidden God' who 'hides' his face, and even the 'Wholly Other God' whose thoughts and ways are not our thoughts and ways (Isa. 55.8, 9), is called upon by name, and allows his Word to be proclaimed in his name. His Word and his Name do not belong to the world of the *analogia entis* and the perception of similarity in still greater dissimilarity.

In Gregory of Nyssa we find the important idea that the 'living God' cannot be held fast in human concepts. 'If the life-giving nature of God surpasses all our understanding, then something understood cannot be life.'[152] 'The living God' escapes human concepts, images and likenesses, just as lived life is more than a life that is conceptually grasped. Images fix a history or a process, tying them down to a situation and 'eternalizing' them, as we say. Through images we transpose time into space, and movement into a fixed state. The same thing happens in the sequence of pictures in a film or video. Once something has been introduced into the picture, it remains there unalterably. Anyone who makes a picture of someone else in order to form a judgment allows that person no further openness to the future. He is pinned down to his past. Pictures create distance. Yet at the same time we need pictures in order to bridge distances. When my wife is away for a time, I like to look at a picture of her, so as to bring her before me; however, when she is present, I don't put up any picture of her, but live together with her. The prohibition of images protects life lived with the living God, and with living and loved human beings. It opens men and women for love of God and their neighbour.

What is true of 'images and likenesses' applies even more to *concepts*. We form them out of our experiences, for without experiences our concepts would be empty, as Kant said. From experiences which are historically changeable and unrepeatable we abstract those which can be more or less repeated, and for these we form the timeless *concept*, which transcends history and hence is continually applicable. If we hold the phenomena of time fast in the concept, the concept then eliminates time and itself has no time, because it must not be altered but must always remain unequivocally the same. In this way concepts acquire a rigidity which does not befit the life embraced by the concepts. This makes it clear that there can be no concepts for 'the living God', that source of life which continually brings forth what is new. A God understood conceptually would be a far-off God, an absent God, a dead idol which we 'grasped'. It is therefore right to say that *Deum definiri nequit* – God cannot be defined.

Is *unknowability* a divine attribute? We can no doubt say that God is unknowable, but not that unknowability is divine. The negations of knowing, of changing, of manifoldness, and of the temporality of life do not circumscribe the divine, for they can just as well be applied to what is deadly. Nothing positive can be deduced from negations. It is only if the positive is experienced that negative paraphrases for it can be found. *Negative theology* is theology first of all, otherwise it insensibly becomes the atheistic *negation of theology*. So negative theology remains bound to affirmative theology as a necessary corrective, just as apophatic theology remains necessarily bound to cataphatic theology. It is a corrective, not a paradigm.

5. Dialectical knowing: unlike knows unlike

Ernst Bloch once asked 'whether only like can apprehend like, or whether, conversely, what is unlike would not be more qualified to do so?'[153] I have elsewhere presented the idea of a 'divine revelation in contradiction' and a corresponding 'dialectical knowing',[154] and then followed up Bloch's hint historically.

'Other is only known by other.' This epistemological principle also has its roots in ancient Greek philosophy, though in a tradition which acquired very little influence on our culture. Euripides, quoting Aristotle, wrote:

The parched ground yearns for rain,
and the high heavens, great with rain,
desire to fall to earth.[155]

'Everything living springs out of strife,' said Heraclitus. Opposites attract each other. But it was Anaxagoras who first formulated the epistemological principles which were the precise opposite of the ones maintained by Empedocles:

Anaxagoras holds that sense perception comes to pass by means of opposites, for the like is unaffected by the like . . . We come to know the cold by the hot . . . the sweet by the sour, the light by the dark . . . All sense perception, he holds, is fraught with pain, for the unlike when brought into contact [with our organs] always brings distress.[156]

This final comment about the connection between perception and pain is important. If our organs of perception encounter something like, something familiar, or something that already corresponds to ourselves, we feel endorsed, and that is pleasing to our senses and feelings. But if our organs of perception encounter something strange, something different or new, we feel pain. We sense the resistance of what is alien, the contradiction of the other, the claim of the new. The pain shows us that we must change ourselves if we want to understand the alien, perceive the other, and comprehend the new. The pain shows that we must open ourselves if we want to take in the other, the alien or the new, and that we cannot adapt it to ourselves or make it like ourselves without destroying it.

But how do we perceive it? We perceive it, not through its correspondence or similarity, but through its contradiction. We first perceive its strangeness, difference in kind or novelty through that in us which does not correspond to it. We perceive the other with what is opposite in ourselves. We become alive and sensitive to what is new not through consonance but through dissonance. To use Anaxagoras's imagery: the darker it is in us, the more we perceive the brightness of the light; the colder we are, the more intensely we feel a fire's warmth; once we have tasted the sour, we savour the sweet. We can carry over this kind of knowing from difference to other experiences too. When we are among people who are black, we notice that we are white. Among people who are white we see that we are black. When we are with children we discover that we are getting old. Among women we see that we are men, or among men that we are women. If everyone is the same – if there are no longer any differences – we know nothing any more, for what is no different is to the one who is no different a matter of complete indifference. In a transferred sense, we can say with the young Schelling, 'Every being can become manifest only in its opposite – love only in hate, unity only in strife.'[157]

To put it somewhat less dramatically: it is only in the foreign land that we understand what home is. It is only in the face of death that we sense the uniqueness of life. It is only in strife that we know how to appreciate peace. It is in our encounter with the difference of others that we experience the character of our own selves. Among people who are like us we do not notice ourselves at all. We are so much a matter of course to ourselves that we are not aware of ourselves. It is first in the *distance*, even more in the *difference*, and then finally in the *contradiction* that we perceive the other, and in perceiving that other at the same time perceive our own selves.

Here too the 'knowledge-constitutive interest' is union, eros. But what comes into being is not a unity through uniformity, but a unity in diversity. Those who are different can long for reciprocal complementation, like the Yin and Yang in Tao. What is contradictory can produce new life through the contention, if the differences are accepted as challenges. Then *agon*, strife, is 'the father of all things'. Dynamic and dialectical communities of the different and the contradictory come into being: unity in division, and division in unity, and the unity of division and unity, as the young Hegel described the dialectic of love.[158]

Applied to knowledge of God, this dialectical principle leads to the recognition of difference in community. The principle of likeness says that 'God is only known through God'. The principle of analogy says that we perceive what is similar to God in what is still more dissimilar to him. But the principle of dialectical knowing says that God is perceived as God only in the sphere of what is essentially different from him: in the realm of what is creaturely, finite, transient, and in the sphere of the human beings who are in contradiction to him. For them, God is 'the Wholly Other' and they perceive his God-ness from their own godlessness. It is not when human beings see themselves as 'divine' and feel 'God's own power' in them that they can perceive the wholly-other Being of God, but only when they are human beings, wholly and entirely and nothing else than that – human beings who recognize their weakness and their misery. When they cease to be proud and unhappy 'gods' and become true human beings, they let God be God, as Luther aptly put it.[159] It is only when men and women become wholly godless, in the sense that they dispense with all self-deification and presumptuous similarity to God, that they can perceive the wholly other reality of the true God.

But this only happens where God himself becomes human, and disperses our self-deification by bringing back to us the humanity we have forsaken. That is the revelation of God and ourselves in Christ. Revelation is the divine crossing of the frontier into the human existence which is 'other' for God and into the human misery of sin which contradicts him. That is why the inner-trinitarian principle of likeness which Matthew uses – only the Father knows the Son and only the Son knows the Father, 'and anyone to whom the Son chooses to reveal him' – ends with Jesus' cry 'Come unto me all you who are weary and heavy-laden' (Matt. 11.28). The weary and the heavy-laden know God.

'To know God means to suffer God', says a wise old Greek saying, drawn from experience. The human perceptions of God in the biblical narratives entirely correspond to it. It is with pain that men and women first perceive the wholly other reality of God which they encounter. It is the pain of their own fundamental change. According to Christian experience, these are the pains of dying from God and the joy of being born again out of God's Spirit. Christian baptism symbolizes the dying with Christ and the rising in Christ to new life (Romans 6). Only through a fundamental change in our own existence do we perceive the wholly other reality of God. This kind of suffered knowledge of God received its ultimate and concentrated theological form in the theology of the cross of the young Luther, according to which God is hidden beneath cross and suffering, and can only be perceived '*e contrario*'. The place where God encounters us, the *locus theologicus*, is the God-forsaken misery of the cross. Today's liberation theology knows this theology of the cross too. It calls it the 'epistemological breach. In the moments of God's profoundest revelation there was always suffering of some kind: the cry of the oppressed in Egypt, the cry of Jesus on the cross, the birth pangs of the whole creation as it waits for its redemption.'[160] 'In so far as God is revealed in his opposite, he can be known by the Godless and the Godforsaken, and it is this knowledge which brings them into correspondence with God and, as I John says, even to have the hope of being like God.'[161]

6. Counter-images, counter-histories and counter-worlds of subversive talk about God

The 'similarities in still greater similarity' to God, and the earthly metaphors and parables for the kingdom of heaven, would seem to be formulated in a space free of conflict and domination. In an unscathed and ideal earthly world, they seem to picture the lovely, heavenly world of God. It is only in a world like this that the analogies and parables of God would seem to be possible without confutation. But in actual fact we do not exist in worlds of that kind at all. If we are ruled by other lords, we can be in conformity with 'God the Lord' only if we resist and protest against them. But what does this *language of resistance* look like?

'O Lord our God, other lords besides thee rule over us, but thy name alone we acknowledge' (Isa. 26.13). This verse was printed at the top of the announcement of Ernst Käsemann's death on 14 February 1998. Käsemann has been called the 'theologian of the New Testament'. All his life he was a militant and rebellious theologian, 'God's partisan'.[162] It is in line with his own thinking when I say: peace with God brings us into continual conflict with the godless powers of this unpeaceful world. It is only in resistance to them that we can be in conformity with 'the Lord our God'. It is true that we have to use their language, but it is not their language we speak. They have power over us, but we remain strangers to them. What language do oppressed people in a dictatorship speak? We need only think of Hitler and Stalin to discover the subversive language of the people. Because dictators are afraid of it, they very speedily introduce their own prescriptive language. Things must only be called by the names the dictators have thought out for them. Under Hitler, the German people had to feel threatened by 'Bolshevism' and 'plutocracy'; under Stalin there were not two world powers, the United States and the Soviet Union; there was only the 'belligerent power' and 'the peace-loving power'. Political correctness was invented long ago in dictatorships of this kind, as a way of controlling the language of the people, and with their language their souls. People react by distancing themselves through their speech, through subversive language and political jokes which only rouse a liberating laugh in dictatorships. Subversive distancing language can be studied in the slave language of the Rastas in Jamaica.

In the biblical and apocryphal traditions of Israel and Christianity we by no means find merely the beautiful, divinely corresponding language of analogies, metaphors, images and parables. What is much more evident is the subversive underground language of the oppressed, the enslaved, the persecuted, and people who are resisting the lords 'of this world' and the collaborators among their own people and in their own religion. This underground language is sometimes prophetically and openly turned against the rule of priests and kings; sometimes it is apocalyptically and subversively aimed at foreign rulers; but it is always developed in conflict. Even the parts of the histories and psalms which are not overtly prophetic and apocalyptic still reflect the original historical situation: the experiences of foreign rule and the subjugation of the people. Of course histories in different situations with different concerns are told differently; nevertheless, with the help of a cautious 'investigative Bible criticism' and a 'hermeneutics of suspicion' critical of power, we can discover the traces of these experiences. The best example in the Old Testament is the Exodus story itself, to which Israel owes its God and its existence. In 'the promised land' and in liberty it reads differently from the way it reads in Babylonian exile and by 'the waters of Babylon'. The same is true of the psalms. They can be sung differently in the home country from in 'the foreign land'. The best example in the New Testament is the story of Jesus' crucifixion. In countries where Christians live in peace it is told differently from the way it is told in the Gulag Archipelago and other places of persecution. It speaks to victims differently from the way it speaks to perpetrators.

Subversive talk about God gives voice to *counter-images* to the self-portrayals of the powers of the present, *counter-histories* to the stories of the victories and successes of the tyrants, whole *counter-worlds* to the powers and conditions of 'this world'. We can spontaneously pick out a few examples.

The story in Ezekiel 37 about the resurrection in the valley of dead bones is a divine counter-history to Israel's fields of the dead, which are strewn among the other, endless and omnipresent fields of the dead in the history of human violence. In the New Testament, the story of the Easter appearances of the risen Christ are counter-histories to the story of his death on

Golgotha, which was present in the memories of the people concerned. In Babylonian exile, under theocratic Babylonian rule, the remembrances of the liberation from slavery in the Egyptian theocracy are related as alternatives, and awaken hope for the 'new Exodus' about which Deutero-Isaiah speaks; and they naturally enough also roused the suspicion of the guards and the foreign rulers. In Christian apocalyptic, the images of 'the heavenly Jerusalem', where God will finally 'dwell' among mortal men and women, and 'will wipe every tear from their eyes', are counter-images directed against Rome, the allegedly 'eternal city', with its state gods and its Caesars, the city alluded to under the subversive name of 'Babylon', the city of sin. Its state gods are the demons of power. Even the title Kyrios for the crucified Christ, the title used in the Jewish Septuagint for 'the Lord' (in accordance with the First Commandment), became for Christians living in the Roman Empire a subversive counter-title aimed at the Kyrios in Rome, the ruler of all the known world. The Christian martyrs thoroughly understood what this apocalyptic alternative meant: *aut Christus – aut Caesar* – either Christ or Caesar; and they refused to conform to the cult of Caesar so as not to fall into the hands of the demons of power and lies.

We need not take the list of examples any further. Jews and Christians can discover them in the history of their persecutions and in the language of their martyrs. The consequence for talk about God is that we can detach ourselves from the reality at hand in order to imagine alternatives and counter-worlds ('alternity', to use George Steiner's word). With the help of these counter-worlds we can conceive of possibilities in a world which otherwise leaves us no chances.[163] Of course the creative imagination can lose its force. Then we dream ourselves into alternative counter-worlds in order to forget the pain of present failures. Every prisoner knows dream worlds of this kind, in which the dreamer lets himself be rapt away so as to forget 'what can't be cured and so must be endured'. But the creative imagination can also conceive ways out, and see how things might be otherwise.[164] Then the counter-images, counter-histories and counter-worlds capture the future, and the pain of the present becomes the past. If these alternatives are linked with hope for the coming of God, then they cease to be unreal possibilities and become real ones, and the mystical dream worlds become alternatives for changes in 'this world'.

We always encounter a godless, unjust, alien world in these two ways: mysticism and revolt. The mysticism of the inner light can become a consuming flame flaring outwards (Karl Marx), but vain resistance can also turn again to inner mysticism, or at least be kept alive there. 'Ascetic Christianity called the world evil and left it. Humanity is waiting for a revolutionary Christianity which will call the world evil and change it,' declared Walter Rauschenbusch, talking about his Social Gospel movement.[165] He was right, although doors for a 'revolutionary Christianity' are not open always and everywhere – not in America either. But then the true Christianity, which calls the world what it is in the light of the crucified Jesus, will become a resistance movement and will not, at least outwardly, fall into line and will inwardly remain independent. A Christianity which is completely 'in line' with the state of the world and the rule of 'other lords' is a Christianity without remembrance of 'Christ crucified', and is therefore a Christianity without Christ.

7. Sacramental language: the faith-creating word

As an example of sacramental language we may take the charge given by the risen Christ to the disciples, according to John 20.21–23: 'If you forgive the sins of any, they are forgiven; if you retain the sins of any, they are retained' (v. 23). According to the Israelite view, only God can forgive sins. According to the Christian view, Jesus forgave sins in God's name and in the power of God's Spirit. Here, that commission, and with it that authority, is passed on to the disciples. The risen Christ declares: '*As* the Father has sent me, *even so* I send you' (v. 21). This is, as it were, an analogy 'from above', a true analogy, without a distinction between image and the thing imaged.

Jesus' divine mission is passed on to the disciples. The disciples
are drawn into Jesus' messianic mission. The risen Christ
'breathes' on to the disciples the 'Spirit who is the giver of life',
just as the Creator once breathed on Adam and made him a
living being. What the disciples then do in the power of the
Spirit 'corresponds' to what Jesus did in the power of the Spirit,
and is yet more than merely an analogy, a 'similarity in still
greater dissimilarity'. When they forgive sins 'they *are* forgiven'. What they say happens. It is not just an analogy or a
metaphor for something which might possibly happen. It is not
that the words correspond to the facts; the fact corresponds to
the word. If someone's sins are 'forgiven', and he asks whether
they have really been forgiven, and by God himself, we cannot
respond by saying: perhaps – it was an analogy; possibly – it
was a metaphor; it might be so, but it might also not be so, for
every statement is at once true and false. We must be able to
answer: Amen, it is assuredly true in time and eternity.

We call this faith-creating, assurance-creating talk of God
sacramental, because here God's Word can be heard *in* the
human word, and the authority for it is found in the indwelling
power of the Holy Spirit. Here the one is not *like* the other, but
the one is *in* the other. For this sacramental understanding
of language about God Luther used the rhetorical figure of
synekdoche, where the part is used for the whole, the one being
in the other. Between likeness and unlikeness there exist not
merely the analogies, metaphors and parables of similarity, but
also the *identification* of the one with the other. That does not
create an identity: the human word remains the human word,
and God's Word God's Word. But God lays his word in the
human word, and identifies himself with what the human word
says: 'if *you* forgive the sins, they *are* forgiven.' It is only in this
assurance that there can be kerygmatic talk of God. That distinguishes it from religious language in a general sense. And
that is why it begins like every sacramental action with the
epiklesis – the invocation – *of the Holy Spirit*. That is not a
ceremonial elevation of human language; it enfolds human
language in the assurance that what is said in God's name

happens: 'Your sins *are* forgiven. You *are* free.' Sacramental talk about God is 'absolute' inasmuch as it contains at heart the *word of absolution* – the free pardon for new, free life in the life-giving Spirit. When the divine speech which forgives sins takes this form, what happens is what John describes: 'Receive the Holy Spirit.' The 'outpouring of the Holy Spirit' extends to all flesh.

In this sense Christian talk about God is at heart sacramental talk about God. That distinguishes it from analogous talk about God and from the metaphorical language of parabolic speech, but makes it possible for this talk about God to use fitting analogies, felicitous metaphors drawn from colloquial speech, parables from the everyday life of the listeners, and subversive underground language, in order to make clear its true and innermost concern.

If we know what we have to say and want to say, there are no bounds to the wealth of linguistic possibilities which we can use in order to express the 'one thing that is needful' in a way that is appropriate and comes home to its listeners.

III. Mirror Images of Liberating Theology

The two sides of oppression

In this chapter we shall be looking at the contextual theologies of the Third World which are engaged in critical dispute with the world of the West. These are theologies of liberation from colonialism, capitalism, racism and sexism. That is to say, they are turned against phenomena and structures which have plunged their world into misery. These theologies have their location among the people who live on the downside of the history which the victors term 'world history', and they have grown out of the praxis through which people who are oppressed, impoverished and discriminated against free themselves from the coercions and constraints which lie heavy on them. We shall not be looking at the contextual theologies which have developed in other cultures – the African or Asian theologies. These are important if we are to perceive the riches of Christian theology, which has come to be at home in such different cultures, so that we can banish the narrow-minded Eurocentricism of our own theology to the confines of its own limitations. But here we shall consider only the liberating theologies of the oppressed, because they are mirror images of the Western world as their victims see it.

In our selection we shall look at *black theology* in the United States, the *liberation theology* that has developed in Latin America, Korean *minjung theology*, and the *feminist theology* which is ubiquitous. These theologies are as contextual as the others. But they have been quite consciously *developed* in their political, social and cultural context, in their historically conditioned *kairos*, and for the social class, group or community which is characterized by the exploitation, oppression and estrangement from which it suffers. Because these theologies try to promote the liberation of these particular groups, they are simultaneously critically related to the dominating oppressors and exploiters, and the authors of the estrangement. We shall therefore view them, not through their own eyes, but through our own, and describe them in their critical and liberating relevance for the world in which we ourselves live and which puts its impress on us, either consciously or, most often, unconsciously. So I shall describe these theologies 'crosswise':

Black theology for whites;
Liberation theology for the First World;
Minjung theology for the ruling classes;
Feminist theology for men.

This selection also makes it clear, on the other hand, that here we cannot go into the *kairos* theologies which have grown up in recent years in South Africa, Central America and Europe.[1] We must also leave out the peace theology which developed in both Germanys round about 1980, in the era of the peace movement, but whose *kairos* became a thing of the past after East Germany's *Anschluss* to the Federal Republic in 1989, and once the nuclear missiles had disappeared from German soil.[2] That does not mean that we have no need to learn from the Kairos documents and from prophetic peace theology so as to to arrive at a liberating theology in the depressing conditions of the so-called First World – on the contrary. But in this chapter we must confine ourselves to longer-term periods, contexts and forms of oppression.

My choice of liberation theologies has been influenced not least through my own close personal connection with them. My *Theology of Hope* (1964, ET 1967) already gathered historical liberations and eschatological expectation of the kingdom of God into a single coherent perspective, and in this eschatological future-looking perspective did not permit the metaphysical distinction between time and eternity: hope is realized in liberating and healing action, and casts its eschatological light into actions in solidarity of this kind. Early on, the political theology which Johann Baptist Metz and I developed from 1967 onwards released the 'revolutionary spirit' of the original Christian faith.[3] This immediately brought it into contact with social-critical and revolutionary freedom movements in Europe and the United States, as well as in the countries of the Third World. Let me introduce the account of the theologies I have mentioned with some reminiscences of my personal involvement with them. This was supportive, but my solidarity occasionally took critical form as well.

The oppression of human beings by other human beings has many different faces. It can take the form of political oppression, economic exploitation, social exclusion, cultural estrangement and sexist humiliation. It takes other forms too. But it is always a crime against life. For human life is life in community and communication. Life means 'loving your neighbour as yourself', not 'subdue him and make him submissive'. To oppress other people means to cut oneself off from God too, 'for if a man does not love his brother whom he has seen, how can he love God whom he has not seen?' (I John 4.20).

Oppression always has two sides. On the one side stands the master, on the other side lies the slave. On the one side is the arrogant self-elevation of the exploiter, on the other the suffering of his victim. Oppression destroys humanity on both sides. The oppressor acts inhumanely, the victim is dehumanized. The evil the perpetrator commits robs him of his humanity, the suffering he inflicts dehumanizes the victim. Where suffering is experienced in the pain of humiliation on the one hand, evil spreads on the other. This polarization of society is conspicuous in many areas of the world. On one side of the street, behind barbed wire, are the golf courses and the gated communities of the rich, guarded by the police; on the other side are the stinking slums of the poor and unemployed, with their rising crime rate. We see it in Rio de Janeiro, in Johannesburg, in Los Angeles and in Seoul. The children of the rich keep to themselves in private schools with highly paid teachers, the children of the poor go to run-down state schools, if they go to school at all. The protected life in the gated communities is pleasant, but inhuman. These are gilded prisons where fear stalks. The unprotected life of the slums is unpleasant, but for all its inhumanity, it has more potential for human closeness and community. The surrender of the privileges of the rich is not too high a price to pay for a humane society, with dignity and justice on both sides.

Because oppression always has these two sides, the liberation process has to begin on both sides too. The liberation of the oppressed from their suffering must lead to the liberation of the oppressors from the evil they commit; otherwise there can be no liberation for a new community in justice and freedom. The goal of these reciprocal liberations cannot be anything less than a community of men and women, free of fear, in which there are no longer any oppressors, and no longer any oppressed. In order to achieve this goal, the oppressed will have to free themselves from the constraints of oppression and cut themselves off from their oppressors, so as to find themselves and their own humanity. It is only after that that they can try to find a truly humane community with their previous oppressors. The oppressors will first of all have to see themselves in the suffering eyes of their victims, and recognize themselves as oppressors, so that by surmounting their compulsions to oppress the others they can then overcome the isolation they have brought on themselves. They will have to withdraw their violence and their structures of violence if they want to turn back again to the community of human beings.

The liberation of the oppressed is a moral duty, and in many situations a duty that is self-evident, at least for the oppressed. The liberation of the oppressors is in most cases not a self-evident duty, at least not for the oppressors, who profit from the oppression of the others. They are blind, and fail to see the suffering they inflict on their victims. They are blinded, and find many grounds to justify their baseness. The liberation of the oppressors, so that they can arrive at their own human dignity and at true human community with the others, is an experience which requires more than good will: the master has to die so that the brother can be born. Control over others must give way to community with others.

Whether it be black theology, liberation theology, minjung theology or feminist theology, the liberation theologies familiar to us from the Third World are without exception theologies focussed on the liberation of the poor and oppressed masses from the rule of the oligarchies which exploit them. At their best they express the suffering of the victims and their hopes, and grow up in the context of praxis: the praxis of the people's self-organizations, and movements for their liberation and their human rights. It is a matter of course that they should be 'one-sided', because they have taken up cudgels for the victims of violence and discrimination. It is also a matter of course that for them the problem of the evil involved has to take second place to the need to make people aware of the misery, and that the call to reconciliation has to recede behind the cry of the tortured. It is really also self-evident that the oppressed should not adopt a public 'victims'' role, so as to let themselves be helped and thus to become dependent, but that they should get up and liberate themselves. No one else can do that for them. It is also self-evident that they must avoid falling into the trap of self-pity. They would then be doubly imprisoned, by their oppressors and by themselves.

But it is a deplorable fact that after more than thirty years of liberation theology among the poor in the countries of the Third World, there should still be no comprehensive theology for the liberation of the oppressors among the ruling classes in the countries of the industrial West. Here the European Kairos Document of 1998 is a first approach. But that theologians in the West should do no more than shrink back from black theology, Latin American theology, Korean minjung theology and feminist theology, or allow themselves to be entertained by them, without having the faintest perception of the changes in themselves which are required, is a reflection of 'hardness of heart' in the biblical sense of the phrase. For theologians in the West, under the pressure of these theologies to display mere tolerance or benevolence, as much as to say 'How splendid – for you', and for them then go on as before, is a sign of stupidity, not intelligence.[4] The reason is probably that members of the white, male, middle-class world are ready enough to recognize the need for the poor in the Third World to be liberated, but are not prepared to see themselves as accomplices of the forces that have oppressed them. They show good will by contributing to development aid projects, disaster funds and so forth, but avoid painful insights into the unjust structures of their own world. It is easy to be liberal where it doesn't cost too much; and through this very attitude we waste the chances for our own liberation from structures incompatible with human dignity, a liberation which would free us for community with the people in the countries of the Third World.

But those who want to stand up for the liberty of the oppressed must stop participating in their oppression, and must therefore begin to liberate themselves. That is not a matter of having a guilty conscience in social questions. It has to do with conversion – striking out a new direction towards the future of one's own humanity. Good deeds are not the fruit of a guilty conscience. They ensue of themselves out of joy in a new community, without oppressors and without victims.

In the political and economic systems of our world many people are themselves oppressed, and in their turn play their part in oppressing other people: they are 'oppressed oppressors' or 'victimized perpetrators'. Because of this it is important to recognize the need for liberation on both sides and, it may be, to perceive that need in our own existence too.

2

Black theology for whites

1. My personal access to black theology

In 1967/68 I was invited to spend the academic year as visiting professor at Duke University in Durham, North Carolina. We and our four children lived in a white district, and I taught theology at the white divinity school. The first thing that struck me was the invisibility in white circles of the black majority of the population. Unless one just happened to run across a porter, at Duke University one met only whites. Black people could be seen in the white areas only if they were maids or shop assistants, road-menders or dustmen. They lived in their own black areas or ghettos. But our friend Fred Herzog[5] was involved in the Civil Rights movement, and he and his wife Kristin took us into the country in order to show us the literally naked misery of the black sharecroppers, but also the crosses of the Ku Klux Klan (highly active among the poor whites) which had been burnt as a warning.

At that time Duke University was somewhat withdrawn from what went on in the world. But that changed abruptly on 4 April 1968. We were sitting with theologians from all over the country in one of the university halls at a 'Theology of Hope Conference'.[6] I was just arguing with Van Harvey about the distinction between *Geschichte* and *Historie** when Harvey Cox burst into the room crying 'Martin King has been shot'. We immediately broke off the conference, and the participants hurried home, for by the same evening shops and businesses in

---

* In German *Historie* means history as a scholarly discipline, *Geschichte* the historicity of human existence.

the American cities were going up in flames. The black population rose with a cry of rage, while the whites tried to protect
themselves. Then the unbelievable happened: 400 students sat
down in the quadrangle of Duke University and mourned for
Martin Luther King for six days and six nights, in rain and heat.
At the end of that week of shame and mourning, black students
from a college nearby came and danced through the rows of
white students and we all sang together: 'We shall overcome.'
From that day, the blacks in Durham became more self-
confident and the conscience of the whites woke up.

I first met Jim Cone, the creator of 'black theology', at the
annual meetings of the American Academy of Religion in 1969,
in one of the huge New York hotels. I had talked about hope
and poetry under the title 'How can I sing the Lord's song in a
strange land?'[7] He came up to me to say that he was working on
a theological interpretation of the black blues and spirituals.
We got on at once and became friends. His pioneer book *Black
Theology and Black Power* had just appeared that year (1969).
We published it at once in German in our series Gesellschaft
und Theologie ('Society and Theology'). It came out in 1971,
Fred Herzog writing the German introduction and a chapter
which is still worth reading on 'God: Black or White? Black
Theology's Challenge to Christian Faith' (165–85). In 1973 I
wrote the foreword to the German translation of Cone's book
The Spirituals and the Blues. An Interpretation. In 1974 I edited a double issue on black theology in the periodical *Evan-
gelische Theologie*, but this proved controversial and brought
the periodical no friends.

We had Jim Cone twice in Tübingen, but the political and
religious problems of the descendants of the African slaves in
the two Americas and the Caribbean make little impact on
Germans, even though they are in fact the inner problems of the
whole Western world on the downside of the modern history it
shares. Without the slavery of the black masses there would
have been no investment capital for the build-up of Western
industrial society.

During many lecture tours throughout the United States I

always enjoyed my time in black universities, such as Howard in Washington, and black seminaries, such as the Interdenominational Theological Center in Atlanta, Georgia. In 1971 *Black Awareness. A Theology of Hope*, by Major Jones, was published. In 1974 Deotis J. Roberts wrote *A Black Political Theology*. Later, in Trinidad and Jamaica, I discovered the traces of Marcus Garvey's 'Back to Africa' movement, and came to know something of the dreams of the Rastafarians.

2. *African slavery (1518–1888) and the building of the modern world of the West*

Slavery was an institution in most pre-modern societies. Aristotle defended it on the grounds of practical reason. In his letter to Philemon, Paul did not call it fundamentally in question: there are freemen and slaves, but in the Christian congregation they have all been one since their baptism. 'Here there is neither slave nor free . . .' (Gal. 3.28). Nevertheless, in Christendom, whether this principle applies only before God or in the social world too remained an open question. It was only the democratic movement which grew up during the Enlightenment and the Industrial Revolution which put an end to slavery as a social institution, since 'all men have been created equal' and are endowed with inalienable human rights. In United States waters the last slave ships were seized in 1880. Brazil was the last country to abolish slavery, in 1888. In the Ottoman Empire the Arab slave trade continued until the First World War.

Serfdom existed in the European countries into the eighteenth and nineteenth centuries. Peasants were sold like other commodities. Press-ganged soldiers were bought and sold by absolutist potentates. Mercenaries from Hessen fought for England in the American War of Independence. In Venice even today one is shown the place where slaves were sold up to to 1789. The mass enslavement of Africans must therefore certainly be seen in the social context of its time. At the same time, it falls outside that framework because it made the plantation empires in

America possible, and the industrial development of the Western World.

'Discovered' in 1492, in 1495 Hispaniola (Haiti) experienced a rising of the 'Indigenas' against the Spaniards. The Indios were massacred on a massive scale, and those that were left died in the gold mines, or committed suicide. In 1517 Bartholomé de Las Casas, priest, landowner and a former slave-owner, thereupon presented himself to Charles V and accused him of the genocide of these people.[8] Prompted by pity for the weaker Indios, he made the fateful suggestion that black slaves should be imported from Africa, because they were stronger. Charles V agreed. But Las Casas bitterly regretted his proposal later, when he saw the consequences. The famous 'Asiento' was produced, the import licence for the slave-trade in the Spanish colonies, which could then be sold on. Africa had been assigned to the Portuguese by the pope. In this way a European slave-trade developed in which slaves were carried from West Africa to the Spanish and Portugese colonies in America.[9] Elmira (1481) was the first slave-trader's fort. From the middle of the sixteenth century almost all the other European countries (Brandenburg-Prussia among them) followed suit, in order to profit from the growing demand for black slaves in America. From 1540 onwards more than 10,000 slaves were transported every year; by the end of the century a total of about 900,000 had been brought into the islands of the West Indies alone. There are no exact figures but those we know are terrible enough: alone between 1575 and 1591 52,000 slaves were shipped from Angola to Brazil; between 1680 and 1700 300,000 were carried on English ships; between 1680 and 1688 the Royal African Company had 249 slave-traders under contract, shipped 60,783 slaves and unloaded 46,396. In the seventeenth century about 2,750,000 slaves were sold. But the climax of the slave-trade was only reached at the beginning of the nineteenth century, when the four 'slave crops', sugar, rice, tobacco and cotton, reached the peak of their production in the American plantations. All in all, it is thought that there were over 15 million African slaves who survived, and 30 to 40 million who did not.

The slave trade with which the modern Western world was built up was far and away the biggest international trading business in modern times.[10] It was part of the world-wide 'triangular commerce': products of the mercantilism that was now beginning were exported to Africa, together with weapons – slaves from Africa to the two Americas and the islands of the West Indies – gold, silver, lead and then above all sugar, rice, tobacco and cotton ('colonial produce', as it was called) to Europe. The merchantmen were never empty. The result was the downfall of West African kingdoms, the 'Balkanization' of the tribal territories, and the cultural decay of the African coastal population. A further consequence was the destruction of the local subsistence economy and the build-up of colonial plantation empires in America, with the monocultures we have mentioned. And the necessary investment capital was thereby made available for the industrialization of Western Europe which – in the form of the Spanish, Portuguese, French, Dutch and British empires – seized power over the world, in the face of India, China and the Ottoman empire.

Although England abolished the slave trade after 1807, it took the American Civil War later in the nineteenth century to put a final end to slavery in the Western world. The economic presupposition was the displacement of the plantation economy by industrial society, which needed 'a work force' but not slaves. In the United States, the industrialized North, with its immigrant workers who had voluntarily come to America from Europe, proved superior to the agrarian South, with its non-voluntary slave labour.

On the one side Christians, especially Quakers, fought with mind and spirit, as well as with the methods of civil disobedience, for the abolition of slavery: in 1641 it was forbidden in Massachussetts; in 1652 in Rhode Island; in 1761 in Pennsylvania. But on the other side resistance and revolts by the African slaves themselves also led to the end of slavery. The slaves were by no means so teachable, obedient and docile as white literature depicted them as being – *Uncle Tom's Cabin*, for example. The history of black slavery was an endless history of mutinies, rebellions and flight, as well as of active and passive resistance. Famous examples are the Negro revolts on Haiti between 1791 and 1798, under the victorious leadership of Pierre Dominique Toussaint l'Overture, which were only beaten down under Napoleon; the struggles of the Maroons against the English in Jamaica; and Nat Turner's revolts in Virginia in 1837.[11] An important source of the power behind these risings lay in the religion of the oppressed, which we find expressed in the spirituals. The biblical stories about Exodus and homecoming, Babylon and Zion, Moses and Elijah, kept alive resistance and the hope for freedom.

> Oh Freedom, oh Freedom!
> Oh Freedom, I love you.
> And before I'll be a slave,
> I'll be buried in my grave
> and go home to my Lord
> and be free.[12]

Of this appalling slave trade pursued by the Western world, more that 22 million blacks or Afro-Americans are left in the United States, more still in Brazil and in the West Indies. These people are African in origin but live in English, Spanish and Portuguese-speaking countries. They were cut off from their roots, in most cases know nothing of their origin, and bear the names of their former slave-owners – Little, King, Garvey, Armstrong, Marley. Many of them have the blood of earlier slave-owners in their veins and are not purely black. As Malcolm X deplored, they bear within themselves the violation of their grandmothers. And yet, involuntary though their coming was, they have put a definitive impress on the development and culture of the countries in which they now live, and are true Americans, or Brazilians, and so forth.

The political abolition of slavery by no means put an end to the white racism which went hand in hand with it, serving as its justification. Until the civil rights movement in the years between 1960 and 1970, blacks in the southern states of the

USA were subject to legal discrimination, and lived under the strict segregation laws imposed on them by the 'white supremacy', which was restored after the Civil War had been lost.

Even today black Americans constitute the mass of the unemployed, the homeless, the sick – and the army. The United States may be a 'melting pot' for immigrants (although that is not true either), but black Americans have always been left outside. Today 'pluralism' is practised as a democratic ideology. But black Americans have never shared in this pluralist tolerance, because there can be no pluralism between descendants of the former perpetrators and their victims. The sickness of white racism is a legacy of slavery.

The 400 years of enslavement of the blacks has profoundly infected the souls of the whites with this *disease of racism*, even if today the whites are generally unconscious of it.[13] But we only need to be aware of the role played by the colour black in the psycho-pathological symbolism of white people in order to recognize this disease. The contrast between day and night, light and darkness, shows that in the world of 'the white man' black symbolizes wickedness, evil and threat. In America the hangman was a black man. Satan is black, dirt is black, black clothes are a sign of mourning. When people are slandered, their names are 'blackened'. When we are angry we 'look black'. Strike-breakers are 'black-legs'. For people who are white, those who are black symbolize whatever is irrational, compulsive, unclean, uncontrolled and sensual, characteristics which white self-control and the light of white reason are supposed to rise above.

The special Negrophobia of the whites (which has no parallel where people with red or yellow skins are concerned) is a projection of the parts of their own souls they have shut away, and the guilty fear they have suppressed. We project on to those who are black our own suppression of the body, the senses and the drives, a suppression which, ever since the beginning of the modern world, we have laboriously had to learn through self-mastery and self-control – the lesson impressed on modern men and women by the Puritans and the Jesuits. We also project 'nature' on to those who are black – after all they are 'children of nature', while we have risen to become nature's 'lords and possessors', as Descartes said. Liberation from the disease of racism and especially from Negrophobia therefore cannot be seen as something subsidiary and by the way; it requires a kind of collective psychotherapy for whites, and nothing less than a new cultural revolution. Martin Luther King always acutely diagnosed this sickness in the eyes of the whites.

If we follow the UNESCO definition, which was taken over by the General Assembly of the World Council of Churches in Uppsala in 1968, we understand by racism:

> The ethnocentric pride in one's own racial group, the preference given to the particular characteristics of this group, the conviction that these characteristics are fundamentally biological in kind, negative feelings about other groups, linked with the urge to discriminate against groups belonging to other races and to exclude them from full participation in the life of society.

In its listing of the modes of behaviour which must be called racist, this definition (paraphrased here) is not complete.[14] But the essential point is clear. The characteristics of one's own 'race' are identified with the characteristics of humanity itself. To be human is to be white, and people of different races become non-persons, sub-human, or people of inferior value and inferior capacities. One's own self-esteem is based on one's white skin. One's own race legitimates the right to rule over races that are inferior. In this legitimating function racism becomes a dangerous means of psychological warfare waged by the rulers over the ruled. As 'second-class citizens' the people belonging to this dominated group are denied civil rights; as itinerant workers they are kept permanently dependent; homeless, they are open to every police action. The feelings of superiority cherished by the dominating race then produce feelings of inferiority among the races who are dominated. They are systematically made to hate themselves.

In its concrete form, racism always has these two sides: it is both a psychological mechanism of self-righteousness on the one hand, and on the other an ideological mechanism for the domination of others. Racism therefore destroys humanity on both sides. The white racist displays superhuman pride in his white 'race', and is yet obsessed by an inhuman fear. Those for whom to be human is the same as to be white destroys their own humanity. Because they must continually translate their fear into aggression towards others, they also destroy their community with them. They see in black people only their blackness, not other people like themselves. Racist humiliation of others is at heart deadly self-hatred.

3. *Marcus Mosiah Garvey (1887–1940) and the 'Back to Africa' movement*

Before we come to the black theology of James Cone, we shall look at three different ways in which black Americans reacted to their situation after the abolition of slavery. There were three different liberation movements: 1. back to the liberation offered by Africa; 2. separation from white supremacy in America; 3. integration in the 'American dream'. The name of Marcus Garvey stands for African nationalism, the name of Malcolm X for separation from the American 'nightmare', the name of Martin Luther King for integration into a better America. We must give at least brief accounts of these movements in order to make black theology comprehensible.

Marcus Garvey was the charismatic leader of black nationalism between 1919 and 1930.[15] Although much of his important work was done in the United States (to which he emigrated in 1916), he was born on 17 August 1887 in St Ann, Jamaica. His second name Mosiah (Moses) was given him by his mother: 'I hope he will be like Moses, and lead his people.' On his father's side he was descended from the rebellious Maroons, who had pursued guerrilla warfare against the British in the mountains of Jamaica. Even after the abolition of slavery in 1834, the black population in Jamaica could only survive as labourers in the white plantations. Garvey came to know the exploitation of the blacks in Kingston, Costa Rica and Panama. Booker T. Washington's autobiography *Up from Slavery*[16] made him ask: 'Where is the black man's Government? Where is his King and his Kingdom? Where is his President, his country, and his ambassador, his army, his navy, his men of big affairs?' In order to answer his questions he founded the UNIA (the Universal Negro Improvement Association) with branches both in Jamaica and in the United States. In 1919 it became the largest mass organization of black Americans. He also founded the newspaper *Negro World*, an African Legion and the shipping line Black Star Line, and called himself the provisional president of Africa.

Most important of all was Garvey's attempt to boost the self-confidence of the poor black population by reminding them of their African home. We are part of the proud African nation and descendents of the Pharaohs, he maintained. Our home is not this country of our white exploiters, but free Africa – 'Ethiopia' as he called it (Ethiopia being then the only African country which had never been subjugated and colonized). Garvey's attempt to raise up the bowed-down black people in America was directed towards the liberation of the African continent. 'Back to Africa' was synonymous with 'Africa for the Africans'. Here Garvey took his inspiration from Herzl's Zionism, which purposed both to make Israel the home of the Jews and to defend the rights of Jews all over the world. The echoes of the stories about Israel's liberations are not only prompted by the love of black people for the Old Testament. The first step on this long road out of American slavery to the freedom of Africa was for Garvey the inner separation from the dominant white world. He stood for 'black segregationalism' and hated racial mixing, mixed marriages and mulattoes.

The founding of the black shipping line for the return to Africa proved to be an economic failure. Garvey was not a businessman. In 1925 he was sentenced to five years' imprisonment because of taxation problems, and was deported to Jamaica in 1927. But his great Africa vision found a real point of reference.

Turn your eyes to Africa, he proclaimed in Jamaica: when a black king is crowned the day of redemption will be at hand. In 1930 Haile Selassie I, previously Ras Tafari Makonennen, was crowned emperor of Ethiopia. In Jamaica this triggered off the new religious Rastafari movement, in which many people saw the fulfilment of Marcus Garvey's message.

When Fascist Italy under Mussolini attacked Ethiopia in 1936 and Haile Selassie fled to England, Garvey's expectation that the day of redemption was imminent collapsed. He died in 1940 in England. But ever since Jamaica's independence (1962) he has been revered there as a national hero. His attempts to build up an independent black economy failed, but not his thrusts towards a new black self-esteem. The later Black Panther, Black Power, and Black is Beautiful movements were also influenced by him, as was African nationalism in African countries after independence. 'Africa for the Africans – those at home and those in exile' is an enduring demand.

The new religious movement of the *Rastafarians* can on the one hand be seen religio-critically as a shift away from the political demand for a return to Africa in the direction of a religious dream world; but on the other it can also be seen as a stabilization of the inner liberation from mental and spiritual oppression, and a preservation of African nationalism.[17] It is at all events one of the most interesting modern forms of expression of the 'religion of the oppressed' (Laternari). Without laying claim to a judgment of my own, I should like to stress and interpret the following points from the material available to me.

How can slaves and their descendants, living in a foreign land, express their own hopes in the culture, language and religion of their oppressors, and find their own identity? By changing the English language of the rulers into their own Rasta language. The Rastas escaped the English linguistic and cultural conformity imposed on them, and Africanized it by way of linguistic twists and re-interpretations. The Rasta language is called 'I-yaric' and is a sacred language for the initiated. The 'I' has a special importance because it stands for the link with both the divine and the brothers. The 'little I' enters into mystical association with the 'big I' of the divine, and the human being becomes holy. The link with the divine is achieved through meditation, which is stimulated through the 'sacrament', the sacred plant ganja/marihuana. The divine name is JAH, an abbreviated form of the Old Testament YHWH, and goes back to the JAH-God of the Maroons in Jamaica. Jah-man is the man of God and Jah-maica what has been made here by JAH.

The world of white rule in which black people have to exist is 'Babylon', as the apocalyptic language says in encoded form. The Rasta have to separate themselves from this despicable system. So numerous antitheses are developed. Where the churches use incense as the perfume of God, the Rasta community uses ganja. Where the whites have houses of God, for the Rasta the body of every human being is holy as 'temple of the Spirit'. Whereas in the religion of the whites the Lord 'Jeesaz' reigns, here the 'victorious Lion of Judah' is expected, as redeemer of the black race, his 'chosen people'. Haile Selassie I is this longed-for redeemer, who will bring the oppressed black people to 'Ethiopia', free Africa. Garvey held the Ethiopian ruler to be a human being, but the Rasta invested him with divine attributes. After his death in 1975, Haile Selassie lived on in the hearts of all 'I-and-I brothers'. The Rasta acknowledge him through their 'dreadlocks' (their lion's manes), their ceremonious, upright walk, and their knitted woollen caps in the Ethiopian colours, red, gold and green. 'Babylon' dictates the working hours of the day, so the Rasta meet at night, the time which is free. Babylon dominates the great cities, so the Rastas prefer to withdraw to the lonely mountains. Whereas white people eat meat, the Rasta are vegetarians. They share with the Jews the exilic situation which they call 'Babylon', following the Christian book of Revelation. They are hence the true Jah-people, who are waiting for their Exodus.

The Rastafarians have become known not least through the reggae music of Bob Marley and Peter Tosh. The three drums which are used carry the rhythm of the earth to heaven. Singing and dancing draw the initiated into the harmony of heaven and earth and therefore bear within themselves the holy and healing power of the Spirit of 'I-and-I'.

Rastafari has been called a messianically millenarian cult: messianic because of its hope for the redeemer Haile Selassie, millenarian because of the expectation of a golden future in 'Ethiopia'. But that is not an adequate description, nor is it sufficient for an understanding. Rastafari represents a turning away by the black Jamaicans from the white culture enforced on them, and from its Christian tradition. The transference of Marcus Garvey's Back to Africa movement into the world of religion, Rastafari's development of its own underground culture, a counter-culture to the culture of the white rulers, the transformation of the dominant language into a counter-language, and the conversion of the dominant religious symbols into a subversive religion: these are unique achievements of this 'religion of the oppressed', which serves to raise up and liberate the descendants of black slaves. In the language and music of the Rasta, in their way of life and their cults, the home country 'Africa' lives as a utopian world which does not yet exist. 'Ethiopia' is a transferable symbol for 'the promised land' and for 'heaven on earth'. The 'Babylon system' is an expandable symbol for the slavery of body and soul in its old and new forms, a symbol used for thousands of years by the oppressed and persecuted Jews and Christians and their martyrs. The fact that in Garvey's time, and even today, hardly a single black person in Jamaica and the United States wants to return to Africa as it really exists, but that black people can nevertheless present themselves as independent, free human beings in the alien culture which oppresses and humiliates them, gives the utopia 'Ethiopia' its critical justification. 'Free our minds from mental slavery,' as Bob Marley sang.

4. Malcolm X (1925–1965) and black separation

Slavery, far more than imprisonment, left profound traces in the souls of those enslaved and their descendants. These traces make themselves felt in the inferiority complex which develops in people humiliated by masters with a superiority complex. I am speaking out of the experience of long years as a prisoner of war, from 1945–1948. One faces a hostility against which one cannot defend oneself. One creeps into the shell of one's own inner life, and reacts outwardly with impassive indifference. One blocks off one's own vital energies and comes to terms with the barbed wire and the forced labour: 'Bent down so low 'til down don't bother you no more,' said the black slaves. One accustoms oneself to the chains, so that they no longer chafe; makes oneself unnoticeable so as not to run into difficulties; smiles in order to keep the masters in a good mood. These are the experiences of hostages in kidnapped aircraft as well. The mental and spiritual consequence is self-contempt and the inner temptation to self-destructiveness.

In the former slave states, the fight for legal equality with the whites was only one side of all the black movements. Their other purpose was to raise up the bowed-down souls of the blacks so that they could achieve self-respect through consciousness of their own dignity. That meant nothing less than black self-determination according to their own values, not the values of the white world. 'Rather die standing up than live on one's knees.'

The Black Power movement (its name was introduced into the Civil Rights movement by Stokely Carmichael in 1966) wanted to be the power to say Yes to one's own blackness, and to make the whites either recognize it or accept the conflict.[18] But in order for this to be possible the blacks had to destroy the picture which the white masters had made of them so as to keep them down. They had to find their own image, with which they could raise themselves up. 'The worst crime the white man has committed has been to teach us to hate ourselves,' proclaimed Malcolm X. His leader in the Black Muslim movement, Elijah Muhammad, had ironically complained: 'The Negro wants to be a white man. He processes his hair. Acts like a white man. He wants to integrate with the white man, but he cannot integrate with himself or his own mind. The Negro wants to lose his identity, because he does not know his own identity.'[19] But the victims cannot be integrated into the society of the perpetrators. That is why the motto of Black Power was: first separation from the dominating white culture and its values, then the discovery of black identity and values, and finally perhaps – one day – a new integration on the basis of mutual recognition, but not 'on the terms of the white race'.

Consequently it was and remains false to criticize Black Power and black theology as being 'racism in reverse' – blacks against whites. What is at stake is something different: 'Black consciousness is the key to the black man's emancipation from his distorted self-image'[20] – the image he has made of himself because he was forced to it by the whites.

But the problem is that the blacks in the United States have been doubly oppressed, first through racism and secondly through poverty. It is therefore difficult to gather together a 'black community' and to motivate it to fight against white racism. The black population is already divided into poor and rich, and the black middle class is not prepared to put at risk the privileges that it has achieved. Martin Luther King therefore first led the March on Washington, but later the March of the Poor as well. He saw the double oppression, but was from birth onwards more on the side of integration. Malcom X saw it too, but stressed the racist humiliation, and was from birth onwards on the side of separation. Both sides were faced with the question: where to? Separation yes, but where is the land of liberty? Integration yes, but under whose conditions?

Malcolm X was a representative of the poor blacks in the North. Born as Malcolm Little in Omaha, Nebraska, on 15 May 1925, the seventh child of a Baptist assistant preacher who never had a steady congregation, he grew up in Lansing, Michigan. His father was a black Nationalist and an organizer of Marcus Garvey's UNIA. His mother worked there too. So he grew up with the idea 'Africa for the Africans' and with the hope that 'Africa's redemption is coming'. The Ku Klux Klan drove his family out of Omaha, a white hate group set their house in Lansing on fire. After the death of their father the children were distributed among different families as 'state children' – wards of court. Malcolm's schooling ended when he was fourteen: 'I finished the eighth grade in Mason, Michigan. My high school was the black ghetto of Roxbury. My college was the streets of Harlem, and my master's was taken in prison.'[21]

While he was in prison Malcolm got to know the disciplined Black Muslims and in 1958 was converted to Elijah Muhammad's 'Nation of Islam'. For them devils were white and God black, and blacks have God's true religion and culture. This strange Muslim faith gave Malcolm self-respect and self-education while he was in prison. He had overcome the temptation to 'self-destruct'. He continued to educate himself and after he was released from prison joined Temple Number One in Detroit. The founder of the Black Muslims gave him the name 'X', which was intended to symbolize the African surname which he did not know, and thus freed him from the 'white, blue-eyed devil' who had given his slave the name 'Little'. He took Malcolm in like a son, making him No. 2 in the movement, as his personal messenger. This was the radical continuation of the Garvey movement: 'The solution of the problem is separation, not integration.'

Malcolm X was one of the best and most intelligent speakers in the United States of his time. His personal problem was only that he was not pure black. 'Malcolm was red because his maternal grandmother was raped by a white man.' Malcolm hated himself for this: 'I hate every drop of the rapist's blood that is in me.'[22]

In the 1950s and 1960s Malcolm X was the great alternative in the black community to Martin Luther King. In his famous Washington speech in 1963, 'I have a dream . . .', King was casting back to the 'American dream' and the declaration of human rights in the American Constitution: 'All men are created equal.' But Malcolm summed up the cry of the wretched in the black ghettos: 'I have a nightmare.' What the whites call their American dream has always been for the blacks only a nightmare. In order finally to wake up from that nightmare, cried Malcolm, the blacks have to take up the struggle against the 'white devils'. But the search for self-confidence and identity is hard: we know neither our names, our language, our homeland nor our religion. 'We are like dry bones in the valley.' But, Malcolm proclaimed, 'The great day of separation is at hand', for God will destroy white America. Only fools want to be 'integrated' into a sinking ship. But Malcolm too did not know the place where the blacks would be saved on America's downfall. His proposals for a territorial separation were meant as a utopia.[23] This was what Elijah Muhammad had taught too. Like 'Babylon', America has become subject to God's judgment. 'No one shall escape the doom except those who accept Allah as God, Islam as his only religion, and the Honorable Elijah Muhammad as his Messenger to the twenty-two million ex-slaves in America.'[24] This was once again an Exodus story with a white Pharaoh, a black Israel, an Islamic Moses and 'Africa' as the promised land.

After 1960 Malcolm broke with Elijah Muhammad. He wanted to see the Nation of Islam in political action, whereas Elijah Muhammad wanted to keep it as a strictly religious community. Malcolm wanted to intervene politically 'now', but Elijah waited for God to act in the year 1970. In February 1965 Malcolm X was shot in Harlem, as he was addressing a great crowd of people.

For the whites Malcolm counted as a radical, a black racist, a preacher of hate; for many blacks he was an apostle of the new black self-respect. He led young blacks in the ghettos away from their self-destructiveness through drugs, crime, prison sentences and so forth. As James Cone says, freedom is always first of all one's own perception of one's own self-esteem and dignity. But for the separation which Malcolm X taught, there was no 'promised land'; nor were there any 'liberated zones' in society, not even for Indians, to whom the land belonged. And yet this utopia has acted as an inspiration in the criticism of the imposed values of the whites, and in the build-up of black self-confidence.

As Malcolm X shows, the socio-psychological problem of

self-contempt is a problem from which the descendants of black slaves and victims of white racism have to suffer every day. But it is not a problem of racism alone. It is also a human problem imposed by the capitalist achievement-orientated society.[25] If the sense of one's own value depends solely on achievement and possessions – that is to say, on the market value of human beings – then it is ultimately founded on profound existential anxieties. The person who 'doesn't make it' is a failure, and is forced to retire from the competitive struggle. The achievement-orientated society has to evoke permanent depression among its members in order to goad them on to particular achievements. If people are judged according to their market value, the result is a new justification through works, and a nihilist mood of anxiety. Private and public pastoral care in this society therefore has only one theme for all concerned, irrespective of their race: self-esteem and success. You aren't just nothing. You are someone who can make it. God loves you if you only want it. In capitalist society the gospel is self-acceptance, self-esteem, self-love. The message 'black is beautiful' reaches only those who have been humiliated by white racism, but not those who have been exploited by the market economy. And yet they can all learn from black theology that human dignity is more than the humiliating image of the black man or woman painted by whites, and more too than the market value of a human being. The emancipation of black men and women from racism can become the model for the human emancipation of human beings.

5. Martin Luther King (1929–1968) and American integration

The blacks in the United States have two souls in their breasts, an African and an American one. W. E. B. Du Bois recognized this early on: 'Am I an American or am I a Negro? Can I be both?'[26] Malcolm X had answered: I am black first of all. My sympathies are black. My affiliation is black. I am not interested in being an American because America was never interested in me. Martin Luther King, in contrast, stood for the full integration of the blacks in American society. His dream of the equality of the blacks, proclaimed in his remarkable speech before the Capitol in Washington on 28 August 1963, was, as he said, 'a dream deeply rooted in the American dream'. We simply want the realization of the American dream, he proclaimed, a dream which is still unfulfilled, a dream about equality of opportunities, rights, property, a dream about a society in which people are judged not according to the colour of their skins but according to their character, a dream about the brotherhood of all, a dream about America as 'land of the free and home of the brave'.[27] He therefore claimed, logically and rightly, in the name of the humiliated and poor blacks, the great promises of the American constitution. Because the American dream is still unfulfilled, the liberation and integration of the blacks can still become part of it.

Martin Luther King felt himself to be American first of all, and then black. Many black people after him have had the same experience: after having looked for their roots in Africa, they have discovered there that they are Americans. That is also the conclusion Keith B. Richburg, a journalist on the *Washington Post*, draws from his experiences in Africa, as he records in his book *Out of America. A Black Man Confronts Africa*.[28] But what does the 'American soul' of the blacks look like? Do they become 'Americans' only under the conditions of the white world? Or can this integration lead to a new world of free and equal partners?

Martin Luther King Jr was born in Atlanta, Georgia, on 15 January 1929 as son of the Baptist pastor Martin Luther King Sr. His house is only a few steps from the famous Ebenezer Church, which became the centre for the Civil Rights movement in Atlanta. His father was the son of a poor sharecropper in Georgia, but he had worked himself up and in the end became an influential personality in the black community. This family, this church, and the self-determining will ('Help yourselves, then you can succeed in the world of the white man too,' as Booker Washington had said) were the essential influences in

Martin's childhood. But it was still the world of legal segregation, with 'Whites only' notices in buses, hospitals, parks,
shops, restaurants, and so forth. In short, it was the Jim Crow
world of the white police and the Ku Klux Klan. It was only in
the churches that the blacks could be themselves, and think,
talk and sing as they really were. The Christian congregation
and the black community belonged closely together.

When he was eighteen, Martin Jr was ordained, and went on
to study at Croser Seminary in Chester, Pennsylvania. He too
had unpleasant encounters with white racists, but he did not
live in the black slums like Malcolm X. He was determined 'to
get on' and both in the seminary and later at Boston University
counted as one of the best students. His later thinking and
actions were deeply influenced, first, by Gandhi's writings and
the non-violent protest movement in India; second, by the
philosophical personalism of Edgar Brightman; and third, by
the Christian theology of Reinhold Niebuhr, Paul Tillich
and Henry Nelson Wieman. In Boston he studied Hegel's
Phenomenology of Mind (or *Spirit)*, and learnt from Hegel's
dialectic that progress can only be made through conflict. His
study programme extended to white theology – European theology as far as possible, German theology included; there was no
question of a black theology. In Boston he met Coretta Scott.
They married in 1953, and Martin accepted a pastorate at the
Dexter Avenue Church in Montgomery, Alabama.

It was there that the famous story of Rose Parks took place.
On 1 December 1955, as she travelled home from work, tired,
she refused to give up her place in the bus, a place reserved 'for
whites only'. She was arrested, and the long and total boycott
of all municipal buses in Montgomery by the blacks began.
Martin Luther King was the organizer and leader. This boycott
was followed by a massive number of sit-ins and freedom
marches, which finally culminated in the great March on
Washington in 1963. Law was on the side of the blacks, for as
early as 1954 the Supreme Court had declared that the segregation of schools and buses was unconstitutional; but power was
in the hands of the whites. For Martin Luther King, racial

discrimination was at first in the forefront, but after 1965 he and the Southern Christian Leadership perceived the close connection between racism, poverty and militarism in American politics. It was not by chance that he was murdered on 4 April 1968 in Memphis, Tennessee, when he and others organized the strike of black trash collectors.

The great themes of King's public speeches were *justice* and *love*, in that order. He justified the Montgomery boycott through the right of the blacks to their own rights: 'The right to protest for rights.' That right is constitutional and is in conformity with God.[29] For King, the question of love entered the discussion only in connection with the mode of the protest: civil disobedience, but in non-violent action. Non-violent action puts the violent in the wrong. Violence destroys the violent inwardly. Non-violence frees them from their self-destructiveness. Violence creates enemies; non-violence can turn enemies into friends. Non-violence has a reconciling power, so only the methods of non-violence can be used for the integration of black and white in a new, just society. But non-violence has nothing to do with the powerlessness of the powerless, for whom nothing is left but to surrender. Non-violence is the royal way of liberating the oppressed and the oppressors from hate and fear. For the person who cannot take this path, self-defence, if necessary with violence, is better than the surrender into impotence, as Gandhi had already said. Because of this commitment to non-violence, many black people saw in King only 'a religious Uncle Tom' and preferred to follow Malcolm X's morality of self-defence.

Martin Luther King always directly set the local actions and experiences of the blacks in the southern states of America in a global context. Things began in Montgomery on a December evening with Rosa Parks, but all over the world exploited people were rising against their oppressors. For King, this was a movement for a new world-wide community of people of all races on the basis of justice. He then also met with agreement and support from all over the world, and he soon went on to develop this 'dream of the better America' into a hope for the whole world, contending that it was impossible to be free in America as long as the peoples of the Third World were not free. For him, freedom was always universal and indivisible. Through their struggle for their rights the blacks in America were to deliver the whites too from racial fear and racial hatred. They were to redeem the soul of America and create 'a beloved community'. 'The Negro is God's instrument to save the soul of America.'[30] So at the beginning of the 1960s King himself became the public spokesman not only of the blacks but of the whites too for 'the dream of our American democracy' – the better, true America.

It was only after 11 August 1965 that he began to have doubts.[31] On that day, following a revolt of the blacks in the Watts ghetto of Los Angeles, the police shot thirty-four people and laid the whole quarter waste. The white reaction was more violent than he had expected, and the blacks turned away from his non-violent methods: 'Burn, baby, burn.' That year the Vietnam war took on new brutality, and King threw himself completely into the anti-Vietnam war movement. The face of America changed. It was no longer the dreamland of freedom. It was a country of repression, internally and externally. 'The judgment of God is now on America,' proclaimed King, just as Malcolm X had also done. He felt that he was called to be a prophet for America, but his sermons no longer fostered the official American optimism.

Martin Luther King always said that he was a 'man of God' and a preacher of the gospel, nothing else. But history made of him an eminently *political theologian*. His best sermons were public speeches, and his public speeches were sermons. This made the American public his congregation, and not the American public alone. The reason was that King had his roots in the black congregation which had always been the centre of the black population. There was no separation there between church and society, religion and politics. King had only made this unity country-wide and world-wide. Adam Clayton Powell Jr complained that the white churches had turned Christianity into a 'churchianity', and in so doing had betrayed the prophetic message about universal freedom and the equality of all.[31] For King, the God of the Bible was the God of world history. Experience of God was present in human experience of life and suffering. The cross of Christ was always linked with the cross of Christ's oppressed, black fellow-sufferers. For King, the righteousness and justice of God was divine and human justice at the same time.

King's theology derived *contextually* from the suffering of the blacks in the United States of America, but it was *universally* related to the freedom of all men and women. He began with the liberation of the oppressed, but at the same time aimed to liberate the oppressors too. *In partisan terms* King was on the side of the blacks, but *dialectically* he also wanted to win over the whites. Practically and in concrete terms he acted *locally*, but he thought *globally*. And that can count as a model for every political theology.

6. James Cone and black theology

There have always been black theologians in the United States. But black theology is a name which James Cone has given to his theological interpretation of the Black Power movement,[33] and since 1969 it has been generally adopted.[34] We shall consider the relevance of black theology for whites by looking at some of its problems.

The name indicates a programme: 1. liberation from 'white theology', with its choice of topics and its methods drawn from the dominant white culture; 2. to make Christian theology as a whole aware of black theology's own subject, context and *kairos*, as well as its own community; 3. to develop a theology based on the particular experience of God and life of black men and women, as this is expressed in the sermons, songs and liturgies of the black churches. The term 'black' means the situation of the descendants of the slaves in the dominant white culture of America, since the colour of their skins was used by white racists as a sign of their degradation to the status of 'niggers'. Black theology is therefore not African theology.

Over against a theology in the African cultural context, this is the theology of the oppressed in the white cultural context.

Does the gospel about the kingdom of God have any special relevance for humiliated people deprived of their rights, who are suffering under the burden of the slavery of their forebears?

Neither in the past nor in the present has European theology made the mass enslavement of black people at the beginning of modern times one of its chosen themes.[35] Luther took no notice of the 'discovery' of America, and Schleiermacher was equally unconcerned about the slave-trade, which was at its height in his time. For Barth, Bultmann and Tillich too, this was not a subject for theology. Consequently it was only in our generation, in the ecumenical context and in the light of the apartheid regime in South Africa, that a discussion emerged about the impossibility of reconciling Christian existence and racism. But that is *the* theme of black theology, its sole purpose: 'to apply the freeing power of the gospel to black people who are under white oppression'.[36] Black theology knows no other authority than the misery of the oppressed and is therefore not prepared to maintain any biblical or theological doctrine 'which contradicts the black demand for freedom now'.[37] For in the sense defined above, to be black is 'holy' and a symbol for the saving and judging presence of God in history for the sake, and for the benefit, of oppressed men and women. 'Where there is black, there is oppression, but . . . where there is blackness, there is Christ, who has taken on blackness so that what is evil in men's eyes might become good.'[38]

In his second book, *A Black Theology of Liberation*, Cone drew on Tillich's concept of symbol to describe concrete blackness in the USA in its universal meaning for all the damned of this earth. He wrote: 'The focus on blackness does not mean that only blacks suffer as victims in a racist society, but that blackness is an ontological symbol and a visible reality which best describes what oppression means in America.'[39] If God's liberating presence in history is to be found at the place where people are suffering from the injustice of oppression by other people, then blackness is also 'the most adequate symbol for pointing to the dimensions of divine activity in America.'[40]

This leads to the theological question: *is God 'black'?* Quite early on, black preachers and poets saw God like this, but it was Cone who first justified this talk of God theologically: the 'blackness of God' is at the heart of every black theology, for it says that God identifies himself with the oppressed and makes their humiliation his own. Cone points to God's identification with the enslaved people of Israel in their bondage in Egypt, and to the hymn in Philippians 2 which tells how Christ himself took the form of a slave and became 'the Oppressed One', in order to free the enslaved. A moving spiritual tells the same thing:

> Were you there when they crucified my Lord
> Were you there when they crucified my Lord?
> Oh! Sometimes it causes me to tremble, tremble, tremble;
> Were you there when they crucified my Lord?

The answer:

> I know what he went through
> because I have met him in the high place of pain,
> And I claim him as my brother.[41]

For Cone, God the Father identifies himself with oppressed Israel, the Son becomes himself the Oppressed One in order to free the prisoners, the Spirit of this Father and this Son becomes energy in the self-liberation of the oppressed.

But 'God is black' also means: 'We must become black with God.' Bonhoeffer said something similar in his Gestapo cell: 'Only the suffering God can help,' and 'Christians are beside God in his suffering.'[42] In the history of injustice and violence God takes the part of the oppressed and the poor, in order to redeem all human beings from evil. In this history, to be partisan is the dialectical way to the universality of the kingdom of freedom. For Cone, God cannot be colourless or colour-blind, because the human history of violence does not allow him to be neutral or indifferent towards victims and perpetrators. God loves the people at the bottom of the ladder, and puts down the mighty from their seats. The liberal abandonment of talk about God's wrath is false. God's love for the whites can only mean wrath, and that means the destruction of their whiteness and all the privileges which they have associated with it.

It is quite consistent that Cone should develop a *theology for the victims* but not a theology for the perpetrators, or only indirectly. God is the God who creates justice for those who suffer violence, not the God who justifies the sinners. His Christ is the saviour of the sick, the brother of the poor, the liberator of the oppressed. Right down to his death on the cross, he is *the Oppressed One*. The slaves understood the suffering Christ, and knew that he understood them. In this sense Christ is 'the black Messiah' of the humiliated blacks.

That is certainly the picture of the synoptic Jesus of Nazareth rather than the Christ of patristic dogma. But this is not the man Jesus of white, middle-class, liberal theology. This is the assailed, tortured and crucified Son of man and the risen Redeemer of the poor. Here Christ's cross and resurrection acquire paradigmatic significance for the liberation struggle of the blacks. The historical Jesus is the prefiguration of the Christ of the present, and the present Christ is the Christ with, beside and in the blacks who rise up out of their oppression and lethargy. The eschatology of the black spirituals was orientated towards the next world, so that it might give comfort in slavery's vale of tears; but the eschatology of black theology is presentative and aggressive. 'Black Theology has hope for this life.'[43] From the black perspective, Christian hope means participating in the world and making it what it ought to be. Black eschatology 'will not be deceived by images of pearly gates and golden streets' in the heavenly Jerusalem, 'because too many earthly streets are covered with black blood'.[44]

What follows from the black theology of the victims for Christian theology on the other side? As the question suggests: it means first of all that 'white' theology must become truly

Christian theology. The blacks demand that whites abandon their whiteness as a sufficient form of human existence, and at long last take the risk of creating a new humanity, says Cone, rightly. But without the liberation of the blacks from the misery of white racism the whites will not be liberated from the other side of this misery. Until the 'master-slave' system is ended there can be no truly human community.

Black theology opens up for the theology of the whites the unique chance to free itself from the constitutional blindness of white society, and to become Christian theology. If we listen seriously to the stories of the blacks, if we try to understand black theology, we begin to see ourselves and our own history through the eyes of the people who have suffered and are still suffering under our culture and our church. The person who has incurred guilt can no doubt admit his guilt, but only his victims know what suffering his injustice has caused. So we only become free of our own blindness if we see ourselves through the eyes of our victims and identify with them, because it was with them that the Son of man already identified himself (Matthew 25). White Christians should not, one day, have to ask unsuspectingly, 'Lord, when did we see you *black*?' Christ lies before their door as a black. Black theology makes our own task clear in the struggle against the evils of racism, which oppress both victims and perpetrators, even if in different ways.

But people who are personally involved with black theology are also asking whether to describe the blacks only as victims of the ruling whites does not fixate them on the whites in a way that has negative consequences. Black people in America are more than merely descendants of the black slaves. They have also brought into America their own culture and their own forms of religion. So whenever black people in America remember who they are, this brings to the surface their rich culture, even though in many cases it has been suppressed. Black theology must therefore return to the inner traditions of *black religion*, which have been preserved above all in the black churches.[45]

Not least, the symbolic term 'black' for the oppressed must

not reduce to invisibility the particular misery and particular dignity of black women. Today there is a good *black womanist theology*, which on the one hand limits black theology and on the other develops it further.[46]

3

Latin American liberation theology for the First World

1. Personal experiences

It began so hopefully. The year 1973 saw the appearance of the German translation of a book written by Gustavo Gutiérrez, of Lima, Peru – his seminal *Theology of Liberation*.[47] I read it at once with great enthusiasm and held seminars on it, for I found there the perspectives of my own *Theology of Hope* and the praxis of a political theology such as Johann Baptist Metz and I envisaged, though here not in the European context but in the completely different context of Latin America. The way Gutiérrez took up Marxist situation analysis in describing the exploitation and poverty in Latin America was in line with the Christian-Marxist dialogues we had held in Salzburg, Herrenchiemsee and Marienbad in the 1960s. These had been sponsored by the Catholic Paulus Gesellschaft and they had brought us 'from anathema to dialogue', and from dialogue to co-operation in social and economic sectors.

From the theology of liberation that was now beginning we learnt a theology closer to praxis than we were academically used to. It gave us the courage to think again about 'church and people',[48] even though National Socialism had made so frightful a misuse of the concept of 'people'. On the other hand, the first books on the theology of liberation that was just developing in Latin America still reflected an entirely European influence. In Gutiérrez's first book, the philosophers and theologians he cites are almost all European – hardly a single one

from the Latin American traditions. Things were no different in
the work of Juan Segundo, Hugo Assmann and José Miguez
Bonino.[49] Even in their contradiction of the 'First World' in
Europe, they were still living from Europe's revolutionary
ideas. So those of us belonging to the political-theology camp
thought initially of a new 'wonderful friendship' with the new
Latin American theology of this new departure.

It soon emerged, however, that this was an error. The Latin
Americans viewed our approach rather as an attempt to take
possession of their theology for ourselves, an attempt which
they had to resist if they wanted to find their own identity. We
looked for immediate integration into a new, shared community, but what they initially needed was separation. And so
we came face to face with one cut-off after another. They called
their theology a theology of liberation, ours 'liberal theology'
and 'the progressive theology' of the First World; their theology, they claimed, was the fruit of praxis, ours the product of
the study. This seemed to me unfair. Then some of them picked
up the Marxist criticism of *Theology of Hope* and political
theology, criticism they took over from the state ideology of
East Germany (the GDR); and all at once I heard on Brazilian
lips what I had already heard from the GDR state theologians
Müller and Streisand, which had ended in a denunciation to the
East German state security service in 1968, and its imposition
of a speaking ban. The last straw was a visit to Tübingen in
1974 by a group of Marxist-influenced theology students from
ISEDET, Buenos Aires. They came to inform us that they had to
free themselves from all intellectual European influence, and
would therefore no longer be reading Barth, Bultmann, Tillich
– or Moltmann either; for Karl Marx had said that 'all history
is a history of the class struggle'. When asked whether Karl
Marx, then, had been born in Buenos Aires, and what country
their forefathers had emigrated from, they were unwilling to
provide an answer.

At that point I exploded, so to speak. I wrote the 'Open
Letter to José Miguez Bonino', which was also translated into
English and Spanish and in 1976 caused something of a stir.[50] I

asked three questions. 1. What is Latin American about Latin American liberation theology? 2. What is criticism, if in the end the critic says more or less the same thing as the person he criticizes? And 3. Marxism and sociology put theologians on a par with Marxists and sociologists, but do these Marxists and sociologists also bring the theologians to the people? Unfortunately the spontaneous reaction proved to be hostile, as if these questions meant that I rejected liberation theology in general, and had cut myself loose from its advocates. Hugo Assmann was hurt, Rubem Alves embittered. Only Miguez Bonino and Gustavo Gutiérrez seemed pleased about this contribution to the discussion, because they felt that they had been taken seriously. I received no direct responses, but in the next generation I found the liberation theologians turning to their own cultural traditions, pre- and post-Columbian.

In 1977, at the request of the World Council of Churches in Geneva, I undertook a lecture tour through Latin America. I began at ISEDET, Buenos Aires, and finished up in Mexico City.[51] There, after six weeks, a number of liberation theologians were waiting for me at an international conference, 'to crucify me' as Jim Cone put it. They also then tore to bits the 'Theology of Human Rights' on which I lectured. The rupture of communication, which Hugo Assmann especially wanted, depressed me. But next morning, the well-known Cuban theologian Sergio Arce came to my door and asked me to take his son Reinerio Arce Valentin under my wing in Tübingen as a theology student (at that time his son was professor of psychology in Havana). This evidence of trust consoled me. On the flight home I drafted a theology for 'the liberation of the oppressors'.[52]

Through the editorial board of the Catholic reform periodical *Concilium*, I then engaged in a long, friendly discussion with Gustavo Gutiérrez, Leonardo Boff and Jon Sobrino, and finally came to see that my offer of a community to be shared by political theology and liberation theology had been made in a situation when they needed separation in order to come to themselves. I saw that the point where their theology was located – their *locus theologicus* – was different from ours. The *Sitz im Leben* for the theology of liberation is the suffering and dying of the poor. At that time ours was the mutual threat of destruction through the Great Powers with their weapons of mass extermination, which were piled up in both parts of Germany.

In 1991 on a journey through the Goethe Institutes in Central America I then discovered Nicaragua, held lectures and conferences at the great Protestant seminary CIEETS, and threw myself into the foundation of the first Protestant university in Central America, UENIC.[53]

But what bound me most deeply to Latin American liberation theology was a surprising, providential event. On 16 November 1989, in the University of San Salvador, six Jesuits and two women were brutally murdered, so that the courageous voice of Ignacio Ellacuria might be silenced. The soldiers dragged the body of Father Ramon Moreno into the room of the absent Jon Sobrino. A book that had fallen down from the shelves was found lying in Moreno's blood. It was *El Dios Crucificado – The Crucified God*. It now lies there under glass as a symbolic interpretation of the martyrdom of brothers and sisters. I made my pilgrimage there in 1994.

In this chapter I shall treat liberation theology in its own place and situation from the viewpoint of a theologian who lives for it in the First World. I am not in favour of transferring the name 'liberation theology' to other groups of the oppressed, or to other countries. To do so robs it of its originality. So much has been written about the rise and history of Latin American liberation theology that I shall offer no summary, informative account. Whole libraries and many standard works have been written by Latin American liberation theologians themselves,[54] about which I have also already commented.[55] My concern here is only the relevance of their work in Latin America for our work in Europe, and the perspectives for further development in contexts of the threatened world which touch both them and us jointly. I mean by that feminist theology, ecological theology and ecumenical theology.

2. *The exploitation of a continent and the building up of the Western world*

The theology of liberation begins with awareness of the context of the life, actions and thinking of those who want to liberate themselves. In Latin America and the Caribbean this context is the situation of a continent which for more than 500 years was 'discovered', conquered, settled and exploited by Spaniards and Portuguese, and then by the other European nations. What followed the unexpected clash of peoples in unequal civilizations which had developed for more than 40,000 years independently of one another and unconscious of each other? The one civilization came from the neolithic age, the other from the European Renaissance. They had wholly different cultures, mentalities and immune systems. Although they were not numerically superior, these differences brought the Spaniards swift victory, and the Indios certain downfall.

In 1492 the foundations were laid for the new world order which today still reflects the dominance of the Western world. With the 'discovery' of America, Europe moved from its almost peripheral existence in the world as a whole, into the centre.[56] The year 1492 saw the beginning of the European seizure of power over the peoples and continents, and according to Hegel was the hour when 'the modern world' was born.[57]

But what does 'discovery' mean? Ever since the beginning of modern times, discovery has meant more than merely finding something that has been hidden; it has always meant taking possession of what is new and strange as well. Modern 'discoveries' are therefore invested with the names of their discoverers. 'America is an invention of European thinking,' says the Mexican historian Edmundo O'Gorman. The conquistadores found what they were looking for because they invented it. The particular life and independent cultures of the Aztecs, Mayas and Incas were not perceived, and have still not been perceived even at the present day; they were suppreseed, as being different and strange, and were sacrificed to the culture of the conquerors.[58] Islands, mountains and rivers lost their Indian names and were given Spanish 'Christian' names instead. The languages and writings of the indigenas were forbidden and burnt. The conquests were justified with the myth of 'unclaimed property', which belongs to whoever takes possession of it. And with the missionizing of America's subjugated peoples, European Christendom also set out on the road to world hegemony. America's conquerors were motivated to their great deeds and misdeeds by two things: 'God and gold'. We shall look first at the one and then at the other, in order finally to view the end of the Third World and its 'superfluous people' which are now no longer needed.

What hope motivated the Spanish and Portuguese conquerors? It was the messianic vision of the 'New World'.

Columbus evidently sought for both God's Garden of Eden and Eldorado, the city of gold.[59] Apart from personal enrichment, the gold was designed to help the reconquest of Jerusalem by the Christian empire. He appealed to a prophecy of Joachim of Fiore: 'From Spain will come the one who will bring the Ark back to Zion'; for he and the conquistadores who followed him saw their conquests apocalyptically. It was the 'Iberian messianism' of the quintomonarchianists.[60] According to their vision of world history, which was borrowed from Daniel 2 and 7, the rise and fall of the four great empires of Babylon, Persia, Greece and Rome will be followed by the redeeming empire of the divine Son of man: 'His dominion is an everlasting dominion and his kingdom one that shall not be destroyed' (Dan. 7.14). Then 'the saints of the Most High shall receive the kingdom, and possess the kingdom for ever, for ever and ever' (7.18). 'And the kingdom and the dominion and the greatness of the kingdoms under the whole heaven shall be given to the people of the saints of the Most High; their kingdom shall be an everlasting kingdom, and all dominions shall serve and obey them' (7.27).

But whereas according to Daniel this empire of the Son of man is the great divine *alternative* to the 'bestial' empires of the world, the conquistadores interpreted it as 'the fifth empire' which was to consummate previous attempts at world-wide rule. The fifth earthly empire was to be the universal Christian monarchy in which there is only 'one flock and one shepherd': *Fiat unum ovile et unus pastor.*[61] Its capital had to be Jerusalem, according to ancient prophecy, for there Christ's 'second coming' was to take place. For this they transferred the ancient *translatio imperii* theory from the world of the West to world history: the universal Christian monarchy is the true legal heir of the ancient empires and the fulfilment of humanity's dream of the unifying kingdom of the world 'which shall have no end'.[62] The Iberian quintomonarchians – the court theologians of the Spanish kings – set the empire of Charles V in this historical framework, which was both universal and messianic: 'You are on the way to the universal monarchy, when Christendom will be gathered under one shepherd' (Mercurino Gattinara, 1519).[63]

The discovery and conquest of the new continent was one of the final acts in this eschatological drama of salvation, and this apocalyptic interpretation for its part justified the violence which the Christian rulers were bound to use in taking possession of the whole earth and converting the peoples. The rulers also justified the violence through the 'stone', which according to Daniel 2.34f. shatters the kingdoms of the world, a symbol for the eternal kingdom of God which will 'break them in pieces' (2.44).

The sources of this political theology of Christian world conquest are manifold. Some writers point to the strong Jewish influence on Iberian Christendom. Jewish Christians, they claim, transferred the messianic longing for a universal, eschatological kingdom of peace to the Castilian monarchs, later the Catholic kings.[64] But because the 'discovery' of America in 1492 coincided with the final expulsion of the Moors from Spain, we may also think of Byzantium, which had fallen to the Turks in 1453. Just as Turkish Islam was victorious in the East, European Christendom achieved victory in the West, through the Spanish monarchy. Thus Spain also took over Byzantium's political theology in order to justify the conquest of the world, the purpose of which was to establish universal Christian rule. This Byzantine political theology was also quintomonarchian, taking up Daniel's 'image of the monarchies'. The Christian imperium is the goal of the divine salvific plan for all peoples.[65] Yet quintomonarchianism had probably always been the inspiration for the political theologies of the Christian empires, so it is no wonder that we find it again in Columbus too and in the theologians of the Spanish world conquests in America.

The Spanish and then the Portuguese mission in America was merely the religious side of the spread of the end-time universal Iberian monarchy. The *reconquista* of Spain from the Moors and the forcible conversion or expulsion of the Jews was already intended to establish the purely Christian empire. This *reconquista* was merely extended in the *conquista* of America. Whereas in Spain the motto was baptism or expulsion, in America it was baptism or death. Just as the struggle against the Islamic empires took on the apocalyptic features of the struggle against the Antichrist, so the struggle against the Indio empires in America bore the apocalyptic characteristics of the struggle against the idolatory of the devil worshippers. As Las Casas bitterly complained, this was not the fight for the souls of the American peoples with the gospel and in love.

But what gave the conquistadores their superiority over the much larger and more powerful kingdoms of the Aztecs, the Mayas and the Incas? Huge empires were shattered with absurdly small troops. This is not easily explained, but there are two immediately plausible reasons: smallpox and canons.

The epidemics of the smallpox brought in by the Europeans had an appalling effect. The mediaeval epidemics had given the Europeans immunity, but not the Indios. The 'microbe shock' spread much more swiftly than the military conquest.[66] Before Pizarro came to the Incas, smallpox was already there and had decimated the population.[67] It was an unconscious but sustained 'bacteriological warfare', which depopulated whole areas. Even in the nineteenth century the Indian tribes of the Kiowa in North America were still ruined by smallpox epidemics. The conquerors were certainly not aware of the epidemics they brought with them, but they interpreted the mass mortality of the natives as a 'divine punishment' inflicted on them, and a 'providential gift' to themselves.

The modern European canon technology, the armed riders on horses, which were still unknown to the Indians, the trained fighting dogs and, not least, the Spanish method of waging war which was designed to wipe out the opponent completely: all these proved superior to the armies of the Indians, much more numerous though they were, and produced a 'military shock'; for the Aztecs kept to the tradition of ritual warfare. Todorov has shown this convincingly by comparing the mentality of Montezuma (Moctezuma) and Hernan Cortes.[68] The Aztec king had a deterministic understanding of history and a fatalistic submission to fate. Because events take a cyclical course, everything is foreordained and has already been there before. Recurring events are answered by the appropriate rituals, not by the personal free decision with which we react to what is new in history. The Aztec communication system was aligned, not towards contact between human beings, but rather towards cosmic events, as a way of establishing harmony with the forces of nature. Hernan Cortes, on the other hand, was a European, an open and adventurous man of the Renaissance, who could react to new situations with decisions that had no precedent. He could enter into the mind of the Aztec prince in order to outwit him, as a hunter outwits the animal. He knew only 'human communication at the expense of communication with the world'.[69]

European world conquest still always follows the same lines: first come the ethnologists, then Coca Cola; first exploration, then domination, then marketing. But what Europeans gain in power over the other peoples and over the earth they lose in their now-failing ability to integrate themselves into the rhythms and cycles of the earth. The person who only wants to know the world in order to master it, ceases to be in harmony with it. With the European conquest of the world the modern man-made ecological world-wide catastrophes began.

The exploitation of Latin America started with the Spanish

gold fever. According to Marco Polo's fabulous reports, the countries of the Far East were supposed to possess gold in plenty. After the war against the Moors, the Spanish treasury was empty. To acquire gold was therefore in the interests of the Spanish crown. The first question the 'discoverers' put to the natives was always the question about gold. That was how the myth about Eldorado, the city of gold, began. Expeditions looked for it in vain in Florida, on the Amazon, and in the Andes. Their greed for gold and their talk about God made gold and the conquerors' God synonymous for the Indians.[70] 'Gold is the Christian God. Let us sink it in the sea, so that they will leave us in peace,' said one of the chiefs.

After the gold came *silver*. The wealthiest silver town was Potosi. In 1573 the town had as many inhabitants as the European capitals Rome, London or Paris at the same period. The silver mountain was 15,680 ft high. Today it looks like a pierced ant hill, and is an exhausted slag heap. Between 1503 and 1600 three times more silver was taken to Spain from America than the estimated total reserves in Europe.

The precious metals torn out of the new colonies furthered the economic development of Europe – one might even say they made it possible.[71] But at the end of the seventeenth century Spain had control of only 5% of its own trade with its colonies; 95% was in other European hands.

After gold and silver came the great plantation empires. Sugar cane, coffee, cotton and tobacco were crops that needed those enormous numbers of black slaves. Through the exploitation of the colonies by the mother countries, colonial aristocracies developed there which piled up enormous wealth, and continue to do so – but the wealth is invested in Europe, not at home. From this class come the military dictators who put down every revolt by the poor, and the killer gangs who murder protesting and defiant Christians, such as Archbishop Romero and the six Jesuits in San Salvador.

For centuries the Spanish and the Portuguese and the Catholic Church have maintained that the extermination of whole peoples and the destruction of their civilizations in

Central and South America was nothing but a *leyenda negra*, the 'black legend' and defamation which was started by Bartolomé Las Casas and spread by the Anglican English and Calvinist Dutch, in order to discredit the Catholic kings of Spain and the Catholic Church. Las Casas' indictment was certainly spread by Protestant printers in Europe, but it is true for all that. Twenty-five years after the landing of Columbus, all the native people on Guanahani were dead. According to Las Casas' report, Cuba was almost completely deserted a few decades after its 'discovery'. Todorov thinks that c.1500 there were about 80 million people south of the Rio Grande. In 1570 there were only 10 to 12 million. When the conquerors arrived, about 25 million people were living in Mexico; round about 1600 it was only one million. The decimation of the population by approximately 70 million people in seventy years must be viewed even without any 'black legends' as 'the greatest genocide' in the history of humanity.[72] The reasons have already been stated: subjugation, enslavement, conversion and smallpox.

The analysis of *Latin America's present situation* from which the first generation of liberation theologians proceeded was dominated by the *development* theory.[73] With its help, Catholic liberation theologians interpreted the 'signs of the time', as *Gaudium et spes* had proposed. 'Natural theology' was now replaced by sociological analysis as the presupposition for the 'theology of grace', which then became the 'theology of liberation'. Between about 1950 and 1960 the conclusion of the socio-economic analysis was 'under-development', and the therapy for the Latin American countries was therefore called 'development', modernization furthered by every conceivable 'catching-up' strategy. Major projects for producing energy, and for production aimed directly at the world market, were supposed to let Latin America 'catch up' with the developed countries. The educated classes and the political class took over President John F. Kennedy's 'alliance for progress' from the United States. Theologians tried to find a 'theology of development'. After twenty years of a development policy of this kind,

the results were devastating: the ousting of the country population for the benefit of the agro-industry, slums in the growing
cities, debt in the state budgets.

Under the influence of the successful socialist revolution in
Cuba in 1959 and Allende's policies in Chile, from 1960
onwards a different analysis became more relevant: the dependence theory. According to this, economic progress is always
unequal: the progress of the one is at the expense of others. The
differences between poor and rich are growing. At the centre,
power is increasing; at the peripheries dependence. Latin
America was a European colony and its development did not
go hand in hand with progress in the First World, but was
marginalized. If this analysis is correct, the goal can only be
'liberation' from this growing dependence. This interpretation
of the Latin American situation became the current frame of
reference both for the liberation theologies and for the declarations of the Latin American episcopate in Medellin in 1968 and
Puebla 1979 on 'the pastorate for the poor'.[74]

The theory of economic dependence says that between
equally strong economic entities independencies develop, but
between entities of unequal strength, dependencies. That
applies between countries, between social classes, to the relationship between urban and rural areas, and so forth. This
theory seems correct if we look at the consequences in the Third
World. But it provides only exogenous or external reasons and
neglects the endogenous or internal ones. That is to say, it sees
the Latin American countries only in their relationship to the
countries of the First World, but not in relation to themselves.
The dependence theory has a number of different schools,
which differ according to the subject of the liberation in view:
for the nationalist school, it is the state; for the Marxist school,
the exploited classes; for the populist school, 'the people'. The
one looks to the military, the other to the Communist party, the
last to popular organizations. The first generation of liberation
theologians started from the Marxist analysis for the most part,
but not from the therapy offered by the Communist party; it
looked rather to the spontaneous popular organizations of

workers on the land, and people living in the slums. The class-struggle analysis was widespread between the Cuban and the Sandanista revolutions. The repressions of the military dictatorships also proved its justice. Alliances grew up between Christians and socialists in many countries, as is evident from the famous 1972 conference 'Christians for Socialism' in Santiago di Chile, but it was only in a few places that the people were successfully mobilized.

These early dependence theories put forward undifferentiated, monocausal explanations for the impoverishment of the masses in Latin America. But the accusations of guilt levelled at the exploitative First World – justifiable as those accusations are, in our view – did not lend force to the people's own energies in their struggle for liberation. A one-sided, inadequate picture of human beings developed too. It is not enough to define people only as 'the poor' over against 'the rich', and to leave their other qualities unnoticed. 'The poor' do not want to be addressed only in the context of what they *do not have*, but also, and first of all, for what they *are*. 'The poor' in Latin America are also Indios and mestizos with their own culture, blacks and mulattos, women and men. They have preserved a culture which has been repressed for 500 years; they have developed Afro-Brazilian cults, live from their own stories, their music and their dances. The analysis of 'the poor' in comparison with 'the wealthy' must therefore give way to a more differentiated, multi-perspective analysis of the richer and more complex reality.[75]

That is what is happening in the second generation of liberation theologians. There is now an awareness of the situation of women, the race problems, the dialogue with the ancient cultures, the ecological catastrophes. Not least, there is an open question: the question whether the awakening and self-liberating Indios still need a Christian theology at all, or whether they are not rather seeking for their liberation in their own ancient religions.[76]

3. The preferential option for the poor – the option for Christ

We shall now look at some of the most important theological theses of liberation theology, discussing them, but without any attempt at completeness. Critical comments mean that these theses are being taken seriously.

Liberation theology can appeal to two important preparatory statements by the church: the declarations of the bishops' conferences in Medellin in 1968 and in Puebla in 1979. I shall cite them in some detail in order with their help to be in a position to refute Cardinal Ratzinger's biassed criticism of liberation theology.

MEDELLIN 1968

'We are on the threshold of a new historical era in our continent, which is full of *longing to come of age, for liberation from every form of slavery, for personal maturity and the integration of all.* Here we perceive the first signs of the painful birth of a new civilization. We cannot avoid interpreting this gigantic effort for speedy change and rapid development as an evident sign of the Spirit, who leads the history of men and women and peoples towards their calling' (Pope Paul VI, Encyclical *Populorum Progressio*, No. 15). 'We Christians must indeed never cease to anticipate the *presence of God*, who desires to redeem *the whole human being*, soul and body' (Constitution on the Church 3). 'Just as Israel, the first people, once experienced God's saving presence when he freed her from the oppression of Egypt, . . . so we too, the new people of God . . .'

PUEBLA 1979

'With renewed hope in the enlivening power of the Spirit we adopt once more for ourselves the view of the Second General Assembly which expressed *a clear and prophetic, preferential and solidaric option for the poor . . .* We affirm the need for the *conversion of the whole church in the sense of a preferential option for the poor with a view to its comprehensive liberation*. . . If we approach the person who is poor in order to accompany him and serve him, we do what *Christ taught us to do*, when *he, as poor as us, became our Brother.* Hence the ministry to the poor is a *preferential,* even if not an *exclusive, component* of our discipleship of Christ . . . The commitment to the poor and oppressed and the growth of base communities have helped the church to discover the *evangelistic potential* of the poor, since they continually face the church with questions by calling it to repent and be converted, and since many of the poor in their lives translate into action the values of the gospel – solidarity, service, simplicity, and the readiness to receive the gift of God.'[77]

The remarkable points in these two church documents, to which every Latin American Catholic liberation theology appeals, are the following:

1. In *Medellin* the liberation movements on the Latin American continent were interpreted as 'signs of the time', which the church has to accept, so that it may be present where people are living, suffering and hoping. They are signs of the Holy Spirit in human history.

2. In *Medellin* the indivisible wholeness of salvation is stressed: human beings are to be redeemed soul and body. No distinction is made between this world and the next, between well-being and salvation, liberation and redemption, since 'God's presence' is comprehensive and cannot be restricted.

3. The church as 'the new people' of God is seen in the perspective of God's 'first people' and the Exodus story of its liberation. 'As once   . . . so we too . . .'

4. In *Pueblo* the familiar 'preferential and solidaric option of the church for the poor' was firmly established and made an essential component of the ethics of the discipleship of Christ and of Catholic social teaching.

5. In *Pueblo* the 'evangelistic potential of the poor' for the

conversion of the church was perceived, a potential which could bring the church to turn away from oppressive forms of domination to the service of Christ.

6. The person who turns to the poor turns to Christ, who became poor like us, so as to become our Brother.

7. Commitment to the poor and the base communities of the poor leads the church towards the conversion which is required today.

The various theologies of liberation are interpretations and expositions of these preparatory statements made by the church. That is not surprising, since a number of liberation theologians co-operated in the formulation of these official texts.

It follows from what the texts say, first, that the *theological location* of the texts must be looked for among the poor, to whom the preferential option of the church applies. But in addition the original *subject of the theology* must be sought for in the 'commitment of these people' and in 'their struggles to become free human beings'.[78] But this necessarily and essentially leads theology beyond the church as it exists at present. The church becomes the church of the poor when it becomes *the church of the kingdom of God*, a church in which the kingdom arrives at its all-embracing liberty. The preferential option for the poor is first and foremost an *ecclesiological* term for a new orientation and social location of Christ's church, and it is therefore also a political and *moral* term for solidarity with the poor, protest against poverty, and the church's own commitment to the poor. But underlying this option too is the theological concept of *God's* option for the poor, which is already expressed in the Old Testament: '[The Lord] executes justice for the oppressed' (Ps. 146.7). In the New Testament this theological concept is christologically fulfilled through the One who proclaims the kingdom of God to the poor and calls them blessed in the light of the kingdom, the One who himself became poor in order to make many rich, and who called 'the least' among the people his brothers. The link between the ecclesiological and political concept of the option for the poor and the theological and christological concept is seen as it is seen in Phil. 2.5: 'Let *this mind* be among you which was also in Christ Jesus' – and then follows the hymn extolling the Christ who 'emptied himself' and was exalted by God. The God of the poor is manifested in Christ, who emptied himself 'unto death, even death on the cross'. The option for the poor therefore leads to a theology of the cross, as Jon Sobrino made clear from the example of Archbishop Oscar Arnulfo Romero: 'In the poor he came upon that which, understood in the Christian sense, is the scandal in the mystery of God. In the crucified men and women of history the crucified God made himself present to him . . . It was in their faces especially that he glimpsed the disfigured face of God.'[79] But as their hope too 'the God of the poor' is manifested in Jesus' message about the kingdom, and in his resurrection from the dead into the liberty of God. The church comes close to the mystery of redemption when it comes close to the poor. In fellowship with them, it becomes assured of its own hope. The people of God therefore belongs to the community of the fellow citizens of God's kingdom; and according to Christ's message, in this world these are the poor and the children.

Since the option is called preferential, it must not be understood in a one-sided exclusive sense. It is meant in a one-sided *inclusive* sense. God has mercy on the poor so that through them he can save the rich too. The poor are saved through their liberation, the rich through God's judgment on their unjust wealth. So through the one-sided and 'preferential' option, all will finally be saved. For the different dimensions of theology touched on here, the 'preferential option for the poor' is the preliminary decision, or preliminary understanding (*precomprensión*), for absolutely every liberation theology.[80] And that is reason enough for us to look at two critical points:

(a) Is the call for an option *for* the poor directed to the poor or the non-poor? Does the solicitous 'for' not imply a detachment, a distance from the poor – a distance which the option is supposed to bridge, but which is thereby at the same time actually deepened?

In Germany we have already twice had similar discussions about the 'for', the first of them in connection with Dietrich Bonhoeffer's formulations about 'the church *for* the world', 'the church *for* others'. In spite of all the self-relinquishment they call for, they have unintentional undertones of solicitude, advocacy, patronage, and an elitist rule over the others, disguised as 'responsibility', so that it would be better to talk about a church *with* the world and a church *with* others. Anyone who does something 'for other people' must first of all be there 'with the others'. No one can do anything good '*for* the poor' who does not live '*with* the poor'; for it is not just the giving that is a problem for us human beings; it is the taking in dignity too. The preferential option *for* the poor must never make the poor the object of missionary endeavours, charitable care and revolutionary leadership. That would be a fundamental misunderstanding of what it means. The poor do not need any 'carer' or welfare officer, advocate or leader. They need brothers and sisters who live with them and listen to them before they talk to them.

The other discussion was raised in the socialist context. The 'socialism as it really exists' of the Marxist-Leninist state party saw itself as 'socialism *for* the people'. The anarchist 'socialism *of* the people' was already put down in Russia in 1918 with the Kronstadt rising. The socialist state elite therefore lived in their own, protected quarters, cut off from the ordinary population, and no longer knew the people they wanted to create socialism *for*. That was the beginning of the end of the socialist world in Eastern Europe. Marx had still called religion 'opium *of* the people', and discovered in it longing and protest. It was only Lenin who described religion as 'opium *for* the people', so that the role of religion could be taken over by 'the truth of socialism'. But there is no such thing as democracy *for* the people but only *of* the people and *by* the people, and the same thing is true of socialism, religion and the church. The preferential option *for* the poor therefore presupposes the option *of* the poor for a *church of the poor*.[81]

(b) This was what *Puebla* meant by the phrase about the

'evangelistic potential of the poor' which the church had to discover; for in that potential the poor are subjects, not objects. It is not the church which converts the poor; it is the poor who convert the church to Christ. The 'good news' of the poor for all human beings is the presence of Christ among them and the kingdom of God which begins in their midst. It was the poor in El Salvador who 'converted' Archbishop Romero. The poor are recognized as the subjects of a divine mission when we talk about the 'prophecy of the poor', 'the evangelism of the poor' or 'the messianism of the poor'. But one must take care not to burden the poor unduly with surpluses of theological significance of this kind. After all, the poor do not 'opt' for poverty, and people who are suffering from exploitation and oppression, and whose situation is desperate, are not inclined to suffer for the redemption of the world; they want to be freed from their poverty and suffering.

If we take seriously the story about the Last Judgment of the Son of man/Judge of the world in Matthew 25, it carries us a step beyond awareness of the 'evangelistic potential of the poor'. Here the Son of man *identifies himself* with the poor and suffering in this world: 'As you did it to one of the least of these my brethren, you did it to me' (25.40). And in the Last Judgment he *decides* about people according to what they did to 'the least', in whom he himself was present. According to this powerful story, there is a twofold 'fellowship of Christ': the community of the righteous and the community of 'the least'. The one is the manifest fellowship of Christ, the other the hidden fellowship. So the important thing is to bind the fellowship of believers to the fellowship of the least, in whom Christ waits for those who are his.[82] The 'preferential option for the poor' is the option for Christ, who is present in them.

The next step leads us to see in the poor the present Christ, and in their sufferings the sufferings which according to Col. 1.24 'complete' the sufferings of Christ for the redemption of the world.[83] 'The crucified people' is then nothing less than 'the historical prolongation of the suffering servant of God'. That is then another collective interpretation of the 'suffering servant' of Isaiah 53. Even if liberation theologians such as Ellacuria and Sobrino initially establish only analogies between the figure of the suffering servant and the suffering people in Latin America, it was nevertheless their intention to ascribe to the sufferings of their people salvific and redemptive effects. The 'crucified people' then becomes the 'light-bringer and bearer of salvation' and in these functions assumes the position of the true church. This idea is not in itself new or revolutionary. It is a consistent further development of the 'body of Christ' ecclesiology of Catholic tradition. But what *is* new and revolutionary is its transference to the poor. According to Pius XII's encyclical *Mystici Corporis* of 29 June 1943, *the church* is *Christus prolongatus* and *alter Christus* – 'the prolongation of Christ' and 'the other Christ'.[84] So if the real presence of Christ is to be found in the poor, if he shares their fate and they share his, then they too are *'altera Christi persona'*. Just as the sufferings of the martyrs, in supplementing the sufferings of Christ, are co-redemptive sufferings, so the poor today truly bear 'the sins of the world', and logically speaking their sufferings are also 'co-redemptive sufferings of Christ'. If they are 'the body of Christ' in a transferred sense, then – as Pius XII said of the church – they also support Christ 'in carrying out his redeeming work'.

Here two serious objections must be voiced. If the image of 'the crucified people' who literally bear 'the sins of the (violent and brutal) world' because they *have* to bear them is extended to all the oppressed in the Third World, then people who have never heard of Christ, are not baptized, but have other religions (like the mass of Hindus in India) quite involuntarily become 'the body of Christ'. This means that the Christian identity of liberation theology gets lost, and what is left is then only the liberation of the oppressed in general.[85] And if 'the crucified peoples' are to redeem the world, who then redeems the crucified peoples? This objection already suggests itself if Isaiah 53 is interpreted in a collective sense: if Israel is the suffering Servant of God, who then redeems Israel? The sufferings of Christ for the redemption of the world are the sufferings God freely takes on himself. Only divine suffering can reconcile the world. Aren't theologians imposing a burden on the suffering poor if they give their suffering a religious significance of this kind? And aren't they thereby 'eternalizing' this suffering, from which the poor after all want to be freed? For the rich, it is important to see the sufferings of the poor in the image of the suffering Christ, so that they may turn back from their brutal and violent world in order to find Christ, and to become true human beings. But does it help the poor?

It is useful theologically to distinguish between an *exclusive* and an *inclusive* meaning in the sufferings and death of Christ. Reconciling and redemptive sufferings are solely Christ's affair. It is for that reason alone that the divine reconciliation and redemption of the world can be seen in his death on the cross. But at the same time, in Christ's sufferings and death there is also the martyr's suffering endured by God's 'true and faithful witness' (Rev. 1.5). As such his suffering belongs within the great fellowship of God's true and faithful witnesses, before Christ, after him, and with him. According to Hebrews 11, it was the witnesses of Israel who *before* him bore 'the shame of Christ'; *after* him it was the Christian apostles and martyrs who bear this shame *with* him. I believe that Col. 1.24 is thinking of these sufferings of the witnesses when it talks about 'completing' the martyr sufferings of Christ. There is no thought of a 'co-reconciling and co-redemptive suffering' on the part of the apostle. If Christ suffers 'the sins of the world' *vicariously*, then he also suffers 'the sufferings of the poor' *in solidarity* with them, and takes from them the burden of all sacrificial notions, so that they can 'lift up their heads' in his fellowship, and free themselves from the constraints which the violent and brutal have imposed on them.

4. Historical liberation and eschatological redemption

Do liberation theologians maintain a 'pure immanentism'? Do they reduce 'the salvation of the soul' to 'social salvation'? Do they disperse the kingdom of God in the 'progress of history'?

Ought Catholic priests to concern themselves only with 'eternal life', not with the life of society, as John Paul II demanded on his visit to Nicaragua in 1985? These reproaches were the subject of the offensive which the Prefect of the Congregation for the Doctrine of the Faith, Cardinal Ratzinger, started against the liberation theologians in Latin America in 1984 and 1985. They turn up again and again in denunciations. I shall refute them on the basis of Gustavo Gutiérrez's first book, *A Theology of Liberation* (first published 1972, ET 1973/74).

The theology of liberation was initially a theological interpretation of the processes in which human beings free themselves in history from oppression and make themselves the determining subjects of their own history. This presupposes that history is moving progressively towards a goal, and can therefore also be understood as a unified complex of events. That is the general view of history taken by the modern Western world, and the belief in progress which is inherent in it. The classic dialectical formulations can be found in Hegel and Marx, the classic linear formulations in Darwin and Teilhard de Chardin. Catholic theology has always interpreted 'nature' in the light of grace. Ever since *Gaudium et Spes* (1965) it has interpreted 'nature' as history with the help of 'signs of the time' in the light of the eschatological hope; and as Medellin and Puebla show, it admits the historical dynamic of the various peoples. What the liberation theologians call the 'dynamic' of the peoples in their yearning for freedom and their struggles for liberation entirely corresponds to the spirit of the Second Vatican Council, in which the church tried to catch up with the dynamic of the modern world.

On the other hand, liberation theology is itself a liberating force, with its own theological dynamic. It takes this from the prophetic traditions of the Bible, from Maurice Blondel's 'theology of action', and from the rediscovery of the eschatological dimension of Christian theology. Liberation theology belongs together with the Catholic Bible movement and the Catholic base-community movement as part of the new Christian dynamic in Latin America. In its context, its *kairos*, and for the poor people in Latin America, it is the successful synthesis of prophetic theology and the will to be free on the part of the oppressed. It is neither merely a – superfluous – religious interpretation of the political situation, nor an – ineffective – political conclusion from theological postulates; it is Christian theology *in* the political context.

In Gutiérrez, this 'presence' of theology in the real, practical context is to be found on almost every page. He writes that in the degree to which human beings create history, they align themselves towards the gift which gives history its ultimate meaning, and open themselves for it – that is to say for the ultimate encounter 'with the Lord and other people'; for 'it means sinking roots where the pulse of history is beating at this moment and illuminating history with the Word of the Lord of history, who irreversibly committed himself to the present moment of developing humankind to carry that development to its complete fulfilment'.[86]

The strengths of Catholic liberation theology, but some weaknesses too, can be found hidden in the transference of the traditional relationship of nature and grace to history and eschatology. What cannot be consummated through grace or 'the kingdom of God' is occasionally uncritically assumed to be 'nature' or 'the dynamic of history'.

What is *liberty* for the theology of liberation?

When he takes up the modern world's concept of liberty, Gutiérrez calls it 'the possibility of enjoying a truly human existence, a free life, a dynamic liberty which is related to history as conquest'.[87] Human beings create themselves, become aware of themselves, liberate themselves through work, which changes the world and educates men and women: that is the way Hegel, Marx and Freud defined liberty. In defining the theological concept of liberty, Gutiérrez follows Paul: 'St Paul continuously reminds us of the paschal core of Christian existence and of all human life: the passage from the old to the new person, from sin to grace, from slavery to freedom.'[88] How is this theological statement related to the previous secular one? Between nature and grace there is continuity and mutual integration. Everything human is ordered towards completion in 'the free gift of the self-communication of God'.[89] In the history of the world in its most comprehensive sense, Christ became human. Consequently his redemption is the centre of historical development and 'the struggle for a just society is in its own right very much a part of salvation history'.[90] Redemption therefore presupposes the self-liberation of human beings, and completes it. 'This is not an identification,' cries Gutiérrez, in a precautionary reply to the critics he expects.[91] Redemption by God and the self-liberation of human beings interpenetrate one another mutually, and must be seen as 'intertwined'. Redemption cannot in any way be reduced to liberation – nor is redemption a substitute for liberation. The critics have not noticed that here Gutiérrez is no longer thinking in their simplistic alternatives, but *perichoretically*.

But what is the outcome of the 'intertwining' view of self-liberation and redemption according to the pattern of nature and grace? In his first book Gutiérrez seems to accept uncritically the modern aggressive concept of liberty that was behind the European conquest of the world. 'Liberty is *conquista*.' If this was the liberty of the conquerors and rulers, it must also be the liberty of the people who want to free themselves from oppression and dependence. Their determination by others must become self-determination, for they are to become the determining subject of their own history. Human freedom certainly does have this *subjective* side, and means independence. But objectively, freedom is possible only in the community of human beings, and is also *interdependence* in mutual respect and love. Finally, there is personal and shared freedom only if the future is 'full of everything possible'. If nothing more is possible, there is no more freedom either. Freedom has this personal, this shared, and this prospective dimension of future. If we were to describe freedom in these three dimensions only as *conquista*, we would plunge the world into chaos. But the dynamic of the people and of the theology of liberation surely cannot see themselves as a prolongation of Iberian quinto-monarchianism and its messianic conquest of the world!

Those of us who have to live on the side of the perpetrators, not on the side of the victims, perceive another dimension of the history of freedom. In this dimension freedom is not liberation from poverty, suffering and death; it is liberation from historical guilt and its consequences, which are the urge for justification and the compulsion towards repetition. Among us, the history of freedom without redemption from historical guilt becomes the abstract success-story of the Western world, the story of history's victors and the subjugation of weaker peoples and silent nature. But the person who allows only his successes to be ascribed to him, and not his guilt, has not come of age, and makes himself incapable of responsibility. Without redemption from historical guilt the history of emancipation leads to blindness towards the suffering one has inflicted, and to a denial of one's own subjectivity, and hence to the loss of one's own freedom. That is the reason why the liberation theology of the victims cannot be transferred to a liberation theology for the perpetrators.

What is *wholeness* for liberation theology?

Although Gutiérrez does not want to 'identify', his starting point is the unity of history; he no longer wants to distinguish between world history and salvation history. 'There is only one history – a "Christo-finalized" history.'[92] The one history has to do with the salvation of the world. Just as sin is not merely a hindrance to salvation in the next world, but also means a breach with God and the human community in this one, so salvation too is related, not merely to eternal life in the world beyond, but also to the healing of the life that has been broken here through oppression, disease and poverty. The person who fights here against exploitation, participates in the eschatological movement of redemption. [93] Like the Declaration of the Episcopal Conference in Medellin, Gutiérrez relates to each other this world and the world beyond – the world beyond death – in the unrestricted presence of God. 'One looks then to this world, and now sees in the world beyond not the "true life", but rather the transformation and fulfilment of the present life.'[94] Salvation is not another world in the 'beyond'.

It means that this world becomes finally different. In the liberations of the people, their redemption already becomes efficacious in germ: 'Salvation is also an intrahistorical reality.'[95] Here Gutiérrez follows the modern theologians who understand religion no longer as the opium of the next world but as the force for changing this one. This world and the next are no longer two different stages of Being, on earth and in heaven. They are different aeons of the one redemptive process. The times of present and future are *perichoretically* interlaced, as anticipation and consummation.

It is not the holistic thinking for which Gutiérrez is striving that is open to reproach. The criticism which can be made is that he does not think holistically enough, but pays homage to European anthropocentricism. 'Humankind is the crown and centre of the work of creation and is called to continue it through its labour.'[96] Even in 1972 that was no longer true. Even then the extent of the ecological catastrophes had set on foot the reversal process – ecological thinking instead of anthropocentric thinking. Parallel to economic exploitation and racist alienation, industrial pillaging and the destruction of nature is a form of oppression which must be opposed by a holistic process of liberation, if the process is to lead to freedom for the benefit of others and not to freedom at their expense. For a long time the Latin American liberation theologians declared that the 'ecological question' was a typical luxury problem for the First World. But in the last few years they too have become 'green' and ecologically conscious, and recognize the double spoliation of the poor in their country – on the one hand the theft of their freedom, on the other the robbery of the foundations from which they live.[97] Latin America is an eco-logical catastrophe area. To respect the ancient Indian under-standing of nature and to give it new form for the present day is an important contribution which Latin America makes to humanity's problems with the destruction of the environment.

What is *historical progress* for liberation theology?

The idea of the unity of history seen from the perspective of its final goal necessarily leads to the notion of historical progress. If the present is experienced as oppression, and if the future is hoped for as a liberation, it is understandable that history as a whole should be interpreted as the progress of freedom. According to *Gaudium et Spes*, although earthly progress must be distinguished 'from the increase of the kingdom of Christ, such progress is of vital concern to the kingdom of God, insofar as it can contribute to the better ordering of human society'.[98] For Gutiérrez this means: 'There is a close relationship between temporal progress and the growth of the kingdom' although these two processes are distinct:[99] the growth of the kingdom is not indifferent to earthly progress, More, it is the kingdom which first lends earthly progress its value and has a genuine interest in it. In saying this Gutiérrez is picking up Teilhard de Chardin's belief in progress, and his teleology of the Omega Point, and transferring it to political history in Latin America. In his view, whereas traditional Christian circles are often dominated by a certain pessimism, which is the equivalent of a flight from the world, Christians in the Third World take an optimistic view, which aims to reconcile faith and the world, and thus to make an equilibrium possible.[100] The progress of human freedom and the increase of the kingdom of God interpenetrate each other mutually without ever becoming identical in history. In the liberation process the kingdom of God is heralded; in the kingdom of God the liberation process is completed.

Gaudium et Spes, the Latin American Bishops' Conferences and Gutiérrez all give historical teleology the preference rather than historical eschatology. The kingdom of God is in the process of its growing, not in the process of its coming. The end of history is consummation (*telos*), not rupture (*finis*). So the future is that which comes into being *out of* the present, not what *comes to meet* that present; it is not 'the coming', in the sense of that English term for future. Nevertheless, ultimate freedom is not to be the reward for present strivings for liberation; it is God's 'undeserved gift', as Gutiérrez never tires of stressing. But this undeserved gift of completion must already be so present here and now in historical praxis that we can rely on it; for every divine action is dependent on expiation. Bert Brecht put it in secular terms: 'Those of us who wanted to prepare the ground for kindness were unable to be kind ourselves. But you, if the point is ever reached when man becomes man's helper, think of us forbearingly.'[101] Put theologically: Christ is not just the driving power of progress and liberation; he is the redeemer of progress too, and the saviour of the victims of progress and liberation.

Walter Benjamin expressed the intertwining of the historical and the messianic even more cautiously and dialectically: 'Only the Messiah himself completes all historical happening, by himself redeeming, completing and creating its relationship to his messianic future.' That is why 'the kingdom of God is not the *telos* of historical dynamic, and cannot be made its goal. Seen historically, it is not a goal but an end . . . What is secular is therefore not a category of the kingdom, but a category, and the most appropriate category, of its stealthiest approach.'[102]

5. *The Roman fight against liberation theology*

In the spring of 1984, Cardinal Ratzinger, the Prefect of the Congregation for the Doctrine of the Faith, began his fight against the liberation theologians with a 'private study' which was published in *Trenta Giorni* and *Folha di Sao Paulo*. The *Instruction of the Congregation for the Doctrine of the Faith on Certain Aspects of the Theology of Liberation* (*Libertatis nuntius*) then appeared on 6 August 1984.[103] A further, somewhat more differentiated *Instruction* followed in 1986.[104] For his private feud, Ratzinger let fly at Hugo Assmann, Gustavo Gutiérrez and Jon Sobrino – later (and particularly unreasonably) Leonardo Boff – with the aim of proving that their ideas were heretical. Their names did not turn up again in the *Instruction*, but the censure of their alleged ideas remained. It was a matter of wholesale suspicion and the condemnation of 'persons unknown'.

In his previous, private study Ratzinger made 'Rudolf Bultmann' (of all people) 'and his school' responsible for this new political hermeneutic of the Christian faith, and for its revolutionary machinations – which was certainly the last thing Bultmann would ever have thought of; but 'the Bultmann school' was probably also the last thing Ratzinger had clashed with when he was a professor in Tübingen. In the Marxist sector, which was especially censured, only the so-called 'neo-Marxists' Bloch, Adorno, Horkheimer and Marcuse are named. These were important for the students in Tübingen in 1967/68 who had given the professor a hard time,[105] but they hardly meant anything for Latin America. The dependence theory developed by Cardoso (today the President of Brazil) was the starting point for all the liberation theologians; but this is not mentioned at all.

Among the reproaches made in the *Instruction*, Marxism of course takes first place. Objection is taken to 'the insufficiently critical form with which liberation theologians seek refuge in concepts which are nurtured by different trends in Marxist thinking'.[106] But what for the liberation theologians is an analytical instrument – a way of grasping the situations of the poor in Latin America – is for the *Instruction* an anti-church ideology, as Cardinal Höffner observed in an explanatory comment in the same year: 'Marxism is an anti-gospel. If the poor were vehicles of salvation, the salvific work of Jesus Christ would be superfluous.'[107] This judgment about Marxism may perhaps be understandable, as springing from the ideological East–West conflict in the divided Europe of those years; but that Höffner was unable to understand the difference between 'vehicles' of salvation and the 'work' of salvation is astonishing. Leonardo Boff's comment would be apt for most of the liberation theologians: 'If Marxist social analysis can help us to pin down the reasons for oppression, we thank God for it, not Marx. We are not interested in Marxism. Our concern is the praxis of the liberation of our people.' Put in simpler terms: Marxist analysis, yes; communist therapy, no! Hugo Assmann may be an exception, but he is not a 'Protestant', as Ratzinger maintained. The more differentiated the analysis of misery became, with the help of the race question, the culture question, the sexism question and the ecological question, the more the class question became only one among many others. After the disintegration of the Eastern bloc in 1989 and the dissolution of ideological friend-enemy thinking, it ought to be possible to talk about capitalism and Marxism without incurring the reproach of being an enemy of state or church, either from the CIA or by the Congregation for the Doctrine of the Faith.

The second reproach is *'immanentism'*: 'People say that God has become history',[108] and that 'faith' 'is faithfulness to history'. As a consequence, says the document, the kingdom of God is identified with the movements for liberation, class struggle is made a component of salvation history, and the poor are declared to be 'the messianic people of God'. But the traditional doctrine of the church says: first the relationship to God, then social relationships; first sin as a ruptured relationship to God, then sin as injury to one's neighbour. Consequently salvation first of all is a gift of God's grace, conveyed sacramentally through the church, then liberty and justice too, as Catholic social teaching says.

The charge which follows from this is that liberation theologians disperse the salvation of the soul in social salvation, transform personal sins into structural sins, and thus replace the personalism of Catholic philosophy by Marxist socialism. 'The first consequence of sin is to bring into disorder the relationship between the human being and God. We must not reduce this sphere of sin to what is called "social sin".'[109] 'The root of evil is to be found in free and responsible persons, who are to be converted through the grace of Jesus Christ.'[110] But as I have shown from Gutiérrez's book, he neither 'reduces' nor 'identifies'; he thinks strictly in the pattern of 'nature and grace', and presents the one perichoretically 'in' the other. If that is supposed to be 'immanentist', then the declarations of Medellin and *Gaudium et Spes* are immanentist too.

The last alternative propounded (whether to proceed from the person or the community) was, as we all know, already emphasized by Marx as false: 'Change people, then conditions change too' does not work; 'Change conditions, then people change too' does not work either. So in his Third Thesis on Feuerbach Marx already assumed that there is a dialectical, reciprocal relationship: 'The materialist doctrine about change and education forgets that people are changed by circumstances, and that the teacher must himself be taught . . . The coincidence of changing circumstances and human activity or self-alteration can only be grasped and rationally understood as revolutionary praxis.'[111] In order to do justice to the situation in which people are, we must take into account the asymmetry in the effect good and bad conditions have on human beings: bad conditions (such as slavery, hunger, disease and death) leave people no alternatives, whereas good conditions (freedom, health, wealth, etc.) by no means make people automatically good.

The third charge is that of *dispersion*. 'People are striving to identify the kingdom of God and its growth with the human movement for liberation, and to make history the subject of its own development, as a process of the human being's self-redemption through class struggle.'[112] 'In the same way people place themselves in the perspective of a temporal messianism, which is one of the most radical ways of bringing to expression the secularization of the kingdom of God and its disappearance in the immanence of human history.'[113] In the previous chapter we saw from Gutiérrez's book that both reproaches are without foundation. The vague 'people' who are mentioned apparently exist only in the imaginary world of the creator of the suspicion. No evidence whatsoever is offered. The *Instruction* has quite obviously failed to grasp the perichoretic thinking of the one 'in' the other – of nature in grace, and grace in nature – of the kingdom of God in history, and history in the kingdom of God.

In the new German edition of his book (1992) Gutiérrez once again sums up his theology of liberation:

Every healthy, fruitful liberation theology is embedded in the theology of the kingdom of God. As the very heart of Jesus' message, the kingdom is both God's gift and his charge for

the conduct of the person who says Yes to him. *Already*
reaching into history, the kingdom nevertheless does *not yet*
arrive at its full development in history . . . It is true that there
are realizations of God's kingdom in the here and now, but
these are neither *the* coming of the kingdom nor *the whole* of
salvation; they are anticipatory fragments – together with all
their ambiguities – of a full abundance which will only come
about beyond history. Theological criticism must emphasize
the provisional character.'[114]

It must be said, however, that this final declaration is so
broad-based in its correctness that it can be applied to every
particular situation, or to none. In the *kairos* of the necessary
liberation from oppression, it does not justify the demand 'I
want my freedom *now*.' If this necessity – absolute today and
here and now and for us – is to be filled with the dynamic of
faith, the kingdom of God must be identified with the human
will for liberation and experienced in the messianism of the
lived moment. No one can wager his or her life and risk death
for 'anticipatory fragments in all their ambiguity'. It is not the
general relativism of ambiguous anticipations of the future that
is Christian; it is the perception of God's present *kairos*:
'Behold, *now* is the acceptable time, *now* is the day of salvation'
(II Cor. 6.2). The same is true of the kingdom of God: 'If it is by
the Spirit of God that I cast out demons, then the kingdom of
God *has come* upon you' (Matt. 12.28). So as not to give all the
times equal significance through the 'already, but not yet', it is
important to perceive the *presence of the kingdom of God in
the Spirit*, and in that presence to do what is required *today*. It
is the martyrs who tell us what is timely, and the same is
impressed on us by the Jewish understanding of time: 'When, if
not now? Where, if not here? Who, if not us?'

4

Minjung theology for the ruling classes

1. Personal encounters in Korea

I went to Korea for the first time in March 1975, and at the Hankuk Theological Seminary in Seoul met Professor Ahn Byung-Mu.* I had prepared a lecture on 'Hope in the Struggle of the People' for an Urban Industrial Mission Conference in Tokyo, and in this lecture I linked my personal experiences as a member of a defeated people in three years' captivity as prisoner of war (1945 to 1948) with the hopes of the new political theology which Johann Baptist Metz and I had developed in the Christian-Marxist dialogues of the 1960s.[115] But it was the New Testament scholar Ahn Byung-Mu whose Heidelberg dissertation on 'Jesus and the *Ochlos* in the Gospel of Mark' stimulated us to think about the church and the people of Christ. When I arrived in Seoul, I was greeted by Professor Park Pong-Nang, whom I already knew, and in the Yonsei University guest house met Suh Nam-Dong, one of the founders of Korean minjung theology. I gave my lecture first at Hankuk Seminary and then at other seminaries and universities, and was shadowed in unfriendly fashion by the Korean secret service.

At that time Korea was ruled by the military dictatorship of General Park Chung-Hee. Protesting workers and students were thrown into prison and ill-treated. Mothers wearing black

---

* In Korea, what would be our surnames precede what would be our forenames.

scarves protested in front of Seoul Cathedral. Among my listeners at the Hankuk Seminary were many students with shaved heads. They had just been let out of prison. A photo shows sitting next to me the unhappy student who was condemned to death for alleged espionage for North Korea, and who had appealed in court to my *Theology of Hope*. I intervened several times on his behalf with the Korean courts, but achieved nothing. In May 1975 eleven professors were dismissed from the university without notice, eight Christians and four theologians. At that time the writer Kim Chi-Ha, whose poems passed from hand to hand, was confined in the condemned cell. Kim Dae-Jung – today the President of South Korea – was also in prison. At that time we had his letters from prison translated and published in Germany.

Ahn Byung-Mu and I quickly came to understand each other at a deeper level. I always visited him whenever I went to Korea in the years that followed, and he often came to Tübingen for medical treatment. Today our joint student Dr Park Jong-Wha is Secretary General of the PROK. In 1984, together with Günter Baum, I edited a book with relevant texts from the new minjung theology.[116] Divided Korea and divided Germany had much in common. But minjung theology is the first liberation theology to come from Asia, with critical questions put to the First World, and questions too challenging the modernization of South Korea according to Western standards. In 1975 South Korea was still a Third World development country with stringent exploitation of the working people; today it is a high-tech state with horrific debts. It is true that today the minjung drives a car, as my friend David Suh ironically remarked; but the suicide rate is appallingly high.

It seldom happens that an exegetical discovery in the New Testament leads to a new congregational movement and a new theology. Hardly anything of the kind has happened again since Luther's discovery of the righteousness of God in Rom. 3.28, which set on foot the reform movement in church and society. But during his studies in Heidelberg, Ahn Byung-Mu made an exegetical discovery, and it had theological and practical consequences for the minjung movement in Korea.[117] He discovered that in the Gospel of Mark 'the people' – the poor (*ochlos* in Greek) – do not just have subordinate walk-on parts for Christ and his messianic work, as academic exegesis had always maintained, but that there was a highly intimate mutual relationship between Jesus and the *ochlos*, from the time when he began his public ministry in Galilee until his crucifixion by the Roman occupying power in Jerusalem. He identified himself with them, and they were his 'family'. Ahn Byung-Mu introduced this insight into the Korean Urban Industrial Mission, which took to the streets and went to prison on behalf of the human rights of the underpaid, exploited workers.

The 1960s were the years of the military 'development dictatorship' in Korea. The Urban Industrial Mission was the first church organization to penetrate this society.[118] The purpose of the Christian protests was to build up the people's own organizations in co-operatives, trade unions and support groups. During these years Ahn Byung-Mu and his friends founded the famous Galilee Congregation, a congregation of workers and critical intellectuals, who were continually under the surveillance of the police and the secret service, and were often enough physically attacked. Ahn Byung-Mu himself had to stand trial (Bishop Scharf of the Protestant church in Germany appeared as witness in the proceedings) and was condemned to two years' imprisonment. Founding the Galilee congregation was a practical step based on the thesis of the New Testament scholar Ernst Lohmeyer about 'Galilee against Jerusalem', a contrast which is reflected in the story of Jesus' life. So the Galilee congregation was to represent Jesus' people, contrary to the all-dominating and modernizing city of Seoul. Ahn chose the word *minjung* as the Korean translation for the Greek *ochlos*. It is not a word for the Korean nation, or for the proletariat either (that is called *InMin*). The minjung is the whole suffering underside of the dominant society. For centuries it has developed traditions of resistance. It has again and again been the source of rebellion when the pain and anger

(*Han*) became unendurable, for example in the Tonghak revolt of 1890.

The Korean minjung theology links Jesus' gospel of the poor (*ochlos*) with these native popular and resistance traditions in the same original way as the Minjung congregations do in the poor districts of Seoul. Minjung theology is not a theology that has been made culturally indigenous, like 'yellow theology' before it. It is a contextual theology of the suffering people in Korea, and is therefore open for people all over the world, the people of God's kingdom whom Jesus called blessed. Minjung theology is also the first political theology to exist in Korea, inasmuch as it is bound up with the struggle for human and civil rights, and turns Christians from being a 'people of the church' into 'the congregation of the people'.

2. *Jesus and the people (*ochlos*) in the Gospel of Mark*

Form-critical exegesis has always paid a degree of attention to the people round Jesus according to the Gospel of Mark, but hardly any account has been taken of their social character. Liberal hermeneutics was aligned towards historical persons and 'desocialized' Jesus' sayings and acts, so to speak, so that Jesus, 'the man and his work', stood by themselves and could be applied to other individual persons. But the form-critical method is an exegesis which has to do with social history, and with its help the stories about Jesus appear in a different light. From the very beginning, Mark talks about 'the crowd', 'the many', 'the people'; these were the men and women who gathered round Jesus, the people he lived with and addressed, the people whose sufferings he healed, and to whom he knew himself to be sent by God. Generally they are only called 'the nameless background for Jesus' ministry',[119] a 'background choir' for the appearances of the star, as if Jesus performed his ministry to everyone else, only not to these. But for the New Testament scholar Ahn Byung-Mu this 'crowd', these 'many', this '*ochlos*' are the main reason for Jesus' coming and ministry.

In Mark 1.22, 'they' – the crowd – are mentioned, and at the beginning are referred to in the plural, later in the Greek text through the singular *ochlos* (2.4). The word *ochlos* occurs thirty-six times in the Gospel, not including the plural compounds. That betrays a certain intention. In the Septuagint 'the people' are usually called *laos*. But this word is used for Israel as people of God. The other peoples are called *goyim* in Hebrew, *ethne* in Greek. In Mark's Gospel, *ochlos* means neither Israel as God's people nor the people of the Gentiles. It is a 'people' without religious identity and without ethnic coherence. So who are the people as *ochlos*?

Mark always uses the word *ochlos* for the people who gather round Jesus and follow him. The 'crowd' consists of 'sinners', that is, those excluded from Jewish society. They are the impoverished country people, people off the land (*ha'aretz*), without property, as John 7 and 12 show, people who are not economically in a position to keep the Law of Israel, and are hence looked upon by the Pharisees as *massa perditionis*, the multitude of the lost: 'Cursed are the rabble who do not know the Law' (cf. John 7.49). It is about these people that the Gospel now has the following to say:

Jesus teaches the people (Mark 7.14; 8.34; 5.10);

Jesus has mercy on the people (Mark 6.34);

Jesus heals the sick among the people (1.34ff.; 6.56);

Jesus feeds the people (Mark 8);

Jesus preaches to the people from the ship (3.7ff.);

Jesus proclaims to the people the kingdom of God in parables (4.2ff.); according to Matthew 5, the Sermon on the Mount is addressed to 'the people';

Jesus calls 'the people together with his disciples' to the discipleship of the way of the cross (8.34ff.).

The people among whom he sits and teaches are his 'true family', he has his mother and his brothers told when they are outside, looking for him. These people are not 'the disciples' (as Luther interpolated, because he was unable to believe what he read in Mark 3.34).

Jesus' own mission is directed towards these people: 'The

Son of man came to serve, and to give his life for the many'
(Mark 10.45).

His blood, the cup of the new covenant, is shed for 'the
many' (Mark 14.24).

At Easter he appears to the poor women in Jerusalem and the
disciples 'in Galilee' (16.7). Jesus knows that he is not sent 'to
call the righteous, but sinners' (2.16f.). 'Call' (*kalein*) is the
same word that is used at the call of the disciples (1.20), and
elsewhere in the New Testament it has the sense of choosing.

Conclusion: the *ochlos* is the addressee of Jesus' mission; he
came on behalf of the people, his messianic kingdom is meant
for the poor, his love is for the many.

Consequently:

1. Jesus 'teaches' the people. He does not teach the people the
Torah. He teaches them the gospel of the kingdom, the
messianic beatitudes and the discipleship ethic of the Sermon on
the Mount;

2. It is 'the nameless crowd' who are Jesus' people and
family, not his own family physically speaking, and not Israel,
his 'physically' own people either;

3. *Ochlos* is 'God's people', the people of God's kingdom,
the people of the poor who are 'called' and therefore chosen.

4. The healing miracles of the God's kingdom and Jesus'
table-fellowship with 'sinners and tax-collectors' take place
among these people.

5. When he goes to Jerusalem he calls these people to the
discipleship of the cross.

6. He sheds his blood and gives his life for these people.

Who, in terms of social history, were the *ochlos* at the time of
the Gospel of Mark? Ahn thinks that Mark was writing after
the destruction of Jerusalem in AD 70 and was describing the
homeless, driven-out, scattered people of his time who had been
deprived of their rights, Jews and Christians. They share the
fate of the poorest of the poor, the homeless and the displaced
persons in the Roman empire.

Where is God? The first destruction of Jerusalem and the

Babylonian exile was followed by the growth of Shekinah theology. According to this, God too forsook his dwelling on Zion in order to go into exile with his people. Applied to the expulsion after the year 70, this means that the choosing and liberating God is present among his people, suffering with them. In the poor, homeless people who have been displaced and are therefore lost, God's suffering and accompanying Shekinah is present, a homeless, displaced, poor and scattered God, who wanders with the poor through the dust of the streets. The crucified Christ and the divine Shekinah who suffers in the poor belong together.

Ahn sums this up as follows:

1. *Ochlos* is not the term for a social class. It is a relational term – a rulers' term for the subjugated and dominated. The poor are *ochlos* in relation to the rich. Tax-collectors belong to the excluded rabble, in relation to the Jewish establishment. 'Consequently the term cannot be invested with a particular value or used for an idealization.'[120]

2. The *ochlos* are certainly feared by the unjust and powerful, but they are not organized and therefore cannot be reckoned with as a power faction. The *ochlos* are not the Zealots, who fight against Rome for the nation of Israel. They are the poor, not of much use either for building a state or for a revolution.

3. Jesus is unconditionally on the side of the *ochlos*. He quite evidently has no intention of turning the *ochlos* into an anti-Roman fighting force, but he proclaims to them the kingdom of God as their future, the future which already belongs to them here and now, and he fills this people with new hope and with the vision of a way that can be their own. 'Jesus fights together with the suffering minjung (*ochlos*) on the front of this Advent [of God's].'[121]

3. Messiah and minjung

According to the model in Mark's Gospel, minjung theologians bring Jesus and 'the people' so intimately close that the transitions are fluid, and the characteristics are even interchangeable. We shall therefore first try to discover who Jesus is in the eyes of the *ochlos*-minjung, and shall then see what the *ochlos*-minjung, together with Jesus, become for the world.

In the eyes of the forsaken, scattered and sick minjung, Jesus is not the remote 'Christ of the church with his golden crown'. He is the brother in need, who understands them because he experiences their fate himself. As their brother he is related to the poor, not set over them as their lord and master. This makes a practical hermeneutical 'realization' of Jesus possible in the minjung's own experiences of suffering; 'Jesus in our midst' became the gospel of the minjung pastors. 'Jesus is present when an innocent student under torture refuses to reveal the names of the friends who are "wanted", and is therefore killed; or when a young worker sacrifices his life for his mates. The cross of Jesus is a present reality, and people, baptized and unbaptized alike, take the way of the cross together with Jesus.'[122] This is not metaphorical language. It is one and the same reality, described there with the name of Jesus, here with the name minjung. That only sounds strange and disconcerting to modern Western ears because by personal names we mean individuals existing exclusively for themselves. But if the name 'Jesus' does not mean just a person in himself, but also a life and a life-history in community with the social history of his 'people', the transitions from the Jesus of the minjung to the minjung Jesus become more understandable.

Minjung christology is not the exclusive 'representation' christology of the Reformation's *solus Christus*. It is the inclusive solidarity christology of the divine Brother, who suffers with us and who identifies himself with 'the least' among the people. 'As you did it to the least of these my brethren, you did it to me' (Matt. 25.40). So the least of the minjung belong to his community and represent his presence. Without Jesus' solidarity with the people, Jesus' representation for the people is not conceivable either.[123] All representation christology is based on a christology of solidarity. That is true of Jesus' life and ministry among the people, but it is truest of all of his suffering and death on the cross. The minjung understand him in his suffering because they feel that they are understood by the suffering and dying Jesus. In the daily suffering and sacrifice of the people the image of the crucified Jesus acquires a wholly different meaning from the meaning it has in the lives of rich people in the First World, which, even if painless, are often empty of meaning. Third World theology, as I have shown, is everywhere at heart a theology of the cross. In Korea, the picture of the crucified Jesus speaks to the Christian and the non-Christian minjung because it gives a different answer to the question of suffering from the Buddhism which is dominant there.

If Jesus is identified with the fate of the minjung in this way, is the minjung then identified with Jesus and his mission so that they acquire messianic features? If the Messiah belongs to the minjung, do the minjung then become the Messiah?[124] In divided Korea there is in fact a kind of popular messianism, which goes back to the Tonghak revolt. The widespread Maitreya Buddhism also has messianic features in the 'awakening Buddha' of 'the future' world. The North Korean 'Kim Il Songism', with its Juche ideology, was, and still is, definitely a messianism designed for domination. Kim Il Song certainly claimed to be a Marxist, but he was the self-styled religious saviour and father of the people. Contrary to this political messianism, the South Korean minjung theologians have set the true messianism of the minjung, in order to distinguish 'messianic politics' from 'political messianism'.[125]

If we look at the biblical model for the minjung in the *ochlos* in Galilee, the impression is not so uplifting. There the people are not idealized. They are shown as equivocal, and easily led astray. They left Jesus alone on the cross. But that too is part of the poverty of the people, and is not something for moral and theological criticism. The minjung are only romanticized by people who do not belong to them.

Worth discussing, on the other hand, is the messianic elevation of the minjung's struggle for freedom and their human rights. According to biblical traditions, the messianic liberation

leads to redemption in God's new world. The necessary liberation of the minjung makes these people the subject of their own
history. In this historical liberation the people catch sight of
their future in the kingdom of God, but they are not yet there;
for how they will shape their history after they have won their
liberty is an open question. The hoped-for reunification of
Korea is not yet the resurrection into the life of the world to
come, but it corresponds to that and points towards it, whereas
the painful division of a people and its families contradicts the
kingdom of God as harshly as possible. To put it more directly
and dialectically: the final must be identified with the provisional so as to set free energies for what is final; but the two
must also be differentiated, if there are not to be bitter disappointments. The 'today – here – us' on which every liberation
theology must insist includes this double presence of the final in
the provisional and the provisional in the final; otherwise its
presentative eschatology is not a realistic eschatology.

4. *Who is 'the suffering servant of God'?*

It somewhat took my breath away when, during a discussion in
David Suh's house, Ahn Byung-Mu answered this question by
pointing to the minjung. Who, then, must bear the sins of the
First World? The Third World. Who must endure the exploitation and violence of those in power? The minjung, the poor,
forsaken people. When we sing 'Thou who bearest the sins of
the world', we must in a realistic sense think of the minjung.

But does this involuntary, reluctant, passive endurance of
oppression and exploitation by the poor have any redemptive
meaning, such as we mean when we talk about the 'bearing'
and 'taking away' of sins through the vicarious and representative suffering of the Servant of God according to Isaiah 53,
and the narratives of Christ's passion which were shaped
according to the pattern of that image? If the minjung are not
merely the suffering people but are also the people of God
which through its sufferings redeems humanity, then this puts a
question to the christology, and also raises the question about

an excessive burden laid on the people. At that time I asked Ahn: if the minjung is to redeem the world, like the suffering servant of God, who then redeems the minjung? And if the minjung redeem through their sufferings, how can they struggle so as at long last to overcome this suffering? Who, then, has asked the minjung whether it wants to suffer for the redemption of the world? His answer was the one he had already given in writing: 'In Hebrew thinking we find no clear distinction between individual and community. For example, is the suffering servant in Isaiah 53 an individual, or Israel? Western theologians continually try to understand him as an individual. That is not justified by the facts. It is the attempt to identify him with Jesus as an individual . . . In Asia there is no word for "personality". When we say "human being" it means something collective . . . "Buddha", for example, is not restricted to the individual person Siddharta but is universal – that is to say, from the social aspect a collective.'[126] Ahn has therefore always interpreted the story of Jesus' life as told in the Gospels as a 'socio-biography' of the *ochlos*. The narrative of the passion is a 'condensation of the minjung's suffering destiny'. 'Drawing on the history of Jesus' passion, Mark is telling the suffering history of the minjung of his own time. And conversely, Jesus' suffering is 'actualized' in the fate of the minjung at the time when Mark was writing.[127] But does this apt exegetical insight mean that 'Jesus' is a 'symbol for the minjung', as Suh Nam-Dong said?

I do not believe that this reduction is felicitous phraseology. The suffering servant in Isaiah 53 does not seem to me to mean the people of Israel collectively. He is a 'servant of God' like Moses, who does not just represent his people before God, but represents God to his people too. I believe that the image of the 'suffering servant' 'through whose wounds we are healed' (53.5) is a divine figure. He is not an 'individual' in the modern sense, nor is he a self-contained 'personality'; he is a person from God, who is there 'out of the people, with the people and for the people'. This is already evident from the comparison 'we – he': 'All we like sheep have gone astray . . . but the Lord laid all our iniquity on him' (53.6). The righteous one who 'makes many righteous because he bears their iniquities' (53.11) is a name for God himself. Only God can atone by 'bearing' the sins of the people and taking away the burden of them. If we see the suffering servant of God as a figurative embodiment of the 'suffering God', then the alternative between an individual and a collective interpretation of Isaiah 53 and the history of Jesus becomes superfluous. It is replaced by the relation between solidarity and representation. Solidarity and representation are so interwoven, or dovetailed, that solidarity in existence-with-others offers the presupposition for representation in existence-for-others. However, mere solidarity without representation does not overcome any suffering but merely increases the pain.

Bonhoeffer's insights into 'the suffering of God' which he wrote down in the Gestapo cell come closest to the theology of the cross worked out by the minjung theologians: 'The Bible points people to God's helplessness and suffering: only the suffering God can help.' 'The human being is called to suffer with the suffering of God from the godless world.' 'Christians stand beside God in his suffering.'[128] The minjung theologians have localized this 'suffering of God from the Godless world' in the oppressed and exploited minjung. If the minjung congregations stand beside the minjung in their pain, they stand 'beside God in his suffering'. But they do not stand there in order to bear sins for the reconciliation of the world, but so as to rise up with the minjung into the liberty of a juster world, in which the pain of the people no longer exists. So it is after all useful to distinguish between atoning suffering, which is solely God's affair, and the suffering of the people, which has to be overcome. The distinction must be made in the interests of the minjung 'as they really exist'.*

Another question put to minjung theology arises from the Christian-Jewish dialogue in Germany. This dialogue has made

---

* This is a reference to the distinction made between socialism as an ideal and theoretical form of government and the 'socialism as it really exists' of East Germany and the Eastern bloc in general, before its disintegration.

Christian theologians sensitive to conscious or unconscious anti-Judaism and to unreflected transferences of Israel's experiences of God to the people of Christ.[129] In this dialogue we have learnt to read the stories about Jesus in the synoptic Gospels as a social history of Israel. The history of Jesus is shaped according to the pattern of Israel's history with God – the flight into Egypt and the return home from Egypt, the forty days in the wilderness, and, not least, Jesus' exile experience between Gethsemane and Golgotha. According to Daniel 7, 'the people of the Most High' also belongs to Jesus' title as Son of man. Whether this 'people' is the people of Israel remains an open question, if 'the Son of man' is a universal divine figure who overthrows empires and fulfils the hopes of humanity. Is the minjung in Korea now taking Israel's place as 'the new Israel', as German critics – in typically German fashion – have mistrustfully conjectured? The same question was also critically raised in opposition to the proclamation of a Korean Year of Jubilee for reunification and social justice.[130]

I think that both suspicions are wrong. There has never been any antisemitism in Korea, because there were no Jews there. 'Auschwitz' took place in Germany, not in world-wide Christendom. The charges of antisemitism thrown out at large by German theologians are nothing other than transparent attempts to hide the burden of one's own guilt in the alleged collective guilt of Christians as a whole. In his interpretation of Mark's Gospel, Ahn Byung-Mu stated very clearly that, in his view, Mark means by the *ochlos* the inhabitants of Palestine who after the destruction of Jerusalem in the year 70 were homeless and without rights – the Jews first of all, then Christians and Gentiles too. In the Roman empire the people of God, *laos*, is made the homeless people, *ochlos*. If Jesus belongs to this *ochlos*, he lives with Jews and Gentiles, and is there for them both. For the Christian church to take up 'years of jubilee' is not an 'expropriation' of what is Israel's; it is a grateful endorsement of Israel's insight into God's sabbath. The same may be said about the archetypal history of the Exodus.

Fundamentally speaking, we have to say here that all the

traditions of all the peoples become universal, and are directed to everyone once they have been committed to writing. How else could we in Europe learn from Lao Tse, Confucius and Buddha? How otherwise could Asians read Kant and Hegel? Israel's holy scripture is directed to all nations, since it was for this that Israel was chosen. The holy scripture of Christians belongs to all human beings, because it was written for them all. In my view, therefore, the debate pursued by Jews and Christians about the 'possession' of the Bible is not merely out of keeping with the facts; it is godless, if it really is a matter of the Word of God in these writings.

5. 'We are the people' in democracy and church

The Korean word minjung can hardly be adequately translated into German or English because we cannot reproduce the same linguistic and historical connotations, and even if we could, it would not help us to discover the people (*ochlos*) for ourselves in our own situation. We can therefore only allow ourselves to be stimulated to parallel action. For this, the events of 1989 which led to the reunification of divided Germany give occasion enough. '*We are the people*,' cried the demonstrators in Leipzig in November 1989, in protest against the police and military forces of the socialist GDR dictatorship, and thereby initiated the first non-violent revolution in Germany. '*We are one people*', they cried soon afterwards, and united the divided nation.

What is the difference between the two slogans? In the first case the oppressed people became aware that they were the nationals of the German 'Democratic' Republic, and that according to the constitution 'all power proceeds from the people'. In the second case Germans demanded the German national state. In the first case the dominated people rose up against a dominating party clique; in the second case Germans demanded that they be allowed to live together with other Germans in a single state. In the first case it was a matter of democracy, in the second a matter of the nation; in the first case a question of civil rights (which correspond to universal human rights), in the second a question of German citizenship according to inherited nationality, the *ius sanguinis*. In their cry, the Leipzig demonstrators were appealing to two different concepts of 'people'.

The ancient democratic idea which has its roots in Greece, and the new democratic idea which was the fruit of the Enlightenment, both made the people the subject of their own political history. All political power emanates from the people, says the doctrine of popular sovereignty. The political groups and parties merely help to form the will of the people, claims the constitution or Basic Law of the German Federal Republic; they act *with* the people, not *for* the people.

Apart from the renaissance of the classical Greek idea, the modern democratic concept has a Christian root too. We find this in the Protestant Reformed tradition of federal (or covenant) theology and federal, or covenant, politics.[131] The idea of popular sovereignty was biblically justified by the Huguenot monarchomachists, and they used it for a new formulation of the right to resistance. According to the *Vindiciae contra tyrannos* of 1579 (generally thought to have been written by Philipp Duplessis Mornay), Christian states are built up on the pattern of the *politia Moisi*, the state or constitution of Moses: God made his eternal covenant with the people, in which he promised 'You shall be my people and I will be your God.' It follows from this that the people make a contract of rule with their ruler, and hand over to him part of their liberty so that he may act in the people's stead and in their name. If a ruler breaks this contract, then the people through their other representatives are empowered to resist, so as to force the ruler to remain true to the contract. But if the ruler breaks the people's covenant with God, he is a blasphemer and must be removed. 'At the beginning the people had no king other than God.' 'Consequently kings should always remember that they indeed reign by God's grace, but through the people and for the people.' If the people's covenant with God (to which the contract of rule is subordinate) is broken, then the people is freed from all obligations towards the ruler (*Populus jure omni obligatione solutus*).[132]

In the American Declaration of Independence the covenant with God was called *constitution*. The Basic Law (the *Grundgesetz*) of the German Federal Republic entirely accords with this when it says in the Preamble that it was resolved upon in our 'responsibility before God and the people'. Consequently for the people to avail themselves of the right to resist any breach of the constitution is the test case of democracy.

According to this theological justification of popular sovereignty *vis-à-vis* the ruler (that it springs from the people's covenant with God), 'the people' means everyone who lives within the sphere of the covenant, everyone who enters into it and keeps it, irrespective of his or her race, class or ethnic affiliation. It is not the nation which makes the people sovereign; it is the constitution. The constitutional republic bases the fundamental rights of its citizens on universal human rights, not on the 'national ties conferred by inheritance', as in the German *ius sanguinis*. This is the 'open republic'. Its ultimate goal is a universal republican order in which human rights everywhere become the basic rights of its citizens, so that the people everywhere are the subjects of their own political history, and are nowhere treated as the object of tyranny any longer.

The roots of tyranny can be detected in the inherent difficulties of representative institutions. Representative rule rests on deputization. Deputization is a normal form of shared human life. But deputization or representation 'for others' always involves the danger of the estrangement of the others. Political estrangements develop if the political representatives get on top of the people they are only supposed to represent, and if the people bow down to their own government. What then develops is a separate and remote 'political class' on the one hand and a growing political apathy among the people on the other. Participation democracy then becomes an absentee democracy, in which the politicians are left to do what they like as long as they leave the people in peace. This political estrangement is the beginning of political dictatorship and political idolatry. It can only be avoided through active participation by the people in political life, and through factors of direct democracy. Democracy is 'a government of the people, by the people, for the people', as Abraham Lincoln impressively proclaimed in his famous Gettysburg address. A government *for* the people only comes third, and presupposes the government *of* the people and *by* the people.

The Christian idea of the people which, according to the Gospel of Mark, is defined by Jesus' relationship to them (the *ochlos*) was not merely left unimplemented in the history of the hierarchical church; it was actually suppressed. We shall only rediscover it if we rise up with the cry of popular protest – this time on the part of the church's people – claiming: 'We are the church.' This is what has happened since 1994 in Catholic congregations in Europe. Ever since the early Christian development of the monarchical episcopate, we have known the church as a hierarchy 'from above' which delegates the universal episcopate of the pope 'downwards', and demotes the people of Christ to the status of 'the faithful', or 'the people in the pews'. The distinction between clergy and laity has split the people of God into two. The word 'lay' originally meant a member of the *laos*, the people of God; but because the clerics were set apart from the people, the word came to mean the ignorant and incompetent, those with no jurisdiction. A 'complete layman' means someone who doesn't understand what something is about. In the hierarchical perspective, 'the people' are only there as the object of 'holy rule', of caritative care and guidance by their 'shepherds'. For centuries, people in the church have reacted to this godless and un-Christian deprival of their responsibility with growing apathy and with silence. Since they are no longer 'forced' to go to church, they leave the church altogether. The result is people without a church and a church without people. This is a silent falling away from the church which the church itself has brought about. It is only if this 'church for the people' becomes a 'church of the people and by the people', and if the hierarchical church for looking after people becomes a congregational church, with many different kinds of participation, that the ancient schism between church and people will be overcome.

What applies to the Roman Catholic hierarchy in its estrangement from the people can also be said about the Protestant pastoral aristocracy, or its somewhat more modern variation in the form of a theological and pastoral expertocracy. Ideas about a blanket church-management which will cover the religious needs of the people are not enough to create what in Germany is called a *Volkskirche*, a church intended to meet the needs of the whole population. Even the strenuously promoted programmes 'church for the people', 'church for others', or 'church for the world' do not reach the people, because the word *for* cuts the church off from the people and makes the people an object – something to be cared *for*. A 'people's' church which accords with Jesus and the people can grow up only through a congregational renewal that springs from the people and is implemented through the people. For this, the Catholic base communities in Latin America, and the free church, Pentecostal congregations are examples and models.

But there is another picture still for the relationship between the church and the people of Christ, and this leads to an expanded concept of the church.[133] According to the Gospels, there is the *manifest* church of believers and followers of Jesus, and the *latent* church of the poor and those who wait for Jesus. The manifest community of believers lives in the apostolate of Christ: 'He who hears you hears me' (Luke 10.16); 'As the Father has sent me, even so I send you' (John 20.21). In these sayings Christ – the risen Christ, according to the Gospel of John – promises his real presence in the apostolate of the community of his people, who follow his messianic mission to the world; so we proclaim the invitation to be reconciled with God 'in Christ's stead' (II Cor. 5.20). Real presence by virtue of Christ's identification with the community of his people fills the proclamation, the sacraments, the fellowship and the *diakonia* of his congregation with authority. It is an active identification.

We find a similar-sounding but passively meant group of

promises of Christ's real presence in others among the poor, hungry, thirsty and imprisoned – in short the *ochlos*. 'He who visits them visits me.' 'As you did it to one of the least of these my brethren, you did it to me' (Matt. 25.40). That is also true of the children: 'Whoever receives one such child in my name receives me' (Matt. 18.5). Jesus calls the poor and the children blessed because the kingdom of heaven already belongs to them.

If we absorb this latent fellowship of Christ with the poor and the children of the people into ecclesiology, the result is a tremendous tension which 'the church as it really exists' must bridge: *ubi Christus ibi ecclesia* – where Christ is, there is the church. The true church of Christ is at the place where the fellowship of Christ is. The whole Christ is present in the manifest community of believers, and in the latent community of the poor – and therefore in the community of believers and the poor, the community of the lovers of the people and the children of the people. Christ's apostolate says *what* the church is, 'the least' say *where* the church belongs. The *hidden* Christ awaits those who are his in the poor and the children of the people. The *manifest* Christ comes to them with those who are his. In the apostolate the risen, coming Christ is present; in the poor the suffering, crucified Christ looks at us and waits for us.

5

Feminist theology for men

1. The beginnings of my personal sensitivity to feminist theology

I did not come to feminist theology. It came to me through the discoveries of my wife, Elisabeth Moltmann-Wendel.[134] I was drawn into it, and then experienced astonishing changes in myself. Out of respect for her independence, I have never claimed to be a 'feminist theologian', unlike some others who were willingly prepared to jump on to this modern bandwagon. Nor did I ever try to interfere. But from 1972 onwards, feminist theology became an important part of our conversation as man and wife, and in the family, and – whether consciously or unconsciously – it influenced me deeply. If two people are so close, and live together both in space and mind, the mutual influences cannot be unravelled. When I talk in this chapter about feminist theology for men and their liberation, I am not talking objectively about 'men'; I am really speaking subjectively about myself. The influence is unmistakable; but for all that, I am speaking solely for myself, on my own responsibility. The theories and reflections that follow are my own affair, and mistakes and false conclusions must be laid at my door alone. It is for men to judge and describe the liberating (or burdensome) effects which have emerged for them from the new feminist theology, and must still be expected. To make this point clear from the outset: it is not a matter of dressing oneself in borrowed plumes; nor is a matter of benevolent tolerance of 'laudable' efforts on the part of the 'weaker' sex; nor, again, is it a question of integrating a new movement into the ancient edifice of theology. Like every liberation theology, feminist theology also needs:

1. *Separation* from the male theology which is dominant in tradition and at the present time;

2. *Identity*, so that it may find itself and its own concerns undisturbed and in freedom;

3. At the end of these two processes we may then one day arrive at a new common theology in reciprocity and with equal rights in the shaping of this community. But this *integration* must not be looked for before the goal of the liberation process has been reached.

It was not always easy for me personally to understand the necessity for taking this road, when from 1972 onwards feminist theology found its way into our marriage; but I was curious enough to go along with it in keen anticipation, and – for my part and along my own road – to build a male liberation theology, so to speak. In so close a community, if the one changes, the other changes too. In their transformations the two remain related.

Every learning process involves pain, and every process of personal change even more so, if it means surrendering a prejudice to which one has got used. The two of us started off as equal and evenly matched partners. We had met and come to love each other when we were students in Göttingen. She freed me from my existentialist Kierkegaard phase and we worked together on our theological theses. She took her doctorate in 1951, I followed in 1952. We were free and equal in our shared community with each other.

Then came the era of profession and children – the time of family life. I became a pastor and later a university theologian, and after that a globe-trotter. The house was full of four daughters and many students, who came and went. A division of labour followed. What that meant for Elisabeth, she herself has described. For me, one responsibility followed another, making me the father of a family, but in addition a pastor and a professor of theology who was fascinated and eaten up by his work. It was always a bit too much. Of course the burden of responsibility filled me with pleasure over this position too. It was the practical application of feminist theology to myself which for the first time slowly opened my eyes to the estrangements involved. Often enough I became the test case and prime example of 'typical male thinking' and an academic 'objectivity' without 'subjectivity'. I had neither learnt nor deserved anything else. It took some time for me to arrive at my own case history, and for me to realize how I had been turned from a young human being into 'a man': through the upbringing of my father, through training at school and in the army, and through comrades in the prisoner-of-war camp.

It was not easy to surrender the power which went with the responsible role as father of a family. It cost some self-reflection before I was able to link the theological truths I recognized with my own male stance and its limitations, and before I could say 'I' in order to relativize these things. The encounter with black theologians had already made me very much aware that I am a white theologian and that this existence puts its stamp on my perceptions. The encounters with Third World theologians had made me aware that I live in the First World and that that too puts its stamp on my thinking, whether I like it or not. But living with feminist theology brought this necessary self-enlightenment with incomparably more force into the very heart of personal existence.

On the other hand this process of change brought great gain. I learnt to see the world with new eyes. Perception of the social and economic reality of women expanded my political theology. The rediscovery of the senses, the immediate senses and the less immediate ones, led my thinking out of abstractions into life. Through feminist exegesis, I read the Bible with my own eyes and with theirs, and noticed to my shame how much – and how much that was important – I had simply overlooked, because it had never struck me. Elisabeth and I then several times held joint Bible-study sessions at major church conferences, and also conducted a joint television service, and we enjoyed this. But this pleasure was not generally shared. When in 1975 I held my first seminar on liberation theology, and in the second half of the semester came to feminist theology, the women students began to dominate the seminar to such an extent that I had to arrange a separate session with the men, in order to encourage them in a brotherly way. Their initial aggression had given way to depression. The remarkable public reactions to my wife's feminist theology in my own faculty in Tübingen, and among a number of German bishops, became increasingly incomprehensible to me – even from man to man. After about ten years I had evidently drifted far away from my male caste.

Yet the new Christian community which is becoming possible in the churches is a great charismatic gain for women, and perhaps even more so for men. The new human community which is possible in modern societies is a new gain in human rights for humanity as a whole. I have come to understand the growing feminist theology (apart from some excesses, which develop in all new beginnings) as a great invitation to men to develop a consciously limited, masculine liberation theology, through which to overcome the estrangements on both sides brought about by the patriarchal traditions. For this, one pre-condition is essential: the power games must stop, the master in the man must vanish, power must be distributed justly and equally, so that everyone, men and women alike, get the chance to fulfil their talents and callings, so that they can be used.

There have always been chapters in Christian dogmatics and ethics dealing with the proper, divinely willed relationship between men and women in the order of creation, after the Fall, and in the order of redemption. But ever since the beginning of the democratic revolutions in the United States and France, emancipation movements have been set on foot by women who have demanded the same rights as men, since all human beings 'are created equal and are endowed with certain inalienable rights'.[135] In the Anglo-Saxon countries, socio-political movements for the emancipation of women developed; but in conservative church circles in Germany all that happened was a 'women's movement without emancipation', educational reforms, deaconess communities, and 'women's auxiliaries' in the Christian congregations.[136] The social and political 'freedom of the woman' went together with democratic freedom for atheism, and the emancipation of women was associated with the emancipation of the workers for socialism.

This split in German society also influenced theological attempts in the nineteenth and twentieth centuries to find a new 'order' for the relationship between men and women. Typically enough, these attempts were made for preference in the sphere of marriage and the family, not in the legal or the social and economic sectors. With a few exceptions, it was men who concerned themselves with the new relation of wives to their husbands and families, as if the problem was 'the new woman', not the man in his traditional dominating roles. The biblical models based on the creation accounts and the apostolic letters were to be actualized, because their authority as the Word of God must not be infringed, even though they after all derived from a pre-democratic and pre-modern culture. The result could be seen in painstaking but relatively unimportant variations on the old subordination of the woman to male dominance with the aim of 'mutual subordination in love' and a 'partnership in equal grace'; that is to say, women were to be newly integrated into the male world which was the premise.[137]

But theologians who made these attempts, and bishops and synods who responded in this way to the emancipation of women in society, failed to realize the full extent of the cultural revolution which had now come upon them, and simply did not understand what was going on. The so-called women's question was in reality nothing less than the fundamental challenge to the age-old, patriarchal and androcentric male rule, as the theologians could in fact easily have read already in Friedrich Engels, August Bebel and John Stuart Mill.[138] The patriarchy (to give it the shorthand title I shall use here) interpenetrates and dominates everything: religious ideas, the picture of the human being, the legal and economic system, the structure of the family, medicine, and the relation to nature. It was the new feminist theology which made it clear for the first time what the so-called woman's question is really about. It is not just a matter of liberating the woman from her subordinate position; it also means liberating the man from his master's role. That is to say, it has to do with a religion of freedom, a holistic picture of the human being, a humane society, and a new ecology of the earth.[139]

The question, of course, is whether, and in what way, feminist theologies belong within the framework of the liberation theologies of the blacks and the poor in the Third World, since they have after all developed in the white middle classes of American and European society. The reasons why we should nevertheless see them in this context are these:

(a) Whether they view themselves as liberation theologians or not, feminist theologians are concerned contextually and in their involvement with the liberation of oppressed women from patriarchy, masculine sexism, and the generally androcentric character of our culture.

(b) Ever since the beginning of patriarchy, women exploited by men have also belonged to the downside of the history of male dominance, not just black slaves and their descendants, the oppressed and exploited people of the Third World. The difference is that the feminist struggle against patriarchal culture has to change not just the socio-political situation of human beings, but their psycho-social situation too. And this touches the private or intimate sphere as well.

(c) The critical questions and accusations of feminist theology are analogous to those of liberation theology. But they do not only affect the androcentricism of the First World. They touch the machismo in the Third World too, the depreciation of the woman in Confucianism, the mutilation of women in Africa, and the abortion of female babies in India. So the fronts overlap, and that is sometimes a reason for conflicts about priorities. On the other hand, for reasons such as these, black women have named their theology 'womanist theology' (Alice Walker), and Latin American women have called theirs *mujerista teologia,* in order to differentiate themselves from the perspectives of white middle-class women in the United States and Europe.[140]

(d) A culture characterized by patriarchy can be found among nearly all peoples, irrespective of their tradition and the colour of their skins. It is the mark of Asian and African cultures as well as the pre-Columbian cultures which the conquistadores in America came across after 1492. It was in prehistoric times at most that there was a matriarchy as an alternative to this general patriarchal culture.[141] Vestigial remembrances of this can be discovered in prehistoric finds and in the legends of many peoples. But their interpretation goes back to nineteenth-century Romanticism. The feminist theology of the present day sees itself as part of a cultural revolution which aims to change an age-old human culture, and thinks of itself as part of a liberation movement which aims to speak for the feminine part of humanity today, and has to intervene on its behalf. Whether this is still possible as 'Christian' theology is then an open question, since after all the majority of oppressed women today are not Christians.

2. *Patriarchy and its consequences: facts and interpretations*

Max Weber used the term 'patriarchy' sociologically as a way of describing the legal supremacy of the man in family and society.[142] For feminist theology 'patriarchy' is the term for an institutionalized system of sexual hierarchy and a psychological mechanism for its justification, according to which the man is born and made to rule, while the woman is born and made to serve. This can most easily be seen in the ancient Chinese law, according to which the woman has to serve three men: first her father, then her husband, last her oldest son.

Patriarchy means in the first instance that inheritance goes through the male line. So a son has to be born as heir, 'to carry on the family'. Too many daughters are viewed as a misfortune, because the dowry can plunge a family into poverty. The result in many patriarchal cultures is the abortion or killing of female children. Patriarchy also means that the oldest son has to keep up the ancestor cult, and is responsible for the generation contract. The father of the family is also the family priest. In the Roman patriarchy the father of the family, as owner of the women, children and slaves in the house, had the *ius vitae necisque*, the right over their life and death.[143] The emperor, or Caesar, was revered as the father of his country (*pater patriae*). As such he had a father's duty to look after it, but as its lord he also had the right over the life and death of his subjects (who in Germany used to be called *Landeskinder*, the country's children). As the father of his country, the emperor was at once ruler and priest, and *pontifex maximus* (supreme priest) was one of his titles. The Father of the gods whom he had to worship and represent was Jupiter. The Roman patriarchy may be considered as patriarchy in its purest form, whereas at the same time in the countries of the eastern Mediterranean goddesses were worshipped – the great Diana of the Ephesians, for example. The patriarchal sexual hierarchy certainly changed its forms and appearances in the course of cultural history, as feudalism gave way to a middle-class society, rural to urban civilization, and the agrarian to the industrial world; but it has endured with astonishing tenacity.

Today we understand psychologically by a masculine sexism the imaginary yet frequently cherished delusion of 'manliness'. It is a phenomenon consequent on the patriarchal legal system. It will continue to exist and poison the social atmosphere as long as there are men who define humanity in terms of their masculinity, and through this definition exclude women. Then the supremacy of the man over against the woman is seen in his sexually active role, his supposed potency, and his life-long narcissism. The egocentricism which is typically male derives from a separation from the mother which has never been psychologically digested, and which causes him to oppress 'the other', the so-called 'femininity' of his feelings, senses and inner needs. But what he cannot permit himself, he will not endure in the women he encounters either, but will tread it down.

In analogy to racism we can therefore define this male sexism by saying the following: 'By male sexism we understand the domination of the man over the woman on the basis of privileges which the man sees as belonging to his masculinity, and which he ascribes to that. It is the masculine pride in his own sex, the preference given to the particular characteristics of the male sex in culture, economy, politics and religion, the conviction that these characteristics are fundamentally biological in kind, and are therefore a matter of destiny. Along with this goes the belittling of women as "the weaker sex", the undervaluation in public life of allegedly feminine characteristics, and the exclusion of women from full participation in the public life of society.'[144]

To be fully human then means to be a man. The reason given, ever since Aristotle, is that the man provides the seed, and that the male semen contains the homunculus, the woman being merely the vessel for receiving the semen, like the furrow in a ploughed field, or an incubator. Consequently even today the man occasionally calls the woman 'the mother of his children', although biologically, people have known ever since 1923 about the equal part played by the female ovum. Aristotle and Aquinas, because of their lack of biological knowledge, thought that the woman was a deficient, not quite finished man, who was created to serve and help the human being who was complete – the man. The man is the head, and bears responsibility for the woman; the woman looks after his bodily needs. The man lays claim to logical thinking and will-power; the 'warmhearted' woman is at his disposal for emotional services which can be called upon at any time.

In the working world, which is determined by men, the woman's characteristics – innate or acquired – are undervalued. In her work in the house she leads a shadow existence. Her work in bringing up children is unpaid, and only recently in Germany has it come to count towards her pension. If the work is paid, she is punished for possible absences through pregnancy by lower wages or by unemployment. Her body has to be, like the man's, capable of equal performance at all times, so her menstrual cycle cannot be taken into account. But this means that in the working world the man is the norm against which the woman is defined. She is viewed as a deficient man, and must make every effort 'to do a man's job', as people say.

If the man bases his sense of his own value on his sex, he develops an aggressive sexist identity: he defines himself by not being a woman, and does not let himself 'get soft', as they said in men's clubs and army units, in which femininity was equated with weakness.[145]

But this masculine sexism is more than just a group phenomenon. It is also a means of psychological warfare, a war waged by dominant men against the women who have to be dominated. Male feelings of superiority then evoke feminine feelings of inferiority, so that the dependent women content themselves with keeping a low profile and as victims are made to become accomplices in the male delusion. Women then feel that they are men's indispensable auxiliaries, or 'helpmates', or complements; and they adapt themselves.

In its concrete form, masculine sexism has two sides, one internal, one external. It is a psychological mechanism of male self-justification and complacency, and at the same time it is an ideological mechanism for the exploitation of 'the other sex'. It can therefore be overcome only if women free themselves from the roles expected of them, cast away their inferiority complexes, and find their way to their own selves in their humanity – and if men surrender the superiority complex they have been trained to acquire and find their way to themselves in their humanity. These psychological and social changes are not possible without social and economic redistributions of rights and duties – i.e., political and economic power – so that women and men can find more equal and juster chances to fulfil their personhood and can discover a more humane community with each other.

Patriarchy and its consequences in the form of masculine sexism – the consequences described here – have not merely humiliated women. They have robbed men of their humanity too. The drama of the male self lies in the permanent search for security by way of control and repression, because there is no other way of preserving the conscious self, which has been split off from the whole. If the divided and pre-programmed man compensates for his inner anxieties through aggression towards women and by disparaging them, he destroys the humane society. To this the 'women's refuges' in our cities are a daily testimony. Inhumane genital mutilation in Africa takes its toll of two million women every year. World-wide, more than 130 million women suffer under it. Like racism, masculine sexism is basically self-hatred which constitutes a public danger. The feminist liberation of women from their patriarchal and sexist oppression gives men too the chance to free themselves from their delusion of supremacy, and to develop more human qualities.

3. The Bible and patriarchy

The patriarchal order of the sexes did not come into the world through the Bible, but the Bible developed in the patriarchal world.[146] Its testimonies came into being in the era of transition from nomadic to settled existence and from agrarian to urban life. They are testimonies from a period of about a thousand years.

Seen from the aspect of cultural history, the Tenach or Old Testament shows the conflicts between the nomad God of 'Abraham, Isaac and Jacob' and the Canaanite fertility goddesses who were worshipped in feminine cults in the area of the eastern Mediterranean, and in historical Israel too. In the Israelite belief in God itself, there are strongly masculine traditions, where Yahweh is called the Lord, the Judge, the God of Battles, the Father.[147] Parallel to these there are feminine traditions too, which talk about the divine daughter Hokmah (Wisdom), Ruach (the Spirit of God), and the Shekinah (God's indwelling). Finally, there are internal conflicts between the Israelite traditions of freedom and the patriarchal notions of order.

From the aspect of cultural history, a similar picture can be found in the Christian New Testament. On the one hand there are Jesus' disciples, a community of free and equal women and men; on the other we have the family ethics of the codes in the Pastoral Epistles. On the one hand there is the gospel of freedom in the Spirit – on the other the ordered structure of creation, as a bulwark against the fear of chaos.[148]

But observations about cultural history of this kind have little to say to us about the content of the narratives and testimonies about God in the Old and New Testaments. Plato lived in a slave-owning society and supported the tyrant of Syracuse, but that still does not tell us anything about the truth of his teaching about Ideas. Mozart was a child of his absolutist time, but to say that still does not tell us anything about the beauty of his music. The fact that the Bible grew up in the world of patriarchy and slavery still does not tell us anything about the presence of eternity at that time, or about the future in its past. Yet every historical consideration of the biblical traditions fits them into their own time and presents their ideas in terms of their own world. That time and that world are no longer our time and our world. No one reads the Bible in order to take over a world picture that is past and gone. No one has to adopt the social concepts and the patriarchal sexual hierarchies of the Bible. If that were so, for biblical reasons we should have to reintroduce slavery into Christianity, revert to absolute monarchy instead of democracy, and so forth. I think it is expecting too much to ask us to follow Karl Barth, who in 1934 wrote to the early feminist theologian Henriette Visser't Hooft that 'the whole Bible presupposes patriachy, not matriarchy, as the temporal and earthly order of the relationship between man and woman' and that we must accept this 'fact' as God-given, 'like the fact, for example, that the chosen people to which Christ too belonged just did not happen to be the people of Carthage or the Spartans, but was the people of Israel'. Consequently the patriarchy presupposed in the Bible is one of 'God's particular divine directives in respect of the way he acts with human beings'.[149] Fortunately Barth did not 'just happen' to extend this fundamentalist-sounding 'revelation positivism' (as Dietrich Bonhoeffer called it) to the institution of slavery.

In order to distinguish hermeneutically between what is temporally conditioned and what is eternal, what belongs to the past and what points to the future in the biblical traditions, we have to turn back to objective criteria in the divine discourse to which they witness. Otherwise the only alternative is either a fundamentalistic one – on the basis of the Bible to bring to a halt, and fix, the whole of cultural history – or to write new 'hallowed' scriptures in every new age and new circumstances.[150] The God who is present to his people in promise, Exodus, covenant and law is, in my view, *the first objective criterion* in the Tenach or Old Testament. He is the God of whom human beings are enjoined to make 'no image or likeness', because they themselves are his 'image' on earth, created 'male and female' (Gen.1.26). This prohibition of images also goes for human concepts, metaphors and analogies: God is not like a father, not like a lord, not like a war hero, and so on. It is rather that his presence frees human beings from analogies of this kind, and from the representations of God which are used by earthly fathers, lords and warriors, and which are legitimated by the analogies. If the image of God is 'male and female', then the image-less God is equidistant from male and female images, and cannot have any preference for the masculine analogies. So if we know that God is neither the one nor the other, we can say: God is like a father, and like a mother, like the old and like a child, like an Almighty and like a co-sufferer, and so forth.

The result of this must then be a consistent 'de-theocratization' and 'de-patriarchalizing' of the biblical histories and laws of God. As well as Moses, who led his people to freedom, the prophetess Miriam, with her Reed Sea song, must be stressed with equal weight (Ex. 15.20ff.), since she will have been the leader of a group of the prisoners.[151] The Ten Commandments must then be reinterpreted, now no longer as commandments for men ('You shall not covet your neighbour's wife . . .'), but as commandments for men and women. The Levitical laws about the purity and impurity of the woman, and the 'texts of terror' – the sad, horrible women's stories about Hagar, Tamar,

Jephthah's daughter and the unknown violated woman in Judges 19 – are in need of re-vision, in the literal sense.[152] The misunderstanding of the second creation account and the story of the Fall, according to which the woman was created second but was the first to become 'a transgressor' (I Tim. 2.11ff.), must be revised, even though this misunderstanding can also already be found in the Bible. Adam was formed from the dust, but Eve was formed from Adam; so as the second, she is not secondary, but is rather higher in kind.[153] The statement that 'Adam was not deceived, but the woman was deceived and brought about transgression' (I Tim. 2.14) contradicts Genesis 3 and is a typically male continuance of Adam's malicious accusation of Eve (Gen. 3.12). According to this false exegesis, was the original sin of humanity 'Eve's sin' or – to follow the language Paul uses otherwise – 'the sin of Adam'?

Nor does the patriarchal hierarchy which Paul describes in I Corinthians 11, with its downgrading of the woman's position (God is the head of Christ, Christ is the head of the man, the head of the woman is her husband), correspond to the equal position and equal rights of men and women as image of God according to Gen. 1.26. Paul actually contradicts this when in I Cor. 11.7 he calls the man 'the image and glory of God', but the woman merely 'the glory of the man'. With this graduated hierarchy, Paul also contradicts what he himself says in Gal. 3.28 about the one baptism and spiritual endowment of man and woman: 'There is neither male nor female, for you are all one in Christ Jesus. And if you are Christ's, then you are Abraham's offspring, heirs according to the promise.' In their character as God's children, men and women are equal and free. The faith in Christ to which the New Testament witnesses stands in the same tension to the patriarchal laws and ordinances as to the Yahweh faith in the Tenach/Old Testament. Whereas the Jesus of the synoptic Gospels is quite evidently described as the friend of women and children, the risen head of the community of his people is saddled with a downwardly-graduated hierarchical rule, which later – and already in Ignatius of Antioch – assumed the descending sequence of the monarchical episcopate: one God – one Christ – one bishop – one church. The outpouring of the Spirit originally described in Joel 2 comes upon old and young, masters and servants, men and women alike, and they are all filled with the divine Spirit's energies; but later the 'holy rule' of the 'spiritual pastors' pushed out the Christian liberty of the charismatic congregation.

These may be sufficient instances to initiate critical approaches to a non-patriarchal interpretation of the biblical traditions. The kingdom of the promising God and the gospel of life are 'not fettered' (II Tim. 2.9; Barmen Declaration VI). They are bound neither to the institution of slavery nor to that of patriarchy. They are like the scarlet thread of hope running through in the mutable and transitory forms of life and society in Israel and Christendom. Because the biblical traditions were all written by men, with the experiences and opinions of their time, and because these traditions were also gathered together by men into the canon of 'holy scripture', a critical feminist hermeneutics is necessary, not just for women but for men too, so that we may discover and translate into the present 'the concern of scripture' – which means whatever in the past is pregnant with future.

Like every liberating theology, every feminist hermeneutics begins with 'a hermeneutics of suspicion'.[154] With what intention were the texts written and the stories told? Do they serve to legitimate domination or to liberate from oppression? Are there other stories behind the written ones, stories which we discover only if we read the texts 'the other way round' – for example, the relation of the serpent to the woman in the story of the Fall? In the traditions do we have to do with palimpsests? Every feminist hermeneutics therefore puts to the texts the question about the effect on patriarchally disparaged women. That is not just a contemporary secular interest, but the Bible's very own concern too. The biblical vision of freedom and healing continues to give women the power to fight for their dignity and liberty. Both the hermeneutics of suspicion and the hermeneutics of liberating words and healing visions are gathered together in a *hermeneutics of remembrance,* recollections of the histories of suffering of women in the patriarchal and slave-owning society in which the biblical texts were written. Remembrance hastens the redemption, says an old Jewish saying. Without remembrance there is no hope for healing. So without remembrance of the histories of the patriarchal suppression of women, there is no hope for a new community of equal and free women and men.

4. Patriarchy and the church

There are no theologically relevant arguments against the ordination of women to all the ministries in the church of Christ, even if arguments are still put forward by the Vatican in the Roman Catholic Church, and by some Orthodox bishops. On the level of theological argument, this discussion has been decided. We shall not take it up and summarize it here. I may point instead to the relevant literature.[155] We shall concern ourselves with the next steps. It is not merely a question of the appropriate representation of women in the leading bodies of the churches, but also, and in the churches where women are ordained more than ever, a question of the new quality of the church made up of men and women. Are women to integrate themselves in a church determined by men, or must they free the church from its patriarchal deformations? Quotas will only measure quantities but not qualities. What is there to be? Women in the men's church? A new 'women's church'? Or a church of the Spirit shaped by women and men in mutual respect, for the renewal of creation?

Let us take as starting point a small but typical example. In 1986 the leading bishop of the Protestant church in Germany, Martin Kruse, enlisted support for a study on 'The Woman in Family, Church and Society' with the words: 'Can we in the church afford to take so little advantage of the gifts of many women?' This was well meant, but who are 'we in the church' if it is not the men, and who takes 'so little advantage of the gifts of many women' if not the men? If a new fellowship of women and men is to come into being in the church, this ecclesiastical 'we' must be set aside and newly defined. The 'gifts' of women and men cannot 'be taken advantage of' by either men or women, but only by the source of life from which they come, the Spirit of God. A new community through the development of the rich abundance of their spiritual gifts and energies is experienced by men and women in *the church of the Spirit* which, according to the promise, is 'poured out on all flesh' so that it may become eternally living. After the patriarchal form of the church, in which *God the Father* was the prototype of all authority, and after the brotherly form of the church, in which *God the Son* was the prototype of the brotherly community (Barmen Declaration III), the approaches to a new community of women and men in the church are now bringing us face to face with a new perception of the fellowship of *God the Spirit*.

The re-formation and renewal process of the church which has begun with the ordination of women is going to change the face of the church fundamentally, from its image of God to its praxis. It is the concern and the merit of feminist theology to have initiated this comprehensive renewal process in Christianity. It will be necessary not only because of the secular women's movements of the present day, as a way of bringing the church into line and up to date. This 'unrest among women', as church statements so benevolently put it, is always also an echo of the unrest of the Spirit itself, an unrest which sets in when the church fails to live up to the promises of its existence, and the gospel to which it witnesses remains unfulfilled.

I shall now go into this still undischarged future of the church's own biblical history, in order to take up concerns of feminist theology from the male side.

(a) *The image of God: created free and equal.* One problem in the relationship between women and men is the balance between their likeness as human beings and their particular character as women and men. If the essential likeness is disregarded, inhumane relationships of domination and dependence are the result; if the difference between women and men

is ignored, the result is a uniformity which does justice neither
to her nor to him. If with this in mind we again read Gen.
1.26–27 carefully, we shall be struck by the strange shift
between singular and plural: '*Let us* make human beings, *an
image* after our likeness . . . And God created *the human being*
in his own image . . . male and female he created *them*.' 'Human
beings' in the plural are created and are to be '*an* image' of the
God who is in himself plural. 'The human being' becomes the
image of God in the plurality of men and women.[156] Through
this subtle language, the writer is making the point that it is
wrong to use the fact that there are men and women to deduce
differing species with different rights; they are human beings. It
is equally wrong to make of men and women abstract human
beings *per se;* the human being exists only as woman or man.
What 'corresponds' to the creative God as his image on earth is
solely a human community in which women and men arrive at
their different, feminine or masculine identities, and by way of
these identities are there with one another and for one another,
and together constitute the resonance of the living God in his
earthly creation.

The likeness to God enjoyed by human beings embraces their
wholeness, body and soul, as woman or man, and must not be
restricted to their sexless souls or their bodiless spiritual
natures, as has been usual in the tradition of the Western
church ever since Augustine. If women and men in their bodily
and spiritual wholeness are together God's image, then they are
his image in their sexual difference and their community with
each other too. To be in the image of God is a social concept,
and lends divine splendour and dignity to the full human community of men and women. The exclusion of the body, the
senses and feelings from the soul's likeness to God has led to
the halving of the man and to the repression or demonization
of our bodily nature. The parts that were split off were then
projected on to the woman who – together with the body,
its senses, feelings and drives – was also suppressed and
demonized. The severance of the body from the soul, and of
nature from spirit, as well as the subjugation of both body and

nature, are serious injuries to the man as image of God, and thus to his human dignity. It is only when this de-embodiment of the man, and the 'beheading' of the woman[157] that follows, are surmounted in a new culture of the senses that women and men find their way to their true human dignity.

Although psychosomatic medicine, anthroposophy and the modern movement for the rediscovery of the senses and the return of the body all point in this direction, no new *sensory culture* has developed in the modern or post-modern world. In fact what has been pushed forward still further is the de-sensualizing of a virtual world (which is now perceived only with the remote senses of eyes and ears) and the reduction of human beings (whether women or men) to the status of abstract subjects of understanding and will.

(b) *Called, justified and sanctified through the gospel of life.* A corresponding balance between likeness and difference which accords with the original creation can be found in the testimonies of the redeemed new creation of human beings. In the power of God's Spirit, Jesus proclaimed the imminent and open kingdom of God to the poor, sinners, women and children, and gathered a crowd of men and women disciples. The stories about Jesus and women in the synoptic Gospels show that in his fellowship there were no male privileges. Instead, women who were bent down under their load, and the children who were simply disregarded, were raised up and encouraged.

The apostolic gospel about the *justification of the God-forsaken* (the 'sinners' of traditional language) also creates likeness and difference between women and men in their shared character as children of God. The person whom God 'justifies' he installs as his child with the 'right to inherit' eternal life in his kingdom. The new beginning out of grace makes the women and men concerned citizens of the coming kingdom of God, with equal rights. They have equal rights before God *and* towards one another, and are not bound to the positions assigned to them by the patriarchal rule of this world. The traditional differentiation between 'what is valid before God' and 'what is valid in the world' again splits up their new wholeness and is illogical. The cleavage between a religious 'inward-ness' and an 'outwardness' determined by the world of civil society merely destroys what was healed.

From the very beginning the community of Christ baptized men and women alike and put them on an equal footing through *the one baptism*. That is undisputed, and has never been called in question. By doing so it recognized without qualification the fellowship with Christ and the experience of the Spirit of both women and men. Women were demoted only when the question of their ordination to the ministries of the church came up. But because all the different gifts and tasks in the community of Christ stem from the one baptism, here there can be no fundamentally different treatment of baptized men and women. It is only when faith and baptism are devalued in the churches that the lamentably unequal treatment of men and women in the matter of ordination results. Faith and baptism lose their value through infant baptism. If infants are already baptized, then their confession of faith must be made good later, at confirmation, and the special gifts the Spirit confers on them can be recognized only very much later, if at all. In some Baptist churches, in contrast, believers' baptism and the ordi-nation for the special ministry in church and society coincide.

(c) *Alive through the Spirit and given a part in the renewal of the earth*. Paul makes the balance between likeness and difference in women and men clear when he talks about the *unity and diversity* of the varied energies of the Holy Spirit in the community of Christ: 'There are varieties of gifts but the same Spirit; and there are varieties of service, but the same Lord; there are varieties of working, but it is the same God who inspires them all in everyone' (I Cor. 12.4-6). It is precisely *not* the uniformity of the gifts which constitutes their unity. The unity comes from the source of their plurality. By the energies of the divine Spirit we have to understand everything which people contribute to the common life of the church, 'the body of Christ'. It may be hymns, prophecies, doctrines, prayers, consolations, encouragements, healings, diaconical help, and so on. So through their calling women and men also bring into the community their natural and unique dispositions and gifts: 'Let every one lead the life which the Lord has assigned to him, and in which God has called him' (I Cor. 7.17).

According to Joel 2 and Acts 2, every experience of the Spirit is linked with participation in 'the outpouring of the Spirit on all flesh'. That does not mean just the 'devout flesh' of Israel or Christianity but, as the Hebrew shows, 'all the living' – human life in the warp and weft of all living things which the earth brings forth. The experience of the Spirit does not elevate the people it touches above this world; it brings them into profound solidarity with the whole sighing creation (Romans 8), for the energies of the Spirit which they experience are not super-natural, heavenly powers, but 'the powers of the age to come' (Heb. 6.5). So what is experienced in a small way in the charis-matic congregation belongs within the universal context, and must be seen against the universal horizon of the new creation of all things.

The renewal of the community of women and men in the church is neither an internal church affair nor is it merely the need to catch up with the progress of society. The riches of the gifts and tasks of God's Spirit demand a new variety in the com-munity of Christ. The Spirit gives 'to each his or her own', and involves men and women together in joint work for the kingdom of God, the new creation of all things. So whether women should be ordained and what the new, charismatically experienced community of women and men in the church should look like, are not merely practical questions. They are *questions about God* and questions about the *hope for his coming kingdom*. If God's Spirit is 'poured out on all flesh', then 'your *sons and daughters* will prophesy'. If 'the daughters' are prevented from doing so, then God's Spirit is hindered and injured, and the future of life will be hindered too.[158] Whenever the church has suffered persecution, it is women who have kept the Christian congregations alive, proclaimed the gospel, baptized, celebrated the Lord's Supper, taught, consoled and encouraged, and led the congregations. In the twentieth century that was the case in Russia, China, and in the martyr church in

Latin America. And if this is so 'in case of emergency' it cannot be any different in normal cases either. It is in extreme situations that the truth emerges.

5. *The liberation of the man from the patriarchal God complex*

When we ask about the meaning of feminist theology for men, we are not asking about sacrifices which men ought to make, or about the conciliatory tolerance which they might extend to women. We are asking about starting-points for their own liberation from the deformations of patriarchy and for their own discovery of full life. Every man – at least in my generation – can examine his case-history for himself once he is clear about the way he was brought up from childhood 'to be a man': the feelings he had to suppress, the drives he had to master and the roles he had to adopt in order to become the winner, conqueror, ruler, worker, soldier, bread-winner, head of the family, manager and so forth. So that he should 'be a man' he was made to feel continually afraid of 'not being anything', in order to 'make something of himself'. He was split up into a subject of understanding and will (with which he had to identify himself), and an object of heart, feeling and needs (from which he had to distance himself). Together with his own body, the nature surrounding him and 'the weaker sex' belonged to the sphere of his objectivizing domination. His 'master in the house' standpoint had to be imposed everywhere.

But strangely enough every 'ruler' also needs a throne to sit on. The throne of the dominating man is his mother's lap, as we see from Isis and Horus, Astarte and Baal, Mary and the Child Jesus, and many other religious symbols. This dichotomizing of the woman into the adored mother and the ministering housewife is a product of patriarchy. Unresolved ties with the mother and the humiliations of the woman go together. Consequently mothering and dominating must both stop if men want to be free and to discover full life.[159]

In his supremacy, the God of the patriarchy reflects the

misery of the bisected man, for our image of God and our understanding of ourselves always correspond. This God is one-sided – always only the Almighty, the Absolute, the Lord of the world. He determines everything, but is for his part determined by nothing. He rules over life and death, and is himself immortal and impassible. According to Aristotle, like Narcissus he loves only himself, and moves everything to make it chime in with his self-entrancement. If he is given human features, they are masculine ones. Just as God is the Lord of the world, the human being is to be lord of the earth. Just as God subjugates the universe, the man is to subjugate his body. Then he will correspond to his God and Lord. The God of the patriarchy is the 'always still greater' God of monotheism, inasmuch as monotheism means cosmic and political monarchism. That is the oldest patriarchal legitimation of rule, which can be shown to obtain almost universally, from China to Rome: one God in heaven – one emperor on earth; one universe – one empire. Consequently only a *single* earthly universal monarchy can represent the one heavenly kingdom of the world. And with this conviction the age-old struggle for world hegemony began.

The wretchedness of the male Lord God is that he has no name and is solitary, because he has to be absolute. He is described only through his functions as 'the Almighty' and 'the Lord'. Anyone who is closed within himself remains unknown and ineffable – inexpressible whether he is good or evil. But a God about whom we can say nothing except that he is 'the Almighty' is not a God; he is a monster. The man who emulates him becomes a disaster for his people and himself. Hitler too, after all, when he seized power over the German people in 1933, conjured up 'Almighty Providence' in support of his designs. The person who subjects himself to this God of the patriarchy, or takes him as model, ceases to be a finite, mortal and vulnerable human being. He becomes a proud unhappy god, and perishes on the rock of this superhuman God-complex, first spiritually and then physically too.[160] He turns into a solitary individual, and becomes increasingly insensitive and unfeeling the more powerful he becomes. He knows only self-love and the glory of what he has achieved, and is aware that he is loved by no one; so the reverse side of his superhuman pride is an inhuman anxiety.

How can this image of God and this male self-understanding be overcome? In the Christian faith, through the discovery and experience of God's Spirit, the Spirit who interpenetrates everything and surrounds us from every side.[161] Quite early on, the Syrian Fathers of the church talked about the Spirit of God as 'our mother'. When the Homilies of Makarios (Symeon) were translated in the eighteenth century, Count Zinzendorf proclaimed the 'motherly office of the Holy Spirit' as general doctrine among the Moravian Brethren. Like the Ethiopian church fathers, he used the metaphor of the family for the doctrine of the Trinity. If the Holy Spirit is feminine, and acts like a mother, then human beings do not experience themselves as subjects *subordinate to* an Almighty God but, like a child in its mother's arms, feel themselves in safe-keeping '*in* God'. The idea frees us from monotheistic father images, and helps us to experience the whole God with the whole of human existence and with all the senses. God the Spirit was always experienced in and through human community as the 'God in sociality'. The energies of the Spirit constitute 'the power of relationships'.

This experience of sociality in the Spirit of God frees us from the individualism of the monotheistic image of God. God's presence is not experienced in what we divide so as to make it controllable, but in what binds, in order to make both sides mutually alive. The Spirit of God is experienced as the source of life (*fons vitae*) and as the life that gives life (*vita vivificans*). In the Spirit, the severance between soul and body is ended. The body becomes 'the temple of the Holy Spirit' and God is glorified 'in the body' (I Cor 6.19f.). In Paul there is no question of the exclusive preference of the soul for God; that was Augustine's notion. In the experience of the Spirit it is not merely believing souls and awakened hearts that are born; all the other senses awaken too, allowing the whole world to be newly perceived. So life in God's Spirit opens up new bodily nature and new sensuousness, and with that, not least, a new understanding of the human person. The person is now no longer untouchably enclosed within the self, but takes on form in social and natural processes.[162] These discoveries and experiences of life in God's Spirit help men to find their way out of their dichotomized life, and lead them into life in all its fullness.

Theologically, it is the Christian *doctrine of the Trinity* which gets over patriarchal monotheism. 'Trinity' certainly sounds like just one more male theology 'from above', since all three trinitarian Persons are given masculine names. But if we understand the Trinity as the divine mystery which surrounds our whole, common life from every side, like a wider space for living, then its potential is by no means exhausted through what the theological traditions have to say. As the name already tells us, the tri-une God is the God in sociality, rich in relationships, the God who unites. His nature is not almighty power. It is love. The trinitarian love does not rule through division and separation, on the Roman principle of 'divide and rule'. It rules by healing what has been divided and by uniting what has been separated. The solitary man of power may be an imitation of the Almighty, but the image of the triune God can only be a human community in which free and equal persons, in the difference of their unique characters and endowments, are there with each other, and for each other. The trinitarian idea helps me to seek God's presence not only in the heights of the heavens above us and not only in the depths of the being within us, but also in the community between us human beings, and between everything created.

6

Unanswered questions

I shall end this chapter on contextual theologies by formulating some open theological questions. My intention is not to criticize these theologies in order to facilitate their rejection by the male, white theology of the First World. The purpose is to develop them further and to help them to gain a better hearing. Because these contextual theologies all sprang from the downside of the history of the First World, their claim to truth stands as long as this First World – modernized and globalized as it is today – continues to exist. It is pathological blindness when theologians and the bishops of the churches who live in the midst of the First World neither notice the gaze of the others, nor are willing to endure it, nor are capable of seeing themselves through the eyes of the oppressed and excluded.

In front of me at the moment I have a questionnaire from Sri Lanka which has been drawn up by the well-known Catholic theologian Tissa Balasuriya OMI. The first question is: 'Does the teaching of history in your curriculum include a critical examination of the activity of colonial powers in your country or by your country elsewhere?' The answer of the Protestant theological faculty in Tübingen would surely have to be: No. No one has hit on this idea, if I may except myself. Church history is presented in the framework of European history, theological history in the framework of the history of modern thought. A history of the Third World and of Third World theologies is simply not in evidence. It may perhaps be talked about in connection with missionary history. The following critical questions are intended to point theological interest towards the theologies which have developed in the Third World, and quite consciously so, and which criticize the universal claims made by the theologies of the First World.[163]

1. If praxis is the criterion of theory, what is the criterion of praxis?

The thesis is propounded that 'the first act of theology' is engagement on behalf of the oppressed people, on the basis of an analysis of the causes of their wretchedness. Theological reflection must be the second act,[164] and presupposes the first. I consider this thesis to be one-sided, however, and of importance polemically only in countering the idealistic thesis: first theory – then practice. The relation between practice and theory is always circular, and hence must be defined dialectically, not in a linear way. In every involvement, perception and decision come together, just as in every theory experience and perception act in combination. No one decides blindly and only thinks later about what he has actually committed himself to. The simplistic precedence given to practice ahead of theory appears Anselmian and clerical (*credo ut intelligam* – I believe so that I may understand) without its dialectical reversal (*intelligo ut credam* – I understand so that I may believe). Theology which presupposes that the creed of the church has first been blindly affirmed can only be an internal church study, which has nothing to do with the scientific and scholarly disciplines outside. Its place is the monastery, as in Anselm's case, or the diocesan seminary. The simplistic precedence given to the decision of faith which must be made before there can be theological perception is familiar to us from Pietism. Theology is then 'the theology of the born-again'. If liberation theology were to become a 'theology of the involved', it would become a kind of social pietism of virtuous thinking.

But if the presupposition for theological reflection is to be not merely right thinking about solidarity with the poor, but also the sociological analysis of its wretchedness, we have to ask: what sociological analysis? There is no objective analysis without one's own 'knowledge-constitutive interest'. To put theological reflection second gives rise to the suspicion that the Christian faith is only being used to support previously selected sociological analyses of socio-economic wretchedness, and is being pressed into service so that a presupposed socio-political option may be imbued with Christian engagement. That is a good thing if it moves Christians to social and political involvement, but it is bad as a way of bringing socially involved people to Christianity. 'Christians for Socialism' was an option of this kind in 1972. But it calls for the reversal: '. . . and Socialism for the Kingdom of God and his Righteousness and Justice!', so that through Christianity socialism too may be 'reminded of God's kingdom, God's commandments and righteousness', as Thesis V of the Barmen Theological Declaration of the Confessing Church said in 1934, when talking generally about rulers and ruled.

Faith in Christ has its own praxis: the discipleship of Christ crucified. Because in Christ the kingdom and justice of God for the poor, the sick, the marginalized and the children are thrown open, and are already present, what follows for Christ's sake is 'the preferential option for the poor' and the conflict with the people of power who have made them poor and sick, marginalized and abandoned. That goes beyond socialist options, for it also leads to community in solidarity with people with whom no revolution and no state can ever be made. Who is the criterion of this praxis of justice? It is *Christ*, who is present, hidden, in the poor, the sick and the children (Matthew 25).

2. If the crucified people are to redeem the world, who then redeems the people?

With this redeemer myth both Ignazio Ellacuria in San Salvador and Ahn Byun-Mu in Korea have wished to express the dignity of the tormented and oppressed people. It is true that the poor are exposed without defence to the violent acts of the rich, and that they suffer the sins of the First World, inasmuch as sin is an act of violence towards those who are weaker. It is also true that according to the synoptic Gospels Christ as the coming Son of man-Judge of the world is already present in hidden form in the poor, and waits for the just acts of those who are his, just as he will judge according to what people do for the poor, or against them. But for all that, theologians surely cannot impose on poor, exploited people, in addition to the poverty which they want to overcome, the burden of the redemption of the world through their bearing of the First World's sins. The poor, crucified people are not *Christus prolongatus* – the extension of Christ – nor are they the people of voluntary martyrs who 'complete' what is lacking in 'the sufferings of Christ' for the redemption of the world. How can anyone who wants to help the people out of their involuntary impoverishment, which is not self-inflicted, wish to lend to its suffering this religious sacrificial lustre for the redemption of the world? Which poor man or woman will be helped by that? The collective interpretation of Isaiah 53, the chapter about the suffering servant of God, is false, even in Old Testament terms, because even the first 'servant of God', Moses, was not a collective, and not an individual person, but was a divine figure representing Godself. Simply to transfer this to the poor 'crucified' people is hermeneutically questionable, and in my view completely wrong, if in this way these people are to be turned into a collective Christ.[165]

Behind these theological deductions we catch sight of the nineteenth-century Idealist myth of emancipation. After the emancipation of the bourgeoisie, the proletariat comes forward for the 'human emancipation of man'. The process of the self-liberation of the proletariat from exploitative class rule through self-organization is therefore pursued vicariously on behalf of the human race, and can only end when the whole of humanity has become 'the subject of its own history'.[166] In this respect the proletariat in all countries is an *avant garde* that fights for the liberation of humanity. If this emancipation process is described in terms of the Christian redeemer myth we have just cited, the result is not in actual fact to reinforce the motivation for this struggle; rather, the motivation for it is weakened. The people who break their chains and throw them away cannot have any desire to 'bear' the sins of the world.

3. If the goal of liberation is to make the people the determining subject of their own history, what is the goal of that history?

To make every individual person and humanity as a whole the determining 'subjects of their own history' has been the declared goal of all the democratic, socialist and emancipatory movements of modern times: 'We are the people.' If we wanted to deny this aim to the liberation movements of the colonialized peoples, the descendants of the African slaves, the Korean minjung, and women, we should have to deny all progress in the awareness of freedom and all institutions of freedom in the modern world. This goal is as 'self-evident' as human dignity and human rights. The democratic idea achieves its goal only when all peoples organize themselves democratically, and when all governments derive their legitimating power from the free assent of the governed. The socialist idea achieves its goal only when there are no more classes and no more class rule. The idea of humanity achieves its goal only when the dignity of each and every human being is respected and secured through the protection of their human rights. In short, the goal of every liberation movement is liberty.

But what is this liberty then used for? What does 'the subject of its own history' do with that history? To be the subject of its own history is the presupposition for free decisions, but it is not in itself as yet a salvific goal, for this determining subject can also become the subject of its own destruction. If it is the subject of both good and evil, it can dig its own grave too. The mere seizure of power over one's own history is no guarantee that good will come of it, even if that is better than to be the helpless victim of decisions made by others. Consequently we must add the moral goal of the history to this goal of liberation, and must at least say the following:

The history of which men and women are to be the subject must have as its goal justice, peace and the integrity of creation, in expectation of the coming kingdom of God, which will complete history and put everything to rights.

The kingdom of God which will complete everything begins in this world with the liberation of those who are bound, with the achievement of justice for those who suffer violence, with calling the poor and the children blessed, and with the new beginning of life in hope.

4. Does liberation theology lead to the liberation of the poor and women from Christian theology?

This question sounds somewhat paradoxical, but it arises inescapably if the logic of liberation theology is thought through to the end. The starting point of the Third World theologies is the struggle of the poor and the oppressed against all forms of injustice and the rule of the few over the many. The true determining 'subject of the theology' is therefore 'the poor people with a liberated consciousness', for God is a God of the poor. In Latin America most of the poor are Christians, many of them, however, forcibly converted Catholic Indios and blacks. If these people acquire their political and cultural freedom, they will also free themselves from Christianity in church and theology, and will rediscover their suppressed cultural and religious traditions. This is already happening now among the Mayas. If liberation theology is to be transferred to the oppressed in India (as is being attempted in dalit theology), we come up against the fact that the mass of the poor are Hindus and have no desire whatsoever to become Christians. For their liberation, they ask neither about the Christian faith nor about any other theology. The uprising of the oppressed peoples in Africa was a liberation from the colonial rule of the Christian nations. The participation of Christians in these struggles for liberation therefore by no means merely constitutes 'a new starting point for theological reflection'.[167] It is also the starting point for a departure *from* theological reflection. If the

Christian movement for the liberation of women sees itself as part of the world-wide movement for women's emancipation, its Christian elements can be used as the vehicle for involving Christian women in the struggle; but this is not necessary. So if the contextual liberation theologies in their present forms go beyond Christianity, what is left of their Christian identity? We do not have to think conservatively in order to come up against this question; we must only think liberation theology radically through to the end.

I can well imagine that some theologians, men and women both, who have become involved contextually in one way or another, will feel criticized by these questions. I can also imagine that these critical questions will earn me applause from the wrong side. But I believe that truth compels us to face up to them so that we may arrive at more serviceable answers than the ones we have found up to now.

IV. The 'Broad Place' of the Trinity

I

Personal approaches

The relevance of an understanding of belief in the triune God came home to me in three ways:

(a) *Political theology.* At the end of the 1960s, when we began to think about a new political theology, we were convinced by Erik Peterson's article on 'Monotheism as a Political Problem', with its criticism of the monotheistic justification of monarchist and absolute power, and its postulate: 'For Christians there can be political action only if the premise is belief in the triune God.'[1] First published in 1935, Peterson's article came out at a time when in Germany the fanaticized masses were chanting 'one people – one Reich – one Führer', and when Hitler was legitimating his 1933 seizure of power through the 'providence of world history', whose agent he claimed to be. At the same time, however, with the help of a posse of historical instances, every religious legitimation of a universal monarchy was driven home on Christian grounds: the worship of the one God in heaven – a mode of argument that had been normal practice from time immemorial, from China by way of Persia as far as Rome: 'One God – one emperor – one empire.' The formula was used by Genghis Kahn as well as by Louis XIV, in non-Christian empires as well as Christian ones.[2]

But the Christian doctrine of the Trinity is different. It does not link the eternal God with a godlike ruler. It brings that God together with the Christ crucified in the name of the Roman empire, and with the liberating Spirit of the resurrection, the Spirit of life. Peterson believed that with the development of the doctrine of the Trinity in the concept of God, 'monotheism as a political problem is finished and done with'. 'The doctrine of the divine monarchy was bound to founder on trinitarian dogma.'[3] Historically, however, this was not the case. The 'political theology' of Carl Schmitt (1922, 1934) finally boosted political monotheism into a justification for Hitler's total dictatorship.[4] And after his conversion to Catholicism, Peterson did not even notice the clerical monotheism of the papal hierarchy, the monarchical episcopate: one God – one Christ – one pope – one church.

Yet for all that, Peterson's critical starting point was important for the development of the 'new political theology' – new, because its subject is no longer the state and political sovereignty; it is now the church in society and the political actions of Christians.[5] Once the premise is belief in the triune God, the acts of Christians in church and political life are determined by the discipleship of the crucified Christ and life in the Spirit of God, not through obedience to the powers that be, and loyalty to one's own country and people. Political loyalty and social conformity are possible only to the extent to which they are not in contradiction to the discipleship of Christ and life in the Spirit. In the case of contradiction, we must contradict: 'Do not be conformed to this world . . .:' It is with these words that Paul begins the ethical and political chapters, 12–13, of his Epistle to the Romans.

(b) *The theology of the cross.* When in 1972 I came to concentrate on the theology of the cross, and wrote *The Crucified God*, I turned the traditional question upside down. The question traditionally asked was the soteriological one: what does the cross of Christ mean for us men and women? My question now was the theological one: what does the cross of the Son of God mean for God himself? And I came face to face with the pain of the Father of Jesus Christ who suffered with him. If Christ dies with the cry of profoundest God-forsakenness, then in God the Father there must be a correspondingly profound experience of forsakenness by the Son. If the Son suffers his death on the cross not just as a human death but also as an eternal death of God-forsakenness, and thus as 'the death of God', then – or so we must conclude – the God whom he always called 'Abba, dear Father' suffers the death of his Son and the deadly tornness of his own heart and eternal being. The death of the Son of God on the cross reaches deep into the nature of God and, above all other meanings, is an event which takes place in the innermost nature of God himself: the fatherless Son and the sonless Father. Anyone who thinks about this meaning for God of Christ's death on the cross, discovers the manifested mystery of the triune God: 'One of the Trinity suffered', says Cyril's now accepted theopaschite principle.[6] I would add: if one suffers, the others suffer too. Christ's death on the cross is an inner-trinitarian event before it assumes significance for the redemption of the world.

There are two classic Christian images of the Trinity which can well be used for preaching, instruction and theological meditation. The one is Andrei Rublev's wonderful icon, painted in the fifteenth century in Orthodox Moscow. The three divine Persons are sitting at table. Through the tender inclining of their heads and the symbolic gestures of their hands they show the profound unity which joins them and in which they are one. The chalice on the table points to the self-giving of the Son on Golgotha for the redemption of the world. The situation is the moment before the incarnation of the Son for the redemption of the world. The picture is based on the story in Genesis 18 in which Abraham and Sarah receive 'three men', lavish hospitality on them, and from them receive confirmation of God's promise of a son, a promise over which Sarah admittedly laughs, because of her advanced age. Abraham and Sarah had 'entertained angels unawares', says the later interpretation. They encountered the triune God, declared later Christian theology. Rublev leaves Abraham and Sarah out of the picture and paints the 'three angels' in such a way that it is impossible to discover who depicts the Father, who the Son and who the Spirit. And so this incomparable portrayal of the unportrayable God came into being.

The other image of the Trinity is the mediaeval 'mercy seat' pictured in the Latin Western church. With an expression of intense pain, God the Father carries in his hands the crossbeam of the cross on which the dead Son hangs, while the Holy Spirit in the form of a dove descends from the Father on to the Son. Just as in the icon the eucharistic chalice stands at the centre between the three Persons, so here the cross is at the centre of the triune God. But here what is being shown is the breathtaking situation of Holy Saturday, *after* the death of the Son and *before* his raising from the dead through the life-giving divine Spirit, a situation which justifies the other description of this picture, 'The Pain of God'. Johann Rist's German hymn 'O mighty dread, Godself is dead . . .' was also originally a hymn for Holy Saturday.

In both these pictures, Christ's death on the cross and the making-present in the eucharist of its redeeming significance are the 'heart' of the triune God.[7] I know of no Christian portrayals of the Trinity in which the cross is missing. The redeeming cross of Christ always pierces deep into the eternal divine mystery, and it is only in the crucified Christ, bound to us in solidarity, that the divine mystery reveals itself. The Trinity is the theological background for the happening on the cross; the crucified Christ is the revelation of the trinitarian mystery of God. To put it in scholastic terms: the doctrine of the Trinity must therefore be seen as the formal, or essential, principle of the theology of the cross, and the theology of the cross as the material principle of the doctrine of the Trinity. This becomes manifest in the raising of Christ: it is only when we plumb the depths of the abyss in 'the pain of God' and in Christ's eternal 'death of God' that we are possessed by the immeasurable Easter jubilation at the victory of life over sin, death and hell, and over the beauty of the new creation of all things in the God's eternal presence.

(c) *Orthodox Theology.* I met him during a theological lecture tour through Romania, to which the Patriarch Justin had invited me in 1979. He spoke at the end of my lectures in the Theological Institute in Bucharest, and what he said was always followed by a long respectful silence in the lecture hall. I am talking about Dumitru Staniloae, professor for dogmatics, and acknowledged master of Romanian Orthodox theology and the newly awakened Orthodox spirituality. In ten volumes he translated the famous *Philokalia* into Romanian. His *Teologia Dogmatica Ortodoxa* and his *Teologia Morala Ortodoxa* influenced generations of priests and theologians in Romania after the war. During Communist rule he was imprisoned for five years – on the grounds of 'mysticism'! His *Theology of Love*, he once said, was inspired by the same spirit as my *Theology of Hope*.

In spite of his advanced age, Staniloae played a lively part in the ecumenical consultations in Klingenthal, where we tried to find the solution to the *filioque* problem in the doctrine of the Trinity.[8] The Western church's introduction of the *filioque* into the Niceno-Constantinopolitan Creed for the 'procession of the Holy Spirit from the Father' led to the schism in the ecumenical church in 1054 – a schism which still, right down to the present day, disastrously divides the Christian churches in Europe, as the conflicts in the Balkans show. Staniloae convinced me that the *filioque* addition is superfluous and detrimental.[9] For if the Holy Spirit proceeds from 'the Father', then 'the Son' is always already present, since in the trinitarian perspective the Father is always the Father of the Son. Conversely, without the addition of *filioque*, the Son can proceed not only from the Father but from the Spirit too; and this leads to a richer christology in the reciprocal relationship to pneumatology. The fact that we are still incapable of thinking the relative independence of God the Holy Spirit over against its closer definitions and attributions 'Spirit of God' and 'Spirit of Christ', lies in the fateful introduction into the creed of the supposedly unimportant and 'speculative' *filioque* formula.[10] When in place of the metaphysical impassibility of the Godhead I put the biblically grounded 'passion of the passionate God', it was, perhaps surprisingly, the Orthodox theology of Staniloae which met me half way, and saw in this an expression of 'God's compassion', if we understand that in the sense of the Old Testament.

With financial help from the Protestant churches and the Catholic Bishops' Conference, we were then able to publish and make accessible to the West the German translation of Staniloae's *Orthodox Dogmatics*, the translation being prepared by the Lutheran professor Hermann Pitters in Sibiu/ Hermannstadt.[11]

2

I Believe in the triune God

1. The one name of the triune God

Simply to hear 'the name of the Father, and of the Son, and of the Holy Spirit' is to sense that there must be a marvellous fellowship in the mystery of God. It is *the one name* of God, in which 'the Father, the Son and the Holy Spirit' are so different that they are named one after the other, and are joined with each other through the narrating 'and'. In trinitarian thinking we do not reduce God to a concept. We tell his eternal history. We call the divine mystery a 'tri-unity' when we wish to start from the three Persons and stress their one-ness; we talk of the 'threefold God' when we proceed from God's one-ness and contemplate the three Persons in which this one-ness 'un-folds' itself, since it is a one-ness differentiated in itself. 'The threefold God' has a modalistic sound, 'triunity' a tritheistic one. To talk about God 'one-in-three'[12] is not very helpful, because it brings the one-ness numerically on to the same level as the three-ness of the Persons. I would also prefer to avoid talking about a 'God in three Persons'[13] because the word three is related to the one personal God, and suggests the figure of a body with three heads.

With whatever term we use, however, we are expressing the insight that God is not a solitary Lord of heaven, who sub-jugates everything, as earthly despots have always done in his name. Nor is God a cold, silent force of destiny, which deter-mines everything and is touched by nothing. The triune God is a God in community, rich in inner and outward relationships. It is only of him that we can say 'God is love', for love is not solitary, but presupposes those who are different, joins those who are different, and distinguishes those who are joined. If 'the Father and the Son and the Holy Spirit' are joined together through eternal love, then their one-ness is in their *concord* with each other. They form their unique, divine community through their self-giving to one another. By virtue of their overflowing love, they go beyond themselves and open themselves in creation, reconciliation and redemption for the *other being* of finite, contradictory and mortal creatures, in order to cede them space in their own eternal life, and to let them participate in their own joy.

2. *The trinitarian history of God*

God's history with the world is a trinitarian history.[14] All three Persons of the Trinity are always involved, whether the Father creates the world through the Son in the energies of the Holy Spirit, and preserves it for the coming of his kingdom, whether the Son is sent into the world by the Father through the Holy Spirit, then in his turn sending the Holy Spirit from the Father into the world, or whether the Holy Spirit glorifies the Son and the Father and leads the world into the eternal life of the Trinity. But as this brief summary shows, the divine Persons are involved in the history of the world in different ways in each case. Their interplay changes, because the subject of the action changes from the Father to the Son and to the Spirit. But it is always a co-efficacy of the divine Persons in concurrence, through which their eternal fellowship is thrown open for the time of creation, and its 'wide space' for creation's free development and final glorification.

Out of this a double perspective emerges. In the first, the triune God empties himself in creation, its preservation and redemption, in order finally to dwell there with his eternal glory – as in his temple – so that we can say with Paul that in the end 'God will be all in all' (I Cor. 15.28). And then there is the other perspective: that God's history with the world is played out between the divine Persons. Out of love for the Son/Logos, who is at the same time the Daughter/Wisdom, the Father creates a world of living beings who are meant to correspond to him; out of love for the Father, the Son himself becomes human and Wisdom becomes flesh, in order to redeem humanity and all the living; while the Holy Spirit fills everything that is with life, and holds all created being together.[15] If through the Logos/ Wisdom the Father in the power of the Spirit creates a world differentiated from God, then this world derives 'from God', is formed 'through God' and exists 'in God'. The goal of its redemption is 'that they also may be in us' (John 17.21).

We cannot dispense with any of these perspectives in favour of another. But they can be intertwined with each other in such a way that we can say that the triune God will indwell the world *in a divine way* – the world will indwell God *in a creaturely way*.

The heart of the trinitarian history of God with the world in the changing efficacies of the divine Persons can be perceived in the history of Christ. It is first of all *Jesus' history in the Spirit*. From the time of his baptism Jesus knows that he has been sent as Christ into the world – sent by the Father through the Spirit.[16] The subject of his community with the God whom he calls 'Abba', so as to understand himself as the messianic 'Child', is the Spirit. The Spirit is also the determining subject of his proclamation and his healing acts and, not least, the subject too of his self-surrender to death on the cross. Through the Spirit the Father raises him from the dead. After that the deter-mining subject changes: the risen Christ sends the Holy Spirit from the Father and is himself present in this life-giving Spirit. The Spirit of God the Father becomes the Spirit of Christ, and Christ's history in the Spirit becomes *the history of the Spirit of Christ*. This change of subject in the history of salvation is described by the Gospel of John in Christ's farewell discourses, which indeed are also the advent discourses of the Paraclete, the Spirit. In the trinitarian history of creation and preservation, and of reconciliation through Christ, the determining subject of the action is *God the Father*; but now, in the thanksgiving and the praise of God, and finally in the redemption through the resurrection, and the glorification of reconciled and redeemed creation, this subject changes to *God the Spirit*. Here the Holy Spirit is not merely 'the Spirit of the Father' and 'the Spirit of the Son'. It is God the Spirit, who glorifies the Father through the Son, and through the Son unites the whole creation – now made eternally living – with the Father.

We are drawn into the trinitarian history of God with the world, its creation, its redemption and its glorification, through *baptism* in the name of the triune God. The first trinitarian creeds are baptismal creeds (Matt. 28.19). The life in the Spirit and in the discipleship of Christ which baptism symbolizes is the praxis of the doctrine of the Trinity. That means that this is anything but a speculative theology-de-luxe, without any relevance for life. The person who confesses the triune God begins to live 'in him'. We experience ourselves in God and God in us (I John 4.16). That is the new, true life.

In the fellowship with Christ, just as in trinitarian faith, everything depends on Christ's divine sonship. Those who understand it lay hold of their own 'rank' as children of God and become assured of their future in God's kingdom, which Paul calls the 'right of inheritance' enjoyed by God's children. The divine sonship does not only link Christ with God; it also, conversely, links God with the crucified Christ. What it means is not so much a deification of Jesus as a humanization of God. Anyone who denies the divine sonship of Jesus dissolves this link. What is left is then only the Jesus humanism of the nineteenth century or the Islamization of the Christian God in the twentieth. If Jesus is not 'God's Son', then his suffering and death on the cross has no divine significance for the redemption of the world either. It vanishes in the unending history of the suffering of murdered men and women. But if 'one of the Trinity suffered', then he brings healing into wounded humanity, and hope for life into this murdering and dying world.

3

From the historical hope in God's promise to the spatial experience of God's indwelling

My early theological world was dominated by prophetic concepts such as protest and promise, promise and Exodus, Exodus and liberation. 'The logic of promise' and the expectation of God's coming shaped my theological thinking from the time of *Theology of Hope* (1954; ET 1967).[17] In those years there was a great deal of talk about the presence of God in the dynamic of history, and about God's acts in history. In the historical framework of God's promises and of active human hopes, God 'dwelt', so to speak, 'in time' (Dietrich Ritschl's phrase) because time, not space, dominates the categories of history. But the God who is present in time is also the mainspring of world history. He is 'the God before us', as Johann Baptist Metz put it, the God who goes ahead of us, drives our developments forward, and prepares for us the way into the future of his eternal kingdom. As many people sensed at that time, he is a 'restless God', who leads his people with their 'restless hearts' through the world 'of unlimited possibilities' into that ultimate future in which he together with them will find rest in an all-redeeming new creation.

But what we also had very much in our minds, consciously or unconsciously, was a hectic human history of revolutions and repressions in the Third World, and the increasing acceleration in the thrust towards modernization in politics, culture and the economy in the countries of the West – the 'renewing of the

New', as the Americans said. It was only slowly, at the beginning of the 1970s, that we became conscious of the simple fact that human history is located within the ecological limits of this planet earth, and that human civilization can survive only if it respects these limits, and the laws, cycles and rhythms of the earth. If humanity disturbs, and ultimately destroys, its environment, it will annihilate itself. As we became aware of the 'limits of growth', as the Club of Rome put it in 1972, we found ourselves facing a problem with the all-dominating category of historical time. No one can 'remain' in time, let alone 'dwell' in it. We can at most 'go with the times' by hastening from the past into the future, while time rolls away under our feet from the future into the past, like a lift which persists in going up when we want to go down. This is a symbol of progress which can be applied to more than one sector of the continually modernizing world. In those years we developed new theologies of history (Wolfhart Pannenberg), of hope (Jürgen Moltmann) and of liberation (Gustavo Gutiérrez), in order to come to terms with the historical dynamic; but we were not able to overcome the dichotomy between human history and nature with which our predecessors had justified the anthropocentricism of modern times. In the nineteenth century there were already attempts to 'humanize nature' and to 'naturalize' human beings, and a combination of the two attempts – for example by the young Karl Marx – but they failed to find a way out of the dilemma, either theoretically or practically.

Ever since my work on an ecological doctrine of creation and a social doctrine of the Trinity, I have tried to expand my theological world, which had been one-sided in its orientation towards time. I now tried to extend it through the concepts of space and 'home', the Shekinah and the perichoresis, reciprocal indwelling and the coming to rest in one another. The link between my early theology of time and this later theology of space was for me the discovery of the fundamental importance of *the sabbath* for the doctrine of creation and for the messianic expectation of the future.[18] The periodic interruption of fleeting working time by the sabbath times of rest for human beings and nature in the presence of God also interrupts the dynamic of accelerated modernization. That is why the preservation of the sabbath/Sunday from the flexible working hours of the modern world is a protection for human dignity and God's rights. At that time I found many theological and philosophical studies of time, but almost none of space. The only standard work is Max Jammer's book, with a foreword by Albert Einstein.[19] Time and space are complementary in the space-time continuum of physics, but for our human experience they are not symmetrical: we can experience different times in the same space, but not different spaces at the same time.

The exilic and post-exilic theology of Israel has given us the *concept of the Shekinah*, which means the 'indwelling of God'. It was part of God's covenant with Israel from the beginning. The one who promises 'I will be your God' also promises 'I will dwell in the midst of the Israelites.'[20] Figuratively speaking, the Shekinah comes upon the ark of the covenant, the movable altar which the wandering people of God carried with them. David brought the ark to Jerusalem. Solomon built a temple for it, and in the temple's Holy of Holies God's Shekinah 'dwelt'. But what happened to it after the temple had been destroyed by the Babylonians? Did it return to heaven, or did it go with the people into Babylonian captivity? Because God dwelt 'in the midst of the Israelites' even before there was an ark, there was one convincing answer: God's Shekinah itself became homeless together with the people, and wanders with them through the exile of this world, until one day, united with the Eternal One, it comes to rest, and fills the whole world. According to Franz Rosenzweig's interpretation, the idea of the Shekinah already implies a self-differentiation in God: 'God cuts himself off from himself, he gives himself away to his people, he suffers their sufferings with them, he goes with them into the misery of the foreign land, he wanders with their wanderings.'[21]

An influential background for the development of New Testament christology can be found in this Shekinah theology. 'The Word became flesh and dwelt among us' (John 1.14), in

Christ dwells 'the whole fullness of God bodily' (Col. 2.9), the Holy Spirit 'dwells' in our bodies and in the community of Christ as in a temple (I Cor. 6.19). These indwellings of God in Christ and in the congregations of his people point beyond themselves to the *cosmic Shekinah* in which God will be 'all in all' (I Cor. 15.28). According to Christian theology, incarnation and indwelling are grounded in the kenosis of God. By virtue of his lowering of himself, the infinite God is able to indwell the finite being of creation.

The idea of mutual indwelling, *perichoresis*, goes back to the theology of the Greek Fathers, and makes it possible to conceive of a community without uniformity and a personhood without individualism. The semantic history of the term has been well investigated.[22] The noun means vortex or rotation; the verb means a movement from one to another, to reach round and go round, to surround, embrace, encompass. In the New Testament it occurs only twice (Matt. 3.5 and 14.35), and in both instances it means only 'the world around'. Gregory Nazianzus was probably the first to use the word theologically. John Damascene made it the key term for his christology, and then for the doctrine of the Trinity too. In *christology*, perichoresis describes the mutual interpenetration of two different natures, the divine and the human, in Christ, the God-human being. The examples are red-hot iron, in which fire and iron interpenetrate, or Moses' burning bush, 'which was not consumed'. In *the doctrine of the Trinity*, perichoresis means the mutual indwelling of the homogeneous divine Persons, Father, Son and Spirit. Here the Greek expression *hidrysis* was also used, a word which means mutuality without admixture and without separation. John Damascene wanted to find a definition for the Johannine unity of the Son with the Father: 'I am in the Father, the Father is in me' (14.11); 'He who sees me sees the Father' (14.9). Jesus and God the Father are not *one and the same*, they are *at one* – a unity – in their mutual indwelling.

The perichoresis of the divine Persons describes their unity, their oneness, in a trinitarian sense, not by way of the metaphysical terms 'divine substance' or 'absolute subject'. Its application both to the two natures in christology as well as to the three Persons in the doctrine of the Trinity shows the fruitfulness of the concept. It can delineate not only the link without admixture with 'the others' of the same species, but also the link with 'the other' of a different species. Whereas the three divine Persons form their perichoresis through *homologous love*, deity and humanity are linked in the God-human being by virtue of *heterologous love*.

The Latin translation of the term was first *circumincessio*, later also *circuminsessio*.[23] The first word describes a dynamic interpenetration (*incedere*), the second an enduring, resting indwelling (*insedere*). Eventually the Council of Florence (1438–1445) formulated a dogmatic definition which was intended to serve the ecumenical unification of the Western and the Eastern church:

> On account of this unity the Father is wholly in the Son, wholly in the Holy Spirit; the Son is wholly in the Father, wholly in the Holy Spirit; the Holy Spirit is wholly in the Father, wholly in the Son. No one of them either precedes the others in eternity, or exceeds them in greatness, or supervenes in power.[24]

On the perichoretic level, therefore, no one of the Persons in the Trinity precedes the others, not the Father either. Here the Trinity is a non-hierarchical community. If it is possible to talk at all about the Father's 'monarchy', it can only be on the level of the constitution of the Trinity, not in its perichoretic life. In the Trinity it is not the monarchy of the Father which is the 'seal of their unity';[25] it is the perichoresis. Nor is it the Holy Spirit which in the unity of the Father and the Son constitutes 'the bond of unity' (Augustine's view). This conception would reduce the Trinity to a Binity, and would rob the Holy Spirit of his own Personhood. It is not a single subject in the Trinity which constitutes the unity; it is that triadic inter-subjectivity which we call perichoresis.

The Latin words *circumincessio* and *circuminsessio* bring

out the double meaning of the trinitarian unity: movement and rest. We arrive at the same result if we use the Greek verbs *perichoreo* and *perichoreuo*. These then describe the mutual *resting* in each other and their shared *'round-dance'*.[26] But semantically, perichoresis is derived from *perichoreo*, not from *perichoreuo*. Nevertheless, the shifting and diversified round-dance of three persons can quite well be used as an illuminating description.[27] What is meant, at all events, is that in the Trinity there is simultaneously absolute rest and complete movement, rather as in the eye of a hurricane. On the level of the trinitarian perichoresis, there is complete equality between the divine Persons. No one of them precedes the other in eternity. We cannot even number them, and call the Holy Spirit the 'third Person' of the Trinity.

Each Person 'moves' in the two others. That is the meaning of their *circumincessio*. So the trinitarian Persons offer each other reciprocally the inviting *room for movement* in which they can develop their eternal livingness. For living beings, there is no freedom without free spaces in their social life. In a transferred sense, that is also true for the divine Persons in their perichoresis. They move with each other and round one another and in one another, and change 'from glory into glory'. We might compare this with circular movements or a kaleidoscopic play of colour. In their eternal mobility, the trinitarian Persons fuse with the free scopes they give each other without being absorbed in one another. In their *circumincessio* they are simultaneously Persons and rooms for movement. In the human sphere we call these social spaces in which others can move 'moral space'. If we transfer this to the divine level we have to proceed from a unity of physical and moral spaces, for the perichoresis is as primal as is the life of the trinitarian Persons.

Each Person ek-sists outside himself in the two others. It is the power of perfect love which lets each Person go out of himself to the extent that he is wholly present in the other. That means, conversely, that every trinitarian Person is not merely *Person* but also *living space* for the two others. In the perichoresis each Person makes himself 'inhabitable' for the two others, and prepares the wide space and the dwelling for the two others. That is the meaning of their *circuminsessio.* Consequently we should not talk only about the *three trinitarian Persons*, but must at the same time speak of the *three trinitarian spaces* in which they mutually exist. Each Person actively dwells in the two others and passively cedes space for the two others – that is to say, at once gives and receives the others. God's Being is personal being-there (*Da-sein*), social being-with (*mit-sein*) and, perichoretically understood, being-in (*in-sein*).

The perception of their perichoretic unity leads, not least, to a new version of the trinitarian concept of person. Boethius' traditionally used definition *Persona est individua substantia naturae rationalis* ('a person is an individual existence of a rational nature') is unusable, because in the perichoresis the trinitarian Persons cannot be individual existences or individuals remaining in themselves and existing from themselves. They must rather be understood as ek-static hypostases. We need a *perichoretic concept of person.*[28] This goes even beyond the communitarian concept of person – *persona in communione* – because it has to be moulded by the reciprocal indwelling. By virtue of their selfless love, the trinitarian Persons come in one another to themselves. In the Son and in the Spirit the Father comes to himself and becomes conscious of himself as Father; in the Father and in the Spirit the Son comes to himself and becomes conscious of himself as Son; in the Father and in the Son the Holy Spirit comes to himself and becomes conscious of himself as the Spirit.

If it is the perichoresis which forms the trinitarian unity, then it is that which also leads to the *trinitarian differentiation* between the divine Persons. The Father differentiates between the Son and the Spirit, because he has different relationships to the Son and to the Spirit; the Son forges the difference between the Father and the Spirit because he establishes distinguishable relationships to the Father and to the Spirit. In each case the third Person is the bond between the two others, and also differentiates between them. The counter-check is simple. If there is only the reciprocal relationships between two Persons, then they are easily distinguishable. Because the Person and relationships of the Holy Spirit have been undervalued in the tradition of the Western church, we must stress as emphatically as possible that the Spirit is not simply 'Spirit of God' and 'Spirit of Christ', as the Western church's *filioque* suggests; it is God the Holy Spirit, pre-eminently, and in relation to both God the Father and God the Son. The Spirit does not only 'receive' himself from them, as traditional language says; he also 'gives' himself to them and is wholly in them, as they are wholly in him.

4

The unity of the Trinity:
the concept of perichoresis

There are two points of departure for the development of trinitarian doctrine, the metaphysical one and the biblical one.[29] The metaphysical approach presupposes the proof that God *is* and that God *is One*. In the framework of the ancient metaphysics of substance, Tertullian formulated the famous proposition for the doctrine of the Trinity: *una substantia – tres personae* (one substance – three Persons). The unity of the Trinity subsists in the shared, homogeneous substance of the three divine Persons. They are a single divine Being. They are one substance but not one Person. In the framework of the modern metaphysics of subjectivity, Karl Rahner and Karl Barth identified the unity of the Trinity in God's Personhood and subjectivity: *one divine Person in three modes of being*, one divine subject in three distinct modes of subsistence. The unity of the Trinity lies in the sovereignty of the one God. The divine modes of being are one Person, not one substance. Both ways of thinking presuppose that the unity of the Trinity precedes the threeness of the divine Persons, and is not, therefore, itself first constituted by these Persons. The conclusion to be drawn is that in the threefold God we must assume 'one nature, one consciousness and one will', which then manifest themselves in the three modes of being or subsistence.

The touchstone for dogmatic constructions is the hermeneutics of the biblical history. If we apply this doctrine of the Trinity to the Gethsemane account, for example, we immediately perceive its limitations. Is it one mode of being of the one God who prays there to the other? How can we assume in the triune God only 'a single will' and 'a single consciousness', when Jesus' prayer to the Father ends with the words: 'Not my will but thine be done'?

The biblical starting point for the development of the doctrine of the Trinity is that there are three different actors in the divine history, Son – Father – Spirit; the question about their unity then follows. Whereas Paul and the synoptic Gospels always talk about 'God' when they mean 'the Father of Jesus Christ', explicitly trinitarian language can be found in the Gospel of John: 'He who has seen me has seen the Father', says the Johannine Jesus; 'I and the Father are one'; 'I am in the Father and the Father is in me' (John 14.9; 10.30; 14.11). Jesus and God the Father are related to each other as Persons, as the expressions 'I' and 'thou', 'we' and 'us' suggest. Their unity is not presupposed, but is constituted by the Persons themselves through their reciprocal indwelling.

This perichoretic form of unity is the only conceivable *trinitarian concept of the unity* of the triune God, because it combines threeness and oneness in such a way that they cannot be reduced to each other, so that both the danger of modalism and the danger of 'tritheism' are excluded.[30] If we understand the divine life perichoretically, it cannot be realized by a single subject alone, and cannot be thought without the three divine Persons.[31] Their shared nature, their shared consciousness and their shared will is formed intersubjectively through their specific personhood in each case, by their specific consciousness in each case, and by their own will in each case. The Father becomes conscious of himself by being conscious of the Son, and so forth.

If we see the trinitarian unity perichoretically, then it is not a self-enclosed, exclusive unity. It is a unity which is open, inviting and integrating, as we see when Jesus prays to the Father for the disciples (John 17.21) '. . . that they also may be *in us*'. This indwelling of human beings in the triune God entirely corresponds to the converse indwelling of the triune God in human beings: 'If anyone loves me, he will keep my word; and my Father will love him, and we will come to him and make our dwelling with him' (John 14.23). Perichoresis does not merely link others of the same kind; it links others of different kinds too. According to Johannine theology there is a mutual indwelling of God and human beings in love: 'He who abides in love abides *in God* and *God in him*' (I John 4.16). Paul formulates the ultimate eschatological vista as God's cosmic Shekinah, when God will be 'all *in* all' (I Cor. 15.28). All created beings will then be 'deified' in the eternal presence of the triune God, as Orthodox theology says, following Athanasius. That is to say, all created beings will find their 'broad place where there is no more cramping' (Job 36.16) in the opened eternal life of God, while in the glorified new creation the triune God will come to his eternal dwelling and rest, and to his bliss.

I have called the inviting, integrating and uniting fellowship of the triune God 'the open Trinity',[32] and have differentiated it from the images of the closed Trinity – the 'circle' or 'triangle'. The Trinity is open, not out of deficiency and imperfection, but in the superfluity and overflow of the love which gives created beings the living space for their livingness, and the free scope for their development. Jung was right when he detected in some pictures of the Trinity a 'fourth person', the Virgin Mary; but he was wrong when he made of this the archetype of a 'quaternity'.[33] In actual fact Mary is a symbol for saved humanity and the new creation of all things. She therefore finds her living space *in* the divine Tri-unity. That means that the open Trinity is the inviting encompassing reality of the whole, redeemed and renewed creation, which, for its part, then becomes the encompassing world for the divine indwelling.

5

Trinitarian experience of God

A few years ago, in Granada, Spain, I came across an old Catholic order which I had never heard of before. They call themselves 'Trinitarians', were founded in the eleventh century, and have devoted themselves ever since to 'the liberation of prisoners'. Originally that meant the redemption of enslaved Christians from Moorish prisons, but not only that. The arms on the church of the Trinitarians in Rome, St Thomas in Formis, show Christ sitting on the throne of his glory, while at his right hand and his left are prisoners with broken chains, on the one side a Christian prisoner with a cross in his hand, on the other a black prisoner without a cross. Christ frees them both, and takes them into fellowship, with him and together. 'Trinity' was the name for this original liberation theology more than eight hundred years ago.

But what does the doctrine of the Trinity – 'abstract' and 'speculative' as it sounds, in the opinion of many people – have to do with the praxis of political and social liberation theology? How can the worship of the Holy Tri-unity become a driving, leavening force for the liberation of persecuted, imprisoned and forsaken men and women? If we ask about the inner theological connection between 'Trinity' and 'liberation', we shall first have to identify the Christian experience of God as a trinitarian experience of God, and must then come to the trinitarian structure of the community of Christ and life in the Holy Spirit.

The fact that the Christian experience of God has a trinitarian structure can be seen easily enough from the early Christian benediction formula which Paul quotes in II Cor. 13.13:

The grace of our Lord Jesus Christ
and the love of God
and the fellowship of the Holy Spirit
be with us all.

(a) The trinitarian experience of God begins with the experiences of unmerited and unexpected *grace* in the encounter with Christ and in fellowship with him. In Christ 'one of the Trinity becomes human and suffers in the flesh'; so for men and women Christ is the gateway to the trinitarian experience of God. Through faith in Christ their life *in* the Trinity begins. Faith is trust in God's promise. In this believers experience grace, which frees the victims and the God-forsaken perpetrators of sin from the destructive power of evil, and through Christ, their brother in the humiliation and their redeemer in the guilt, admits them into the divine fellowship. In the fellowship of Christ the new, liberated life begins, with the great Yes of God's love for those he has created.

(b) In the fellowship of Christ, the Father of Jesus Christ becomes our Father too, and we begin to believe in God for Christ's sake. Just as Jesus called God exclusively 'Abba', dear Father, so in his fellowship believers become children of God who, moved by the Spirit, address God with the same intimate word 'Abba'. When Jesus – probably at his baptism – discovered this intimate secret of the present God, he left his family and found his 'family' in the poor, forsaken people in Galilee (*ochlos*). Those who follow him and call God 'Abba', dear Father, do nothing other than that. But this means that 'the Father of Jesus Christ' has entirely different functions in the life of Christ and the lives of those who are his from the patriarchs of the ancient family religions. Christ's 'Abba' has nothing to do with the Greek Zeus, the father of gods and men, and even less with Jupiter, the Roman father of the gods. Consequently he has nothing to do either with the political 'father of his country' and the dominating 'father of the family'.[34] He can also hardly serve as heavenly legitimation for clerical hierarchies. Even if in the Roman empire the Father of

Jesus Christ also came later to be fused with Jupiter in the concept of God, the irreconcilable difference nevertheless remains: between Jesus's God and the Roman Lord God Jupiter stands the cross on Golgotha, on which Jesus was executed in Jupiter's name through the Roman occupying power under Pontius Pilate, even if Pilate certainly 'knew not what he did'. Whereas in Roman Christendom, from the time of Lactantius, 'Father and Lord' became one in the concept of God (so that God must be 'both loved and feared'), Paul always distinguished between 'God, the Father of Jesus Christ' and 'Christ our Lord' (I Cor. 1.13, and frequently). God is the Father of Jesus Christ; Christ is our Lord and liberator; through Christ, in the relationship to God of God's children, we come as children to the Father in heaven.

(c) The 'fellowship' of the Holy Spirit is of course his fellowship with believers first of all.[35] Evidently, however, the endowment of fellowship between people who are different is ascribed to the Holy Spirit in a special way, through his creative energies. For it is through his eternal presence that the fellowship of the Father with Christ is given, and that, on the other hand, the frontiers of division and enmity between human beings are broken down, so that the Spirit can be called 'the Go-Between God' and 'the social God' (Hegel's *Gemeingeist*, or Common Spirit). The experience of the Spirit links Jews and Gentiles, Greeks and barbarians, men and women, old people and children in a new community of the equal and the free. Beyond that, the experience of the Spirit reaches out to 'all flesh' – that is to say, to everything living – and brings nature to its flowering in the first tokens of the springtime of the new creation of all things.[36] So when human beings wake to new life, the Spirit links this awakening with the expectation of 'sighing' nature. 'Community' seems to be the particular nature of the Holy Spirit and his creative energies, just as 'grace' determines the nature and specific action of the Son, and 'love' the nature and efficacy of the Father.

In the co-workings of grace, love and fellowship the trinitarian experience of God is born. Christ accepts us in grace that has no preconditions, God the Father loves us with an unconditional love, the Spirit brings us into community with all the living. The three Persons act in differentiated ways, but they all concur in a unified movement, which creates new and, in its newness, eternal life.

6

The trinitarian experience of fellowship

The other side of the trinitarian experience of God is the trinitarian experience of the fellowship of the church. Here the classic text is Jesus' high-priestly prayer in John 17.21:

> That they may all be one,
> even as thou, Father, art in me and I in thee,
> that they also may be in us,
> so that the world may believe that thou hast sent me.

The fellowship of the disciples with each other, for which Jesus prays, is intended to *correspond* to the reciprocal indwelling of the Father and the Son in the Spirit: or so we may be permitted to add. The trinitarian fellowship of God is here the prototype, the church the reflection.[37] That is the first dimension in Jesus' prayer. 'That they may all be one' is the motto of the ecumenical movement towards the visible unity of the church, for we can assume that this prayer of Jesus was heard by the Father, and that in this prayer all divided churches and Christians are already 'one'.

It is important to stress that the unity of the church 'corresponds' to the perichoretic unity of the three divine Persons, not to a single Person in the Trinity.

From time immemorial the unity of the church in hierarchically structured churches has been based on *'the monarchy' of God the Father*, and this is so even today. The 'monarchical episcopate' – one bishop – one church – as Ignatius of Antioch taught – is the result. It can then, as with the First Vatican Council, be taken even further, in the universal episcopate of the pope. But this *communio hierarchica* does not correspond to that prayer of Jesus' for the unity of those who are his.

In the Reformation movements of the sixteenth century, *Christ, the Son of God*, was then put at the centre of the fellowship of the church. 'The first-born among many brethren' (Rom. 8.29) was the mark of the community of brothers and sisters. 'The Christian Church is the community of brethren in which Jesus Christ acts in the present . . .' says Thesis 3 of the 1934 Barmen Theological Declaration of the German Confessing Church.[38] Brotherliness and sisterliness then take the place of obedience to the bishop, the conferrer of unity. But to base the fellowship of the church on fellowship with Christ in this way does not correspond to that prayer of Jesus' either.

Today, in the Pentecostal movements and the Pente-costalization of the traditional churches, we are experiencing a hitherto unknown *presence of the Holy Spirit* and its energies. Charismatic congregations are growing up in which everyone knows that he or she is accepted and needed, with his or her gifts and powers.[39] There is *one Spirit* but *a variety of gifts* (I Cor. 12.4), and the Spirit gives to each their own. The charis-matic congregation comes into being out of the pluriformity of the Spirit's energies. Its unity is God the Spirit himself, the source of life. This experience of the Spirit may well become the future of the ecclesial community. Brotherliness will give way to the power of the Holy Spirit, which confers unity in diversity.

This new development is fascinating, but even this does not correspond to the prayer of Jesus; for what constitutes the unity of the church in its trinitarian plenitude is neither the monarchy of the Father, nor the brotherliness of the Son, nor the diversity of the Spirit's gifts, each of them on its own; it is their simul-taneity, and the reciprocal interpenetration of all three Persons and their modes of efficacy, and their spaces for living. The church is meant to correspond neither to the Father nor to the Son nor to the Spirit, each for itself, but to their *eternal peri-choresis*. That is what Cyprian meant with his much-quoted dictum: 'The Church is a people brought into unity from the unity of the Father, the Son and the Holy Spirit.'[40] The community of the church comes into being out of the concurring efficacies of the Father, the Son and the Spirit. It was this trinitarian co-operation which Paul no doubt already had in mind when, talking about the abundance of the congregation's gifts, energies and ministries, he gave these a threefold base (I Corinthians 12):

> There are varieties of gifts, but it is *the one Spirit*.
> There are varieties of service, but it is *the one Lord*;
> There are varieties of powers, but it is *the one God* who inspires all of them in every one (12.4–6).

It is only if we see the perichoretic unity of the Trinity in the perichoretic co-workings of the three divine Persons that we understand the second dimension in Jesus' prayer: 'that they may also be *in us*.' That is the *mystical* dimension of the fellowship of the church. It does not merely 'correspond' to the trinitarian unity of God; it also '*exists*' *in* the Tri-unity of God, which is open to the world; for through the operation of the Father, the Son and the Spirit it has been taken into the innermost mystery of God. The open space of the perichoretic community of the triune God is the divine living space of the church. In the community of Christ and in the energies of the life-giving Spirit we experience God as *the broad place* which surrounds us from every side and brings us to the free unfolding of new life. In the love which affirms life we exist *in God* and *God in us*. The church is not just the space for the indwelling of the Holy Spirit. It is the space indwelt by the whole Trinity. The whole Trinity is the living space of the church, not just the Holy Spirit.

What does this community look like, in its correspondence to the triune God and its life in the Trinity? We find the classic text for this in Acts 4.32–37:

> Now the company of those who believed were of one heart

and soul, and no one said that any of the things which he possessed was his own, but they had everything in common . . . There was not a needy person among them.

This so-called 'early Christian communism' was not a social programme. It was the expression of the new trinitarian experience of community.[41] People put their community above the individual and their private possessions. They no longer needed these possessions to give their lives security. In the Spirit of the resurrection their fear of death disappeared, and with it their greed for life. That is why they had 'enough', 'more than enough'. In this community the competitive struggle which turns people into lonely individuals is ended, and the social chill of a heartless world vanishes.[42] The 'strong hand' of the state, which forcibly prevents men and women from becoming 'wolves' for other people, also stops short at this community. The community can deal with its own affairs. It is true that historically speaking this 'early Christian communism' did not last long, but it has by no means vanished for all that. In the Christian monastic orders, and the radical Protestant communities of the Hutterites and the Koinonia Farms, among Mennonites and Moravians, communities of this kind can still be found today. And in the new Latin American base communities people are experiencing the trinitarian fellowship of God. That is why at their meetings in Trinidade, Brazil, in July 1986 their posters bore the words: 'The Trinity is the Best Community.'[43]

I

'The Trinity is our social programme'

This thesis was put forward by Nicholas Fedorov, a friend of Dostoevsky's, and I assume that with it he was looking for a third way between the autocracy of the Russian Tsars and the anarchism of Kropotkin.[44] The Holy Tri-unity in God and its resonance in the *sobornost* of the Orthodox Church were for him models for a truly humane society in freedom and equality. The problem of how to combine personal liberty and social justice dominated the European societies from the time of the French Revolution onwards, and still has not been solved at the present day. Fedorov argued that the unity of the triune God shows just such a unity of person and community, in which the Persons have everything in common apart from the attributes and differences of their personhood. This means that a human society which corresponds to God's Tri-unity, and lives in it, must be a community without privileges, and one where liberty is not infringed. Persons can only be persons in community; the community can only be free in its personal members. The equilibrium between personal freedom and a just society should be possible in the light of the triune God and his resonance in the church, provided that the ecumenically united church can understand and present itself as the avant garde of a redeemed humanity, freed from its divisions and enmities.

Fedorov was unable to win acceptance for his ideas in the Russia of his time, but these ideas can be trend-setting today. For the last two hundred years Western industrial society (and now modern society in general) has experienced one thrust towards individualization after another. The last of them bears the name 'postmodern'. The opportunities for choice open to individualized men and women are enormously increased, and anyone who has the means can also take advantage of these opportunities. But this power is paralleled by the growing powerlessness of the individualized people, who can certainly look on at events in the world through the media, but can do nothing to change them. An individual is not a person, but – as the Latin word *individuum* says – something that in the final analysis is indivisible; it means the same as the Greek word 'atom'.[45] As the end-product of divisions, the individual has no relationships, no attributes, no memories and no names. The individual is unutterable. A person, unlike an individual, is a human existence living in the resonant field of his social connections and his history. He has a name, with which he can identify himself. A person is a social being. The modern thrusts towards individualization in society prompt the suspicion that a modern individual is the product of that age-old Roman principle of dominance: *divide et impera* – divide and rule. Individualized people can easily be dominated by political and economic forces. There is only resistance for the purpose of protecting personal human dignity if people join together in communities and decide their lives socially for themselves.

These few pointers may suffice to show the public relevance of the trinitarian concept of God for the liberation of individualized men and women, and the relevance of the trinitarian experience of community for the development of a new sociality.

Epilogue

'The Fear of the Lord is the Beginning of Wisdom' Science and Widsom

I should like to close this account of some of the methods and forms of theology today with a meditation on the relationship between theological wisdom and scientific knowledge. According to the biblical traditions, *the fear of the Lord* is the beginning of wisdom. According to the early Greek philosophers, all knowledge is the fruit of wonder. Do we have to choose between Jerusalem and Athens? Must we decide between the church and the laboratory? Or does astonishment over the world lead us to the fear of God, and the fear of God to astonishment over the world?

In our discussion of theological epistemology we saw how cognition of the same and the similar leads to the re-cognition of what we already know, and to endorsement, whereas knowledge of what is different and alien evokes pain over the alteration in our own selves.[1] But how do we come to perceive something new?

The roots of the perception of what is new are not to be found solely in the perceiving subject. They also lie in the object to be perceived. We perceive what shows itself – what 'allows itself to be perceived' – not merely what we want to perceive, and therefore bring forth of ourselves. Perceptions which lead to knowledge arise in the encounter between the awakened human senses and impressions of the outside world. Encounters of this kind issue in *astonishment*. If something astonishes us, our senses unfold for the direct reception of the impressions as flowers turn towards the rising sun; and the things or processes perceived penetrate our sensory organs, fresh and unfiltered, like the sun's rays. They quite literally impose themselves on the human being. They im-press us, and we are im-pressed. We still cannot take them in, as we say; we are taken aback, taken by storm, and at first stand there disconcerted – disconcerted by our boundless wonder. That is why alarm and amazement are so close to one another.

In wonder we perceive things *for the first time*. Astonishment is the source of intuitions. The wondering child still has no concepts with which it can grasp the impressions that crowd in upon it from every side, for it cannot remember anything comparable. It is only the second or third time that memories are formed which allow the impressions to be comprehended, and repeatable attitudes spring up to meet the impressions that crowd in. All our concepts presuppose intuitions. After many repetitions, the child has then already become accustomed to the perception. It is no longer surprised and no longer wonders. It reacts as it is accustomed to do, and as it has learnt. That is why grown-ups think of wonder as belonging to the child's eyes, which see the world for the first time. With every child a new life begins, and every child discovers the world in its own way.

But we can go beyond childlike wonder and say in general that astonishment always and everywhere accompanies the perception that a phenomenon is *unprecedented*. Every new piece of scientific knowledge is called a 'discovery' and evokes the astonishment that belongs to something that is 'for the first time'. It can be repeated, and proved, and expands the horizon of our knowledge. And yet we recall 'the first time' by giving to the discovery the name of the discoverer. Because an event of this kind evokes this astonishment over what is new, we talk about dis-coveries, meaning by this the disclosure of what has been hidden and the perception of what was hitherto unperceived.

Ever since the beginning of the scientific age, we have

stressed the active side of these discoveries. People set out on voyages of exploration, or 'make' such discoveries in the course of their experiments. But every discovery also has its foundation in its objective side. That is why we talk about phenomena, and say that what has been concealed has 'shown itself' to us. That is the passive side of such discoveries. These are experiences which 'happen to us'. Expected, they yet involuntarily surprise us. If we consider the subjective and the objective side of discoveries made for the first time, we see a consonance between that which has shown itself and that which has been discovered, The dis-covery corresponds to the re-velation. We have perceived what it has been 'given to us' to know. We have elicited something which we did not invent. The thing is as we have dis-covered it to be. The world can be known by us human beings. It is accessible to our reason. It seems to be determined by a hidden rationality.[2] Wonder is not evoked only through findings made for the first time. Even if we already know something and are familiar with it, an element of astonishment has to accompany all our knowing, since in the strict sense of the world nothing ever 'repeats itself' in the world and in our lives, for time is irreversible. What is past never returns. Consequently every moment in time is unique. Only that element of wonder within us is able to perceive the *uniqueness* of all happening, because it comprehends the dissimilarity in everything that is similar.

A sense for the uniqueness of every happening has been preserved by people who are able to wonder in the primal – we could also say childlike – sense, and can be astonished. They perceive the uniqueness of the present moment with the surprise with which they comprehended the 'first-timeness' of the discovery. The person who can neither wonder nor be astonished perceives only as a matter of routine what seems to be always the same, and what he already knows. He reacts in the customary ways he has learnt – and understands nothing. He expects nothing any more, and life passes him by – or rather, he passes life by.

Every chance in life is unique. Strictly speaking, there is no such thing as a second chance, at least not the same chance a second time. We might also call the attention awakened and heightened through astonishment and wonder literally *presence of mind*. It lets us take the unique opportunity 'by the forelock', like the *kairos* in Greek pictures. *To live attentively* means to be open for surprises and for what is new in every moment. It means experiencing life full of expectation, dis-covering anew the reality we encounter, and laying ourselves trustfully open to whatever happens to us.

We ascribe wonder as the root of knowledge to the child, and to the primal child in every grown-up. What we expect of the old, in contrast, is *wisdom*. The old are supposed to have become wise through their experience of life and through the approach of death. But although we undoubtedly assume that one becomes wise through experiences of life and death, this process is not a matter of course. 'Sixty years old and not a bit wiser' people once sang in a hit which was a favourite with everyone who wanted to remain forever young. But how do we become wise?

Wisdom does not spring directly from experience. It is the fruit of the reflective handling of experiences. It is not spontaneous perception which makes us wise; it is the perceiving of the perception. Wisdom is the ethics of knowledge. If we make a conscience out of consciousness, and hence are cognizant of what we do and leave undone, we become wise. We look over our own shoulder, so to speak, and ask: What are you doing? What purpose do your findings serve? What have experiences made of your life? What will remain when you die? Wisdom is a reflective counter-movement to spontaneous wonder. The wondering discovery of the world is one thing; wise dealings with these perceptions another.

It is of course understandable that we should look for wisdom among the old, but that we should find it there is not a matter of course for all that. In order to arrive at reflection about ourselves, about what we know, and what we do and leave undone, a countervailing force is needed through which we are brought back to ourselves. This cannot be a particular perception; it must transcend all possible perceptions, and hence the perceivable world as well. In the biblical traditions, the transcendence which brings a person back to himself is called '*the fear of the Lord*'. This does not mean the awe and terror of the Wholly Other; nor does it mean the *mysterium tremendum* of primordial religious experiences. It means the *sublimity of God*, the immeasurability of his wisdom and the fathomless complexity of his creative Spirit. The fear of God links reverence before the majesty of the 'ever greater God' with a childlike basic trust in his immeasurable goodness, and curiosity about his creative activity in the history of the cosmos, the history of life, and in personal history. The fear of God does not make people slaves of a unloved Almighty; it is merely the other side of the love of God. 'To fear the Lord is wisdom's full measure' – 'to love God is wisdom' (Sirach 1.16, 14). 'The fear of the Lord is glory and exultation, and gladness, and a crown of rejoicing' (Sirach 1.11). It is not a contradiction to the fear of God when 'the children of God' in the New Testament say: 'There is no fear in love, but perfect love casts out fear' (I John 4.18). The fear of God and the love of God describe the two sides of God's presence, distance and closeness, sublimity and intimacy.

I think it is important that in dealing with the perceptions and capacities of the human being, wisdom should begin with the fear of God, not with the fear of death and of the annihilating nothingness of death. It is true that we learn from Psalm 90, if we read it in Luther's translation, 'to remember that we must die, so that we may become wise' (v.12). But death merely reveals the irreversibility of time and the irretrievability of every lived moment. It reveals, that is, the astonishing uniqueness of life. But this knowledge belongs to wondering perception, not yet to wisdom. In the fear of God we have no need to fear either death or the time of transience, for in that fear we discern the frame of reference for the perceivable world and the knowing of it.

The *frame of reference* for the *perceivable world* is its fundamental knowability. To put it in biblical terms: there is a divine wisdom in all things, and knowledge of it makes human beings wise. 'By wisdom the Lord founded the earth' (Sirach 3.19). His wisdom is 'created before all things' (Ecclus. 1.4) and 'the whole world is full of his wisdom' (Wis. 1.7). This basic trust in the wisdom of God which is presupposed and is spread out before us in the cosmos and in life can be understood as a pre-rational postulate of pure reason. Every scientific discovery dis-covers something of this wise rationality in the world. The structure of the world determined by Wisdom or the Logos hastens invitingly ahead of human knowledge – and yet at the same time, in its divine sublimity, it is immeasurable and unfathomable. That is why human beings in their knowledge of the world become wise through the fear of God. 'Wisdom is with the humble' (Prov. 11.2). We become humble when with every expansion of our knowledge we know how little we know, because the expansion of human knowledge is possible in 'the broad place' of the sublime divine wisdom.

This *frame of reference* for *human knowledge of the world* is to be found in the fear of God and the love of God, because with whatever we know it is wise to respect the dignity of the known object itself. The person who through his knowledge destroys the part of nature he knows, or who knows it for the purpose of destroying it, is neither wise nor does he know anything. Through the fear of God we draw the living into reverence for life. Through the fear of God we respect the existence and unique nature of things, and do not make ourselves lords over their being or non-being, their life or their death. By virtue of the love of God we love God's hidden wisdom in all things. We see things not just with our own eyes but with God's eyes too, as they are 'there' before him; and we are attentive to the inner side of things, their essential being, the *Ding an sich* which, as Kant stressed, lies hidden beyond the boundaries of what we can know. The love of God makes us wise, because it teaches us that we only know the truth of things inasmuch as we love them for themselves. Then we do not want to know them so as to possess them for ourselves and exploit them for ourselves, but in order to live with them in the wise, ordered community of creation. We then perceive them in the coherences of the sympathy through which the divine Wisdom holds all things together.

This frame of reference for knowledge of the world affects the presupposition, the goal and the 'broad place' of the knowable world, but not the methods by which we arrive at secure knowledge. There Descartes' principle applies: *De omnibus dubitandum est* – everything must be doubted. But this is 'methodical' doubt. It is orientated towards results, and has nothing to do with despair over the world, humanity or ourselves. The very frames of reference we have named invite us to this methodical doubt, because they inspire confidence that the results of perception will prevail, contrary to the doubt. Because there is such a thing as assured knowledge, doubt must exclude all sham solutions.

The fear of God makes us wise in dealing with the knowledge that has been acquired. This brings into play, parallel to scientific ethics, ethics in the technological handling of scientific findings. It is wise to distinguish between good and evil. It is wise to make out of what we know only that which furthers life, and not to further whatever disseminates death. But here we come up against problems between pure research and the applied sciences, and in the technological application of discoveries in peace and war.

The first possible conflict – the conflict between pure and applied science – is illustrated by the dilemma in which Albert Einstein involuntarily found himself. His discovery of the theory of relativity in 1907 was, he confessed, 'the happiest thought in my life'. Its proof through the predicted motion of the planet Mercury in November 1915 convinced him 'that nature had spoken to him', as his biographer reports. That was *pure knowledge* in the literal sense, in a splendid harmony with what was already known. But then came the discovery of nuclear fission, and the possibility of applying it to an atomic bomb, either by the Germans, at Hitler's orders, or by the democratic Western powers – a calculated possibility which was already known quite early on. Einstein made his decision in

1939, in his famous letter to President Roosevelt. The Manhattan project began, and led to the destruction of Hiroshima and Nagasaki in August 1945, with the death of hundreds of thousands of people. Pure knowledge and the wondering joy of discovery ended up in the raw reality of the conflict of interests and the struggle for power between human beings.

The German chemist and Nobel prize winner Fritz Haber was faced with a different dilemma. When he discovered how to isolate hydrogen from the atmosphere, he made it possible to produce artificial fertilizers in peacetime, and munitions in war. His researches made the German poison-gas attacks in 1917 possible. His motto for solving his dilemma was a simple one: 'In peace, humanity; in war, the Fatherland.' But his love for the Fatherland had its limits. When his 'non-Arian' colleagues were dismissed from his institute in 1933 he sent in his resignation.

Where does the responsibility of scientists for their scientific knowledge begin, and for what they or other people make of it? And how far does it go? If wars between nations become crises of humanity as whole, and if in these wars the survival or annihilation of humanity itself is at stake, are people not then responsible not just, any longer, for the application of the instruments of mass extermination but for their actual construction and manufacture too? In 1958 German nuclear physicists accepted this responsibility and refused to co-operate in manufacturing these instruments of mass extermination, to the considerable annoyance of a number of politicians. Of course this responsibility is not just a question for the scientists and technologists involved. It is a problem for the whole of society and – because it is humanity which is under deadly threat – for humanity as a whole. The community of nations must rebel against its role as the passive object of possible total extermination through nuclear, biological and chemical weapons, and must become an active determining subject of common survival. This is the task it must and will assume if it wants to prevent humanity's self-destruction.

But experiences such as these with the application of scientific knowledge in our own time make us ask: is there such a thing at all as a disinterested delight in 'pure knowledge' of 'the knowable world'? Are scientific developments and the financing of scientific research not always preceded by economic and political interests? The first scientific theories of the modern world maintained that the acquisition of power for the purpose of dominating nature was the 'knowledge-constitutive interest' prompting the sciences. 'Knowledge is power,' declared Francis Bacon. Science restores to human beings their sovereignty over nature, the role conferred on them with their creation in the image of God, but lost through sin. Through the sciences, the human being becomes *'maître et possesseur de la nature'* as René Descartes maintained at about the same time in his scientific theory.

Yet if human beings cannot control the power over nature which they acquire through science, they have still not learnt wisdom. If the conquest of nature – the subjugation of the earth and other created beings – is the goal of scientific and technological civilization, then it is not surprising that all other living things should encounter human beings with fear and trembling. The person who sets himself up to be nature's master and possessor and forgets that he himself is merely part of nature, destroys nature and in the end annihilates himself. The harmony between the human side of nature and its other elements gives way to the struggle in which the weaker part is defeated. The community of creation shared by human beings and their 'fellow creatures' (as they are termed in the German Animal Protection Act of 1986) is replaced by the exploitation of the fellow creatures who have been subjugated.

The fear of God is a blessing in that it can free modern men and women from the God-complex which has made them drunk with power and induced the mad illusion that the ascendancy they have acquired over nature makes everything possible. The fear of God can beget the wisdom which lends human beings power over their own power. We do not have to do everything we are able to do. The power we have acquired can be used for what furthers life, so as to exclude what kills it.

Goethe's sorcerer's apprentice had learnt from his master the formula for putting the broom into motion, but unfortunately not the formula for banishing it again to its corner. When shall we learn this second formula of power? The fear of God can ultimately engender the *knowledge-constitutive wisdom* which has no desire to dominate its object and take possession of it, but wants to commune with it and live with it in a life-furthering commonwealth. For 400 years science and technology has exploited its seizure of power over nature. We now need another time in which to integrate human civilization in the nature of this planet earth. For our civilization too is only part of nature. The last fifty years have brought an enormous increase in what we have discovered and know; we now need a still greater increase of wisdom and of wise dealings with our knowledge. If humanity is to have a future, that future belongs not to knowledge but to wisdom; for 'wisdom gives life to him who has it' (Sirach 7.12).

Notes

Preface

1. F. Rosenzweig, *Der Stern der Erlösung*, Heidelberg ³1954, Part III, Book II, 127 (*The Star of Redemption*, trans. W. W. Hallo, London 1971).

2. ET nine years later: J.B.Metz, *Faith in History and Society*, trans. D. Smith, London 1980: 'Theology as Biography', 219–28.

I. What is Theology?

1. For an analysis of the semantic field and for the history of the term cf. W. Pannenberg, *Systematic Theology* I, trans. G. W. Bromiley, Grand Rapids, MI 1991, 1–8; O. Bayer, HST I, Gütersloh 1994, 20–32. Zwingli and Calvin avoid using the term 'theology', and prefer to talk about *doctrina christiana*; but Luther uses it deliberately and comprehensively. I am grateful to G. Ebeling for drawing my attention to this point.

2. This is an age-old argument against scholars in the Christian church, one which was – and still is – used by bishops, popes and pietists. Cf. Luke 10.21: 'I thank thee, Father, Lord of heaven and earth, that thou hast hidden these things from the wise and understanding and revealed them to babes.' And Acts 4.13: 'When they saw the boldness of Peter and John, and perceived that they were uneducated, common men (*agrammatoi kai idiotai*), they wondered.'

3. See Part III, section 5.

4. See Part III, sections 5 and 6.

5. The Second Vatican Council makes an essential distinction between 'the common priesthood of the faithful' and the 'ministerial priesthood', not just a distinction of degree, and 'orders one to another' in such a fashion that both, 'each in its own proper way shares in the one priesthood of Christ'. However, only the 'ministerial priest . . . in the person of Christ . . . effects the eucharistic sacrifice' (The Constitution on the Church, *Lumen Gentium*, II.11). But by ele-

vating the special ministerial priesthood, above the congregation, into 'the person of Christ', baptism, as the fundamental Christian sacrament, is devalued. According to Gal. 3.28, all the baptized are 'in Christ'. Consequently they exercise the priestly and the teaching ministry in Christ's church in common.

6. On the identity-relevance dilemma, cf. J. Moltmann, *The Crucified God*, trans. R. A. Wilson and John Bowden, London 1974, 7–31.

7. The following have entered into this particularly: M. Machovec, *Jesus für Atheisten*, with a foreword by H. Gollwitzer, Stuttgart 1973, and from a quite different angle, C. Morse, *Not every Spirit. A Dogmatics of Christian Disbelief*, Valley Forge, PA 1994. See also D. Sölle, *Atheistisch an Gott glauben. Theologie nach dem Tode Gottes*, Stuttgart 1968.

8. G.Steiner, *Tolstoy or Dostoevsky. An Essay in the Old Criticism*, London 1960.

9. M. Horkheimer, *Die Sehnsucht nach dem ganz Anderen. Ein Interview mit Kommentar von H. Gumnior*, Hamburg 1970, 11, 69.

10. Moltmann, *The Crucified God* (n.6), VI.6: Beyond Atheism and Theism, 249ff.; E. Jüngel, *God as Mystery of the World. On the Foundation of the Theology of the Crucified One in the Dispute between Theism and Atheism*, trans. D. Guder, Grand Rapids, MI and Edinburgh 1983.

11. See H. Küng's splendid programme, *The Religious Situation of our Time*: 1. *Judaism*, ET New York 1992; 2. *Christianity, Its Essence and History*, trans. John Bowden, London 1995; 3. *Islam* (in preparation). I myself have expressed my views about dialogue in 'Dient die "pluralistische Theologie" dem Dialog der Welt-Religionen?', *EvTh* 49, 1989, 528–36, and in 'Dialogue or Mission? Christianity and the Religions in an Endangered World', in *God for a Secular Society*, trans. Margaret Kohl, London and Minneapolis 1999, 226–44.

12. W. von Loewenich, *Luthers Theologia crucis*, Bielefeld ⁶1982; E. Vogelsang, *Der angefochtene Christus bei Luther*, Berlin and Leipzig 1932.

13. This is the fundamental idea of Hans Urs von Balthasar's theological study, *Theo-Drama: A Theological Dramatic Theory*, Vols. I–V (= German I–IV), trans. G. Harrison, San Francisco 1988.

14. Verena Wodtke (ed.), *Auf den Spuren der Weisheit. Sophia – Wegweiserin für ein weibliches Gottesbild*, Freiburg 1991; S. Cady, M. Ronan and H. Taussig, *Sophia. The Future of Feminist Spirituality*, San Francisco 1986.

15. J. Moltmann, *Theology and Joy*, trans. R. Ulrich, London 1973; also *God in Creation. An Ecological Doctrine of Creation* (The

Gifford Lectures 1984–85), trans. Margaret Kohl, London and San Francisco 1985, esp. IV: God the Creator, 72–103.

16. Cf. the wonderful article by my friend N. Nissiotis, 'Die österliche Freude als doxologischer Ausdruck des Glaubens', in H. Deuser *et al.* (eds), *Gottes Zukunft – Zukunft der Welt. Festschrift für J. Moltmann*, Munich 1986, 78–88. Nikos died in an accident shortly after writing this contribution. It is his last article.

17. K. Kirchoff, *Osterjubel der Ostkirche* II, ed. C. Scholmeyer, Münster 1961, 25. Cf. also R. Bohren, *Dass Gott schön werde. Praktische Theologie als theologische Ästhetik*, Munich 1975.

18. E. Benz, *Geist und Leben der Ostkirche*, Munich 1957, 40.

19. This has been rightly stressed by W. Pannenberg in W. Pannenberg *et al.* (eds), *Revelation as History*, trans. D. Granskou and E. Quinn, London and New York 1969, 13f.

20. K.-J. Kuschel, *Abraham. A Sign of Hope for Jews, Christians and Muslims*, trans. John Bowden, London and New York 1995.

21. E. Wiesel, 'Longing for Home', in L. Rouner (ed.), *The Longing for Home*, Notre Dame 1966, 17–29.

22. J. Moltmann, *The Coming of God*, trans. Margaret Kohl, London and Minneapolis 1996, IV.1: The Future of Creation – Sabbath and Shekinah, 261–7.

23. A. J. Heschel, *The Sabbath. Its Meaning for Modern Man*, New York [7]1981.

24. W. Schottroff, '*Gedenken' im alten Orient und im Alten Testament. Die Wurzel zäkar im semitischen Sprachkreis*, Neukirchen 1964; Y. W. Yerushalmi, *Zachor: Erinnere Dich! Jüdische Geschichten und jüdisches Gedächtnis*, Berlin 1988; J. Assmann, *Das kulturelle Gedächtnis. Schrift, Erinnerung und politische Identität in frühen Hochkulturen*, Munich [2]1997.

25. J. B. Metz, 'Zwischen Erinnern und Vergessen: Die Shoah im Zeitalter der kulturellen Amnesie' (1992), in J. B. Metz, *Zum Begriff der neuen Politischen Theologie*, Mainz 1997, 142–8, and since then in many other contributions.

26. On the theological concept of 'story' in America and Germany, see the good introduction in H. F. Perry-Trauthig, *Story und Ethik. Eine Untersuchung aus christlich-theologischer Perspektive*, Frankfurt 1997.

27. A. Alt, 'The God of the Fathers', in *Essays on Old Testament History and Religion*, trans. R. A. Wilson, Oxford 1966, 3–66. In what follows I am gratefully indebted to H.-J. Kraus, *Systematische Theologie im Kontext biblischer Geschichte und Eschatologie*, Neukirchen 1983.

28. P. Kuhn, *Gottes Selbsterniedrigung in der Theologie der Rabbinen*,

Munich 1968, II: Gott als Diener der Menschen, 22–33.

29. W. Zimmerli in the sense of the doctrine of God's self-revelation in the Word: 'Ich bin Yahweh', in *Gottesoffenbarung. Gesammelte Aufsätze*, Munich 1963, 11–40, esp. 20f.

30. Pannenberg, *Revelation as History* (n.19), 6ff., in the sense of a 'theology of facts'.

31. J. Moltmann, *Theology of Hope*, trans. J. W. Leitch, London 1967, Ch. II: Promise and History, 95–133.

32. Thomas Aquinas, *STh* III q 60 a 3: 'Hence as a sign a sacrament has a threefold function. It is at once commemorative of that which has gone before, namely the Passion of Christ, and demonstrative of that which is brought about in us through the passion of Christ, namely grace, and prognostic, i.e. a foretelling of future glory' (*Summa Theologiae*. Latin text and English translation, Blackfriars, Vol. LVI, London and New York 1966, 12f.). ['*Unde sacramentum est et signum rememorativum eius quod praecessit, scil. passionis Christi, et demonstrativum eius quod in nobis efficatur per Christi passionem, scil. gratiae, et prognosticon, i.e. praenuntiativum futurae gloriae.*']

33. H.-J. Iwand, *Die Gegenwart des Kommenden. Auslegung von Lk 12*, Siegen 1955; O. Weber, *Grundlagen der Dogmatik* II, Neukirchen 1962, 641 (*Foundations of Dogmatics*, trans. D. L. Guder, II, Grand Rapids 1962). See also ET 642: 'The supper is the first gleaming of the Eschaton.' J. Moltmann, *The Church in the Power of the Spirit*, trans. Margaret Kohl, London 1977, Ch. V, 4.ii: The sign of remembered hope; 4.iii: The presence of the one who is to come, 246–56; M. Welker, *Was geht vor beim Abendmahl?*, Stuttgart 1999.

34. I. Kant, *Der Streit der Fakultäten* (1798), PhB 252, 83. By transferring Thomist sacramental doctrine to historical events of his own time, Kant interprets the French Revolution as a 'historical sign' of the progress of the history of the human race 'towards betterment'.

35. Here I am following G. von Rad, *Old Testament Theology* I, trans. D. M. G. Stalker, Edinburgh, London and New York 1962, reissued 1975, 121–8.

36. H. W. Wolff, '"Wissen um Gott" bei Hosea als Urform von Theologie', *EvTh* 12, 1952/53, 533–54.

37. Ibid., 551.

38. M. Welker, *God the Spirit*, trans. J. F. Hoffmeyer, Minneapolis 1994, 108ff. Welker rightly ascribes to the Spirit-imbued Messiah the spread of 'justice, mercy and knowledge of God'.

39. D. Harvey, *The Condition of Postmodernity*, Oxford 1990.

40. M. Pohlenz, *Die Stoa. Geschichte einer geistigen Bewegung*,

Göttingen ³1964, 198: 'Panaitios distinguished between three classes of divinities: natural forces, which were thought of as persons, the gods of the state religion, and the gods of myth (γένος φυσικόν, πολικόν, μυθικόν) and with this justified the *tripertitia theologia* which came to prevail especially in the rationalistic theology of Rome.'

41. J. Moltmann, *The Way of Jesus Christ. Christology in Messianic Dimensions*, trans. Margaret Kohl, London and San Francisco 1990, I: The Messianic Perspective, 1–37.

42. Moltmann, *The Coming of God* (n.22), III: The Kingdom of God. Historical Eschatology, 129–255.

43. I. Kant, *Critique of Pure Reason* (1781), Transcendental Doctrine of Method, Ch. II.3: Of Opinion, Knowledge and Belief; *Critique of Judgment* (1790), sections 90, 91: The Nature of Conviction.

44. Here I am following H. J. Iwand, *Glauben und Wissen, Nachgelassene Werke* I, Munich 1962, 27, 22.

45. Ibid., 20.

46. Christian belief in God is more than the moral certainty of God, about which Kant and so many of his followers down to the present day maintain: 'I must not even say: *It is* morally certain that there is a God, etc. but *I am* morally certain, that is, my belief in God and in another world is so interwoven with my moral nature, that I am under as little apprehension of having the former torn from me as of losing the latter' (*Critique of Pure Reason*, trans. J. M. D. Meiklejohn, first published London 1979, 469).

47. K. Barth, *Anselm: Fides Quaerens Intellectus. Anselm's Proof of the Existence of God*, trans. I. W. Robertson from the second (1958) German edition, London 1960.

48. Ibid., 27: '*Intelligere* comes about by reflection on the *Credo* that has already been spoken and affirmed.'

49. Over against the traditional, one-sided precedence given to faith before understanding, I would emphatically maintain the dialectical complement: I understand in order to believe.

50. G. Freudenthal, *Atom und Individuum im Zeitalter Newtons*, Frankfurt 1982; G. Rohrmoser, *Subjektivität und Verdinglichung. Theologie und Gesellschaft im Denken des jungen Hegel*, Gütersloh 1961.

51. See E. Busch, *Karl Barth. His Life from Letters and Autobiographical Texts*, trans. John Bowden, London 1976, 205–9: 'Pupil of Anselm of Canterbury'.

52. Barth, *Anselm* (n.47), 132.

53. Ibid., 15: 'As *intelligere* is achieved, it issues – in joy.' It is joy over the beauty of theology. Because this does not have a merely aesthetic

significance, I am justifying it in what follows with the truth-concept of correspondence. Cf. also E. Jüngel, *Entsprechungen: Gott – Wahrheit – Mensch. Theologische Erörterungen*, Munich 1980.

54. Barth, *Anselm* (n.47): 'The fourth line in Anselm along which *intelligere* necessarily follows from faith is the line of eschatology' (20). '*Intelligere* is a potentiality for advancing in the direction of heavenly vision to a point that can be reached and that is worth trying to reach. It has within itself something of the nature of vision and it is worth striving for as *similitudo* of vision, just because it leads men, not beyond, but right up to the limits of faith' (21).

55. In Pannenberg, *Revelation as History* (n.19), 125ff., the impression given is that ultimately the indirect self-revelation at the end of 'revelatory history' would be made up of the individual, fragmentarily revealing events. In that case the 'end of history' would be only the chiliastic completion, but not also, and at the same time, the apocalyptic ending of history.

56. J. Moltmann, *The Coming of God* (n.22), IV: New Heaven – New Earth. Cosmic Eschatology, 257–319.

57. G. Greshake, *Gott in allen Dingen finden*, Freiburg 1986; L. Boff, *Ecology and Liberation*, ET Maryknoll, NY 1995; J. Zink, *Dornen können Rosen tragen. Mystik – die Zukunft des Christentums*, Stuttgart 1997.

58. K. Barth, *Church Dogmatics* I/1, 350f., 436.

59. This theological knowledge of hope emerges parallel to Ernst Bloch's philosophy of hope, *Das Prinzip Hoffnung* I–III (1959) (*The Principle of Hope*, trans. N. and S. Plaice and P. Knight, Cambridge, Mass. and Oxford 1986), and also takes into account his first wholly messianic and hence also theological work 'The Spirit of Utopia' (*Geist der Utopie*, 1918, 1923; Frankfurt 1964; there is no English translation).

60. J. Moltmann, *The Spirit of Life*, trans. Margaret Kohl, London and Minneapolis 1992, VII: The Rebirth to Life, 144–60.

61. C.-A. Bernard, *Théologie de l'espérance selon Saint Thomas d'Aquin*, Paris 1961; J. Pieper, *Über die Hoffnung*, Munich 1949; C. Péguy, *Le porche du mystère de la deuxième vertu* [i.e., hope], 1911, Paris ⁹1933; second German edition revised by H. Urs von Balthasar, Einsiedeln 1980, 5: 'The faith I like most, says God, is hope.'

62. This can clearly be seen from the development of the doctrine of purgatory from 1336, with Benedict XII's constitution *Benedictus Deus*. Cf. J. Le Goff, *The Birth of Purgatory*, London 1984.

63. J. Weiss, *Die Predigt Jesu vom Reich Gottes* (1892; Göttingen ³1964), 264f. (*Jesus' Proclamation of the Kingdom of God*, trans. R.

Hiers and D. L. Holland, London 1971). R. Bultmann was also convinced that, 'as every sane person knows, [history] will continue to run its course'; see his 'New Testament and Mythology', in H.-W. Bartsch (ed.), *Kerygma and Myth*, trans. R. H. Fuller, London 1953, 5 (trans. emended). So all that remains to us is to declare death to be the *eschaton*, and to mean by eschatology 'the meaning of individual human existence', and no longer 'the goal of history'.

64. I. Kant, *Werke* III, 448.

65. This splendid proposal was made by L. Ragaz, *Die Toten und wir*, Zurich ³1966. I am indebted for this reference to B. Klappert, *Worauf wir hoffen? Das Kommen Gottes und der Weg Jesu Christi*, Gütersloh 1997, 30f. Ragaz writes: 'And that would be the significance of the proper "festival of the death". It would really be a festival of life – a continuation and completion of Easter, the Ascension and Pentecost; [it would also be] the festival of the bringing back . . .of all things, the festival of the victory over death' (8).

66. G. W. F. Hegel, Preface to the *Philosophy of Right* (1821), trans. J. M. Knox, Oxford 1947, 12.

67. J. G. Hamann, *Schriften* II, ed. F. Roth, Berlin 1821, 217.

68. H. J. Iwand, *Luthers Theologie,* in Nachgelassene Werke V, Munich 1974, 276; O. Bayer, *Promissio. Geschichte der reformatorischen Wende in Luthers Theologie*, Göttingen 1971; B. Klappert, *Promissio und Bund*, Neukirchen 1976; H.-J. Kraus, *Systematische Theologie*, 331–3.

69. G Gutiérrez, *A Theology of Liberation*, trans. C. Inda and J. Eagleson, revised, with a new introduction, Maryknoll, NY and London 1988. One problem lies in the activist understanding of theory and praxis, through which the subject of theological theory and Christian praxis remains obscure and unconsidered. Does not a passion out of which the subject is born precede praxis and the theory of praxis: the passion of grace and rebirth?

70. I. Ellacuria and J. Sobrino (eds), *Mysterium Liberationis. Fundamental Concepts of Liberation Theology,* Maryknoll, NY 1993, xv.

71. J. Sobrino, *Spirituality of Liberation*, ET Maryknoll, NY 1988.

72. See Part III.4.

73. G. Gloege, 'Offenbarung', *RGG*³, IV 1610.

74. W. Pannenberg has shown this convincingly in his *Problemgeschichte der neueren evangelischen Theologie in Deutschland*, Göttingen 1997, 189–204.

75. K. Barth, *CD* III/1, 196.

76. Gloege, 'Offenbarung' (n.73), 1611.

77. Moltmann, *Theology of Hope* (n.31), Ch. II: Promise and History, 95–138.

78. *STh* I q 2ff.

79. *The Sources of Catholic Dogma*, trans. R. J. Deferrari from the thirteenth edition of H. Denzinger, *Enchiridion Symbolorum*, St Louis and London 1955, No. 1785 and 1806. [Denzinger: '*Sancta mater Ecclesia tenet et docet, Deum, rerum omnium principium et finem, naturali humanae rationis lumine e rebus creatis, certo cognosci posse*' (III,2). And the condemnation: '*Si quis dixerit, Deum unum et verum, creatorem et Dominum nostrum, per ea, quae facta sunt, naturali rationis humanae lumine certo cognosci non posse: anathema sit*' (Can. 1).]

80. H. Schmid, *Die Dogmatik der Evangelisch-lutherischen Kirche*, Gütersloh ⁷1893, 67–86.

81. H. Heppe and E. Bizer, *Die Dogmatik der Evangelisch-reformierten Kirche*, Neukirchen 1958, 1–10.

82. Ibid.

83. This is precisely the way R. Bultmann saw the function of natural theology: see 'The Concept of Revelation in the New Testament', in *Existence and Faith. Shorter Writings*, trans. Schubert M. Ogden, London 1961, 58–91, and, in the same volume, 'The Problem of "Natural Theology"', 313–31.

84. H.-J. Iwand, *Glauben und Wissen*. Nachgelassene Werke I, Munich 1962, 290–1.

85. G. Söhngen, 'Naturliche Theologie', *LThK* VII, 811–16.

86. G. E. Lessing, *The Education of the Human Race*, trans. F. W. Robertson, 1872, reprinted London and New York 1927, Ch. 1, 3: 'That which education is to the Individual, revelation is to the Race.'

87. Ibid, Ch. 76, 20 (trans. slightly altered).

88. Ibid., Ch. 86, 22.

89. I. Kant, *Religion within the Limits of Reason Alone*, trans. T. M. Greene and H.H. Hudson, London and Chicago 1934, 113.

90. Ibid., 120f.

91. Ibid., 122. On this European philosophical eschatology, cf. J. Taubes, *Abendländische Eschatologie* (1947), Berlin 1991; on Kant, 136ff.

92. For more detail see W. Krusche, *Das Wirken des Heiligen Geistes nach Calvin*, Gütersloh 1957, 15ff.: Der Heilige Geist und der Kosmos. Cf. also Moltmann, *God in Creation* and *The Spirit of Life* (nn.15 and 60).

93. See n.57. Thus too John Paul II in his encylical *Dominum et vivificantem* of 18 May 1986, 54: '"God is spirit"; and also, in such a marvellous way, he is not only *close to this world* but *present* in it, and in a sense *immanent*, penetrating it and giving it life from within. This is especially true in relation to man: God is present in the

intimacy of man's being, in his mind, conscience and heart: an ontological and psychological reality, in considering which Saint Augustine said of God that he was *"closer than my inmost being".'*

94. The Orthodox theologian D. Staniloae talks about this 'transparency' in his book *Orthodoxe Dogmatik*, Gütersloh 1985, I, 293ff. With this transparency there begins the spiritualization of creation which ends in its deification.

95. 'In need of parable and capable of being a parable' for the kingdom of heaven was the way K. Barth saw the world, first in 'Church and Culture' (1926), in *Theology and Church*, ET London and New York 1962; then in 'The Christian Community and the Civil Community' (1946), in *Against the Stream*, ET London 1954, and finally in *CD* IV/3, 165. See C. Link, *Die Welt als Gleichnis. Studien zum Problem der natürlichen Theologie*, Munich 1976.

96. Moltmann, *God in Creation* (n.15), 60–5.

97. E. Jüngel, 'Das Dilemma der natürlichen Theologie und die Wahrheit ihres Problems', in *Entsprechungen: Gott – Wahrheit – Mensch. Theologische Erörterungen*, Munich 1980, 158–77, esp. 175. On the Catholic concept of nature cf. H. Urs von Balthasar, *Karl Barth. Darstellung und Deutung seiner Theologie*, Cologne 1951, 263–371. On the whole complex of natural theology – revealed theology – eschatological theology, cf. J. Moltmann, 'Gottesoffenbarung und Wahrheitsfrage', in *Parrhesia. Festschrift für Karl Barth zum 80. Geburtstag*, Zurich 1966, 149–72, also in *Perspektiven der Theologie*, Munich 1968, 13–35.

98. Moltmann, 'Gottesoffenbarung und Wahrheitsfrage', 171. E. Jüngel praises Schleiermacher and Barth because they 'took logical insight seriously'. But he does not discuss this concept of truth, which in my view cannot stand on its own, because it is in itself circular.

99. For this, Barth cites approvingly F. Turrettini and Thomas Aquinas (I/1 6), without entering into the historical consequences of this absolutism, which he himself entirely rejected.

100. K. Barth, *CD*, I/1 5, 7 (trans. emended).

101. I may point here to my controversy with Nicolas Woltersdorff, 'Public Theology vs. Christian Learning', in Miroslav Volf (ed.), *A Passion for God's Reign*, Grand Rapids, MI 1998.

102. Barth, *CD* IV/2, 275.

103. *CD* IV/3, 139.

104. Ibid., 112f. Cf. here H.-J. Kraus, *Karl Barths Lichterlehre*, ThSt 123, Zurich 1978.

105. Ibid., 117.

106. Ibid., 139.

107. Ibid., 143–50.

108. E. Brunner, 'Der neue Barth', *ZThK* 48, 1951, 89–100.
109. M. Luther, *Werke in Auswahl*, V, ed. E. Vogelsang, Berlin 1933, 375–404.
110. This has been expounded by the Dutch theologian A. A. van Ruler in his splendid book, *Gestaltwerdung Christi in der Welt. Über das Verhältnis von Kirche und Kultur*, Neukirchen 1956.
111. K. Barth, *Theological Existence Today*, London 1933; '*Nein! Antwort an Emil Brunner, Theologische Existenz heute* 14, Munich 1934. ET in E. Brunner and K. Barth, *Natural Theology*, London 1946, which also contains Brunner's article, 'Nature and Grace'. See E. Busch's account in *Karl Barth* (n.51), 248ff.
112. Barth, 'The Christian Community and the Civil Community' (n.94).
113. W. Pannenberg, *Systematic Theology* I, trans. G. W. Bromiley, Grand Rapids, MI and Edinburgh 1991, 107.
114. Ibid., contrary to E. Jüngel (trans. emended).
115. Ibid., 116 (trans. emended).

II. Hermeneutics of Hope

1. *Luthers Werke in Auswahl*, V, Berlin 1933, 388, 392: '*Ideo peccatores sunt pulchri quia diliguntur, non ideo diliguntur quia sunt pulchri.*'
2. H. J. Iwand, *Nachgelassene Werke* 1–6, Munich 1962ff. For his influence on me, cf. D. Meeks, *Origins of the Theology of Hope*, Philadelphia 1974, 30–40.
3. H. J. Iwand, *Die Gegenwart des Kommenden*, Siegen 1955, 36.
4. Id., *Predigt-Meditationen*, Göttingen 1963, 345.
5. B. Klappert has rightly reminded me of this. See his *Worauf wir hoffen. Das Kommen Gottes und der Weg Jesu Christi*, Gütersloh 1997, 90. Cf. also J. Seim (ed.), *H. J. Iwand. Eine Biografie*, Gütersloh 1999.
6. D . Mereschkowski (Merezhkovski), *Jesus der Kommende*, Leipzig 1934, is the second volume of a theological trilogy, translated into German by A. Luther (no ET).
7. V. von Bülow, *Ein gebeugtes Leben. Otto Weber 1902–1966*, dissertation Bonn 1997.
8. 'Prädestination und Heilsgeschichte bei Moyse Amyraut', *ZKG* 65/66, 1953/54, 270–303.
9. *Christoph Pezel (1539–1604) und der Calvinismus in Bremen*, Hospitium Ecclesiae II, Bremen 1958.
10. 'Jacob Brocard als Vorläufer der Reich-Gottes-Theologie und der symbolisch-prophetischen Schriftauslegung bei Johann Coccejus', *ZKG* 71, 1960, 110–29.

11. O. Weber, *Karl Barth's Dogmatics: An Introductory Report on Vols. I.1–III.4*, ET London and Philadelphia 1953. Barth ironically called this introduction the 'Baedecker' to his work.
12. O. Weber, *Grundlagen der Dogmatik*, 2 vols, Neukirchen 1955, 1962 (ET *Foundations of Dogmatics*, 2 vols, trans. D. L. Guder, Grand Rapids 1981, 1983). For his doctrine of the Lord's supper see ET II, 614ff.
13. Ibid., 641, 642.
14. *Lebendiges Bekenntnis. Mit einer Einführung von Otto Weber*, Neukirchen 1950.
15. *Kerkorde van de Nederlandse Hervormde Kerk. Eerste Lezing 14. October 1949*, Art. VIII: *Van het apostolaat der Kerk*, 7–8.
16. A .A. van Ruler, *Gestaltwerdung Christi in der Welt. Über das Verhältnis von Kirche und Kultur* (first published in German), Neukirchen 1956; *Theologie van het Apostolaat*, Nijkerk 1954.
17. Cf. my critical discussion of his eschatology in *The Crucified God*, trans. R. A. Wilson and John Bowden, London 1974, 259–62.
18. *Die christliche Kirche und das Alte Testament*, Munich 1955, esp. 34ff.
19. 'Herrschaft Christi und soziale Wirklichkeit nach Dietrich Bonhoeffer', *Theologische Existenz heute* 71, Munich 1959, 61.
20. 'Die Wirklichkeit der Welt und Gottes konkretes Gebot nach Dietrich Bonhoeffer', in E. Bethge (ed.), *Mündige Welt* III, Munich 1960, 67.
21. *Im Gespräch mit Ernst Bloch*, Munich 1976.
22. *Das Prinzip Hoffnung*, Berlin 1969, 240, 17 (*The Principle of Hope*, trans. N. and S. Plaice and P. Knight, Cambridge, Mass. and Oxford 1986).
23. K. Barth, *Letters 1961–1968*, trans. G. W. Bromiley, Grand Rapids and Edinburgh 1981, 175.
24. G. Möller, 'Föderalismus und Geschichtsbetrachtung im 17. und 18. Jahrhundert', *ZKG* 50, 1931, 419. It really began with the contemporizing interpretation of the book of Revelation, which was seen as a reference to the Protestant power, England, in the struggle against 'the Antichrist' Spain, and to the sinking of the Armada in 1588. See Avihu Zakai, 'From Judgment to Salvation: The Image of the Jews in the English Renaissance', *Westminster Theological Journal* 59, 1997, 213–30: 'In 1617 Richard Bernard, a famous Puritan divine, thus summed up the revolutionary character of the apocalyptic tradition in England: "The matter of this prophecy (the Apocalypse) is historicall, as it cometh to be fulfilled. It is therefore not spiritual or allegorical, but an historical sense, which in this booke we must attend unto" (*A Key to the Knowledge for the*

Opening of the Sacred Mysteries of St John's Mysticall Revelation,
1617, 123). ". . . The mystery of sacred, providential history can be
explained only through divine prophecy which is 'a Prophetical-
Chronology of Times' from the beginning of time and history until
the very end, or until 'all the kingdomes of this world should become
the Kingdome of our Lord and his Christ'" (Joseph Mede, *The
Apostasy of the Latter Times* (1641), in *The Works of Joseph Mede*,
ed. J. Worthington, 1664, Vol.II, 807) . . . No wonder, then, that
some could argue, as did the Puritan William Hicks in 1659, that
"the Revelation is no longer mystery, but a Book of History of
memorable Acts and passages"" (226, 227).

25. G. Menken, 'Über Glück und Sieg der Gottlosen' (1795), in
    Schriften 7, Bremen 1858, 82.
26. It is above all Oscar Cullmann's *Salvation in History*, trans. S. G.
    Sowers *et al.*, London 1967, which spread the salvation-history
    interpretation at the present day. (The German title of his book is
    Heil als Geschichte, 'Salvation *as* History'; the change for the
    English title was made at the author's own request.) Cullmann
    goes back to the prophetic theology which the Erlangen Lutheran
    theologian, von Hofmann, disseminated; see J. C. von Hofmann,
    Biblische Hermeneutik, ed. W. Volck, Nördlingen 1889. As
    G. Schrenk has shown in *Gottesreich und Bund im älteren
    Protestantismus vornehmlich bei Johannes Coccejus*, Gütersloh
    1923, this theology in its turn rests on the 'prophetic exegesis' of
    seventeenth-century Reformed theology. There is also an Adventist
    'prophetic' interpretation of scripture. Cf. E. G. White, *Der grosse
    Kampf. Kirche, Politik und die Zukunft der Welt*, Hamburg 1994.
    For critical comment on the Erlangen salvation-history tradition, see
    F. Baumgärtel, *Verheissung. Zur Frage des christlichen Verständ-
    nisses des Alten Testaments*, Gütersloh 1952. In *Grundlagen der
    Dogmatik* I (n.12), 337 (*Foundations of Dogmatics* I), O. Weber
    excellently worked out the qualitative difference between prophecy
    and promise, although he takes no account of the link between
    God's promise and the covenant.
27. J. Searle, *Speech-acts*, Cambridge 1969, esp. 57–62: 'How to
    promise – A complicated way' (C. Morse gives a summary in *The
    Logic of Promise in Moltmann's Theology of Revelation*,
    Philadelphia 1979, 73–5); O. Bayer, 'Poetologische Theologie?
    Überlegungen zur Poesie des Versprechens', *ThLZ* 124, 1999, 4–13.
28. O. Weber, 'Die Treue Gottes und die Kontinuität der menschlichen
    Existenz', *Gesammelte Aufsätze* I, Neukirchen 1967, 99–112.
29. C. McCoy has emphatically stressed the foundation of American
    democracy in the tradition of Reformed federal theology (J.

Cocceius) and federal politics (J. Althusius). See here J. Wayne Baker, *Heinrich Bullinger and the Covenant: The Other Reformed Tradition*, Athens 1980; C. J. Friedrich, Preface to *Johannes Althusius, The Politics of J. Althusius*, trans. and with an introduction by F. S. Carney, Boston 1964; C. McCoy, *Die Bundestradition in Theologie und Politischer Ethik. Anmerkungen zum Verständnis der Verfassung und Gesellschaft der USA, Rechtstheorie*, Vol. 16, Berlin 1997, 29–45; J. Moltmann, 'Covenant or Leviathan? Political Theology at the Beginning of Modern Times', in *God for a Secular Society*, trans. Margaret Kohl, London and Minneapolis 1999, 24–45.

30. Here I am following W. Eichrodt, *Theology of the Old Testament* I (1933), trans. John Austin Baker, London and Philadelphia 1961. Eichrodt put covenant theology at the centre, but I have drawn my own conclusions from his theses. For the contemporary theology, cf. also B. Klappert, *Promissio und Bund. Gesetz und Evangelium bei Luther und Barth*, Göttingen 1976.

31. Eichrodt, *Theology* (n.30), 38.

32. This is brought out particularly finely by W. Pannenberg, 'Der Gott der Hoffnung', in S. Unseld (ed.), *Ernst Bloch zu ehren*, Frankfurt 1965, 209–25. He stresses 'the unity between the promising God and his promise', which finds its completion in the fulfilment of what is promised.

33. In the following passage I am trying to clarify the questions which Christopher Morse raised in *The Logic of Promise in Moltmann's Theology*, Philadelphia 1979, esp. 38–81. See also A. J. Conyers, *God, Hope and History. Jürgen Moltmann and the Christian Concept of History*, Macon, Ga. 1988.

34. Iwand, *Predigt-Meditationen* (n.4), 165.

35. Morse, *The Logic of Promise* (n.33), 165.

36. H. Schlier, *Wort Gottes. Eine neutestamentliche Besinnung*, Würzburg 1958, 18.

37. G. W. F. Hegel, *Philosophy of Right*, trans. T. M. Knox, Oxford 1947, Preface 12–13.

38. Ibid.

39. My hermeneutical contributions from the period of the *Theology of Hope* can be found in *Perspektiven der Theologie* (1968): 'Exegese und Eschatologie der Geschichte' (1962); 'Wort Gottes und Sprache' (1965): 'Verkündigung als Problem der Exegese' (1963); and 'Existenzgeschichte und Weltgeschichte' (1968).

40. *Hope and Planning*, a selection from the German *Perspektiven der Theologie*, trans. Margaret Clarkson, London and New York 1971, includes only the translation of 'Exegesis and the Eschatology of

History' (56–98). Consequently Christopher Morse overlooked the other contributions to the hermeneutics of the history of promise.

41. Bloch, *Das Prinzip Hoffnung* (n.22), 7: 'The rigid divisions between future and past then collapse of themselves, future which has never become present becomes visible in the past – revenged and inherited, mediated and fulfilled past in the future' (ET *The Principle of Hope*). Cf. also R. Koselleck, *Vergangene Zukunft. Zur Semantik geschichtlicher Zeiten*, Frankfurt 1979.

42. Moltmann, *Perspektiven der Theologie* (n.39), 127.

43. P. Ricoeur, *The Conflict of Interpretations. Essays in Hermeneutics*, ET Evanston 1974; see also 'Der gekreuzigte Gott von Jürgen Moltmann', in M. Welker (ed.), *Diskussion über Jürgen Moltmanns Buch 'Der gekreuzigte Gott'*, Munich 1979, 17–26. See here M.J. Raden, *Das relative Absolut. Die theologische Hermeneutik Paul Ricoeurs*, Frankfurt 1988.

44. J. Moltmann, *The Coming of God*, trans. Margaret Kohl, London and Minneapolis 1996, IV, 3.2: The Times of History, 284–92.

45. This development is precisely described in O. Bayer, *Promissio. Geschichte der reformatorischen Wende in Luthers Theologie*, Göttingen 1971, Part II, Ch. 4: Die reformatorische Wende als Neugestaltung des Busssakraments (*promissio absolutionis – fides*), 164–202.

46. M. Luther, *Von der Freiheit eines Christenmenschen* ('The Freedom of a Christian'), *Werke in Auswahl*, ed. O. Clemen, II, 15–16.

47. '*Quod homines non possint justificari coram Deo propriis viribus, meritis aut operibus, sed gratis justificentur propter Christum per fidem, cum credunt se in gratiam recipi et peccata remitti propter Christum, qui sua morte pro nostris peccatis satisfecit.*' Translation in *The Book of Concord. The Confessions of the Evangelical Lutheran Church*, trans. and ed. T. G. Tappert *et al.*, Philadelphia 1959, 30.

48. E. Cremer, *Rechtfertigung und Wiedergeburt*, Gütersloh 1907.

49. Augustine, *Enchiridion*, trans. and ed. A. C. Outler, London and Philadelphia 1855, XIV, 52, 369: 'The death of Christ crucified is nothing other than the likeness of the forgiveness of sins – so that in the very same sense in which the death is real, so also is the forgiveness of our sins real, and in the same sense in which his resurrection is real, so also in us is there authentic justification.' ['. . . *quemadmodum in illo vero mors facta ita in nobis remissio peccatorum, quemadmodum in illa vera resurrectio, ita in nobis vera justificatio.*']

50. '*Ubi enim est remissio peccatorum, ibi est vita et justitia.*' See *The Book of Concord* (n.47), Luther's Small Catechism, VI: The

Sacrament of the Altar, 352.

51. L. Köhler, *Theologie des Alten Testaments*, ⁴1966, 74. See here J. Moltmann, *The Future of Creation*, trans. Margaret Kohl, London 1979, Ch. VIII: Creation as an Open System, 115–30, esp. 119ff.

52. Augustine, *De civ.* XI, 6. See also J. Moltmann, *God in Creation. An Ecological Doctrine of Creation* (The Gifford Lectures, 1984–85), trans. Margaret Kohl, London and San Francisco 1985, Ch. V: The Time of Creation, 104–39.

53. Köhler, *Theologie des Alten Testaments* (n.51), 72.

54. Augustine, *Confessions*, X, 6, 19.

55. E. Käsemann, 'The Cry for Liberty in the Worship of the Church', in *Perspectives on Paul*, trans. Margaret Kohl, London and Philadelphia 1971, 134, 135, 137.

56. J. Audretsch, 'Blick auf das Ganze: Überlegungen eines Physikers zur theologischen Dimension der physikalischen Kosmologie', in J. Audretsch and H. Weder, *Kosmologie und Kreativität – Ein Gespräch zwischen Physik und Theologie*, Leipzig 1999, 23.

57. E. von Weizsäcker (ed.), *Offene Systeme* I. *Beiträge zur Zeitstruktur von Information, Entropie und Evolution*, Stuttgart 1974; K. Maurin (ed.), *Offene Systeme* II. *Logik und Zeit*, Stuttgart 1981.

58. J. B. Metz, 'Kirche und Welt im Lichte einer "Politischen Theologie"' (1967), now in *Zum Begriff der neuen Politischen Theologie 1967–1997*, Grünewald 1997, 9–22.

59. This corresponds to my *Theology of Hope*, trans. J. W. Leitch, London 1967, Ch. V: Exodus Church. Observations on the Eschatological Understanding of Christianity in Modern Society, 304–38.

60. Metz, *Begriff der neuen Politischen Theologie* (n.58), 15.

61. J. Ratzinger, *Aus meinem Leben. Erinnerungen*, Stuttgart 1998: '. . . but when the direction towards political theology became plain, I saw an antithesis emerging which could go deep.'

62. Metz, *Begriff der neuen Politischen Theologie* (n.58), 13: 'His cross does not stand on the private ground of individual and personal territory. Nor does it stand in the Holy of Holies of a purely religious sphere. It stands beyond the threshold of what is guarded as private, or kept apart as purely religious. It stands "outside", as the theology of the Epistle to the Hebrews puts it. The veil of the temple has been rent once and for all. The scandal and the promise of this salvation are public property.' The second saying can be found in the synodical resolution 'Unsere Hoffnung' of 1975, 29, which was largely formulated by Metz.

63. See here J. Moltmann, 'Theologische Kritik der Politischen Religion', in J. B. Metz, J. Moltmann and W. Oellmüller, *Kirche im Prozess der Aufklärung*, Munich and Mainz 1970, 11–52. This

article was my contribution to the 'new' political theology.

64. J. B. Metz, 'Zwischen Erinnern und Vergessen: Die Shoah im Zeitalter der kulturellen Amnesie' (1997), in *Begriff der neuen Politischen Theologie* (n.58), 149–156; also *Trotzdem Hoffen. Mit Johann Baptist Metz und Elie Wiesel im Gespräch*, Mainz 1993.

65. Moltmann, *The Crucified God* (n.17).

66. C. Schmitt, *Politische Theologie. Vier Kapitel zur Lehre von der Souveränität*, Munich and Leipzig 1922, ²1934.

67. Ibid., 83.

68. N. Sombart, *Die deutschen Männer und ihre Feinde. Carl Schmitt – ein deutsches Schicksal zwischen Männerbund und Matriarchatsmythos*, Munich 1991, is considerably more illuminating than H. Meier's apologia, *Die Lehre Carl Schmitts. Vier Kapitel zur Unterscheidung Politischer Theologie und Politischer Philosophie*, Stuttgart and Weimar 1994.

69. M. Bakunin, *Gott und der Staat* (1871), Berlin 1995.

70. Schmitt, *Politische Theologie* (n.66), 75.

71. Preface to the second edition of his *Politische Theologie*: 'We have meanwhile recognized that the political is the whole . . .'

72. W. Dilthey, *Gesammelte Schriften*, Vol. V, Stuttgart 1965, 332.

73. In this section I am pursuing ideas which I put forward in 1968 in 'Existenzgeschichte und Weltgeschichte. Auf dem Wege zu einer politischen Hermeneutik des Evangeliums', in *Perspektiven der Theologie*, 128–46. (This article is not included in the translated selection, *Hope and Planning*.)

74. Dilthey, *Gesammelte Schriften*, Vol. VII, 147.

75. Ibid., 233.

76. Ibid.

77. Although G. Gutiérrez would not like to be understood in so one-sided a way, in his *Theology of Liberation* he does in fact put the praxis of love before theology, just as Anselm already put faith before understanding; see the new English edition of his book, Maryknoll and London 1988, and his introduction, xvii ff.

78. I could never understand why Bultmann investigated the biblical texts form-critically and sociologically, but interpreted them from the viewpoint of existential history and individualistically, without seeing any contradiction here.

79. Rosemary Radford Ruether, *Sexism and God-Talk. Toward a Feminist Theology*, Boston and London 1983; Letty Russell, *The Liberating Word. A Guide to Nonsexist Interpretation of the Bible*, Philadelphia 1976; Elisabeth Schüssler-Fiorenza, *Bread not Stone. The Challenge of Feminist Biblical Interpretation*, Boston 1984, Edinburgh 1990; Annette Noller, *Feministische Hermeneutik zu*

einer neuen Schriftauslegung, Neukirchen 1995. On the whole topic
see *Wörterbuch der Feministischen Theologie*, Gütersloh 1991.

80. This development prompted F. Fukuyama in 1989 to announce 'the
end of history'. See *The End of History and the Last Man*, New
York and Toronto 1989.

81. Ricoeur, *The Conflict of Interpretations* (n.43).

82. M. Luther, 'Through faith God changes us into his word, not his
word into us (*Ex ita Deus nos in verbum suum, non autem verbum
suum in nos mutat*)', *Der Römerbrief*, ed. J. Ficker, II, 65. Cf. here
H. J. Iwand, *Glaubensgerechtigkeit nach Luthers Lehre*, Theologische Existenz heute 75, Munich 1941, 15.

83. Unfortunately, in the Small Catechism Luther changed the Bible's
First Commandment in such a way that Israel's liberation from
Egypt fails to appear.

84. Elizabeth Cady Stanton, *The Women's Bible*, Part I, 1895, Part II,
1898; reprinted New York 1974.

85. H.-J. Kraus has impressively taken account of both in his
*Systematische Theologie im Kontext biblischer Geschichte und
Eschatologie*, Neukirchen 1983.

86. G. Friedrich, 'Basileia', *TDNT* II.

87. H.-J. Kraus, *Geschichte der historisch-kritischen Erforschung des
Alten Testament*, Neukirchen ³1982, 18–24.

88. Iwand, *Predigt-Meditationen* (n.4), 149.

89. M. Luther, WA VII, 97.

90. Weber, *Foundations of Dogmatics* (n.12) III, 305 (trans. emended).

91. G. Gutiérrez, *The Power of the Poor in History*, ET Maryknoll, NY
1973, esp. 16–22. How far this viewpoint is present in the theologies
of the Third World is shown by *Herausgefordert durch die Armen.
Dokumente der Ökumenischen Vereinigung von Dritte-Welt-
Theologen 1976–1986*, Freiburg 1990.

92. See G. Lohfink, *Wem gilt die Bergpredigt?*, Freiburg 1988.

93. See J. Moltmann, *The Church in the Power of the Spirit*, trans.
Margaret Kohl, London and New York 1977, Ch. III.7, The Place of
the Church in the Presence of Christ, 121–32. Unfortunately this
view of the two sides of the people of Christ has played hardly any
part in the succeeding ecclesiological discussions.

94. In discussing the founder religions E. Bloch spoke of a 'growing
human penetration into the religious mystery': *Das Prinzip
Hoffnung*, Section 53, 1392–550 (see *The Principle of Hope*).

95. R. Otto, *The Idea of the Holy: An Inquiry into the Non-Rational
Factor in the Idea of the Divine and its Relation to the Rational*
(1917), trans. J. W. Harvey, London ⁶1931.

96. Weber, *Foundations of Dogmatics* (n.12) I, 248–86: Holy scripture

and the church, esp. 250f. on 'the circle'.

97. See ibid., I, 228–48 on 'theopneusty'. According to the Reformed orthodoxy of the seventeenth century, scripture does not merely contain the Word of God; it is 'God's written Word', verbally inspired right down to the Hebrew punctuation, although this is of a relatively late date. Cf. H. Heppe and E. Bizer, *Die Dogmatik der Evangelisch-reformierten Kirche*, Neukirchen 1958, 10–14.

98. Elisabeth Schüssler-Fiorenza (ed.), *Women's Sacred Scriptures*, *Concilium* 1998/3.

99. Weber, *Dogmatics* (n.12) I, 254f. On page 257, however, he speaks of the canon as being 'factually' closed.

100. H. Kirschstein, *Der souveräne Gott und die heilige Schrift. Einführung in die Biblische Hermeneutik Karl Barths. Mit einem Vorwort von Jürgen Moltmann*, Aachen 1998, 211.

101. K. Barth, *Epistle to the Romans*, Preface to the Second Edition (1921), trans. E.C. Hoskyns, London 1933, 7–8 (trans. emended).

102. Kirschstein, *Der souveräne Gott* (n.100), 281.

103. Basil of Caesarea, *On The Holy Spirit*, 38 b (PG 32).

104. A. Zakai, 'From Judgment to Salvation: The Image of the Jews in the English Renaissance, *WTJ* 59, 1977, 213–30.

105. R. Bultmann, 'The Problem of Hermeneutics', in *Essays*, trans. J. C. G. Greig, London 1955, 234–61.

106. G. Ebeling, 'Word of God and Hermeneutics', in *Word and Faith*, trans. J. W. Leitch, London 1963, 305–32.

107. The best account is given by A. C. Thiselton, *New Horizons in Hermeneutics. The Theory and Practice of Transforming Biblical Reading*, London 1992.

108. E. Bloch, *Atheismus im Christentum*, Frankfurt 1968, 89–114: 'Bibelkritik als detektorisch: roter Faden und Enttheokratisierung im unterdrückten Text' (*Atheism in Christianity*, trans. J. T. Swann, New York 1972). The 'hermeneutics of suspicion' is generally traced back to Paul Ricoeur's psycholanalytical hermeneutics. But in *Freud and Philosophy. An Essay on Interpretation*, ET New Haven and London 1970, he talks only about interpretation as the practice of doubt: Marx, Nietzsche and Freud have opposed their forms of doubt to the encodements of guile, in order to arrive at the truth. All three tried in different ways to bring their 'conscious' decoding methods into line with the 'unconscious' work of encodement which they ascribed to the will to power, the being of society, the unconscious life of the soul. The doubting human being implements in reverse the work of falsification of the guileful human being. Cf. M. J. Raden, *Das relative Absolute. Die theologische Hermeneutik Paul Ricoeurs*, Frankfurt 1988.

109. Basil, *The Holy Spirit*, 39 e. For more detail see J. Moltmann, *The Spirit of Life*, trans. Margaret Kohl, London and Minneapolis 1991, 312–15.

110. Weber, *Dogmatics* (n.12), 240–8.

111. J. Moltmann, *The Trinity and the Kingdom of God*, trans. Margaret Kohl, London 1981 (= *The Trinity and the Kingdom*, New York 1981), 64; Kirschstein, *Der souveräne Gott* (n.100), 286: 'Perhaps the strong emphasis on the *three* divine Persons, such as that given by J. Moltmann in his doctrine of the Trinity, offers the best possibility for further development here.'

112. P. Stuhlmacher, *Vom Verstehen des Neuen Testaments. Eine Hermeneutik*, Göttingen 1979.

113. See J. Moltmann, *The Source of Life. The Holy Spirit and the Theology of Life*, trans. Margaret Kohl, London and Minneapolis 1997, 19–22.

114. In opposition to Darwin, see P. Kropotkin, *Mutual Aid. A Factor of Evolution*, London 1902. For the following passage see M. Welker, 'Konzepte von "Leben" in Nietzsches Werk', *Marburger Jahrbuch Theologie IX: Leben*, ed. W. Härle and R. Paul, Marburg 1997, 41–52. I am indebted to him for stimulating me to think about 'life' as ecumenically 'comprehensive orientation term', in contrast to Nietzsche.

115. *Metaphysics* II, 4, 1000 b.

116. *Nicomachean Ethics* VIII, 4, 1155 a.

117. On this section see J. Moltmann, *God for a Secular Society*, trans. Margaret Kohl, London and Minneapolis 1999: 'The Knowing of the Other and the Community of the Different', 135–52.

118. See W. Capelle, *Die Vorsokratiker*, Berlin 1958, 217, 236.

119. J. W. von Goethe, *Zahme Xenien* III.

120. E. Spranger, '*Nemo contra Deum nisi Deus ipse*' (1949), in *Philosophie und Psychologie der Religion*, Tübingen 1974, 315ff. See also Moltmann, *The Crucified God* (n.17), 152f.

121. See Barth, *Epistle to the Romans* (1921, n.101); Otto, *The Idea of the Holy* (n.95).

122. '*Inter creatorem et creaturam non potest tanta similitudo notari, quin inter eas major sit dissimilitudo notanda*' (H. Denzinger, *Enchiridion Symbolorum.The Sources of Catholic Dogma*, trans. from the thirteenth edition. by R.J. Deferrari, St Louis and London 1957, No. 432, p.171).

123. E. Przywara, *Religionsphilosophie katholischer Theologie*, Munich and Berlin 1926, 22–5. See E. Mechels, *Analogie bei Erich Przywara und Karl Barth*, Neukirchen 1974. From the American sector I should like to draw particular attention to D. Tracy, *The Analogical*

Imagination. Christian Theology and the Culture of Pluralism, New York and London 1981, 405–55.

124. Przywara, *Religionsphilosophie* (n.123), 22.
125. Ibid., 23.
126. Ibid,. 24.
127. Ibid., 25.
128. D. Bonhoeffer, *Act and Being* (1931), ed. W. W. Floyd Jr., trans. H. M. Rumscheidt, Minneapolis 1996, uses this argument in his criticism of Przywara. Cf. Christiane Steiding's dissertation, *Ratio in se ipsam incurvata. Eine Untersuchung zu Dietrich Bonhoeffers früher Erkenntnistheorie*, Tübingen 1999.
129. In this he was followed by Karl Rahner, who was able without any difficulty to relate the fundamental openness of human existence to the Roman Catholic Church as the place of God's revelation. Cf. *Hörer des Wortes*, ²1969, 218 (ET *Hearers of the Word*, New York 1969), and 'Die anonymen Christen', *Schriften zur Theologie* VI, 546 (ET *Theological Investigations* VI, London 1969, 390ff.). For critical comment see E. Jüngel, *God as Mystery of the World. On the Foundation of the Theology of the Crucified One in the Dispute between Theism and Atheism*, trans. D. L. Guder, Grand Rapids and Edinburgh 1983, 262 n.1. Jüngel would like to see the self-transcendence of the human being and the self-communication of God 'ecumenically' mediated.
130. K. Barth, *CD* I/1, Preface xiii. On this see W. Pannenberg, 'Analogie', *RGG*³, 1957, I, 350–353, and his *Systematic Theology* I, trans. G.W. Bromiley, Grand Rapids and Edinburgh 1991, 343ff. Jüngel, *God as the Mystery of the World* (n.129), on the problem of analogical talk about God, with further literature on the philosophical and theological concept of analogy. On Barth's misunderstanding of the *analogia entis*, see H. Urs von Balthasar, *The Theology of Karl Barth*, ET New York 1971.
131. The first and best account of the cosmos analogy in Barth's *Church Dogmatics* was given by H. Urs von Balthasar in his *Karl Barth*, 95–140: 'Analogy in Full Bloom.' However, in view of more recent studies his analysis of a 'shift' from dialectic to analogy in Barth's thinking (70–94) can no longer be maintained.
132. W. Pannenberg rightly points out that in the 'threefold way of knowledge of God', the *via negationis*, the *via eminentiae* and the *via causalitatis*, the last two are closely linked, if we assume that the cause communicates something of its being to the effect, since as causative being it is higher than the being effected. Then the conclusion from the effect to the cause – in this case from the effected world to the divine *causa prima* – is possible. That is the *via eminentiae*.

See *Systematic Theology* I (n.130), 337ff.

133. Jüngel, *God as the Mystery of the World* (n.129), 282–98: 'The Gospel as Analogous Talk about God. On the new linguistic theology', cf. I. U. Dalferth's extensive work *Religiöse Rede von Gott*. Munich 1981.

134. In this section I am drawing above all on E. Jüngel, *Metaphorische Wahrheit. Erwägungen zur theologischen Relevanz der Metapher als Beitrag zur Hermeneutik einer narrativen Theologie*, in a special number of *EvTh*; P. Ricoeur and E. Jüngel, *Metapher. Zur Hermeneutik religiöser Sprache*, Munich 1973; and Sallie McFague, *Metaphorical Theology. Models of God in Religious Language*, Philadelphia and London 1982. Cf. also M. J. Raden, 'Hermeneutik der Entsprechung oder Hermeneutik der Nichtentsprechung. Eine Gegenüberstellung der theologischen Hermeneutiken von E. Jüngel und P. Ricoeur', *EvTh* 48, 1988, 217–32.

135. That is a felicitous metaphor about metaphors coined by Jean Paul. It is quoted by G. Eichholz in *Gleichnisse der Evangelien. Form, Überlieferung, Auslegung*, Neukirchen 1971, 18.

136. McFague, *Metaphorical Theology* (n.134), 16.

137. My critics have occasionally interpreted this as a weakness on my part. But in most cases I have chosen the shift of style deliberately.

138. McFague, *Metaphorical Theology* (n.134), 19. She believes that this is a feature peculiar to liberal Protestantism.

139. Denzinger, nos. 1838, 1839. Cf. H. Küng, *Infallible? An Enquiry*, London 1972, with the postulate that 'statements' can never be true or false in an absolute sense, for they can fall behind reality, be misinterpreted, are only translatable to a limited degree and are open to the influence of ideologies. The truths of statements are historical and as such neither infallible nor irreformable.

140. Jüngel, *Metaphorische Wahrheit* (n.134), 119.

141. J. Derbolay, quoted in ibid., 115.

142. Eichholz, *Gleichnisse der Evangelien* (n.135), 14; Jüngel, *Metaphorische Wahrheit* (n.134), 76.

143. Eichholz, *Gleichnisse der Evangelien* (n.135), 19ff., whom I am following here.

144. Ibid., 26. Cf. here G.M. Martin, *Sachbuch Bibliodrama. Praxis und Theorie*, Stuttgart 1995.

145. Eichholz, *Gleichnisse der Evangelien* (n.135), 31–8. This insight seems to me particularly worth thinking about.

146. Jüngel, *God as the Mystery of the World* (n.129), 289; McFague, *Metaphorical Theology* (n.134), 18: 'A metaphorical theology, then, starts with the parables of Jesus and with Jesus as a parable of God.'

147. L. Keck, *A Future for the Historical Jesus: The Place of Jesus in Preaching and Theology*, Philadelphia 1981, 244.

148. Jüngel, *God as the Mystery of the World* (n.129), 289.

149. J. Moltmann, *The Way of Jesus Christ*, trans. Margaret Kohl, London and San Francisco 1990, 137–50: Jesus – The Messianic Person in His Becoming.

150. Capelle, *Die Vorsokratiker* (n.118), 125.

151. M. J. Rainer and H. G. Janssen (eds), *Bilderverbot*, Munich 1997.

152. Gregory of Nyssa, *De Vita Moysis*, PG 44, 404 B.

153. E. Bloch, *Tübinger Einleitung in die Philosophie* II, Frankfurt 1964, 16.

154. Moltmann, *The Crucified God* (n.17), 25–8.

155. *Nicomachean Ethics*, VIII, 2, 1155 b.

156. Theophrastus, *De sensibus*, 24ff., quoted by G. M. Stratton, *Theophrastus and the Greek Physiological Psychology before Aristotle*, New York and London, 1917, 90ff.

157. F. W. Schelling, *Über das Wesen menschlicher Freiheit* (1809), Reklam ed. 8913–5, 89 (*Of Human Freedom*, trans. J. Gutmann, Chicago 1936).

158. H. Nohl (ed.), *Hegels theologische Jugendschriften*, Tübingen 1907, 345ff; *Systemfragment* of 1809.

159. '*Humanitatis seu (ut Apostolus loquitur) carnis regno, quod in fide agitur, nos sibi conformes facit et crucifigit, faciens ex infoelicibus et superbis diis homines veros, idest miseros et peccatores. Quia enim ascendimus in Adam ad similitudinem dei, ideo descendit ille in similitudinem nostram, ut reduceret nos ad nostri cognitionem. Atque hos agitur sacramento incarnationis. Hoc est regnum fidei, in quo Crux Christi dominatur, divinitatem perverse petitam deiiciens et humanitatem carnisque contemptam infirmitatem perverse desertam revocans*'. ['Through the rule of his humanity or his "flesh", which rules in faith, as the apostle says, he makes us like in form to himself, and crucifies us, in that he turns us from being unhappy and proud gods into true men, that is, the wretched beings and sinners (which we are). For because in Adam we have ascended to be like unto God, he descended into this similarity of ours, so that he might bring us to knowledge of ourselves. Thus does God act in the sacrament of the incarnation. This is the realm of faith, in which the cross of Christ rules, rejecting the divinity for which we perversely strive, and bringing back to us the humanity and weakness of the flesh which we perversely forsake' (WA V, 128).]

160. J. Sobrino, 'Theologisches Erkennen in der europäischen und der lateinamerikanischen Theologie' in K. Rahner (ed.), *Befreiende Theologie*, Stuttgart 1977, 138.

161. Moltmann, *The Crucified God* (n.17), 27f.
162. P. F. M. Zahl, *Die Rechtfertigungslehre Ernst Käsemanns*, Stuttgart 1996. An obituary by Zahl, with a translation of Käsemann's last letters, appeared in the *Anglican Theological Review*, LXXX, No. 3, Summer 1998, 382–94.
163. G. Steiner, *After Babel. Aspects of Language and Translation*, Oxford ²1992, Ch. 3: Word Against Object, 115–247.
164. Trevor Hart, 'Imagination for the Kingdom of God? Hope, Promise and the Transformative Power of an Imagined Future', in R. Bauckham (ed.), *God Will Be All In All*, Edinburgh 1999, 49–76.
165. W. Rauschenbusch,*Christianity and the Social Crisis*, ed. R.D. Cross, New York 1964, 91.

III. Mirror Images of Liberating Theology

1. *Christliches Bekenntnis in Südafrika. Das Kairos-Dokument – Herausforderung an die Kirchen*, Weltmission heute 1, Hamburg 1987; *Der Zentralamerikanische Kairos. Eine Herausforderung an die Kirchen und an die Welt*, EMW-Information 82, Hamburg 1988; *Der Weg nach Damaskus. Kairos und Bekehrung*, *EMW-Information* 84, Hamburg 1989; *Europäisches Kairos-Dokument für ein sozial gerechtes, lebenfreundliches und demokratisches Europa*, May 1998, *Junge Kirche*, Beilage zu Heft 6/7, June 1998.
2. J. Moltmann (ed.), *Friedenstheologie – Befreiungstheologie. Analysen, Berichte, Meditationen*, Munich 1988.
3. See here my early writings *Religion, Revolution and the Future*, New York 1969; 'Gott in der Revolution: "Siehe, ich mache alles neu"', Thesen für die SCM Welt-Konferenz in Turku, Finland, 1968, *EvKomm* 1/1968 (English: 'God in the Revolution', *Student World* 61, 1968, 241–52; also in *Religion, Revolution and the Future*, 129–47, and in Swedish, Dutch, French, Spanish and Polish); E. Feil and R. Weth (eds), *Diskussion zur 'Theologie der Revolution'*, Munich and Mainz 1969; 'Theologische Kritik der Politischen Religion' in J.B. Metz, J. Moltmann and W. Oelmüller, *Kirche im Prozess der Aufklärung*, Munich and Mainz 1970, 11–51. This last article was my first contribution to political theology and to the theology of the liberation of the oppressed. It is centred on the political theology of the cross.
4. As representative of the many others who have rightly complained about this, see R. S. Sugirtharajah, 'Dritte-Welt-Texte in westlichen Metropolen', *Zeitschrift für Mission* XXIV, 1998, 2, 105–18.
5. His first book on the subject was *Liberation Theology. Liberation in the Light of the Fourth Gospel*, New York 1972.

6. F. Herzog (ed.), *The Future of Hope. Theology as Eschatology*, New York 1970, with contributions by Harvey Cox, Langdon Gilkey, Van A. Harvey, John Macquarrie and Jürgen Moltmann.

7. This lecture was a preparation for my little book *Theology of Play*, ET New York 1972 (= *Theology of Joy*, London 1973).

8. The standard work here is G. Gutiérrez, *Las Casas. In Search for the Poor in Christ*, trans. R. R. Barr, Maryknoll, NY 1993. See also his *Gott oder das Gold. Der befreiende Weg des Bartolomé de Las Casas*, Freiburg 1990 (German trans. of *Dios o el oro en les Indias*, 1989).

9. D. P. Mannix and M. J. Cowley, *Black Cargoes. A History of the Atlantic Slave Trade*, New York 1962; E. Galeano, *Open Veins of Latin America*, New York 1962.

10. E. Williams, *Capitalism and Slavery*, Chapel Hill 1944.

11. W. Styron, *The Confessions of Nat Turner*, New York 1966.

12. H. Thurman, *Deep River and the Negro Spiritual Speaks of Life and Death*, Richmond, Va 1975, 33; J.H. Cone, *The Spirituals and the Blues*, New York 1975, 44. On Martin Luther King's gravestone in Atlanta is the following inscription:
    'Free at last!
    Free at last!
    Great God-a-mighty,
    Free at last.'

13. F. Fanon, *Schwarze Haut, weiße Masken*, Frankfurt 1985, 132ff.; P. Martin, *Schwarze Teufel, edle Mohren*, Hamburg 1993, 19–27.

14. See my article on racism and the right to resistance in *The Experiment Hope*, ET London 1975, 131–46.

15. Amy Jacques-Garvey, *Philosophy and Opinions of Marcus Garvey*, two vols in one, New York 1968; E. David Cronon, *Black Moses. The Story of Marcus Garvey and the Universal Negro Improvement Association*, Madison 1955; T. Witvliet, *The Way of the Black Messiah. The Hermeneutical Challenge of Black Theology as Theology of Liberation*, London 1987.

16. Booker T. Washington, *Up from Slavery* (1895), New York 1967.

17. For the following account I am indebted to my earlier assistant Carmen Rivuzumwami, who lived for a time in Jamaica and devoted intensive study to Rastafari religion and reggae music. See also J. Owens, *Dread. The Rastafarians of Jamaica*, Kingston, Jamaica 1976, ²1989.

18. Stokely Carmichael and Charles V. Hamilton, *Black Power. The Politics of Liberation in America*, New York 1967.

19. In the following passage I am drawing on J. H. Cone's account, *Martin and Malcolm and America: a Dream or a Nightmare*, New

York 1991, as well as on *Malcolm X. The Autobiography of Malcolm X as told to Alex Haley*, New York 1973, and on P. Goldmann, *The Death and Life of Malcolm X*, New York 1979. The quotation may be found in J. M. Cone's book, *Black Theology and Black Power*, New York 1969, 19.

20. Cone, *Black Theology and Black Power* (n.19), 19.
21. Cone, *Martin and Malcolm and America* (n.19), 42.
22. Ibid., 56.
23. Ibid., 110.
24. Ibid., 159.
25. J. Moltmann, 'Freedom in Community between Globalization and Individualism: Market Value and Human Dignity', in *God for a Secular Society*, trans. Margaret Kohl, London and Minneapolis 1999, 153–66.
26. Cone, *Martin and Malcolm* (n.19), 3.
27. In the following passage I am following, as well as J. H. Cone's account: Coretta Scott King, *My Life with Martin Luther King*, New York 1969; D. L. Lewis, *King. A Critical Biography*, New York 1970; and N. L. Erskine, *King among Theologians*, Cleveland, Ohio 1984.
28. New York 1997.
29. Quotation in J. H. Cone, *Martin and Malcolm* (n.19), 62: 'If we are wrong, the Constitution of the US is wrong. If we are wrong, God Almighty is wrong. . . If we are wrong, justice is a lie . . .'
30. Ibid., 71.
31. Ibid., 232ff.
32. A. Clayton Powell Jr, *Marching Blacks*, New York 1972.
33. J. H. Cone, *Black Theology and Black Power*, New York 1969.
34. G. S. Wilmore and J. H. Cone, *Black Theology. A Documentary History 1966–1979*, Maryknoll, NY 1979, revised ed. 1993.
35. Exceptions are K. P. Blaser, *Wenn Gott schwarz wäre . . . Das Problem des Rassismus in Theologie und christlicher Praxis*, Zürich 1972, and 'Warum "Schwarze Theologie"?', *EvTh* 1974/1.
36. Cone, *Black Theology and Black Power* (n.19), 31.
37. Ibid., 120.
38. Ibid., 69.
39. J. H. Cone, *A Black Theology of Liberation*, New York 1970, 29.
40. Ibid., 27.
41. H. Thurman, *The Negro Spiritual*, 27; J. H. Cone, *God of the Oppressed*, New York 1975, new revised edition, New York 1997, 109.
42. D. Bonhoeffer, *Letters and Papers from Prison*, ed. E. Bethge, [fourth] enlarged ed., trans. R. H. Fuller *et al.*, London 1971, letter

of 16 July 1944, 361ff.; poem 'Christians und Pagans', 348f..

43. Cone, *Black Theology and Black Power* (n.33), 123.
44. Ibid., 127.
45. Wilmore and Cone, *Black Theology. A Documentary History* (n.34), 1979, 617; J. H. Cone, 'Looking Back, Going Forward: Black Theology as Public Theology', *Criterion*, Winter 1999, 18–27.
46. Dolores Williams, *Sisters in the Wilderness. The Challenge of Womanist God-Talk*, New York 1994.
47. G. Gutiérrez, *A Theology of Liberation* (1971), trans. C. Inda and J. Eagleson, New York 1973, London 1974; revised ed. with new introduction, 1988.
48. See J. B. Metz's chapter on 'Church and People', in *Faith in History and Society*, trans. D. Smith, London 1980; J. Moltmann, 'Hope in the Struggle of the People', in *The Open Church. Invitation to a Messianic Lifestyle*, trans. M. D. Meeks, Philadelphia and London 1978, 95–112 (= US edition *The Passion for Life*).
49. H. Assmann, *Die Götzen der Unterdrückung und der befreiende Gott*, trans. from Spanish by A. Reiser, Münster 1984; J. L. Segundo, *The Liberation of Theology* (1975), ET Maryknoll, NY 1976; J. Miguez Bonino, *Doing Theology in a Revolutionary Situation* (1975), ET Philadelphia and London 1975.
50. In German, 'Offener Brief an José Miguez Bonino', *EvKomm* 9, 1976, 755–7; in Spanish, 'Lettera aperta a José Miguez Bonino', *Selecciones de teologia* 15, 1976, 305–11; in English, 'On Latin American Liberation Theology. An Open Letter to José Miguez Bonino', *Christianity and Crisis* 36, 1976, 57–63; in Italian, in *Giornale di theologia* 92, 1976, 202–17. In response F. Herzog wrote an 'Open Letter to Jürgen Moltmann', now in J. Rieger (ed.), *Theology from the Belly of a Whale. A Frederick Herzog Reader*, Harrisburg, Pa 1999, 173–6.
51. *Temas para una Teologia de la Esperanza*, Buenos Aires 1978.
52. *EvTh* 38, 1978, 527–37 (for Helmut Gollwitzer).
53. Opening lecture 'Relación intima entre fe critiana y libertad humana', *Sacuanjoche* 2/3, Vol. 1, Nov. 1997, 13–26.
54. Bibliothek Theologie der Befreiung, Patmos Verlag, Düsseldorf, with more than 16 volumes. I. Ellacuria and J. Sobrino (eds), *Mysterium Liberationis. Fundamental Concepts of Liberation Theology*, 2 vols, Maryknoll, NY 1993.
55. *Teologia politica y Teologia de la Liberacion*, Universidad Ibero-Americano Mexico City 1991; *Carthaginensia* VIII, 1992, 489–502; *Union Seminary Quarterly Review* 45, 1991, 205–18; 'Die Zukunft der Befreiungstheologie', *Orientierung* 59, 1995, 207–10; 'Die

Theologie unserer Befreiung', *Orientierung* 60, 1996, 204–6. For a summing-up see 'Political Theology and the Theology of Liberation', in J. Moltmann, *God for a Secular Society* (n.25), 46–70.

56. P. Kennedy, *The Rise and Fall of the Great Powers*, New York 1987, shows how unimportant the little European nations were compared with the Ottoman empire, the India of the Moguls and the Chinese empire.

57. G.W.F. Hegel, *Die Vernunft in der Geschichte*, PhB 171a, Hamburg 1955, 189: 'America is thus the country of the future . . .' (*Lectures on the Philosophy of World History. Introduction: Reason in History*, trans. H. N. Nisbet, Cambridge 1975).

58. B. Dietschy, 'Die Tücken des Entdeckens. Ernst Bloch, Kolumbus und die Neue Welt', *Jahrbuch der Ernst-Bloch-Gesellschaft* 1992/93, 234–51.

59. E. Bloch already detected this from Columbus's journals. Cf. *Das Prinzip Hoffnung*, Frankfurt 1959, 873ff.: Eldorado und Eden, esp. 904 (*The Principle of Hope*, trans. N. and S. Plaice and P. Knight, Cambridge, Mass. and Oxford 1986).

60. I am indebted for this reference to M. Delgado, 'Die Metamorphosen des Messianismus in den iberischen Kulturen. Eine religionsgeschichtliche Studie', *Neue Zeitschrift für Missionswissenschaft*, Vol 34, Immensee 1994, which I am following here.

61. Ibid., 40.

62. Ibid., 33.

63. Ibid., 40. Curiously enough they are not mentioned in G. Gutiérrez's book on Las Casas.

64. Delgado, 'Metamorphosen' (n.60), 30–7. That Iberian quintomonarchianism was the result of the strong Jewish influences on Iberian Christianity is his own theory. For him, the metamorphoses of Iberian messianism are 'the expression of the profound longing that a messianic and eschatological role of planetary relevance should be be reserved for Iberian cultures in the divine plan for history' (31). He even believes that he can perceive an 'underlying history' of this messianic longing in present-day liberation theology (31).

65. F. G. Maier, 'Byzanz', *Fischer Weltgeschichte* 13, Frankfurt 1973, 22–3. I wrote about the scheme of the four world empires according to the book of Daniel in *The Coming of God*, trans. Margaret Kohl, London and Minneapolis 1996, under the title 'Eschatological Orders of Time in History', 141–6. But at that time Iberian quintomonarchianism was unknown to me.

66. This has been convincingly put forward by A. W. Crosby, supported by medical knowledge, in *Ecological Imperialism*, Cambridge and New York 1986.

67. T. Todorov, *La conquête de l'Amérique: la question de l'autre*, Paris 1982 (German trans. *Die Eroberung Amerikas. Das Problem des Anderen*, Frankfurt 1985, to which the page references in the present section refer; here 165).

68. Ibid., 8off., 121ff.

69. Ibid., 296.

70. Gutiérrez, *Gott oder das Gold* (n.8). For the following quotation see p.197.

71. Galeano, *Open Veins of Latin America* (n.9).

72. Todorov, *Die Eroberung* (n.67), 161; on the 'black legend' cf. Delgado, 'Metamorphosen' (n.60), 47.

73. Gutiérrez, *Theology of Liberation* (n.47), 78ff.; Miguez Bonino, *Theology in a Revolutionary Situation* (n.49), Ch. 1; B. Kern, *Theologie im Horizont der Marxismus. Zur Geschichte der Marxismusrezeption in der lateinamerikanischen Theologie der Befreiung*, Mainz 1992.

74. N. Greinacher (ed.), *Konflikt um die Theologie der Befreiung. Diskussion und Dokumentation*, Zürich 1985.

75. In this respect Gutiérrez has corrected himself and expanded his viewpoint. See his preface to the new German edition of the *Theology of Liberation*, Mainz 1991, 27 (the German preface differs from that in the new English edition): 'The dependence theory, to which we turned again and again in the first years of our encounter with the Latin American reality, (is) today in spite of all positive results much too blunt an instrument to allow us to see clearly enough the inward dynamic of each country, and also the extent of the world of the poor as a whole.'

76. G. Müller-Fahrenholz, '500 Jahre "Entdeckung" Amerikas – aus der Sicht der "Entdeckten"', *EvTh* 51, 1991, 492–503.

77. Greinacher (ed.), *Konflikt um die Theologie der Befreiung* (n.74), 23, 40.

78. See G. Gutiérrez, *We Drink from Our Own Wells: The Spiritual Journey of a People*, trans. M. J. O'Connell, Maryknoll, NY and London 1988.

79. J. Sobrino (ed.), *Romero, die Notwendige Revolution*, German trans. from the Spanish by E. Págan, Munich and Mainz 1982, 'Einführung', 17.

80. Nancy E. Bedford, *Jesus Christus und das gekreuzigte Volk: Christologie der Nachfolge und des Martyriums bei Jon Sobrino*, Concordia Reihe Monographien 15, Aachen 1995: 'Die Option für die Armen und die Option der Armen', 61–72. Cf. also Gutiérrez on 'The Poor and the Fundamental Option', in *Mysterium Liberationis* (n.54).

81. See I. Ellacuria on 'The Church of the Poor, A Historical Sacrament of Liberation', in *Mysterium Liberationis* II (n.54).
82. J. Moltmann, *The Church in the Power of the Spirit*, trans. Margaret Kohl, London and New York 1977, III.7: 'The Place of the Church in the Presence of Christ', 121–32.
83. See I. Ellacuria on 'the crucified people' in *Mysterium Liberationis* II (n.54). For a detailed account see Bedford, *Christus und das gekreuzigte Volk* (n.80), 136–80; for justifiable criticism, 196–200.
84. 552: The church is *quasi altera Christi persona* . . . Also 72: *Christum dicimus Caput et Corpus, Christum totum.*
85. Bedford, *Christus und das gekreuzigte Volk* (n.80), 200. The Final Declaration of the International Conference of the Ecumenical Association of Third World Theologians (EATWOT) in New Delhi, 1981, says the following: 'Although in Latin America and on the Philippines most people are Christians, in the rest of Asia and in Africa, to which three-quarters of the Third World population belongs, the great majority belong to other religions. If this majority irrupts into the world of Christians, then Third World theology, if it is to be really useful and liberating, must speak to this non-Christian world, and through it. Otherwise theology will become an esoteric luxury of the Christian minority . . . We Christians . . . must also learn to recognize the presence of God among the oppressed of other religions, who in the Third World today are struggling for full humanity. Their sacred scriptures and traditions are a source of revelation for us too.' (See also the translation in V. Fabella and S. Torres [eds], *Irruption of the Third World: Challenge to Theology. Papers from the Fifth International Conference of the EATWOT, 17–29 August 1981, New Delhi*, Orbis Books, Maryknoll, NY 1983.)
86. Gutiérrez, *A Theology of Liberation* (trans. emended) (n.47), 12.
87. Ibid., 18.
88. Ibid, 23.
89. Ibid., 100.
90. Ibid., 97.
91. Ibid., 104.
92. Ibid., 86.
93. Ibid., 91.
94. Ibid., 91.
95. Ibid., 86 (trans. emended).
96. Ibid., 90.
97. R. Arce Valentin, 'Die Schöpfung muss gerettet werden. Aber: für wen? Die ökologische Krise aus der Perspektive lateinamerikanischer Theologie', *EvTh* 51, 1991, 565–77.

98. *The Conciliar and Post-Conciliar Documents*, ed. A. Flannery, revised ed., Dublin and Leominster 1988: *Gaudium et Spes*, 39.
99. Gutiérrez, *Theology of Liberation* (n.47), 99.
100. Ibid.
101. B. Brecht, *An die Nachgeborenen. Gedichte*, Frankfurt 1981, 725.
102. W. Benjamin, *Illuminationen. Ausgewählte Schriften*, Frankfurt 1961. (*Illuminations*, trans. H. Zohn, with an introduction by Hannah Arendt, London 1970, reprinted 1992. In spite of its title, this is not identical in content with the German volume. It includes a translation of *Theses on the Philosophy of History* but not the *Theological-Political Fragment*. The quotations in the present text have been translated directly from the German: see *Illuminationen*, 268ff.)
103. *Instruction on Certain Aspects of Liberation Theology*, published by the Catholic Truth Society, 1984. The quotations from this and the following *Instruction* (see n.104), with the references, have been taken from the German version in *Verlautbarungen des Apostolischen Stuhles*, Fulda 1984 and 1986. Cf. also H. Meesmann's report, 'Kardinal Ratzingers Offensive gegen die Befreiungstheologie', *Publik Forum* 9, 27 April 1984, 25–9.
104. *Instruction on Christian Freedom and Liberation* (for references see n.103 above).
105. J. Ratzinger, *Aus meinem Leben. Erinnerungen (1927–1977)*, Stuttgart 1998, 151: 'Jürgen Moltmann was invited to a chair in the faculty for Protestant theology at about the same time as I came to Tübingen. With his fascinating book *Theology of Hope*, Moltmann had conceived theology in a new and wholly different way, in the light of Bloch's ideas . . . The reception of existentialism into theology, which Bultmann had brought about, was not without its dangers for theology . . . But the destruction of theology which now went forward through its politicization along the lines of Marxist messianism was incomparably more radical . . . because God was set aside and replaced by the political activity of the human being.' Ratzinger tired of the struggle, and in 1969 went to Regensburg 'because I wanted to develop my theology further there in a less disturbing context, and did not wish to let myself be pushed into a continually "anti" position' (153). So in the intellectual and spiritual struggles of those days he left us to ourselves, which to him himself 'seemed like a betrayal' (150).
106. *Instruction* 1984, Preface.
107. J. Höffner, *Soziallehre der Kirche oder Theologie der Befreiung*, 4 September 1984, 18.
108. *Instruction*, IX, 3.

109. Ibid., IV, 14.

110. Ibid., IV, 15.

111. K. Marx, *Die Frühschriften*, ed. S. Landshut, Stuttgart 1953, 339. The practical criticism of liberation theology, admittedly, is provided by the Pentecostal movement. John Burdick, in his book *Looking for God in Brazil. The Progressive Catholic Church in Urban Brazil's Religious Arena*, Berkeley 1993, has shown that the Catholic base communities have failed to bring liberation theology to the poor through education. In a village, chosen as being typical, more than four times more people participate in what the Pentecostal Asambleia de Deus offers, because its 'cults of affliction' free the poor emotionally through experiences of the Spirit and healings through prayer, and do not impose on them even more burdens through liberation than the burdens which they have to bear in any case.

112. *Instruction*, IX, 3.

113. Ibid., X, 6.

114. Gutiérrez, *Theologie der Befreiung*, 1991 German edition (n.75), 242, appended note B.

115. See J. Moltmann, 'Hope in the Struggle of the People', in *The Open Church*, trans. M.D. Meeks, London 1978 (= *The Passion for Life: A Messianic Lifestyle*, Philadelphia 1978).

116. J. Moltmann (ed.), *Minjung Theologie des Volkes Gottes in Südkorea*, Neukirchen 1984. On the political ideas cf. Kim Dae-Jung, *Korea and Asia. A Collection of Essays, Speeches and Discussions*, Seoul 1994.

117. Ahn Byung-Mu, *Draussen vor der Tür. Kirche und Minjung in Korea*, ed. W. Glüer, Göttingen 1986.

118. On the history and profile of minjung theology, see W. Kröger, *Die Befreiung des Minjung. Das Profil einer protestantischen Befreiungstheologie für Asien in ökumenischer Perspektive*, Ökumenische Existenz heute 10, Munich 1992. Krüger lived in Korea for four years and worked with Ahn Byung-Mu.

119. See the article '*Ochlos*' in TDNT.

120. Ahn Byung-Mu, in J. Moltmann (ed,), *Minjung* (n.116), 121.

121. Ibid., 132.

122. Kröger, *Befreiung des Minjung* (n.118), 142. This is expounded in more detail by Kim Yong-Bock in *Messiah and Minjung. Christ's Solidarity with the People for New Life*, Christian Conference of Asia, Urban Rural Mission, Hongkong 1992, 16–18. Cf. also *Minjung Theology. People as the Subject of History*, a CTA-CCA publication, Singapore 1981, and Noh Jong-Sun, *Liberating God for Minjung*, Hanul Seoul 1994.

123. J. Moltmann, *Jesus Christ for Today's World*, trans. Margaret Kohl, London and Minneapolis 1994, 38–40.
124. Kröger, *Befreiung des Minjung* (n.118), 143.
125. Kim Yong-Bock has gone into this question (see n.122 above). Since the end of the Korean war, the *Han* (pain) of divided Korea has thrown up a number of messianic sects, the best known of them the Mun sect.
126. Ahn Byung-Mu in J. Moltmann (ed.), *Minjung* (n.116), 163 n.110.
127. Ibid., 167.
128. Bonhoeffer, *Letters and Papers from Prison* (n.42), letters of 16 and 18 July 1944; poem 'Christians and Pagans'.
129. Kröger has taken up this question; see *Die Befreiung des Minjung* (n.118), 130–6: 'Zur Problematik der "Enteignung Israels" in der AT-Rezeption der Minjung-Theologen (Überlegungen aus dem jüdisch-christlichen Dialog)'.
130. Thus A. Hoffmann-Richter, *Ahn Byung-Mu als Minjung-Theologe*, dissertation, Heidelberg 1988, Erlangen 1990, 159.
131. J. Moltmann, 'Covenant or Leviathan? Political Theology at the Beginning of Modern Times', in *God for a Secular Society* (n.25), I.2, 24–45.
132. L. Wyss (ed.), *Wider die Tyrannen*, Basel 1946, 67. That is the precise opposite to Jean Bodin's absolutist principle: *Princeps legibus solutus* – the prince is the dissolution of the law.
133. I have gone into this in more detail in *The Church in the Power of the Spirit* (n.82), III.7: 'The Place of the Church in the Presence of Christ', 121–32.
134. Cf. Elisabeth Moltmann-Wendel, *Autobiography*, trans. John Bowden, London 1997. For details about feminist theology I would point to the very informative *Wörterbuch der feministischer Theologie*, Gütersloh 1991, and Letty M. Russell and J. Shannon Clarkson (eds), *Dictionary of Feminist Theologies*, Louisville 1996.

In this chapter I shall be describing feminist theology in in its relevance for men, and shall not make the impossible attempt at a survey. Feminist theologies, psychologies and philosophies have been developed in abundance, and have by no means to do only with criticism of male domination.

My personal history with a feminist theology which viewed itself as liberal theology began with Dorothee Sölle's attack on my theology of the cross (*The Crucified God*, 1972; ET 1974) in her book *Suffering* (1973; ET 1975). In it she saw signs of a 'theological sadism'. For me the God-forsakenness of Christ on the cross was the profoundest expression of his solidarity with God-forsaken men and women. In the misery of a prisoner-of-war camp his death cry brought me to faith. Dorothee Sölle read the story morally, however, and rose up in arms against such a 'sadistic God' who abandons and sacrifices his own Son; she even compares this God with the concentration-camp murderer Heinrich Himmler. This viewpoint was so alien to me that I had not even considered it. But ever since then, the legend has gone the rounds that in my view God 'killed his own Son' on Golgotha. Feminist theologians in Germany and the United States have frequently and willingly picked up this moral criticism of the theology of the cross, without realizing that it is an ancient Socinian and Enlightenment criticism of Christianity which goes back to the sixteenth, seventeenth and eighteenth centuries, and that ever since Kant it has been standard polemic levelled by liberal theology against sacrificial theology, the sacrifice of the mass and sacrificial morality (cf. Rebecca Chopp, *The Praxis of Suffering. An Interpretation of Liberation and Political Theology*, New York 1986). Recently the reproach of *victimization* has been raised, in an attack on patriarchal male religion and masculine power politics in general, and has been theologically justified through the defamation of the Christian theology of the cross (cf. Christine Gudorf, *Victimization: Examining Christian Complicity*, Philadelphia 1992; Joanne Carlson Brown and Sharon Bohn [eds], *Christianity, Patriarchy and Abuse. A Feminist Critique*, New York 1989). The 'sadistic God' of Golgotha is now turned into a heavenly practitioner of child abuse, on the pattern of the atrocious fathers who abuse their own daughters. The difficulty for feminist theology at this point is that both on Golgotha and on Mount Moriah what we have are 'father-son' narratives; women and daughters play no part. So first of all the sons are required to abolish the ancient sacrificial religions, as well as the wars in which sons were 'sacrificed' in their millions for their country; while these sons for their part are to require no 'sacrifices' of mothers, wives and daughters. But this has nothing to do with the Christian theology of the cross. It is not a general theology of suffering, and even less a sacrificial theology open to generalization; it is the definitive end of the sacrificial cult, just as the story of the non-sacrifice of Isaac indicates the end of child sacrifice as a religious requirement.

135. Elisabeth Moltmann-Wendel (ed.), *Menschenrechte für die Frau*, Munich 1974.
136. Elisabeth Moltmann-Wendel, *Frauenbefreiung – Biblische und Theologische Argumente*, Munich 1976.
137. Letty M. Russell, *The Future of Partnership*, Philadelphia 1989.
138. F. Engels, *The Origin of the Family, Private Property and the State* (1884), ET London 1902, new trans. by A. West, London 1972;

A. Bebel, *Die Frau und der Sozialismus*, 1879; J. S. Mill, *The Sub-jection of Women*, London 1869.

139. Rosemary R. Ruether, *New Woman – New Earth*, New York 1975.
140. Dolores Williams, *Sisters in the Wilderness. The Challenge of Womanist God-Talk*, New York 1994; A. M. Isai-Diaz, *Mujerista Theology*, New York 1996. See here now Eske Wollrad, *Wildniser-fahrung. Womanistische Herausforderung und eine Antwort aus weisser feministischer Perspektive*, Gütersloh 1999.
141. J. J. Bachofen, *Das Mutterrecht* (1861), Basle 1948; H. Zinser, *Der Mythos des Mutterrechts*, Frankfurt 1981; Heide Göttner-Abendroth, *Die Göttin und ihr Heros. Die matriarchalen Religionen in Mythos, Märchen und Dichtung*, Munich 1980.
142. E. Bornemann, *Das Patriarchat. Ursprung und Zukunft unseres Gesellschaftssystems*, Frankfurt 1975; G. Lerner, *The Creation of Patriarchy*, New York 1976; Kate Millett, *Sexual Politics*, Garden City NY, 1970.
143. H. Tellenbach (ed.), *Das Vaterbild im Abendland*, Vols I–III, Stuttgart 1978.
144. J. Moltmann, 'Die Befreiung der Unterdrücker', *EvTh* 38, 1978, 529.
145. Carl Sombart describes the German male trauma of the Wilhelmine era excellently in *Die deutschen Männer und ihre Feinde. Carl Schmitt – ein deutsches Schicksal zwischen Männerbund und Matriarchatsmythos*, Munich 1991.
146. Letty M. Russell, *Feminist Interpretation of the Bible*, Philadelphia and Oxford 1985; Luise Schottroff and Marie-Theres Wacker (eds), *Kompendium Feministische Bibelauslegung*, Gütersloh 1998.
147. Phyllis Trible, *God and the Rhetoric of Sexuality*, Philadelphia 1978 and London 1992.
148. Elisabeth Schüssler Fiorenza, *In Memory of Her. A Feminist Theo-logical Reconstruction of Christian Origins*, New York and London 1983; ead., *Bread not Stones. The Challenge of Feminist Biblical Interpretation*, Boston 1984 and Edinburgh 1990.
149. Letter to Henriette Visser't Hooft in '*Eva, wo bist du?' Frauen in internationalen Organizationen der Ökumene. Eine Dokumenta-tion*, Gelnhausen 1981, 16; see also the comment in J. Moltmann, 'Henriette Visser't Hooft and Karl Barth', *Theology Today* 55, no. 4, January 1999, 524–32.
150. See II.3 above.
151. Heidemarie Langer, Herta Leistner and Elisabeth Moltmann-Wendel, *Mit Mirjam durchs Schilfmeer. Frauen bewegen die Kirche*, Berlin 1982.
152. Phyllis Trible, *Texts of Terror*, Philadelphia 1984 and London

1992; Helen Schüngel-Straumann, "'Von einer Frau nahm die Sünde ihren Anfang, ihretwegen müssen wir alle sterben" (Sir 25, 24). Zur Wirkungs- und Rezeptionsgeschichte der ersten drei Kapitel der Genesis in biblischer Zeit', *Bibel und Kirche* 53, 1998, 11–20.

153. Helen Schüngel-Straumann, *Die Frau am Anfang. Eva und die Folgen*, Freiburg 1989; Rosemary R. Ruether, *Sexism and God-talk: Toward a Feminist Theology*, London 1992; Pnina Nave Levinson, *Eva und ihre Schwestern. Perspektiven jüdisch-feministischer Theologie*, Gütersloh 1992.

154. Schüssler Fiorenza, *In Memory of Her* (n.148), Introduction, xxiii.

155. Ida Raming, "'Die zwölf Apostel waren Männer . . ." Stereotype Einwände gegen die Frauenordination und ihre tieferen Ursachen', *Orientierung* 56, 1992, 143–6.

156. For more detail see J. Moltmann, *God in Creation. An Ecological Doctrine of Creation* (The Gifford Lectures 1984–85), trans. Margaret Kohl, London and New York 1985, IX: 'God's Image in Creation: Human Beings', 215–43, following Phyllis Trible, *God and the Rhetoric of Sexuality* (n.147), 21.

157. Following Henriette Visser't Hooft,; see *'Eva, wo bist du?'* (n.149), 19.

158. M. Welker, *God the Spirit*, trans. J. F. Hoffmeyer, Minneapolis 1994, 147–82.

159. Elisabeth Moltmann-Wendel and Jürgen Moltmann, *God: His and Hers*, trans. John Bowden, London 1991.

160. H. E. Richter, *Der Gotteskomplex. Die Geburt und die Krise des Glaubens an die Allmacht des Menschen*, Reinbek 1979.

161. J. Moltmann, *The Spirit of Life. A Universal Affirmation*, trans. Margaret Kohl, London and Minneapolis 1992; ead., *The Source of Life. The Holy Spirit and the Theology of Life*, trans. Margaret Kohl, London and Minneapolis 1997.

162. Catherine Keller, *From a Broken Web*, Boston 1986. Cf. in contrast M. Grabmann, *Die Grundgedanken des Heiligen Augustinus über Seele und Gott*, Darmstadt 1957, no.2: 'Substantialität der Seele', 25–8, esp. 34: 'The main characteristic of substance is the resistance against the alternations of becoming and passing away . . . The "I" is, as it were, the firmly supporting rock over which the billows of the stream of consciousness unceasingly break'; 37: 'The monarchical adaptation of our consciousness appears. The "I" sits on the throne and performs the acts of rule . . .'

163. In the following passages I am drawing especially on the compendium *Herausgefordert durch die Armen. Dokumente der Ökumenischen Vereinigung von Dritte-Welt Theologen* (*EATWOT*

[The Ecumenical Association of Third World Theologians]) *1976–1986*, Freiburg 1990, as well as on the Kairos documents *Challenge to the Church. A Theological Comment on the Political Crisis in South Africa*, 1987; *Kairos Central America. A Challenge to the Churches of the World*, 1988; *The Damascus Document*, 1990.

164. *EATWOT* (n.163), 143.

165. *Kairos Central America* (n.163), 47: 'From the perspective of faith, we see our people as collective "servants of Yahweh" elected and called to actively redeem the world by fruitful sufferings, and establish justice among the nations.'

166. Ibid., 45; *EATWOT* (n.163), 34: 'We began to organize ourselves and became a people, the subjects of our own history, El Pueblo, Minjung.'

167. *EATWOT* (n.163), 181.

IV. The 'Broad Place' of the Trinity

1. E. Peterson, *Theologische Traktate*, Munich 1951, 45–148; see A. Schindler (ed.), *Monotheismus als politisches Problem? Erik Peterson und die Kritik der politischen Theologie*, Gütersloh 1978.

2. Genghis Khan to Louis IX of France in 1254: '*Praeceptum aeterni Dei: In coelo non est nisi unus Deus aeternus, super terram non sit nisi unus Dominus Chingischan, filius Dei. Hoc est verbum quod vobis dictum est.*' ['God's eternal precept: in heaven there is none except the one eternal God, on earth there is none except the one Lord Genghis Khan, the Son of God. This is the word declared to you.]

3. Peterson, *Theologische Traktate* (n.1), 103, 104.

4. C. Schmitt, *Politische Theologie. Vier Kapitel zur Lehre von der Souveränität*, Munich and Leipzig 1934.

5. J. B. Metz, *Zum Begriff der neuen Politischen Theologie 1967–1997*, Mainz 1997; J. Moltmann, *Politische Theologie – Politische Ethik*, Munich 1984 (ET *On Human Dignity. Political Theology and Ethics*, selections trans. M. D. Meeks *et al*, Philadelphia 1984); ead., *God for a Secular Society. The Public Relevance of Theology*, trans. Margaret Kohl, London and Minneapolis 1999.

6. Cf. Denzinger, *Enchiridion Symbolorum*, Freiburg [26]1947, No. 202 on the thesis 'One of the Trinity suffered', which the Emperor Justinian had taken over from the twelfth anathema of Cyril: 'Whosoever does not confess that the Logos of God suffered in the flesh and was crucified in the flesh and tasted death in the flesh, in order then also to be the first born from the dead . . . let him be anathema.' See here H. Urs von Balthasar, *Theodramatik* II/2,

Einsiedeln 1978, 207f. (*Theo-Drama: A Theological Dramatic Theory*, trans. G. Harrison, San Francisco 1988).

7. F. Buchheim, *Der Gnadenstuhl. Darstellung der Dreifaltigkeit*, Würzburg 1984, with G. Greshake's pertinent comments in *Der Dreieine Gott. Eine trinitarische Theologie*, Freiburg 1997, 550–1. See also W.H. Vanstone's apt verse:
    Thou art God, no monarch Thou
    Thron'd in easy state to reign;
    Thou art God, whose arms of love
    Aching, spent, the world sustain.
   (in *Love's Endeavour – Love's Expense. The Response of Being to the Love of God*, London [13]1993, 120).

8. L. Vischer (ed.), *Geist Gottes – Geist Christi. Ökumenische Überlegungen zur Filioque-Kontroverse*, Beiheft zur Ökumenische Rundschau 39, Frankfurt 1981

9. D. Staniloae, 'Der Ausgang des Heiligen Geistes vom Vater und seine Beziehung zum Sohn als Grundlage unserer Vergöttlichung und Kindschaft', in ibid., 153–63.

10. J. Moltmann, 'The Wealth of Gifts of the Spirit and their Christian Identity', *Concilium* 1999/1, 30–5.

11. D. Staniloae, *Orthodoxe Dogmatik*, Zürich and Gütersloh, Vol. I, 1985; Vol. II, 1990; Vol. III, 1995.

12. Thus G. Greshake, *Der dreieine Gott* (n.7).

13. I. Dalferth and E. Jüngel, 'Person und Gottebenbildlichkeit', in *Christlicher Glaube in moderner Gesellschaft*, Vol.24, Freiburg 1981, 83.

14. For more detail see J. Moltmann, *The Trinity and the Kingdom of God*, trans. Margaret Kohl, London 1981 (= *The Trinity and the Kingdom*, New York 1981), 99–128.

15. H. Urs von Balthasar lays a one-sided stress on this perspective of the world created, reconciled and finally redeemed in the Trinity. Cf. S. Lösel, *Kreuztheologie bei Hans Urs von Balthasar. Eine ökumenische Perspektive*, dissertation, Tübingen 1999.

16. For more detail see J. Moltmann, *The Way of Jesus Christ*, trans. Margaret Kohl, London and New York 1990.

17. M. D. Meeks, *Origins of the Theology of Hope*, Philadelphia 1974; C. Morse, *The Logic of Promise in Moltmann's Theology*, Philadelphia 1979; A. J. Conyers, *God, Hope and History*, Macon, Ga 1988.

18. Celia Deane-Drummond, *Towards a Green Theology through Analysis of the Ecological Motif in Jürgen Moltmann's Doctrine of Creation*, dissertation, Manchester 1992.

19. M. Jammer, *Concepts of Space*, Cambridge, Mass. 1954, Oxford

1955. Only D. Staniloae, *Orthodoxe Dogmatik* I, 182–92, offers an exhaustive reflection on God and space: 'The Super-Spatiality of God and the Participation of Spatial Beings in It'. He starts from the thesis that 'both the origin and the unity of space are grounded in the Holy Trinity', because 'just as the trinitarian Persons reach into one another, so that one is contained in the other, so also the human persons partially (reach) into one another spiritually, and by doing so in a sense (can) go beyond space and become present in the whole of space' (184). God called space into being by virtue of a possibility 'included in his inner-trinitarian life' (189).

20. B. Janowski, *Gottes Gegenwart in Israel. Beiträge zur Theologie des Alten Testaments*, Neukirchen 1993, esp. 119–47.

21. F. Rosenzweig, *Der Stern der Erlösung*, Heidelberg ³1954, III, 3, 192 (*The Star of Redemption*, trans. W.W. Hallo, London 1971).

22. S. Sorč, 'Die perichoretischen Beziehungen im Leben der Trinität und der Gemeinschaft der Menschen', *EvTh* 58, 1998, 100–18.

23. A. Deneffe, 'Perichoresis, circumincessio, circuminsessio', *Zeitschrift für katholische Theologie* 47, 1923, 497–532; C. A. Disandro, 'Historia semantica de perikhoresis', *Studia Patristica* XV, 1984, 442–47.

24. H. Denzinger, *Enchiridion Symbolorum*, 704: '*Propter hanc unitatem Pater est totus in Filio, totus in Spiritu Sancto, Filius totus est in Patre, totus in Spiritu Sancto, Spiritus Sanctus totus est in Patre, totus in Filio. Nullus alium aut precedet aeternitate, aut excedit magnitudine, aut superat potestate.*'

25. For a different view see W. Pannenberg, *Systematic Theology* I, trans. G. W. Bromiley, Grand Rapids 1991, 325.

26. Patricia Wilson-Kastner, *Faith, Feminism and the Christ*, Philadelphia 1983, 127, was the first to depict the trinitarian perichoresis in the 'image of dancing together'. 'Because femininism identifies interrelatedness and mutuality – equal, respectful, and nurturing relations – at the basis of the world as it really is and as it ought to be, we can find no better understanding and image of the divine than that of the perfect and open relationship of love.'

27. At the quatercentary celebrations at Trinity College, Dublin, I saw a fantastic trinitarian round-dance, performed during the service of worship by three women. They danced all the trinitarian figures dogmatically used since the time of Basil.

28. M. Wolf, *After Our Likeness. The Church as the Image of the Trinity*, Grand Rapids and Cambridge 1998.

29. This seems at the moment to be generally accepted. Cf. Pannenberg, *Systematic Theology* I (n.25), 259ff.; Greshake, *Der dreieine Gott* (n.7), 48ff. I have already criticized the metaphysical approach to

the doctrine of the Trinity in detail; cf. *the Trinity and the Kingdom of God* (n.14), 129–50.

30. In the discussions about trinitarian theology, the charge of tritheism has no objective foundation, because there has never been a Christian theologian who maintained a doctrine of three gods. It is an ancient, first Arian and then Islamic, charge levelled at orthodox Christianity. Later it became a charge directed by the Western church at the theology of the Eastern church. Today it serves to conceal one's own modern modalism. But from the perspective of Islamic monotheism, all Christian theologians – whether it be Augustine or Aquinas, Barth or Rahner, Pannenberg or Greshake, or whoever – are 'tritheists' as long as they adhere to the divine Sonship of Christ and call God 'the Father of Jesus Christ'. It therefore seems to me eccentric when Greshake (*Der dreieine Gott* [n.7], 168–71) thinks that he can show that I have a 'tritheistic understanding of Person', while overlooking the perichoretic understanding of Person which I have in fact developed.

31. W. Pannenberg, *Systematic Theology* (n.25) I, 319: 'If the trinitarian relations among Father, Son, and Spirit have the form of mutual self-distinction, they must be understood not merely as different modes of being of the one divine subject but as living realizations of separate centres of action.' Instead of the 'not merely' we should surely read 'not'.

32. Moltmann, *The Trinity and the Kingdom of God* (n.14), 94–6.

33. Greshake, *Der dreieine Gott* (n.7), 552–3, goes into Jung's construction in detail.

34. J. Moltmann, '"I Believe in God the Father." Patriarchal or Non-Patriarchal talk of God?', in *History and the Triune God*, trans. John Bowden, London 1991, 1–18.

35. Ibid., 57–69: '"The Fellowship of the Holy Spirit." On Trinitarian Pneumatology.'

36. J . Moltmann, *The Source of Life*, trans. Margaret Kohl, London and Minneapolis 1997, 22–5.

37. This is emphasized rightly, though one-sidedly, by B. Nitsche, 'Die Analogie zwischen dem trinitarischen Gottesbild und der communialen Struktur von Kirche', in *Communio – Ideal oder Zerrbild von Kommunikation*, QD 176, Freiburg 1999, 81–114, esp. 86, following *Unitatis redintegratio*, 2. Cf. here also M. Kehl, *Eine katholische Ekklesiologie*, Würzburg 1992; B. J. Hilberath, 'Kirche als communio. Beschwörungsformel oder Projektbeschreibung?', *ThQ* 174, 1994, 45–65. On this from the Protestant side see M. Volf, *After Our Likeness* (n.28), 224–30.

38. A. Burgmüller (ed.), *Kirche als 'Gemeinde von Brüdern'. Barmen*

III, Gütersloh 1980.
39. I am using the expression 'charismatic congregation' in the sense of G. Eichholz's New Testament study, *Was heisst charismatische Gemeinde?*, ThEx 77, Munich 1960, not in a modern denominational sense. Cf. also W. J. Hollenweger, *Pentecostalism: Origins and Developments Worldwide*, Peabody, MA 1997.
40. Cited, for example, in *Lumen Gentium*, Ch. 1 (in *Vatican Council II. The Conciliar and Post Conciliar Documents*, ed. A. Flannery, revised ed., Dublin 1988).
41. Geevarghese Mar Osthathios, *Theology of a Classless Society*, London 1979, and *Sharing God and a Sharing World*, Thiruvalla 1995.
42. D. M. Meeks, *God the Economist. The Doctrine of God and Political Economy*, Minneapolis 1989.
43. L. Boff, *Trinity and Society*, trans. P. Burns, Maryknoll, NY and Tunbridge Wells 1988. Cf. T. R. Thompson, *Imitatio Trinitatis. The Trinity as Social Model in the Theologies of Jürgen Moltmann and Leonardo Boff*, dissertation, Princeton 1996.
44. For more detail here see M. Volf, ' "The Trinity is our Social Program." The Doctrine of the Trinity and the Shape of Social Engagement', *Modern Theology* 14, 1998, 412ff.
45. G. Freudenthal, *Atom und Individuum im Zeitalter Newtons*, Frankfurt 1982, has convincingly shown the inner connection betwen the atomization of nature and the individualization of the human being in the first modern age between Newton and Descartes.

Epilogue

1. See Part II, 4.
2. J. Polkinghorne, *Belief in God in an Age of Science*, New Haven and London 1998, 1.

Index of Names